DK EYEWITNESS

KT-872-931

JAPAN

CONTENTS

INSPIRE / PLAN / DISCOVER / EXPERIENCE

JAPAN

DISCOVER 6

Welcome to Japan.................................. 8
Reasons to Love Japan........................... 10
Explore Japan......................................14
Getting to Know Japan 16

Japan Itineraries................................22
Japan Your Way 36
A Year in Japan....................................70
A Brief History.......................................72

EXPERIENCE TOKYO 78

Western Tokyo......................................82

Central Tokyo 102

Northern Tokyo..................................122

Beyond the Center...........................136

EXPERIENCE JAPAN 146

Central Honshu...................................148

Kyoto City...180

Western Honshu............................. 210

Shikoku...246

Kyushu..260

Okinawa 282

Northern Honshu..............................294

Hokkaido..314

NEED TO KNOW 326

Before You Go.......................................328
Getting Around....................................330
Practical Information...........................334

Index...336
Phrase Book.. 346
Acknowledgments................................351

Left: Sake barrels at Meiji Shrine, Tokyo
Previous page: Oarai Isosaki-jinja, Northern Honshu
Front cover: The iconic silhouette of Mount Fuji

DISCOVER

The glowing lights of Nagasaki

Welcome to Japan...8

Reasons to Love Japan...............................10

Explore Japan...14

Getting to Know Japan..............................16

Japan Itineraries..22

Japan Your Way...36

A Year in Japan..70

A Brief History..72

WELCOME TO
JAPAN

Konnichiwa from one of the most fascinating countries on earth. Japan is a land of contrasts - of tranquil zen gardens and steaming *onsen*, teeming crowds and robot restaurants - and it has charmed visitors for centuries because of it. Whatever your dream trip to Japan includes, this DK Eyewitness Travel Guide is the perfect companion.

1 A stone statue of the Buddha at Eikan-do, Kyoto.

2 Neon lights of Tokyo's frenetic Akihabara Electronics District.

3 A delicate plate of sushi.

4 Kiyomizu-dera Temple, surrounded by fall foliage.

Formed of thousands of scattered islands, Japan's impossibly varied landscape stretches 1,864 miles (3,000 km) from the edge of Siberia in the north to tropical Okinawa in the south. In between, you'll discover the snow-covered slopes of Hokkaido, majestic Mount Fuji, the otherworldly Arashiyama bamboo grove, and much more besides. This is a land of eternal natural beauty, as well as the yearly flowering and falling of ethereal cherry blossoms.

Japanese efficiency is no myth – these islands may be some of the most densely populated on the planet, but the country's thronging cities really do run like clockwork. Tokyo, the capital, where it sometimes feels that the only constant is change, is a science-fiction movie brought to life, with its cosplaying locals, cat-filled cafés, and psychedelic neon street scenes. To the west,

the ancient capital of Kyoto – the ying to Tokyo's yang – with its gilded shrines and graceful geisha, is a heritage wonderland, and – whisper it – a cosmopolitan city. And don't forget Osaka, where proud locals, a chaotic downtown and vibrant food scene meet under the enormous shadow of the country's largest castle.

Even with its unparalleled rail networks, Japan can still overwhelm with the sheer number of unmissable sites on offer. We've broken the country down into easily navigable chapters, with detailed itineraries, expert local knowledge and colourful, comprehensive maps to help you plan the perfect visit. Whether you're staying for a few days, weeks or longer, this Eyewitness guide will ensure that you see the very best Japan has to offer. Enjoy the book, and enjoy Japan.

REASONS TO LOVE
JAPAN

An avant-garde capital that pulsates with quirky cosplayers and raucous karaoke bars, hovering trains that rocket through awe-inspiring countryside, engrossing traditions, and an obsession with etiquette – what's not to love?

1 FAST TRAINS

When Japan launched the *shinkansen* in 1964, they left the rest of the world in the dust. Silently speeding at 200 mph (320km/h), you'll feel as if you're already in the future.

STAYING IN A RYOKAN 2

These guesthouses provide the ultimate Japanese experience. Don a *yukata* (kimono), indulge in a communal bath and savour a home-cooked meal, washed down with plenty of sake.

3 CELEBRATING OTAKU

Once an offensive term for a super fan, more and more people are calling themselves *otaku*. Explore the world of manga, anime, and cosplay in Tokyo's Harajuku district *(p94)*.

4 RIOTOUS FESTIVALS

Don't let its introvert reputation fool you – Japan hosts some raucous celebrations. Expect loin-cloth-clad revellers, sumo wrestlers, and tantalizing scents drifting from stalls *(p70)*.

FANTASTICAL CASTLES 5

From the imposing fortresses of the Warring States Period, such as Kumamoto Castle *(p274)*, to Himeji-jo's graceful donjon *(p224)*, Japan's castles seem straight out of a fairy tale.

SIPPING SAKE 6

Made from a large-grain rice and *koji* (yeast), sake gets its rich flavor from its unique fermentation process. Hot in winter, or cold in summer, it's the perfect thirst quencher *(p65)*.

HISTORIC KYOTO 7
With 1,600 Buddhist temples and more UNESCO-listed World Heritage Sites than any other city on earth, the majestic city of Kyoto is an absolute must for any culture vulture *(p180)*.

CHERRY BLOSSOM SEASON 8
Each spring, as the cherry blossom front sweeps north-wards, the Japanese population indulges in one of its all-time favorite pastimes: *hanami* - picnicking under blooms.

9 ZEN GARDENS
Some think that the rocks represent islands, while others believe that they symbolize emotional obstacles. Search for your own meaning in these mysterious gardens *(p48)*.

10 RELAXING IN AN ONSEN

As one of the most active volcanic regions in the world, in Japan, *onsen* are everywhere you look. Wash away your troubles in one of these bubbling pools *(p61)*.

SAVORING SUSHI 11

You'll find this dish on the menu at swanky Michelin-starred eateries and neighborhood dives. Get your chopsticks at the ready to sample sushi at its most authentic *(p140)*.

KARAOKE NIGHTS 12

Everyone from giggling teens to suit-clad businessmen belt out tunes in soundproof booths. Grab your earplugs, have your song at the ready, and enjoy the ultimate singalong.

EXPLORE
JAPAN

This guide divides Japan into nine color-coded sightseeing areas, as shown on this map. Find out more about each area on the following pages.

OKINAWA

Kyushu

Yaku

East China Sea

Amami

OKINAWA
p282

Okinawa

Miyako

Ishigaki

0 km   200
0 miles   200

N ↑

Sea of Japan (East Sea)

Toyama
Kanazawa
Takayama

Tottori
Izumo

WESTERN HONSHU
p210

KYOTO
p180

Nagoya

Hiroshima
Okayama
Osaka
Matsusaka
Takamatsu

Kokura
Ube
Matsuyama

SHIKOKU
p246

Wakayama

Fukuoka

Kochi

Nagasaki
Kumamoto

KYUSHU
p260

Kagoshima
Miyazaki

0 kilometers   150
0 miles   150

N ↑

Yaku

Wakkanai

Asahikawa
Kitami
HOKKAIDO
p314
Sapporo
Kushiro
Obihiro

Hakodate

Aomori
Hachinohe

Morioka
Akita
**NORTHERN
HONSHU**
p294
Tsuruoka

Yamagata
Sendai
Sado
Niigata
Fukushima

Joetsu
Koriyama

Nagano
Utsunomiya

Mito
**CENTRAL
HONSHU**
p148
TOKYO
p78
Narita

Yokohama

hizuoka
Fuji

*Pacific
Ocean*

EAST ASIA

RUSSIA

MONGOLIA

NORTH
KOREA

SOUTH
KOREA

JAPAN

CHINA

NEPAL

INDIA
MYANMAR

VIETNAM

TAIWAN

*Pacific
Ocean*

THAILAND

CAMBODIA

PHILIPPINES

MALAYSIA

INDONESIA

PAPUA NEW
GUINEA

GETTING TO KNOW
JAPAN

Made up of four main islands - Honshu, Hokkaido, Kyushu, and Shikoku - and several thousand smaller ones, Japan is a land of buzzing metropolises, rural seaside villages, and much more besides. Becoming familiar with each region will help when planning your trip to this sprawling country.

TOKYO

PAGE 78

Japan's capital may be rooted in the past but it is also a vision from the future. Traditional low-slung houses sit beside sleek skyscrapers, and historic Ueno Park is a few streets away from the Akihabara Electronics District. This city really comes alive after dark when serious-faced businessmen and giggling teenagers caterwaul beside each other in karaoke booths, and the glowing lanterns outside cozy, hole-in-the-wall *izakaya* tempt passersby. On top of this, Tokyo's restaurants have garnered more Michelin stars than any other city in the world, but there also many cheap eats to sniff out here.

Best for
That world-famous relentless buzz

Home to
Ginza, Ueno Park, and more

Experience
Everything from watching morning sumo wrestling practice to dining at the bizarre Robot Restaurant

CENTRAL HONSHU

PAGE 148

Although it is home to the charming cities of Kamakura and Kanazawa, Central Honshu is best known for its breathtaking scenery. This stunning region is home to both Mount Fuji and the sprawling Japanese Alps, making it the perfect destination for those who yearn to explore the great outdoors. Despite being well-connected, parts of Central Honshu are still remote enough to have kept their traditional rural lifestyles, buildings, and festivals, making it seem far away from Tokyo.

Best for
Getting lost in nature

Home to
Yokohama, Kamakura, Mount Fuji and the Fuji Five Lakes, Takayama, Kanazawa

Experience
Watching snow monkeys relax in the hot pools outside of Nagano

PAGE 180

KYOTO CITY

To truly understand Japan, you must spend time in its old imperial capital, where scores of the country's famous monuments are preserved within a lively modern city. Kyoto is home to graceful parasol-carrying geisha, beguiling temples and towering bamboo groves. Life here is still largely tied to nature's rhythms. *Kyo-ryori*, Kyoto's celebrated cuisine, for example, makes much of seasonality, and the city's exquisite gardens go through striking seasonal transitions, from fall's bright-red maple leaves to spring's blush-pink cherry blossom.

Best for
Traditional temples

Home to
Nijo Castle, Fushimi Inari shrine

Experience
A tour of the wooden-clad district of Gion

→

WESTERN HONSHU

Osaka, western Japan's largest city, is the cultural counterweight to the economic dominance of Tokyo. With its unique dialect, rough-and-tumble streets, and superlative foodie scene, it's one of Japan's unmissable cities. Away from Osaka, Western Honshu has many allures, including heavenly Himeji-jo and thought-provoking Hiroshima, as well as some of the country's most stunning scenery. The giant Otorii gate of Miyajima, which seems to float above the waves, is a must-see for any visitor, while Yoshino is the best place to walk beneath pink blooms during sakura season.

Best for
Cherry blossom

Home to
Nara, Osaka, Kobe, Himeji-jo, Hiroshima Peace Memorial Park, Miyajima Island, and Horyu-ji Temple

Experience
Watching the diving women searching for pearls in the water surrounding the Mikimoto Pearl Island

PAGE 246

SHIKOKU

Isolated for centuries, Shikoku still feels like a backwater, and is all the more charming for it. The least explored of the Japanese islands, it offers a glimpse of the country as it used to be. The charming castle town of Matsuyama, with its clattering trams and ancient hot spring, is a great base from which to explore the island, while the more adventurous might attempt to master the famous 745-mile- (1,200-km-) long 88 Temple Pilgrimage.

Best for
Rural charm

Home to
Benesse Art Site Naoshima

Experience
Walking the historic 88 Temple Pilgrimage, which white-robed pilgrims believe atones for the worst transgressions

PAGE 260

KYUSHU

Active volcanoes, rolling grasslands, bubbling hot springs, and outgoing locals combine to give this island a very different feel to the rest of the archipelago. City-wise, bustling Fukuoka and beautiful Nagasaki are two of Japan's most cosmopolitan metropolises, showcasing Kyushu's historic role as Japan's gateway to the rest of the world. The menu on the island reflects this cultural melting pot: unctuous Hakata ramen or crisp lotus roots satisfy hungry tummies, while *shochu*, made from sweet potatoes, leaves a fiery taste.

Best for
Steaming onsen

Home to
Fukuoka, Nagasaki

Experience
A soak in the outdoor hot springs of Sakurajima, an active volcano

$\rightarrow$

PAGE 282

OKINAWA

More than 1,242 miles (2,000 km) south of Tokyo lies a tropical paradise. Okinawa's pristine beaches, spectacular diving, and slower pace of life have made it the local's favorite holiday destination. Although it could be easy to just flop on the sand here, the islands reward a deeper look. Naha, the main city, is a heady mix of refined civilization and neon glitz. Here, traditional red-tiled Okinawan houses, topped with ceramic *shisa* lions, stand alongside pulsating karaoke bars. Outside the city, you'll find poignant war memorials, sacred groves, and brimming craft stores to explore.

Best for
Rest and relaxation

Home to
Beautiful beaches

Experience
Awamori, *the local tipple made by distilling fragrant rice into a powerful liquor*

PAGE 294

NORTHERN HONSHU

This part of Japan's largest island is steeped in myth and legend. Home to sacred mountains, dense forests, and vibrant folk traditions, Tohoku – as the Japanese call it – is a rugged and remote wonderland. The region overflows with literary connections, most famously to the haiku poet Basho, who chronicled his intrepid journey into the region in *The Narrow Road to the Deep North*. These days, with easy transport to the capital, this poem no longer holds true, and this tranquil region is as well connected as anywhere else in the country.

Best for
Literature and music

Home to
Nikko

Experience
A powerful performance of taiko *drumming on Sado island*

PAGE 314

HOKKAIDO

The northernmost of Japan's major islands, and the country's largest prefecture, Hokkaido is a land of fire and ice. Characterized by fertile plains, perfect skiing conditions, and looming volcanoes, this spectacular island sometimes feels like a different world. The gateway to Hokkaido, Hakodate is famed for its bounteous morning market, supplied by the fertile seas that surround the island, while Sapporo – the capital – is best known for the intricate ice sculptures that take over the city during its annual snow festival.

Best for
Winter sports

Home to
Boundless National Parks

Experience
Snowboarding on the powder-covered pistes of Niseko Ski Resort

←

1 Dinosaur skeletons on display at Intermediatheque.

2 Toji Temple in Kyoto.

3 The elaborate entrance to Ginza Six.

4 Cosplay participants in Tokyo's Harajuku District.

A land of dramatic contrasts, Japan rewards visitors who have the luxury of time. This itinerary is the perfect introduction to the country.

2 WEEKS
in Japan

Day 1

Start in Tokyo, getting your bearings by jumping aboard the Nihonbashi loop of the free Hinomaru Limousine sightseeing bus *(www.hinomaru.co.jp)*. Get off at Showa Dori Street for a spot of Japanese paper-making at Ozu Washi *(www.ozuwashi.net)*, followed by lunch at Mitsukoshi's huge food hall *(p110)*. Next, walk to the Imperial Palace *(p112)*. If the weather is good, check out the gardens; otherwise, the free Intermediatheque museum will keep you entertained *(www.intermediatheque.jp)*. For dinner, try Edomae – the original Tokyo-style sushi – at Yoshino Sushi Honten *(3-8-11 Nihonbashi)*, followed by a nightcap at the bar at the top of the Mandarin Oriental Hotel, overlooking the neon-lit city *(www.mandarinoriental.com)*.

Day 2

Once dismissed as a clubbing hotspot, Roppongi *(p90)* has fast developed a reputation as a cultural hub. Purchase the ATRo Saving ticket and spend the day exploring the Roppongi Art Triangle; the Mori Art Museum, which specializes in contemporary art, is up first. Pause for lunch at Afuri *(afuri.com)*, famed for its delicately scented ramen, before continuing your whistle-stop art tour at the National Art Center and the Suntory Museum of Art. Stick around Roppongi as the evening draws in; there's no place better for a night on the town.

Day 3

Today you'll meet Tokyo's quirky side. Start on the brash and bustling Takeshita-dori in the Harajuku District *(p94)*; packed with trendy boutiques and vintage stores, it'll easily absorb your morning. Indulge your sweet tooth at Marion Crepes for lunch *(www.marion-crepes.com)*, then take the metro to Ikebukuro for more pop culture madness on Otome Road. Be sure to call into K-Books *(www.k-books.co.jp)* and take tea at Swallowtail, the butler café *(www.butlers-cafe.jp)*. Round off your dive into Tokyo's subcultures at the Robot Restaurant *(www.shinjuku-robot.com)*.

Day 4

Rise and shine before the dawn for an early morning visit to the Toyosu Fish Market *(p138)*. Copy the locals and power up on some early morning ramen, before hitting the shopping mecca of Ginza *(p106)*. Ginza Six is the district's largest shopping complex, which even has a Noh theatre in its basement – buy a happy hour ticket before 2:30pm to see part of one of the plays staged here *(kanze.net)*. After browsing the shops for the rest of the afternoon, arrive early (no reservations) at Umegaoka Sushi no Midori Sohonten *(www.sushinomidori.co.jp)* for a sushi dinner.

Day 5

Board the *shinkansen* to Kyoto. After arriving in under 2.5 hours at the striking Kyoto Station *(p189)*, make your way to Toji Temple *(p188)* for an introduction to Kyoto's religious heritage. Marvel at the 1,001 goddess statues in Sanjusangen-do *(p189)*, then grab lunch at Tsuruki Mochi Hompo Shichijo *(561 Nishinomoncho)*. Next, head to the Fushimi Inari Shrine *(p186)*, where a pretty tunnel of *torii* lead to great views over the city. Return to central Kyoto come evening for a riverside stroll and dinner at Gyoza Shop Gion *(p195)*.

→

Day 6

Delve into Kyoto's past at the Imperial Palace (p195), learning its history on a free tour. At lunchtime, make a beeline to bustling Nishiki Market to fuel up before embarking on the Philosopher's Walk (p208). It ends at Nanzen-ji (p194), where you can enjoy a traditional *matcha* tea. Round off your day sampling different sakes at the Jam Sake Bar (p192).

Day 7

Spend your final morning in Kyoto at the Kitano Tenman-gu Shrine (p198) and the glittering Kinkaku-ji (p199). Enjoy a quick tofu meal at nearby Maboya (9-1 Kinugasa Somoncho) before boarding the train to Osaka (p218). Head into lively Dotonbori in downtown Osaka for dinner and drinks – Tachinomi Nikou (p221) is a top option.

Day 8

Spend the morning exploring Osaka Castle (p218). For lunch, sample marinated eel at Unagi Nishihara (4-12 Kita Shimmachi),

then continue learning about the city's history at the 6th-century Shitenno-ji (p221). As the sun goes down, leave the past behind and head to the top of the sleek Conrad Osaka – with epic city views, this is the perfect cocktail spot.

Day 9

Start by exploring Osaka's subterranean National Museum of Art (p219), then make your way to Michelin-starred Kashiwaya (www.relaischateaux.com) for lunch in a traditional tearoom-style setting. Next, head to the distinctive Umeda Sky Building for panoramic views from its Floating Garden Observatory (p220). In the evening, explore the retro charms of the Shinsekai district, famed for its narrow lanes and old school bars.

Day 10

Spend today in Nara (p214), just a one-hour train ride from Osaka. Pick up picnic supplies near the station before heading to Nara Park to visit Todai-ji (p216). After

1 The West Gate at Osaka's Shitenno-ji Temple.

2 A stall at Nishiki Market.

3 Colorful signage in Osaka's Shinsekai district.

4 Kobe's Maritime Museum and Port Tower.

5 Benesse House at the Benesse Art Site Naoshima.

your lunch, explore the shops and *machiya* (merchant homes) in the Naramachi district before returning to Osaka.

Day 11

Journey 30 minutes from Osaka to Kobe *(p222)*. Start by walking up Kitano-zaka to Kitano-cho and touring the European-style villas. No trip to Kobe would be complete without trying its famed beef, so order it for lunch at Steak House Garaku *(2-14-25 Yamamotodori)*. Spend the afternoon sampling sake at the Ginjo Brewery *(p223)*, then take a sunset walk around the harbor to admire the striking Port Tower and Maritime Museum. Head to the city's lively Chinatown for dinner.

Day 12

From Kobe take the *shinkansen* to Okayama *(p236)*, famous for its beautiful Korakuen Garden. The garden is close to Okayama's castle, as well as the city's museums, so there's plenty to fill the morning. After lunch at Shiroshita Cafe *(1-1-8 Omotecho)*, catch a ferry to the Benesse Art Site

Naoshima *(p250)*. Spend the night at stylish Benesse House, enjoying artfully presented *kaiseki* (small plates) for dinner.

Day 13

Rise early for a morning exploring Naoshima's museums, before heading back to Okayama and taking the *shinkansen* to Hiroshima. Have lunch at Okonomiyaki Nagata-ya *(www.nagataya-okonomi.com)*, then pay your respects at the monuments and museum in the Hiroshima Peace Memorial Park *(p228)*. Oysters are a Hiroshima staple – try them for dinner at Kakifune Kanawa *(www.kanawa.co.jp)*.

Day 14

Discover Hiroshima's forward-thinking attitude at the Hiroshima Museum of Art *(www.hiroshima-museum.jp)* and Hiroshima Orizuru Tower. After slurping some slippery noodles at Bakudanya *(2-12 Shintenchi)*, fly back to Tokyo. If you have the energy, go bar hopping in Shimokitazawa, or treat yourself to a meal at the renowned Inua *(inua.jp)*.

←

1 Shibuya Crossing, one of the busiest crosswalks in the world.

2 The vermilion Tokyo Tower in Shiba Park.

3 Tuna being prepared at the Toyosu Fish Market

4 Shoppers at one of the stalls that line the street up to Senso-ji Temple.

5 DAYS

in Tokyo

Day 1

Head straight to the Shibuya Crossing *(p93)* to catch a glimpse of one of the city's most iconic sights. After enjoying a ramen lunch at Ichiran *(en.ichiran.com)*, ride the Yamanote line to Yoyogi and make a beeline through Yoyogi Park *(p96)* to the Meiji Shrine *(p86)*. Stroll the leafy avenues, before continuing to Takeshita-dori in Harajuku *(p94)*, an epicenter for youth fashion. In the evening, rent a karaoke booth and belt out some classic hits – Shibuya's Karaoke Kan *(karaoke kan.jp)* featured in *Lost in Translation*.

Day 2

Make your way to Shiba Park *(p118)* and take the elevator to the top of the Tokyo Tower for stunning city views. Continue the morning with a stroll through the park, exploring the Zojo-ji temple before a fresh tuna lunch at nearby Itamae Sushi *(itamae.co.jp)*. Spend the afternoon browsing the huge stores of nearby Ginza; for traditional items, check out Mitsukoshi in Nihonbashi *(p110)*. Have a pick-me-up at legendary hole-in-the wall bar MOD *(3-4-12 Ginza)* before dinner at Takashimaya *(p110)*, then end the day with a Kabuki show at the Kabukiza theatre *(p114)*.

Day 3

Set your alarm for an early jaunt to the Toyosu Fish Market: the tuna auctions kick off at 5:30am *(p138)*. Spend the rest of the day exploring the artificial island of Odaiba *(p145)*, pausing for a lunch of battered octopus balls at the Odaiba Takoyaki Museum *(p143)*. Call in at the seven-story Diver City Mall to explore the amazing array of shops and see the giant robot statue, then marvel at the technology displays in the National Museum of Emerging Science and Innovation *(p145)*. For dinner, head to Shin-Toyosu Station for a barbecue with a view at Wild Magic – The Rainbow Farm *(wildmagic.jp)*.

Day 4

You could spend days exploring all the sites that Ueno Park *(p126)* has to offer, but today settle for a visit to the Honkan building at the Tokyo National Museum *(p128)* for an introduction to Japanese art. After lunch at Yamabe Okachimachi *(p128)*, walk to the splendid Senso-ji temple complex *(p132)*. Cross over the Sumida river and visit the Tokyo Skytree *(p135)* for uninterrupted panoramic views of the city, before heading to the tangled lanes of Asakusa *(p133)* for dinner at Nakasei, a tempura restaurant that has been going strong since 1870 *(nakasei.biz)*.

Day 5

Embrace your inner *otaku* at the myriad manga stores and cafés in Ikebukuro *(p142)*, one of Japan's cosplay capitals. Be treated like royalty at Swallowtail, Ikebukuro's famous butler café *(www. butlers-cafe.jp)*, then head to the Sky Circus at Sunshine 60 for an out-of-this-world virtual reality experience. Afterwards, stroll to Jiyugakuen Myonichikan for a tour of Frank Lloyd Wright's "House of Tomorrow" *(2-31-3 Nishiikebukuro)*. Round off your day in *otaku* paradise at the ultimate geek attraction – the Robot Restaurant, which is 20 minutes away on the Saikyo line *(www.shinjuku-robot.com)*. Here, your dinner will be accompanied by a bizarre robot-themed burlesque show.

←

1 The modern cityscape of Yokohama, with Mount Fuji in the background.

2 The famous Giant Buddha in Kamakura.

3 A skier competing on the slopes of Nagano.

4 Shopping at a stall selling fresh fish at Wajima's early morning market.

5 DAYS
in Central Honshu

Day 1

Begin your tour in the buzzing young city of Yokohama *(p152)* at the world-class Yokohama Museum of Arts. When you've finished browsing the collection, and are ready for lunch, head to the atmospheric streets of Chinatown to try some *nikuman* (steamed buns) – Edosei *(192 Yamashitacho)* serves the best. Next, join the locals in praying for prosperity at the Kanteibyo Temple, then catch a bus to the beautiful Sankeien Garden. Head back into the city for a *katsu* dinner at Katsuretsu An *(katsuretsuan.co.jp)*, followed by a stroll along the waterfront. End the day with a ride on the ferris wheel for glittering views.

Day 2

Catch a train to historic Kamakura *(p154)*, famed for its hillside temples. Start at the Tsurugaoka Hachiman-gu Shrine, then walk to the waterfront to enjoy the city's seaside vibe. For lunch, try vegan-friendly Sairam *(sairam-kamakura-en.link)*. Check out the iconic Great Buddha, pausing to cool down with some *kakigori* (shaved ice) if the weather is warm, then take the 40-minute train ride from Hase Station to Enoshima. This island's enchanting beaches are ideal for a lazy afternoon. Enoshima's speciality is *shirasu* (fresh whitebait) – try it at Tobiccho Sandoten *(tobiccho.com)* before heading back to Kamakura.

Day 3

Nagano *(p174)* is nearly three hours away on the train so set off early. Make your first stop the Zenko-ji, where you walk through a dark passage in search of the "key to paradise". Once you've found it, reward yourself with some tasty soba noodles at Uzuraya *(3229 Togakushi)*. Spend the rest of the day on the slopes or hiking, depending on the season. Either way, indulge in a relaxing dip in one of Nagano's *onsen* before dinner. Splash out on a meal at Fujiya Gohonjin *(www.thefujiyagohonjin. com)*, or enjoy budget-friendly ramen at Misoya *(1362 Minaminagano)*.

Day 4

Catch the *shinkansen* (bullet train) to Kanazawa *(p164)*. This city is renowned for its sushi, so be sure to sample some at Honten Kaga Yasuke, near the station *(www.spacelan.ne.jp/~kagayasuke)*. A 30-minute stroll will take you to the disc-shaped 21st Century Museum of Contemporary Art. Explore the innovative installations, leaving enough time to make the three-hour bus ride to Wajima *(p176)*. Check into Wajima Yashio, a *ryokan* with ocean views and tasty treats for dinner *(www.wajima-yashio.com)*.

Day 5

Wajima is famed for its morning market along Asaichi-dori, near the port. Seek out local seafood delicacies, before walking to the Wajima Nuri Kaikan *(wajimanuri.or.jp/ kaikan/file12.html)* to learn about the city's famous ceramics. Head back toward the market for a seafood lunch at Naruse *(2-16 Kawaimachi)*, then spend the afternoon sampling sake at Hiyoshi Sake Brewery. Finish in time to catch the bus from Banbacho to the Shiroyone Senmaida rice fields for a picturesque rural sunset. Return to Wajima and, after another top meal, relax in the *onsen* at your *ryokan*.

←

1 The glittering exterior of the Golden Pavilion.

2 The bustling approach to Kiyomizu-dera Temple.

3 Locals cycling along the streets of Kyoto.

4 One of the delicious dishes served at Kikunoi.

With its easily navigable grid layout, Kyoto rewards exploration on foot or by bicycle. Rentals are commonly available, and many hotels provide bicycles to their guests for free.

2 DAYS

in Kyoto

Day 1

Morning Start your trip at Ryoan-ji (*p200*). This extensive temple serves as a mausoleum for several emperors, but its crowning glory is its zen garden, an ideal place to relax and reflect. The complex also houses a tofu restaurant called Ryoanji Yudofu, where visitors can drop in for a *shojin-ryori* meal – traditional Buddhist vegan cooking.

Afternoon The park surrounding Royan-ji offers a number of walking trails, which are particularly lovely in autumn and spring. After exploring these, cycle the short distance to the Golden Pavilion (*p199*). This is one of Japan's most famous sites, and you cannot fail to be enchanted by its golden silhouette. The pavilion also offers the opportunity to take part in a traditional tea ceremony.

Evening Join a walking tour of the evocative Gion district (*p192*). Tours start every night at 6pm in front of the Gion Omoide Museum (*www.getyourguide.com*). Be sure to book a table for a late dinner afterwards at Kikunoi (*kikunoi.jp*). Run by the famed chef Yoshihiro Murata, this eatery is renowned for its *kaiseki*, a decadent multi-dish meal of reimagined traditional plates. Round off your night with a tasting course at the Jam Sake Bar (*p192*), where the staff will be delighted to walk you through the nuances of Japan's national drink.

Day 2

Morning Spend your morning exploring Nijo Castle (*p184*), the former home of the Tokugawa shoguns. Listen out for the squeaking "nightingale floors", designed to protect the occupants from assassins by making a noise when anyone walks on them. For lunch, a good option is Kaiseki Hyoki, a Michelin-starred restaurant located near Shijo Station that offers reasonably priced lunches (*hyoki.jp*).

Afternoon Cycle to Kiyomizu-dera Temple (*p191*) for spectacular views over the city. The approach to the temple along the steep and busy lanes of the charming Higashiyama District is part of the fun, but it might be wise to park your bike before the start of the hill. The many shops and restaurants in the area have been catering to tourists and pilgrims for centuries – seek out local specialties such as sweets, pickles, and Kiyomizu-yaki pottery.

Evening A gentle five-minute cycle ride away is Pontocho Alley (*p191*), one of the most atmospheric streets in the city. It runs parallel to the broad gravel path of the Kamogawa river, a popular place for a nighttime stroll. For dinner, eat at the world famous Kichikichi (*p195*), home to Japan's most celebrated maker of *omurice* (you'll need to book in advance). Grab a drink afterwards at Hello Dolly, a jazz bar known for its impressive collection of vinyl LPs (*hellodolly.hannnari.com*).

←

1 The historic Todai-ji Buddhist temple in Nara.

2 The famous Otorii gate of the Itsukushima Shrine on Miyajima Island.

3 The distinctive green-and-white exterior of Osaka Castle.

4 The skeletal roof of the A-Bomb Dome, Hiroshima Peace Memorial Park.

5 DAYS

in Western Honshu

Day 1

Begin your trip at Osaka's grand castle (p218); tours take in the excellent collection of art and weaponry. For lunch, head to Kuromon Ichiba market, a foodie hotspot 50-minutes' walk to the south. Travel back into the city center to check out some cutting-edge Japanese fashion at the Hankyu department store (www.hankyu-dept.co.jp), before exploring the eye-catching National Museum of Art. In the evening, take a relaxing dip in one of the baths at Spa World (p220). For dinner, head to Tachinomi Nikou (p221), one of Osaka's tachinomi (small standing bars).

Day 2

Take a one-hour train ride to the ancient city of Nara (p214). Instead of leaving the station, first make the short train journey to Horyu-ji (p232) to see the oldest wooden building in Japan. Head back to central Nara for an unagi (eel) lunch at Edogawa (43 Shimomikadocho), then take a stroll through Nara Park. Huge wooden guardians mark the entrance to Todai-ji, home to the towering Great Buddha (p216) – see if you can squeeze through the hole behind him to be blessed with everlasting luck. Choose Kura (16 Komyoincho) for dinner, an atmospheric izakaya (pub) housed in a traditional art storehouse.

Day 3

After a 2.5-hour train journey from Nara, you'll be greeted on arrival in Himeji by the breathtaking Himeji-jo fortress (p224). Explore the main donjon and the verdant grounds of the castle, before having a late lunch at Wabisuke (2 Wabisuke), an elegant restaurant by the moat. Next, catch a bus to the Shosha-Ropeway to visit the 1,000 year-old Engyo-ji temple. Then, head to Nadagiku Shuzo (www.nadagiku.co.jp), an ancient sake brewery near Himeji station. The brewery shuts at 6pm, but the restaurant, which specializes in tofu and suminabe (a type of hotpot cooked over charcoal), is open until 9pm.

Day 4

Catch the 90-minute shinkansen to Hiroshima. Make your way to the Peace Memorial Museum (p228) to learn about the atomic bombing of the city in 1945, then pick up a bento box from Onigiri Nitaya (www.nitaya.jp) and spend lunchtime in quiet contemplation in the Peace Memorial Park (p228). After paying your respects at the park's poignant monuments, catch the 45-minute ferry to Miyajima Island (p230) from the park's pier. Unwind in the onsen at Kurayado Iroha Ryokan, before enjoying the traditional meal prepared by your host (www.visit-miyajima.jp).

Day 5

Rise early to view the world-famous Otorii of Itsukushima Shrine at high tide, when it seems to float on the sea. Explore the rest of the shrine at your leisure, then follow your nose to Kakiya (www.kaki-ya.jp) for a delicious lunch of fried oysters. Enjoy a moment of calm at the Daisho-in Temple nearby, then make the 90-minute hike up Mount Misen for spectacular panoramic views. Take the ferry back to Hiroshima in time for dinner at Okonomi Mura (www.okonomimura.jp), which serves delicious okonomiyaki (savoury pancakes).

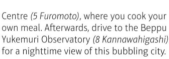

Although public transportation on the island is excellent, Kyushu is best explored by car, providing plenty of opportunity to head off the beaten path whenever temptation strikes.

7 DAYS

in Kyushu

Day 1

Start your trip in the modern city of Fukuoka *(p264)*. First stop is the fascinating modern art collection at the Fukuoka Asian Art Museum, followed by lunch at the *yatai* (food stalls) on Nakasu Island. Your next port of call is Fukuoka Tower, a mere 30-minutes away by subway. Whizz to the top to admire the view, then head back down to ground level to visit the Fukuoka City Science Museum. Here, you can face the future and interact with almost 250 different robots. Round off your day with a meal of fusion cuisine at Bassin *(1-9-63 Daimyo)*.

Day 2

Pick up your rental car and make the two-hour drive to Beppu *(p271)*. Plan to arrive in time for lunch – the *toriten* (chicken tempura) at Tokyoken *(www.toyoken-beppu.co.jp)* is an excellent option. In the afternoon, check out one of Beppu's hot spring resorts; Myoban Hot Spring, perched high above the city, is a nicely secluded option. Keep the temperature up in the evening at the Jigokumushi Kobo Steam Cooking

Centre *(5 Furomoto)*, where you cook your own meal. Afterwards, drive to the Beppu Yukemuri Observatory *(8 Kannawahigashi)* for a nighttime view of this bubbling city.

Day 3

The attractive hot-spring town of Kurokawa *(p276)* is less than two hours' drive from Beppu. Check into the beautiful Fujita *ryokan (6-5-4-1 Manganji)*, then spend the rest of the morning walking the main crater of Mount Aso *(p276)*; tender beef from the Akaushi cattle that graze its slopes can be ordered for lunch at Imakin Shokudo *(aso.ne.jp)* in Aso Town. Next, drive to Takachiho Gorge *(p276)*, where you can rent a rowing boat to get a close-up view of the waterfall. Head back to Fujita in time for dinner and a soak in the *onsen*.

Day 4

Set out early for Takachiho *(p276)*, a town steeped in Japanese mythology. The surrounding area is blessed with some of the island's most dramatic scenery, making for a fabulously picturesque drive. Reach

1 *Yatai* food stalls on Nakasu Island in Fukuoka.

2 Rowing to the waterfall at Takachiho Gorge.

3 A road bridge between Amakusa and Kumamoto.

4 The impressive Suizen-ji garden in Kumamoto.

Kumamoto *(p274)* in time for lunch at Aoyagi *(aoyagi.ne.jp)*, a beautiful spot in which to enjoy sushi. Walk across the river to view Kumamoto's striking black castle, before making the short drive to Suizen-ji, a superlative garden that re-creates sites from elsewhere in Japan. If you're feeling adventurous, try the local *basashi* (horse meat sashimi) at Iroha *(p277)* for dinner. Don't worry if it's not for you – there are plenty of other dishes to choose from.

Day 5

The mist-shrouded islands of Amakusa, less than a two-hour drive away from Kumamoto, were once home to Kyushu's hidden Christian communities, who were driven out of the Shimabara Peninsula *(p275)*. Learn more about this persecution at the Christian Museum in Amakusa City *(19-52 Fumenoomachi)*, before lunch at Yakko Sushi *(76-2 Higashimachi)*. It's a 2.5-hour drive to Nagasaki *(p266)* through epic scenery, including a car ferry trip across the Hayasakiseto Strait. Once you've settled into your hotel, walk to Kagetsu *(p267)* for a fusion meal.

Day 6

Spend the morning exploring Dejima in Nagasaki harbour to learn about the Dutch, Portuguese and Chinese influences on the city. Continue this theme with a lunch of *champon* – a Chinese-style noodle soup – at Shikairou *(4-5 Matsugaemachi)*. Dedicate the afternoon to the affecting Atomic Bomb Museum and Peace Park, then make the short drive to Kagetsu *(p267)* for fusion-style *shippoku*. After dark, park your car at the top of Mount Inasa and enjoy amazing views of the city.

Day 7

Head back to Fukuoka via the Saga Pottery Towns *(p280)*; Yobuko's market offers a selection of affordable ceramics. Once back in Fukuoka, return your hire car before slurping a "pork bone cappuccino" at Hakata Issou *(p265)*. Walk it off on a stroll to the Hakata Machiya Folk Museum, where you can watch a hypnotizing display of silk weaving. In the evening, go *yatai*-hopping on Nakasu Island again, resisting the temptation to go to the same stall as before.

Palatial Pads

Over the centuries, the imperial family's patronage led to the construction of impressive buildings across the country. Perhaps the most famous example is the Katsura Imperial Villa *(p203)*, which was originally built as a princely estate in the early 17th century. This elegant mansion has shaped what is commonly understood to be traditional Japanese architecture, but was also hailed as the ideal modernist prototype by Bruno Taut, the German architectural theorist, in 1937. Book a tour of the villa and other sights, including the Kyoto Imperial Palace *(p195)* and Shugaku-in Imperial Villa *(p204)*, through the Imperial Household Agency *(sankan.kunaicho.go.jp)*.

↑ Elegant 19th-century Kyoto Imperial Palace, the former ruling palace of the emperor

JAPAN FOR
ARCHITECTURE

Architecture is one of the most influential expressions of Japan's culture and creativity. Whether it's the elegant minimalism of the Ise Shrine, or the utopian optimism of the 20th-century Metabolist movement, the country's buildings encompass its multifaceted personality.

Modern Mountains

Roppongi is home to one of Japan's modern marvels of engineering – the Mori Tower. This cutting-edge skyscraper mitigates the risks posed by earthquakes with 192 fluid-filled shock absorbers. These semiactive dampers are filled with a thick oil and, as the tower begins to sway – as a result of tremor or high winds – the oil sloshes in the opposite direction to balance the structure. Another modern wonder in the capital is the Tokyo Skytree. Completed in 2012, and designed to evoke a traditional pavilion, this tower stretches 2,080 ft (634 m) above Tokyo. This latter-day pagoda is ostensibly a TV broadcasting tower, but also has restaurants and observation decks that offer tremendous views of the city's incredible skyline.

The Tokyo Skytree piercing the clouds high above the city's inimitable skyline

↑ The undulating exterior of Tokyo's cutting-edge Yogogi National Gymnasium

Postwar Parks

Built for the 1964 Toyko Olympics, the Yoyogi National Gymnasium in Yoyogi Park *(p96)* fused tradition with cutting-edge design, and symbolized the country's rebirth after the devastation of World War II. The architect Kenzo Tange also designed the Peace Memorial Museum in the Hiroshima Peace Memorial Park *(p228)*. Along with the nearby A-Bomb Dome, it is an affecting memorial and symbol of peace. Join a community-led architectural walk of Hiroshima to understand how the city has reconciled with its tragic past *(oa-hiroshima.org)*.

WHAT WAS METABOLISM?

Postwar reconstruction efforts in Japan's cities spawned new ideas about the future of urban planning and design. One of the most important of these was Metabolism. This movement came about during preparation for the 1960 Tokyo World Design Conference, embraced the idea of modern cities in flux – constantly changing and adapting to meet the needs of their residents. This called for modular megastructures that could grow and shrink according to necessity. Although frustrated in their desire to build Tokyo anew, Metabolist devotees, such as Kenzo Tange and Kisho Kurokawa, exerted a major influence on the country's architecture. Check out Kurokawa's Nakagin Capsule Tower in Ginza *(p106)*.

Sacred Structures

Shrines and temples are some of the most distinctive buildings in Japan. Common features to look out for include vermilion *torii* gates, troughs for ritual washing, and *shimenawa*, the straw rope with white zigzag paper strips that marks the boundary between the everyday and spirit worlds. The Tosho-gu shrine *(p300)* in Nikko symbolizes the power of the Tokugawa shogunate. Take a two-week tour to hear an expert unpack Japanese religious architecture *(www.architecturaladventures.org)*.

←

The five-story pagoda at the entrance to Nikko's Tosho-gu Shrine

JAPAN
IN THE WINTER

While Japan is most often associated with its springtime cherry blossoms, winter is also a superlative time to visit. With perfect pistes, riotous festivals, and steaming hot springs – for people and primates – this season has something for everyone.

TOP 5 RELAXING ROTENBURO

Kita Onsen
w kitaonsen.come
A secluded Honshu bath over 1,000 years old.

Ginzan Onsen
Obanazawa, Northern Honshu
Charming hot springs at "Silver Mountain".

Yagen Onsen
Shimokita Peninsula, Northern Honshu
Free open-air pool.

Asahidake Onsen
Higashikawa, Hokkaido
Soak at the foot of the island's tallest peak.

Noboribetsu Onsen
Noboribetsu, Hokkaido
Eleven kinds of water.

A Good Soak

Sit in a steaming *rotenburo* (outdoor *onsen*), overlooking wintry surrounds, for the ultimate relaxing experience. Hokkaido, with its smoldering volcanoes, has more *rotenburo* than any other prefecture, but there are many more across the country. In Northern Honshu, there is even a bath that caters solely to monkeys. Red-faced macaques soak in the hot pools at the Jigokudani Monkey Park *(p174)*.

Hit the Slopes

Blessed with a mountainous landscape and some of the heaviest snowfall in the world, is it any wonder that Japan boasts some 600 ski resorts? Although the mountains might not compare to the scale of the Alps or the Rockies, the region of Hokkaido compensates by offering the most reliable ski season in the world, with certain resorts averaging 60 ft (18 m) of snowfall annually. The best-quality powder is arguably found in Niseko *(p319)*, where you can take advantage of the excellent skiing and snowboarding conditions, as well as the buoyant après ski.

←

A snowboarder turning on a piste in Furano, one of Hokkaido's many resorts

→

A little girl, crafted out of snow, at the Sapporo Snow Festival

EAT

Kotogaume

Nabemono, or *nabe* for short, is enjoyed throughout the cold winter months. Traditionally, this hotpot is eaten by groups sitting around the gas burner on which the dish bubbles. This Tokyo eatery, owned by a former sumo wrestler, is one of the best places to sample *nabe*.

🅰F4 🏠3-4-4 Kinshi, Sumida-ku, Tokyo 130-0013 📞(03) 3624-7887 🕐L

¥ ¥ ¥

↑ A sculpture of a church, Sapporo Snow Festival

It's Snow Time!

Japan receives more snow for its latitude than any other country on earth, and the Japanese celebrate this epic snowfall with enthusiasm. The most famous snow festival is held in Sapporo *(p320)*, where hundreds of incredible sculptures, crafted from ice and snow, punctuate the city. Look around at night, when the sculptures of global landmarks and sci-fi characters are illuminated with neon lights. Step inside one of the ice huts – or *kamakura* – at the Yokote Kamakura Festival, to enjoy a *mochi* (rice cake), chased down with warming *amazake* (rice wine).

←

Relaxing in a *rotenburo* overlooking a lake in the Akan National Park

Oodles of Noodles

In Japan, you're never far away from a steaming bowl of this much-loved staple. There are three main forms of noodles here: Chinese-style ramen wheat noodles, light soba (buckwheat noodles), and unctuous udon (white wheat noodles). Each region has their own twist; sample them all at the Shin-Yokohama Raumen Museum in Yokohama *(www. raumen.co.jp/english)*.

A serving of soba noodles with a side of tempura, a staple at Japanese tables

JAPAN FOR
FOODIES

The Japanese menu, featuring slippery noodles, hearty hotpots, and delicate tasting dishes, is about so much more than just sushi. Whether you're in the backstreets of Tokyo or the refined restaurants of Kyoto, here you can find the most memorable meals of your life.

Let's Roll!

There are hundreds, possibly even thousands, of different flavours and types of sushi, but at its most pure form, this delicacy is about two things: rice and fish. Chefs train for a lifetime before they can claim to master this myriad dish. Don't let this put you off trying your hand at rolling your own: the world-famous Toyosu Fish Market *(p138)* is a fitting place to learn with Sushi Mafia *(www.sushi.tokyo.jp).*

💬 INSIDER TIP
Secret Tokyo Food Tour

Peek under the lid of local foodie scenes in Japan's biggest culinary cities on a foodie experience with Arigato Food Tours *(arigatojapan.co.jp)*. They will guide you through the warren of *izakaya* in Tokyo, the upmarket *kaiseki* scene in Kyoto, or Osaka during sakura season.

Eat the Streets

Downtown Fukuoka *(p264)* is full of *yatai*, glowing stalls providing hungry workers or revelers with late-night sustenance. While these stalls used to be common around Japan, around 40 percent are now found in this bustling city. Follow your nose, and the smell of creamy *tonkotsu* ramen, to find spots, or discover the stalls most likely to have you shouting *"oishii"* on a tour with a local guide *(www.govoyagin.com)*.

$\rightarrow$

Frying up Osaka's famous fried octopus ball, *takoyaki*, at a *yatai*

Seasons Greetings

Visiting Japan during winter? *Nabemono* (hot pot) dishes will keep you warm. In spring, cherry-blossom ice cream is the perfect accompaniment for sakura spotting. Light noodles will cool you down in sweltering summer, while mackerel is an autumn must.

$\leftarrow$

A delicious swirl of cherry-blossom ice cream

$\leftarrow$

Elevating Japanese dining to a fine art at Kikunoi in Kyoto

Delicate Dishes

Kaiseki, a tasting menu involving tens of delicate dishes, is the pinnacle of fine dining in Kyoto. Here, everything from the serving ceramics to the seasonality of the ingredients is taken into consideration. No trip to the city would be complete without sampling this refined dining style. Eat on a budget at Kyoto Hyoki *(hyoki.jp/en)*, or splash out at Kikunoi *(kikunoi. jp)*, which is run by a third-generation *kaiseki* chef.

$\leftarrow$

Showcasing the endless variety of sushi types, from *nigiri* to *maki*

Hiking the Heights

Pulling on walking boots and heading into the mountains is a popular pastime in Japan, and trails are easy to access and well-maintained. Our favourite is the three-day circuit through the North Japan Alps from Kamikochi *(p175)*. Those looking for a once in a lifetime experience can hike Mount Fuji, which, at 12,390 ft (3,776 m) high, is Japan's highest peak *(p158)*.

→

Hikers in the final stages of ascending Mount Fuji

JAPAN
OUTDOORS

Although Japan is one of the most densely populated countries in the world, over 70 percent of its terrain is mountainous or forested. Such an untamed landscape offers a rich array of outdoor activities – a veritable nature playground for the adventurous.

TOP 3 MOUNT FUJI TRAILS

Mount Fuji is divided up into 10 stages, with most hiking routes starting from the 5th stage, the last place accessible by vehicle.

Kawaguchi-ko
Takes five to six hours from the 5th stage, and three hours down.

Subashiri
This route is four hours 30 minutes up from the 5th stage, and three hours down.

Gotenba
The longest route at eight hours up from the 5th stage, followed by three hours down.

Snorkelling in Okinawa

This island nation provides plenty of opportunities to get up close to charming sea turtles, neon-colored clownfish, and flapping mantaray. The tropical island of Okinawa *(p282)* offers some of the best experiences – Cape Maeda's blue cave is one of the most popular spots. Odo Kaigan, near Gyokusendo Cave *(p288)*, is a more off-the-beaten-path option. Set in shallow water, just off the beach, this coral reef is perfect for families.

→

Snorkeling with a turtle in the tropical waters off Okinawa

Camping in Yakushima

Spend the night in a fairy-tale setting of gnarled tree trunks and moss-covered rocks at this UNESCO Biosphere Reserve. Jerry's campsite offers bicycles, snorkelling gear, and even the chance to try bee-keeping *(www.eu-guesthouse-in-yakushima.net)*. You can learn more about Yakushima's unique fauna and flora on a private hiking tour *(www.yakushimaexperience.com)*.

→

The atmospheric ancient forest of Yakushima

Surfing in Miyazaki

With 1,864 miles (3,000 km) of coastline, Japan offers waves aplenty. The year-round consistency of its swell has made Miyazaki, on Kyushu, a surfer's paradise. Kisakihama – a big beach to the north of the city – is one of the most popular places to ride the waves. Book a lesson at one of the local surf schools to learn the secret to riding the waves. On Shikoku, the area around Kochi *(p254)* offers an array of surfing spots that cater for all abilities.

←

A surfer preparing to hit the waves from the beach in Miyazaki

←

Fly fishing in Hokkaido's Akan National Park

Fly Fishing in Hokkaido

Unsurprisingly for a nation that prizes its sushi, you will see plenty of fresh fish across the country. Try your hand at catching your own in Hokkaido, where crystal-clear rivers and flawless lakes are home to salmon and trout. One of the most spectacular places to fish is the majestic Akan National Park *(p322)*.

→

Built for speed, the
shinkansen at
Shin-Osaka Station

JAPAN ON A
SHOESTRING

Billed as one of the most expensive countries in the world, Japan can be surprisingly affordable. Savvy visitors can go far using reasonably priced public transport, while low-cost fast food and happy hours make evenings a pleasure.

Cheap Eats

Vending machine restaurants offer affordable and filling food in the cities. Insert some yen into the slot, select the meal you want, and your change and ticket will pop out of the machine. Give this ticket to the cook at the counter, and receive a steaming bowl of ramen or a piled plate of fluffy rice. Yoshinoya, the most historic fast-food restaurant in Tokyo, has served up *gyudon* – a hearty dish of rice, beef and onion – since 1899 *(www.yoshinoya. com)*. If you're out and about, lunch at a *conbini* (convenience store) is a great way to save yen.

→

Eating *gyudon* at a communal
table at Tokyo's Yoshinoya

Smart Travel

Buses are an inexpensive way of getting around Japan. Long-distance buses often have reclining seats and footrests, making them both comfortable and practical. If travelling overnight, you'll even save the cost of a hotel. Savvy train travellers should buy a Seishun 18, which permits anyone, regardless of their age, unlimited rides on local and rapid JR trains over five days *(www.jreast.co.jp/ e/pass/seishun18.html)*. For those who want to travel faster and further, the multi-day Japan Rail Pass allows unlimited journeys on every form of public transport, including the bullet train *(www. jrailpass.com)*.

← The friendly-looking Asakusa sightseeing panda bus

STAY

9h 9 hours Capsule
A "smart sleep" system in a high-end capsule.

📍 2-9-4 Kajicho, Chiyoda-ku, Tokyo 101-0044 🌐 ninehours.co.jp

¥ 🚫 🚭

The Millennials
Beer and coffee come with the capsule.

📍 235 Yamazaki-cho, Nakagyo-ku, Kyoto-shi Kyoto 604-8032 🌐 themillennials.jp

¥ 🚫 🚭

Book and Bed Fukuoka
Sleep in bunks hidden between bookshelves.

📍 PARCO, 2-11-1 Tenjin, Chuo-ku, Fukuoka 810-0001 🌐 bookandbed tokyo.com

¥ 🚫 🚭

Tokyo Tips

Japan's capital is an expensive city, but there are plenty of free, or inexpensive, things to do if you know where to look. Buzzing Roppongi's street-scape is an open-air gallery of fascinating sculptures, such as Louise Bourgeois' *Maman (p90)*. At the Arashio Stable, you can watch the sumo wrestlers' morning practice for free *(www.arashio.net)*. Free sightseeing buses navigate city sites – the cutest are undoubtedly in Asakusa. For more tips, see Tokyo Cheapo *(tokyocheapo.com)*.

→

Sumo wrestlers working up a sweat during morning practice at Arashio Stable

Today's Voice

Haruki Murakami is arguably Japan's most famous contemporary novelist. Fans of *Norwegian Wood* (1987) should visit DUG in Tokyo *(www.dug.co.jp)*, the bar in Shinjuku where Toru Watanabe sinks whiskeys with sodas. In Takamatsu *(p253)*, discover why Nakata, protagonist of *Kafka on the Shore* (2002), described the city as "udon central."

A still from a television adaptation of Murakami's novel *Norwegian Wood*

JAPAN ON
PAGE AND SCREEN

With its awe-inspiring scenery and unique ways of life, it's little wonder that Japan has captured the imagination of so many great writers and filmmakers. Follow the trail of your favourite books and movies to see the sights behind the set and pen.

TOP 5 ESSENTIAL JAPANESE FILMS

Late Spring (1949)
Looks at the relationship between a widowed father and his daughter.

Rashomon (1950)
Different characters give conflicting versions of events in this thriller.

Tampopo (1985)
A "ramen" version of a spaghetti Western.

Spirited Away (2000)
The tale of a little girl who is magicked into the spirit world.

Our Little Sister (2015)
Three sisters invite their younger half-sister to live with them.

Be Spirited Away

For many, the quintessential Japanese filmmaker is Hayao Miyazaki, cofounder of Studio Ghibli. Step into the animator's imagination at Tokyo's Ghibli Museum *(p143)*, with its recreated sets, original sketches, and showreels of his films. For full immersion, why not visit one of the real-life spots that inspired Miyazaki's fantastical worlds? The bathhouse in *Spirited Away* is said to be modeled on Dogo Onsen Honkan in Matsuyama *(p256)*.

Windows into the Past

Written in the early 11th century by Murasaki Shikibu, a lady-in-waiting at the imperial court, *The Tale of Genji* is thought to be the oldest work of fiction in the world. Visit the room where Shikibu began to write this historic romance on a moonlit night in 1004 at the Ishiyama-dera temple in Otsu, near Kyoto. Japan is also home to another ancient art form – the haiku. Learn more about these concise poems at Tokyo's Basho Memorial Museum *(1-6-3 Tokiwa)*, dedicated to the masterful Matsuo Basho. You can also recreate his long-form poem *The Narrow Road to the Deep North* by climbing up Mount Haguro *(p308)*. As you walk the forest path, surrounded by towering trees, it is easy to see how Basho was inspired to write his meditative verses. And at the end of your trip, why not summarize your trip in your own haiku?

↑ Illustration depicting Lady Murasaki writing the *Tale of Genji*

←

A still from Hayao Miyazaki's Oscar-winning animated movie *Spirited Away*

Through International Eyes

For many people, *Lost in Translation* (2003) perfectly renders the realities of being a foreigner in Tokyo. Visit the New York Bar at the top of the Park Hyatt Tokyo *(p89)* to recreate the most iconic moments from Sofia Coppola's film. Wes Anderson fans, meanwhile, should take a boat trip to Gunkanjima from Nagasaki *(www.yamasa-kaiun.net/en)*. As well as being the inspiration for *Isle of Dogs* (2018), this abandoned industrial island also featured in the 2012 James Bond film *Skyfall*.

←

Exploring the wonderful Ghibli Museum in Tokyo

↑ Scarlett Johansson and Bill Murray in *Lost in Translation*

Paradise Gardens

Introduced to Japan by Buddhist monks during the Heian Period, a Paradise Garden is designed to evoke the Pure Land, or Buddhist paradise. You can easily imagine the Buddha meditating on an island in one of the gardens' lotus ponds. Byodo-in in Uji City *(p240)* is one of the most famous examples, while the Motsu-ji garden in Hiraizumi *(p306)* makes use of "borrowed landscape" – trees or mountains outside the garden that appear to be part of it.

IKEBANA

The practice of using flowers as temple offerings originated in the 7th century, but formalized flower arranging, or *ikebana*, didn't take hold until the late 15th century. Nowadays, it is seen as a meditative art. Arrangements are supposed to be created in silence, to allow the designer to observe the beauty of nature and gain inner peace.

The Phoenix Hall and lotus pond in Byodo-in garden in Uji City ↑

JAPAN'S
GARDENS

Reflecting the Shinto love of nature and the Buddhist ideal of paradise, Japan's gardens may seem like heaven on earth. From strolling in Western-style parks to meditating among curious rock formations in a zen garden, there are plenty of ways to appreciate these outdoor spaces.

Zen Gardens

Looking to be more mindful? Seek out a *karesansui* (Japanese rock garden) and focus on one of the stones, seemingly floating in a sea of raked gravel. Kyoto is home to some of the best examples, including Ryoan-ji *(p200)* – where the plain earthen walls enhance the abstract arrangement of the stones – and Daisen-in *(p198)*. Kyoto Garden Experience *(www.kyotogardenexperience.com)* offers private tours and the chance to access gardens usually barred to the public.

←

Visitors soaking up the peaceful atmosphere at Ryoan-ji in Kyoto

TOP 3 GARDENS IN JAPAN

Kenroku-en
One of Japan's "three great gardens," this expansive park is equally breathtaking in every season (p165).

Kairaku-en
Located in Mito, the second of the "three great gardens" is at its most spectacular when its 3,000 plum trees blossom in February and March.

Koraku-en
The last of the "three great gardens," this picturesque stroll garden in Okayama is unusual for its spacious lawns (p236).

Stroll Gardens

The landscape comes to life on a walk through one of Japan's stroll gardens, as vistas are concealed and revealed with every step. Suizen-ji Jou-en (p274) is one of the country's finest, while the garden of the Katsura Imperial Villa (p203) replicates famous Japanese landscapes. Tokyo's Rikugi-en Garden (p144) was inspired by famous poems.

→

The undulating landscape of the Suizen-ji Jou-en garden in Kumamoto

Tea Gardens

To reach a teahouse for the tea ceremony, you must first pass through a *roji*. Lined with sweet-smelling moss, this garden is designed to resemble a mountain trail, leading from reality into the magical world of the teahouse. Head to the Kenroku-en Garden (p165) or the Ise Shrine (p244) to take part in this unique ritual.

←

The secluded surrounds of a teahouse

Horse Around

Perfected in the 12th-century *yabusame* (horseback archery) involves an archer galloping down a 837-ft- (255-m-) long track, controlling his horse with his knees, while shooting an arrow at three targets. The best place to witness this feat is at the Kamakura Festival *(p154)*, held each September. The inspired can attempt to master this art at Ibraki *(www.govoyagin.com)*.

→

Showcasing the art of *yabusame* at the Kamakura Festival

JAPAN FOR
SAMURAI STORIES

While samurai may be a thing of the past, the legend around these mythical and honorable warriors has not been forgotten. Step into the world of these ancient military elite by visiting their old haunts or trying your hand at mastering skills, from sword fighting to archery on horseback.

TOP 5 SAMURAI MOVIES

Seven Samurai (1954)
Farmers hire samurai to fight against bandits stealing their crops.

Yojimbo (1961)
A samurai convinces two competing crime lords to hire him.

Harakiri (1962)
Conflict arises over the practice of ritual suicide, *seppuku*.

Twilight Samurai (2002)
A reluctant samurai is forced to fight.

Samurai Rebellion (1967)
A samurai risks death to save his son's wife.

Fight Club

A samurai's sword was said to be his soul – naturally, these weapons could only be made by expert craftsmen. See swords on display at the Sword Museum in Tokyo *(p144)* or visit the Seki Traditional Swordsmith Museum near Nagoya *(p170)* to witness this incredible craft in action.

→

A model in samurai regalia, clutching a prized sword

Silent Assassins

While samurai were military nobility, dressed in elaborate suits of armor, ninja were mercenaries, clothed in all black. The samurai – ruled by elaborate codes of honor – looked down on the ninja, who specialized in espionage, sabotage, and guerilla warfare. Experience the world of these dark assassins for yourself at the Koka Ninja Village, where the brave are put through their paces in a ninja training class (p233). Afterwards, watch the experts at work at the Iga Ninja Museum (p235).

↓ The dark arts of the ninja, on display at Koka Ninja Village

Looking up at the ↑ towering fortress walls of Kumamoto castle

Capture the Castle

Forget about the fairy-tale Himeji-jo or the domineering structure at Osaka - the mightiest fortress is Kumamoto (p274). Alas, this castle wasn't as impenetrable as hoped: it was ravaged during the 1877 Satsuma Rebellion. Currently undergoing reconstruction due to damage sustained during the 2016 earthquake, this fortress can still be viewed from the outside.

The Last Samurai

As warfare changed, the samurai transformed from mounted archers to master swordsmen, and finally to desk-bound bureaucrats. Find out about their evolution at the Samurai Museum in Tokyo (p96). Here, the enthusiastic English-speaking guides will take you through this history, while demonstrating a number of sword moves. After the tour, try on armour for size, adopt an imposing stance, and draw your *katana* like a true warrior.

→

Intimidating medieval armour, displayed at the Samurai Museum

Rainy-Day Activities

When the weather outside is frightful, head into an amusement arcade. Often located near major train stations, these flashing alleys are a great place for kids to burn off excess energy. The country's big game companies, such as Sega, and Capcom, churn out new titles for these arcades, keeping young and old gamers entertained. For gentler distractions, dive into the mammouth Osaka Aquarium *(p221)*, home to around 30,000 marine animals, including a pair of graceful whale sharks.

→

Young visitors getting up close to the fishes at Osaka Aquarium

JAPAN FOR
FAMILIES

Japan is a great place for a family holiday. The people are friendly, the crime rate is low, and the public transportation system is easy to use. With a huge mix of attractions and activities, you won't fail to keep the kids entertained.

Make-Believe Worlds

Creative cosplay is a great way to introduce children to Japanese culture. Kids will love dressing up as samurai, ninja, daimyo and geisha *(www.toei-eigamura.com)*, and reliving the days of yore at the epic Toei Kyoto Studio Park. For rather more contemporary culture, the Ghibli Museum *(p143)* immerses visitors in the worlds of *Totoro, Princess Mononoke,* and *Spirited Away.* Don't miss the life-sized robot from *Castle in the Sky* that dominates the rooftop garden.

←

Children playing on the "Cat Bus" at the interactive Ghibli Museum

EAT

Shinyokohama Ramen Museum
A range of ramen.

 F5 🏠 2-14-21, Yokohama
🌐 raumen.co.jp

¥¥¥

The Gundam Café
Robot-themed waffles.

 F4 🏠 1-1 Kanda Hanaokacho, Tokyo
🌐 g-cafe.jp/en

¥¥¥

Active Fun

Japan's clean, fast, and affordable public transportation system provides ready access to the Japanese countryside. The densely forested mountains, lush green of rice paddies, and pristine beaches are ideal natural playgrounds. Take the kids to Niseko's slopes for some of Japan's best skiing (p319), or to learn to surf (p43) in the waves of Miyazaki.

← Plowing through the snow on cross-country skis in Niseko

Theme Parks

Children will clamor to visit Tokyo Disneyland, home to Mickey Mouse and his pals. Here you can ride hair-raising roller coasters, and have your photo taken with one of Disney's iconic characters (www.tokyodisneyresort.jp). If you only have time for one of the parks, choose Tokyo DisneySea for its under-the-sea theme. To explore the worlds of some of your favorite movies, head to Universal Studios (p220) in Osaka or, for a wackier experience, go to Huis Ten Bosch, near Nagasaki (p269). Occupying a seafront plot the size of Monaco, this vast park re-creates a 17th-century Dutch town, with windmills, canals, and narrow houses.

→ Posing in front of the iconic Disneyland Castle

Kimono Dragons
A kimono-clad *geiko* is an enduring image of Japan. For a peek at this nonpareil apparel, check out the fabulous silks at the Itchiku Kubota Art Museum *(p158).* Then create your own at the Nagamachi Kaga Yuzen Silk Center *(p164).*

A trio of elegantly adorned *geiko*, dressed in colorful silk kimonos

JAPAN FOR
TRADITIONAL
CRAFTS

Hailed as "Living National Treasures," Japan's *shokunin*, or artisans, venerate tradition, continuity, and attention to detail. Across the country you can visit workshops and markets brimming with hand-turned pottery, delicately painted silks and exquistely crafted paper – and even design your own.

TOP 5 OTHER CRAFTS

Origami
Folding paper into unexpected treasures.

Shodo
The art of calligraphy arrived in Japan from China in AD 600.

Bonsai
Carefully pruned, perfectly formed tiny trees.

Ikebana
Beautiful flower arrangements originally used as offerings.

Kodo
An "art of refinement" – the practice of appreciating incense.

Dyeing to Meet You
For centuries, strict sumptuary laws restricted all but the wealthiest from wearing certain colors and fabrics, such as silk. Learn more about the history at Kyoto's Little Indigo Museum *(shindo-shindigo.com).* Get a feel for creating your own textiles at the Mingei Iyo Kasuri Kaikan in Matsuyama *(p256),* or scour flea markets for vintage pieces.

Take a Leaf Out of Their Book

The Genda Shigyo company has been handcrafting paper since 771 and in Kyoto since 794. Pop into the ancient store to admire the *mizuhiki* – twisted paper ribbons. Give the tradition a go: head to Ozu Washi in Tokyo *(p23)* to pour a mixture of bark and water into a sieve, before sifting to form a perfect piece of paper. Just like panning for gold.

→

A traditional paper craftsman working in his studio

Lustrous Lacquerware

Made from the sap of the urushi tree, lacquer is durable, waterproof, and shiny – the perfect varnish. Lacquerware is as ornate as it is resilient. The birthplace of this craft, Wajima is the perfect place to try your hand at designing your own *(p176)*. At the Wajima Kobo Nagaya workshop, you can engrave a set of chopsticks and talk to experienced artisans about their work *(4-66-1 Kawai-machi)*.

←

Sumptuous lacquerware plate inlaid with pearl

Seize the Clay

In the 16th century, advanced techniques from Korea revolutionized Japan's ceramics industry. Kyushu – on the Korea Strait – has since been Japan's greatest ceramics producer. Hop between ancient workshops and laden market stalls in the Saga pottery towns *(p280)*. At Rokuro-za in in Arita, take to the potter's wheel to mould your own masterpiece *(1-30-1 Izumiyama)*.

←

Hand-wringing freshly dyed silk at a textile plant's dye workshop

→

Spinning clay by hand at a Kyushu potter's workshop

The Inspiring Island

One of the country's most atmospheric islands, Sado is studded with wooden villages bleached grey from wind and salt *(p307)*. Despite its bleak appearance, this island has inspired some of Japan's greatest art forms. It was here that *taiko* drumming truly took off. Feel the beat as you strike one of these massive drums at the Sado Island Taiko Center *(www.sadotaiken.jp)*.

→

The windswept landscape of Senkaku Bay on the island of Sado

Did You Know?

Only 430 of Japan's 6,852 islands are inhabited.

JAPAN
OFF THE
BEATEN PATH

Japan is endlessly fascinating, and taking a trip to the country feels like a journey off-the-beaten path even when you're surrounded by crowds. But, beyond the well-worn tourist trail between Kyoto and the capital, there are 7,000 islands to explore, as well as myriad sites to experience.

Galapagos of the Orient

Located 620 miles (1,000 km) south of Tokyo, the UNESCO-protected Ogasawara Islands are an unspoiled Eden. This isolated archipelago, made up of over 30 tropical and subtropical islands, is home to countless endemic species, from tiny Bonin white-eye birds and jewel-like tiger beetles to the elusive Bonin flying fox.

The seculded Kominato Beach on one of Japan's Ogawawara islands ↑

Land of the Diving Women

These days, the tiny island of Hegura, located off the coast of Ishikawa, is best known as a paradise for bird-watchers. In the 1960s, however, it was made famous by the Italian anthropologist Fosco Maraini when he published his photographic book about the ama (diving women) of the island. Amazingly, many of the same women that he photographed still work on the island during summer. The last survivors of a dying tradition, they can still be seen sorting seaweed and diving for abalone.

←

The famous ama (diving women) of Hegura island hauling a net

ANIMAL ISLANDS

Of the dozen cat islands that are found around Japan, the most famous is Aoshima, where cats outnumber humans by an astounding six to one. More than 100 felines prowl about this island, curling up in abandoned houses, and strutting about in the quiet fishing village. If cats aren't for you, check out the unusual Zao Fox Village in Miyagi Prefecture, or try visiting Okunoshima. This island was where Japan produced poison gas during World War II, but it's now crowded with 1,000 cute and fluffy rabbits.

The Hidden Christians

When Christianity was banned at the end of the 16th century, many believers fled to Amakusa, a series of islands between Kumamoto and Nagasaki. Here, the community lived in secrecy for more than 300 years, disguising their faith under a veil of Buddhism. The Christian Museum in Amakusa City *(p35)* displays Buddhist statues, with crucifixes carved into their backs, as well as images of the Virgin Mary that were made to look like Kannon, the Buddhist goddess of Mercy. Explore Amakusa by boat to see why these mist-shrouded islands made the perfect hiding place *(www. seacruise.jp/cruise-english)*.

→

One of the elegant churches found on the islands of Amakusa

Quirky Nights

As twilight hits, Japan's dark side is unleashed. Ghosts and ghouls join handcuffed diners at Lock Up in Shinjuku *(www.lock-up.jp)*, while writhing women and robo-pandas dance to *taiko* techno at Tokyo's Robot Restaurant *(p27)*. Order a bento box, grab a drink, and enjoy the spectacular show.

→

Diners ensconced in shell-shaped chairs at the Robot Restaurant

JAPAN
AFTER DARK

When the sun sets, Japan's streets transform under bright neon lights. From deliciously dingy dive bars to psychedelic robot cabaret, frenetic nightclubs to chilled out live music events, the country's heady nightlife is not to be missed.

Japan Live!

Music lovers flock to Tokyo everything from mellow guitarists to roaring punk bands. Try Shimokitazawa Three for the next big thing *(www.toos.co.jp/3)*, while AKB48 Theater in the Akihabara Electronics district *(www.akb48.co.jp)* is the place for sickly sweet J-Pop. Outside the capital, Osaka Muse is altogether more gritty *(www.arm-live.com/muse/osaka)*.

←

Jazz drummer on a cabaret stage tapping out a beat

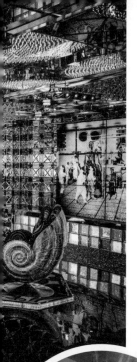

Dive Deep

The shabby alleys and arcades of Tokyo's Golden Gai are home to some of the country's moodiest dive bars *(p96)*. Hidden within this warren-like area is Albatross *(www.alba-s.com)*, a legendary drinking den frequented by artists, students, expats, and salarymen, who chat away into the night. In Osaka, seek out a *tachinomiya*, such Tachinomi Nikou *(p221)*, and rub shoulders with Japan's Everymen. Tucked into the gaps in the cityscape, these modest "standing bars" are as authentic as can be.

→

Tending bar at
Ishinohana Bar in
Tokyo's Golden Gai

Join the Club

Fans of electro-funk, techno, or house music, look no further - Japan's got you covered. The stand-out venue of Tokyo's Shibuya district *(p100)* is Womb, an enormous club throbbing across four floors *(www.womb.co.jp)*, while Sound Museum Vision keeps the party pumping *(www.vision-tokyo.com)*. Dance till dawn at Nagoya's sprawling ID Café *(www.idcafe.info)*, or join the crowds at Osaka's Club Joule *(club-joule.com)*.

←

Sound Museum
Vision in Tokyo's
Shibuya district

INSIDER TIP
Dotonbori

Osaka's glittering lights and the extravagant signage of seemingly endless bars and restaurants are best seen at night. Take a night cruise *(www.ipponmatsu.co.jp)* along the canal to suss out where to go, or find out on foot, with a night walk *(www.magical-trip.com)* hopping from *izakaya* bar to *izakaya* bar.

LGBT+ Venues

Ni-chome, in Shinjuku, has the highest concentration of gay bars in the world. Take a nighttime tour with OutAsia Travel to discover the best of the 300 bars on offer *(outasiatravel.com)*. In Osaka, follow in Lady Gaga's footsteps and head to Frenz Frenzy for a night of karaoke *(frenz-frenzy.website)*.

↑

Costumed
partygoers
atop a float
at Tokyo's
Pride march

Embark on a Pilgrimage

Japan's rich religious tradition has left the country peppered with numerous pilgrimage routes. The most famous is the 88-Temple Pilgrimage *(p258)*. On this journey around Shikoku, Buddhist devotees follow a circuit shaped like a mandala. At around 745 miles (1,200 km) long, it can take between 30 to 60 days to complete; get a taster by walking a section of the course.

Buddhists walking part of the 88-Temple Pilgrimage around Shikoku

JAPAN FOR
WELLNESS

If you're looking for a little rest and relaxation, there's nowhere better than Japan. Whether it's chilling out in hot springs or trying "forest bathing", becoming a pilgrim or immersing yourself in temple life, this tranquil country offers endless ways to maximise your wellbeing.

Time in a Temple

The country's Buddhist heritage has imbued it with a deep spirituality. Find inner peace by staying at a tranquil temple. Secluded from the modern world, visitors can fully immerse themselves in an often silent Buddhist community. Sacred Mount Koya *(p234)* is home to over 50 temples where visitors can meditate, sample traditional *shojin ryori* (vegan) cuisine, and soak in hot springs usually reserved for the monks.

Test the Waters

Soak away any aches and pains at one of Japan's many *onsen* - devotees claim that these hot spings have a number of health giving properties, including the alleviation of neuralgia. For those of a metaphysical mindset, Shinrin-yoku, or "forest bathing", might be just the ticket. This new age practice is said to reduce blood pressure and increase "energy flow".

→

People relaxing in an outdoor *onsen* at dusk

Find Your Ikigai

There's much to be said for the Japanese concept of *ikigai*, or reason for being, for aiding mindfulness. Infuse each day with meaning by trying an activity such as zen gardening at the Kyoto University of Art and Design *(www.jghh.jp/center)* or learning the art of *washoku* (Japanese cuisine) at the Tsukiji Cooking School in Tokyo *(tsukiji-cooking.com)*.

←

A man carefully tending his garden

Eat Yourself Well

The traditional Japanese diet of fish and fermented foods has been linked to the country's longevity, giving you an excellent excuse to devour more of Japan's delicious fare. Take a cookery class at Mayuko's Little Kitchen *(www.mayukoslittlekitchen.com)* to learn how to make this mouthwatering cuisine yourself, or find out how fermentation can improve your health with a visit to the traditional miso factory at the Kyushu Yufuin Folk Art Village in Yukuin *(p270)*.

↑ Monks outside Kongobuji Temple on Mount Koya

→

A delicious bowl of mouthwatering homemade ramen

▽ Cosplay Central

Cosplay, where people dress as their favourite comic book characters, is huge in Japan, thanks to its love of manga and anime. Expect to see locals strolling the streets in costume, especially in Tokyo's Harajuku *(p94)*, Ikebukuro *(p142)*, and Akihabara *(p116)* districts. Pick up your own costume at Studio Crown in Akihabara *(studio-crown. com/experience)* and join in the fun.

△ Gotta Catch 'Em All

Japan is the birthplace of Pokémon, and wannabe trainers will love visiting the Pokémon Center Mega Tokyo in Ikebukuro *(p142)*. Packed full of colorful merchandise, from sweets to pillows, it's *the* place to pimp your Pokédex.

JAPAN FOR
POP CULTURE

It might be renowned for its timeless traditions, but Japan is also home to a fascinatingly futuristic pop culture. From quirky anime to cute cat cafés, kitsch karaoke bars to quick-witted robots, the country's eclectic culture has taken the rest of the world by storm.

△ Bubblegum Pop

Born in the 1990s, Japan's kitschy J-pop – known for its focus on bubblegum pop, catchy tunes, and wacky outfits – has spawned many imitators, including K-pop. Sing along to hits from AKB48 or SMAP at a karaoke booth, or visit Karaoke Kan *(karaokekan.jp)*, the popular chain featured in *Lost in Translation*, to warble with the locals.

▽ Robot World

Japan is at the forefront of robotics, with these mechanical miracles increasingly part of day-to-day life. Visit the Robot Kingdom in Huis Ten Bosch *(p269)* to build your own robotic wonder, then dine in its robot-staffed restaurant. Also in the park is the Henn-na Hotel *(www.h-n-h.jp/en)*, where animatronic dinosaurs greet you at reception.

Did You Know?

A robot priest has been developed to recite mantras at funerals.

▽ Fashion Forward

Renowned as one of the most influential areas in the fashion world, Harajuku's two main shopping arteries - Takeshita-dori and Omotesando - are populated by stalls selling an eye-watering array of outfits *(p94)*. Spy black "Gothic Lolita" dresses, leather "visual kei" skirts, and 1950s-style "rockabilly" headbands - all items beloved by the area's quirky Harajuku girls *(p95)*. With so many outfits to choose from, hire a professional trend watcher to guide you through the various subcultures *(invitation-japan.com/plan/1563)*. After finding the perfect outfit, transform yourself into a living anime at a *purikura* (photo booth).

△ Sticking to a Theme

Sparking a global craze for cat cafés, Japan's eateries cater to every predilection. Take tea with a feline friend at Calico Cat Café *(catcafe.jp)* or sink your teeth into Dracula-themed treats at the Vampire Café in Ginza *(6-7-6 Ginza)*. Final Fantasy fans will love Eorzea Cafe *(www.pasela.co.jp)* for its Ninja amazake - a cocktail made from fermented rice, and topped off with a *shuriken* (throwing star).

Get a Grape

While legend has it that the first wine grapes were grown in Japan as early as 718 AD, local wine did not win acclaim overseas until recently. The country's signature grape, Koshu, is mainly grown in the lush mountains of Yamanashi Prefecture; tours and tastings are offered at most of the 90 vineyards here, but Sadoya (www.sadoya.co.jp), is a particular favorite.

→

Furano wine flavored with lavender, produced in northern Hokkaido

JAPAN
RAISE A GLASS

From flavorful sake to refreshing beer, ceremonial matcha tea to biting whiskey, the Japanese drinks cabinet is overflowing with tasty tipples. Alongside these classic beverages, there are surprising new additions, drawing on international influences. Don't miss these must-drinks.

TOP 5 TEAS IN JAPAN

Matcha
These powdered green tea leaves are used in everything from ice cream to noodles.

Sencha
While the green tea used in matcha is grown in the shade, Sencha is reared in the full sun.

Hojicha
This green tea has less caffeine than others.

Mugicha
Chilled barley tea is popular in summer time.

Genmaicha
Made from green tea and brown rice, this is used to settle stomachs.

Hopping Mad

Japan's big four - Kirin, Asahi, Sapporo, and Suntory - are known around the world, as are a number of craft breweries. For a hopping good time, visit the Sapporo Beer Garden and Museum (p320) to learn about the history of beer, and to sample some delicious brews.

→

On Japan's northernmost island, Sapporo entices visitors in from the cold

INSIDER TIP
Hit the Cider Trail

Japanese cider is on the march – check out the cider trail in Niigata to taste the latest addition to Japan's drinks menu (*www.pommelier.net*).

Neat Drinks
Nursed in dimly lit bars across the world, Japanese whiskies – often award-winning – are firmly on the tastebuds of the whisky world. See where the magic happens at noted brand Suntory's distillery and museum in Yamanashi (*www.suntory.com*).

↓ Award-winning Ichiro, famously Japan's smallest distillery

A girl practising the elaborate ritual of a tea ceremony ↑

Traditional Tea
Japanese monks brought tea to Japan after travelling to China in the 6th century. Since then, tea has become a quintessential part of local culture. It is sipped everywhere, from Tokyo's cool cafés to elaborate tea ceremonies in temple gardens (*p197*). Wazuka, near Kyoto, is a beautiful land of undulating tea bushes. Pick your own leaves at one of these plantations, before sampling different teas alongside traditional Japanese sweets at Kyoto Obubu Tea Farms (*obubutea.com*).

For Goodness' Sake
Traditionally served in small ceramic cups, sake is Japan's national drink. Made from rice, water, and yeast and served warm, it's the perfect accompaniment to Japanese food. There are hundreds of varieties, each with a unique flavour. Attempt to try them all with Sake Tours, whose excursions visit all the best breweries (*www.saketours.com*).

→

Colorfully decorated barrels of sake stacked up in Tokyo

Try Hard

Japan's love affair with rugby started in the mid-19th century with the end of isolationism, and it was soon a regular fixture at elite universities. The country now has more rugby clubs than any other in the world. Following a legendary last-minute victory over South Africa in 2015, Japan hosted its first ever Rugby World Cup in 2019. Japan rugby travel packages are available from InsideJapan (*www. japanrugbytravel.com*).

→

Japan playing South Africa in the 2015 Rugby World Cup

JAPAN FOR
SPORTS FANS

Japan's sporting calendar is packed with both quintessential traditional offerings, such as sumo and kando, and Western games like baseball. Alongside the usual events, the country staged the 2019 Rugby World Cup and will host the 2020 Olympics, cementing it as a sports lover's paradise.

No Kendo

Kendo, a traditional style of fencing using bamboo swords, traces its roots back to the samurai. Take a lesson, visit an armourer, or eat with the professionals on a tour with Samurai Trip (*www.samuraitrip07.com*).

→

Competitors fighting kendo-style with bamboo swords

Hit a Home Run

Baseball was imported to Japan from the US during the early Meiji Period, and almost immediately gained popularity among amateur athletic clubs and universities. Despite being banned during World War II, when it was seen as a corrupting American influence, it is now the most watched and played sport in the country. Housed in Tokyo Dome – the home stadium of the Yomiuri Giants – the Baseball Hall of Fame and Museum displays a fascinating array of memorabilia *(www.english.baseball-museum.or.jp)*. Try out your swing at the Shinjuku Batting Centre *(2-21-13 Kabukicho)*.

← Yomiuri Giants fans at the Tokyo Dome

DRINK

MLB Cafe Tokyo
This shrine to baseball is packed with memorabilia.

F4 **1-3-61 Kouraku** **mlbcafe.jp/en**

Los Cabos Shinjuku
Mexican-style sports bar with great tequila.

F4 **1-3-16 Kabukicho**

Legends Sports Bar
Burgers and craft beer accompany the rugby.

F4 **3-16-33 Roppongi** **legendsports.jp**

RINGS OF GLORY

In 2020, Japan hosts the Olympic Games for the second time. The 1964 competition symbolized Japan's rebirth after World War II, and there are hopes that the 32nd Olympiad in 2020 will mark the end of 21st-century austerity. Although there have been controversies, including a major redesign, the massive New National Stadium, designed by Kengo Kuma, promises to be a monument to match those in Yoyogi Park *(p96)*. Hire a bike, and cycle around the park to admire some of the original 1964 venues that will again be used as sporting stages in the 2020 games.

↑ Wrestlers and a *gyoji* (referee) at a traditional sumo match

Want Sumo This?

The rituals around sumo may be complicated, but the rules are simple: the first wrestler to exit the ring, or touch the ground with any part of his body besides his feet, loses. Tournaments only take place six times a year *(p70)*, but there are other ways to experience sumo. Exhibitions are held between tournaments and *beya* – where the wrestlers live and train – open their doors to visitors. To catch an early morning training session, contact the Japan Sumo Association *(sumo.or.jp)*.

Modern Masters

Immerse yourself in Tokyo's vibrant contemporary art scene at the Mori Art Museum *(p91)*. Located in the Mori Tower, it features constantly rotating exhibitions. At the extraordinary Benesse Art Site Naoshima - Japan's "art island" - visitors can walk among Yayoi Kusama's iconic, spotty sculptures, and Tandao Ando's concrete masterpieces *(p250)*.

The magnificent Mori Art Museum in Tokyo's impressive Mori Tower

JAPAN FOR
ART LOVERS

Art has long been one of the country's most successful exports, with the world clamoring over ukiyo-e prints and screen paintings for hundreds of years. Now, a host of exciting museums and innovative contemporary artists are stealing some of the spotlight from these traditional artforms.

 INSIDER TIP
Arty Stay

Palace Hotel Tokyo offer bespoke tours of the capital for art fans. Led by art historians, you can take in the world-class museums, browse for pieces, and visit some offbeat galleries *(www.en. palacehoteltokyo.com)*.

Traditional Scenes

To understand how Japan fuses traditional art with modern design, visit Tokyo's Nezu Museum *(p92)*. Designed by award-winning architect Kengo Kuma, it showcases over 7,400 works of Japanese and East Asian art, including *Irises*, an exquisite screen painting by Ogata Korin (c. 1701–05). Another site for traditional art in the capital is the Tokyo National Museum *(p128)*. Seek out the the museum's haunting collection of Noh masks for a fleeting glimpse into one of Japan's most idiosyncratic traditional art forms.

Striking Sculptures

The Hakone Open-Air Museum *(p169)* displays works by Rodin, Miro, and Picasso, as well as one of the world's largest collections of Henry Moore. The Kirishima Open-Air Museum, on Kyushu, is home to sculptures by Gormley, Turrell, Kapoor, and Yayoi Kusama *(www.open-air-museum.org)*.

↑ Emil-Antoine Bourdell's *Hercules the Archer* at the Hakone Museum

Asian Art

The Fukuoka Asian Art Museum *(p265)* showcases some of the continent's most daring artists. Spanning the early 20th century to the present, the collection includes everything from traditional oil paintings to video art. For a deep dive into contemporary Asian art, check out the Lee Ufan Museum at Benesse Art Site Naoshima *(p250)*.

← The entrance to the Fukuoka Asian Art Museum

Fantastic Photography

As Hiroshi Sugimoto is known for his long-exposure shots of seascapes and structures, it is appropriate that his Odawara Art Foundation Enoura Observatory juts out over Sagami Bay *(www.odawara-af.com/en)*. This eccentric museum features a minimalist exhibition space, a teahouse, and an outdoor Noh theatre.

→ Hiroshi Sugimoto's Odawara Art Foundation Enoura Observatory

↑ *Irises* by Ogata Korin (c. 1701–05), at the Nezu Museum, Tokyo

A YEAR IN
JAPAN

JANUARY

△ **New Year** *(Jan 1)*. At midnight, Buddhist temples ring their bells a total of 108 times.
Nanokado Hadaka-mairi *(Jan 7)*. Young men, dressed only in loincloths, rush to climb a rope to the ceiling of Nanokado temple in Yanaizu.

FEBRUARY

△ **Setsubun** *(Feb 3)*. To celebrate the start of spring, beans are thrown to scare away evil and bring good fortune.
Sapporo Snow Festival *(early Feb)*. Large-scale snow and ice sculptures take over the city for one week.

MAY

Aoi Matsuri *(May 15)*. Magnificent pageantry takes place in Kyoto, as revelers process to the Shimogamo and Kamigamo shrines.
△ **Sanja Matsuri** *(3rd weekend in May)*. Tokyo's wildest festival, featuring parades, dancing, and traditional music.

JUNE

△ **Rice-Planting Festival** *(Jun 14)*. Dressed in brightly colored traditional outfits, participants plant seedlings in the rice paddies of Sumiyoshi Ward, southern Osaka.
Chagu-chagu Umakko *(2nd Sat in Jun)*. Decorated horses parade to Hachiman-gu shrine in Morioka.

SEPTEMBER

△ **Hachiman-gu Festival** *(Sep 14–16)*. A procession of floats and horseback archery at the Hachiman-gu shrine in Kamakura draws a big crowd.
Sumo Autumn Basho *(mid-Sep)*. Tokyo hosts a fortnight of professional competitions.

OCTOBER

Nada Fighting Festival *(Oct 14–15)*. At Matsubara Shrine in Himeji, men carrying portable shrines compete to ring the lucky bell in the courtyard.
Tosho-gu Fall Festival *(Oct 17)*. Armor-clad samurai escort a portable shrine through Nikko.
△ **Fire Festival** *(Oct 22)*. Enormous fires in the shape of Chinese characters are burned into the hills that surround Kyoto.

MARCH

△ **Hina Matsuri** (*Mar 3*). Families with young daughters set up displays of elaborately dressed dolls, representing the imperial court in the Heian period.

Sumo Spring Basho (*mid-Mar*). Osaka hosts its annual tournament, which builds in intensity as the best wrestlers compete later in the competition.

APRIL

△ **Sakura Season** (*throughout*). Blooms ornament temples and parks nationwide, and cherry blossom is celebrated in classical poetry and literature.

Kanamara Matsuri (*1st Sun*). At Kanayama Shrine in Kawasaki, a 6-ft- (2-m-) tall phallus is paraded through the streets to offer prayers for conception, safe childbirth, and marital happiness.

Buddha's Birthday (*Apr 8*). All over Japan, believers bathe small statues of the Buddha and decorate them with flowers to signify his birth.

JULY

Gion Matsuri (*throughout*). Kyoto's largest festival features beautiful traditional costumes.

△ **Tanabata Matsuri** (*Jul 7*). An ancient festival celebrated by writing wishes on paper and hanging them from trees.

Fuji Rock Festival (*last weekend in Jul*). Japan's largest outdoor music event.

AUGUST

△ **Awa-Odori** (*Aug 12–15*). The city of Tokushima sings and dances for four days and nights to commemorate the building of the castle here in 1587.

Obon (*Aug 13–16*). Buddhists across the country visit their family tombs for the festival of the dead, in which riotous dances are performed and lanterns are lit to guide the deceased.

Daimonji Bonfire (*Aug 16*). Five large bonfires are lit on the hills around Kyoto to mark the end of Obon.

NOVEMBER

△ **Daimyo Gyoretsu** (*Nov 3*). Hakone hosts the re-enactment of a feudal lord's procession along the old Tokaido road between Edo and Kyoto.

Kyokusui-no-En (*Nov 3*). At Kyoto's Jonan-gu Shrine, poets dressed as Heian nobles must compose a 31-syllable poem, while drinking a glass of sake.

DECEMBER

Winter Illuminations (*throughout*). Light installations ornament cities across the country, from Sapporo to Tokyo.

△ **Okera Mairi Ceremony** (*Dec 31*). Head to the Yasaka Shrine in Kyoto to witness locals lighting lengths of bamboo rope with the sacred flame, so that they can ignite candles on their household altars.

A BRIEF
HISTORY

Japan's history is characterized by its separation, both geographically and politically, from the Asian continent. When centuries of isolationism ended in the 19th century, the country embraced new technologies, and today Japan is a world leader in everything from fashion to robotics.

The Emergence of Japan

Japan's first inhabitants arrived over 40,000 years ago, possibly via land bridges from the Asian continent. The Jomon hunting and gathering society emerged around 14,500 BC, and from 300 BC to AD 300 the Yayoi people spread from Kyushu to Honshu and Shikoku. In the west of Japan, between 538 and 710, a local clan – the forebears of today's imperial family – began to consolidate its power. It was during this period that Buddhism and Chinese writing arrived in the islands, and a system of laws based upon Confucianism and Chinese legal standards were established.

[1] A map showing the prefectures of Japan.

[2] Yayoi period dwellings in Yoshinogari Park.

[3] Murasaki Shikibu, author of the *Tale of Genji*.

[4] An illustration of the Mongol invasion in 1281.

Timeline of events

300 BC– AD 300

Methods of farming, metalwork, and pottery reach Japan from the continent.

239

Queen Himiko sends an envoy to the Wei kingdom in China.

710

Heijo-kyo (Nara) is made capital the capital of Japan.

794

Heian-kyo (Kyoto) becomes the capital, which it remains until 1868.

823

Kukai, an advocate of Shingon Buddhism, is made head of Toji temple.

From Nara to Heian

Beginning with the establishment of an imperial capital in 710, the Nara Period saw spectacular literary, artistic, architectural and religious advances. The era ended with the relocation of the capital to Heian-kyo (Kyoto) in 794. There, Chinese influences blended with native Japanese elements in painting, calligraphy, poetry and prose. After the collapse of the Chinese Tang dynasty in 907, Japan began to distance itself from its neighbor and developed a culture that was more distinctly Japanese.

Kamakura Period

In 1185, the elegant world of the Heian court was shattered by the struggle between the Taira and Minamoto warrior clans. The result was the establishment of Japan's first shogunate – rule by warriors – and power shifted from the imperial court to Kamakura, near modern Tokyo. The Mongols launched two invasion attempts in 1274 and 1281, both of which were halted by the weather, leading the Japanese to coin the term *"kamikaze"* – divine wind. In 1333, the Kamakura shogunate collapsed after the emperor Go-Daigo attempted to reassert imperial control.

PERIODS OVERVIEW

Jomon 14,500–300 BC
Yayoi 300 BC–AD 300
Yamato 300–710
Hakuho 645–710
Nara 710–794
Heian 794–1185
Kamakura 1185–1333
Muromachi 1333–1568
Momoyama 1568–1600
Tokugawa (Edo) 1600–1868
Meiji 1868–1912
Taisho 1912–1926
Showa 1926–1989
Heisei 1989–present

c 1000

Tale of Genji - possibly the world's oldest novel - is written by court lady Murasaki Shikibu.

1087

Emperor Shirakawa abdicates and becomes first cloistered emperor.

1180–85

Minamoto clan defeats the Taira and establishes Kamakura shogunate.

1274

The first Mongol invasion attempt lands in Kyushu.

1333

The Kamakura shogunate collapses.

Warring States Period

After years of civil war, the Muromachi shogunate emerged victorious in 1336. Whereas Kamakura had existed in equilibrium with the imperial court, the Muromachi took over the remnants of the imperial government. Rebellions followed and, in 1467, the Ōnin War broke out, leaving Kyoto devastated and effectively ending the national authority of the shogunate. For the next century, Japan was racked by debilitating warfare between increasingly autonomous samurai sections. Oda Nobunaga – a *daimyo* (feudal lord) who rose through military ranks in the provinces – set out to unify the nation, but died unsuccessful in 1582. Nobunaga's deputy, a former peasant named Toyotomi Hideyoshi, continued the work of unification. To achieve this, he set about destroying as many of the country's castles and forts as he could and confiscating weapons belonging to farmers. After Hideyoshi died, *daimyo* from eastern and western Japan fell into dispute and sent their samurai, led by Tokugawa Ieyasu and Ishida Mitsunari respectively, to battle in Sekigahara. Ieyasu emerged victorious in 1600 and subsequently founded the Tokugawa shogunate in 1603.

1️⃣ General and statesman Oda Nobunaha.

2️⃣ Statue of Toyotomi Hideyoshi outside Osaka.

3️⃣ The landing of Commodore Perry.

4️⃣ The Great Kanto Earthquake of 1923.

Did You Know?

The Japanese imperial family were believed to have succeeded from the sun goddess, Amaterasu.

Timeline of events

1467
The devastating Ōnin War begins, destroying much of Kyoto.

1600
Tokugawa Ieyasu establishes the Tokusgawa shogunate.

1635
All foreign commerce is confined to the artificial island of Dejima in Nagasaki.

1641
Only the Dutch and Chinese are allowed access to Japan.

1707
Last eruption of Mount Fuji.

The Edo Era and the Meiji Restoration

Peace was achieved by forcing the *daimyo* to reside every other year in Edo (Tokyo), the new seat of the shogunate. While Kyoto remained the official capital, Edo greatly eclipsed it in size. Japan isolated itself from the rest of the world until 1853, when the American Naval officer Commodore Perry challenged Japan's refusal to enter into international relations. Weakened by internal unrest, the shogunate could only accede to Perry's demands. Imperial power was restored in 1868, and Japan swiftly embraced Western technology under Emperor Meiji. Tokyo became the capital and seat of the emperor, the samurai class was abolished and the first prime minister was appointed in 1885. Conscription was introduced to create a modern fighting force, which proved effective with victories in the Sino-Japanese War of 1894–5 and the Russo-Japanese war of 1904–5. During the subsequent Taisho Era, party politics flourished, suffrage was extended and new labour laws were enacted, but World War I, the 1918 Rice Riots, the Great Kanto Earthquake of 1923, and the repressive Peace Preservation Laws challenged this liberal atmosphere.

↑ A portrait of Emperor Meiji, instrumental in the modernization of Japan

1853

US Naval officer Commodore Matthew Perry anchors in Edo Bay.

1854

The Kanagawa Treaty between the US and Japan is signed.

1868

Imperial power is restored and Tokyo becomes the capital.

1894

The First Sino-Japanese War begins.

1905

The Russo-Japanese War ends with the Treaty of Portsmouth.

World War II

Following the end of the Taisho era, hardliner army officers began assassinating moderates in an attempt to manipulate Japan's policies. These militarists believed that seizing land from China and Russia would secure raw materials and improve national security. By 1937, the country was embroiled in a war with China that estranged it from the rest of the world. When the US cut off Japan's access to oil, Tokyo made the decision to attack Pearl Harbour in Hawaii, in December 1941. American bombers decimated Japanese cities in retaliation, but the military government refused to surrender. In August 1945, the US dropped atomic bombs on Hiroshima and Nagasaki, and the Soviet Union entered the Pacific War. Emperor Hirohito ordered the cabinet to sue for peace and the US occupied Japan.

An Economic Bubble

By 1952, when the American occupation finally ended, Japan was beginning to find its feet. A new atmosphere of freedom unleashed a creative shockwave that saw intense innovation in art, film, literature and architecture. The country profited

↑ A newspaper reporting surrender of the Japanese in World War II

Timeline of events

1932
Young naval officers assassi-nate the prime minister and attempt a coup.

1933
Japan withdraws from the League of Nations.

1941
Japan enters World War II.

1945
Atomic bombs are dropped on Hiroshima and Nagasaki.

1964
The first journey is made by *shinkansen* (bullet train).

3

4

further from the Korean War, as it supplied the US forces with vehicles and technology. Industrial production surged and exports, such as cars and electronics, made Japan one of the world's richest nations. It all came to a screeching halt in 1992, however, when the economic bubble that inflated real estate and stock market prices burst. Decades of stagnation followed.

Japan Today

In March 2011, Northern Honshu was hit by an earthquake with a magnitude of 9.0, resulting in a tsunami. The disaster caused problems at four nuclear power plants, leading to a serious case of radioactive contamination and a continued loss of confidence in the government. In 2012, Shinzo Abe was elected prime minister after promising to put an end to deflation but, due to a rise in sales tax, Japan entered another recession just two years later. The Japanese economy has also been hampered by a workforce that is both aging and declining – between 2010 and 2018 the population had shrunk by about 1.3 million people. Nonetheless, the country remains prominent on the world stage as the host of events such as the 2020 Olympics in Tokyo.

1 Japanese troops on the march in 1939.

2 The Hiroshima Peace Memorial.

3 A *shinkansen* in Tokyo.

4 People praying for the victims of the 2011 earthquake.

Did You Know?

The average delay of a *shinkansen* (bullet train) is only 30 seconds.

1997
Economic recession in Southeast Asia, spreading to Japan

2013
Tokyo is selected as the host city of the 32nd Olympiad.

2017
Emperor Akihito announces he will abdicate on 30 April 2019.

1989
Emperor Hirohito (Showa) dies; his son, Akihito, assumes his role.

2011
Major earthquake and tsunami causes destruction to Honshu.

2020

EXPERIENCE
TOKYO

The frenetic Shibuya Crossing

Western Tokyo 82

Central Tokyo 102

Northern Tokyo 122

Beyond the Center 136

EXPLORE
TOKYO

This section divides Tokyo into three
sightseeing areas, as shown on this map,
plus an area beyond the center.

SUGAMO

SENGOKU

OTSUKA

KOHINATA

KASUGA

WASEDAMACHI

HYAKUNINCHO

Koishika
Koraku
Garde

TOYAMA

YARAICHO

KAGURAZAKA

KITA-
SHINJUKU

WAKAMATSUCHO

FUJIMI

KABUKICHO

TOMIHISACHO

ICHIGAYA

Kitanon
Park

SHINJUKU

NISHI-
SHINJUKU

Shinjuku
Station

YOTSUYA

SANEICHO

ICHIBANCHO

DAIKYOCHO

KOJIMACHI

CHIYO

YOYOGI

Shinjuku Gyoen
Garden

WAKABA

SHINANOMACHI

National
Theatre

Tokyo
Opera City

SENDAGAYA

Meiji Jingu
Outer Gardens

NAGATACHO

Meiji
Shrine

WESTERN TOKYO
p82

National Diet
Building

YOYOGI

AKASAKA

NISH
SHINBA

Yoyogi
Park

HARAJUKU

KITA-
AOYAMA

Aoyama
Cemetery

National
Art Center

TORANOMON

UEHARA

TOMIGAYA

JINGUMAE

MINAMI-
AOYAMA

ROPPONGI

AZABUDAI

UDAGAWACHO

Taro Okamoto
Memorial Museum

Roppongi
Hills

Tokyo
Tower

SHIBUYA

Shibuya
Station

NISHI-
AZABU

HIGASHI-
AZABU

Shiba
Park

DOGENZAKA

HIGASHI

AZABU-
JUBAN

OHASHI

SAKURA-
GAOKACHO

HIROO

SHIBA

AODABI

EBISU-
NICHI

MINAMI-
AZABU

EBISU

SHIROKANE

TAKANAWA

0 kilometers 1

0 miles 1

N
↑

TABATA

NISHI-
NIPPORI

MINAMI-
SENJU

SUMIDA

HIGASHI-
NIPPORI

MINOWA

SENDAGI

KIYOKAWA

TSUTSU
MIDORI

*Yanaka
Cemetery*

NEGISHI

SENZOKU

YANAKA

UENO-
SAKURAGI

IRIYA

IMADO

HIGASHI-
MUKOJIMA

NEZU

*Tokyo
National Museum*

Tokyo Metropolitan
Museum of Art

MATSUGAYA

ASAKUSA

MUKOJIMA

HIKATA

HONGO

*Ueno
Park*

Senso-ji
Temple

Tokyo
Skytree

INARICHO

NORTHERN TOKYO
p122

UENO

AZUMABASHI

NARIHIRA

KOTOBUKI

YUSHIMA

TAITO

MISUJI

HONJO

SOTOKANDA

KURAMAE

ISHIWARA

AKICHO

ASAKUSA-
BASHI

KAMEZAWA

KINSHI

KANDA

RYOGOKU

KOTOBASHI

IWAMOTOCHO

TATEKAWA

UCHI-
KANDA

*Imperial
Palace
Grounds*

OTEMACHI

HAMACHO

SARUE

CENTRAL TOKYO
p102

NIHONBASHI-
NINGYOCHO

TAKABASHI

nperial
alace

YAESU

*Imperial
Palace
Plaza*

NIHONBASHI

KIYOSUMI

MARUNOUCHI

SENGOKU

*Tokyo
International Forum*

SHINKAWA

*Hibiya
Park*

SHINTOMI

EITAI

FUYUKI

TOYO

GINZA

MINATO

CHISAI-
/AICHO

AKASHICHO

JAPAN

NBASHI

TSUKIJI

IBA-
MON

*Hama Rikyu
Garden*

KAIGAN

TOYOMICHO

HARUMI

TOKYO

WESTERN TOKYO

Shinjuku and Shibuya, the dual centers of Western Tokyo, three stops apart on the Yamanote line, began to boom only after the 1923 earthquake and the opening of the Tokyu Toyoko line, linking the capital and Yokohama, in 1932. Despite its short history, the area still has stories to tell, from Hachiko – the dog who faithfully waited for his owner outside Shibuya Station everyday from 1923 to 1935 – to the US occupation of Yoyogi Park, or Washington Heights as it became known, between 1945 and 1964. The park remained on the world stage for the 1964 Summer Olympic Games.

This part of the city is new Tokyo – all vitality and energy, fast-paced, constantly changing, and challenging the more traditional pleasures of Central and Northern Tokyo. When the Imperial Japanese Army moved to Roppongi in 1890, the area became a nightlife hot spot, and this reputation was only reinforced with the influx of expatriates after World War II. Although no longer burdened with a sleazy reputation, people still flock here after dark for Roppongi's cosmopolitan clubs, bars, and music venues, and the neon lights and pachinko parlors of East Shinjuku. On top of this, Shibuya, along with neighboring Harajuku and Minami-Aoyama, have been the epicenters of both young and haute-couture Japanese fashion since the 1980s.

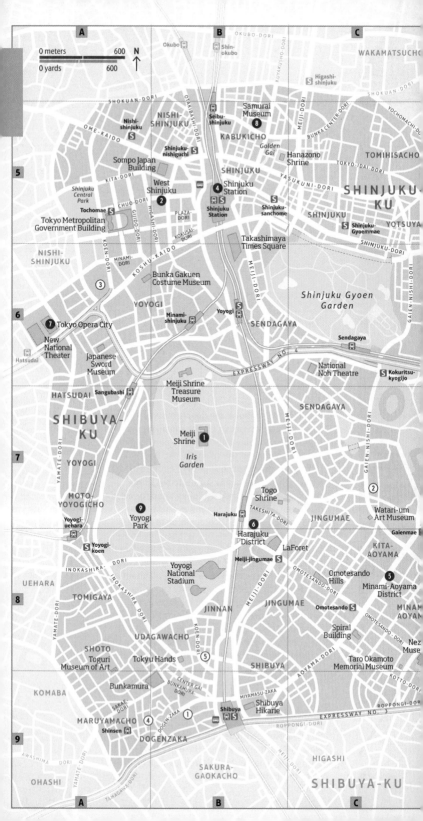

WESTERN TOKYO

Must Sees
1. Meiji Shrine
2. West Shinjuku
3. Roppongi District

Experience More
4. Shinjuku Station
5. Minami-Aoyama District
6. Harajuku District
7. Tokyo Opera City
8. Samurai Museum
9. Yoyogi Park
10. Akasaka District

Eat
1. Maruhachi
2. Den

Drink
3. New York Bar

Stay
4. Hotel Beat Wave
5. The Millennials Shibuya

① ✥

MEIJI SHRINE
明治神宮

📍B7 🏠1-1 Yoyogikamizonocho 🚉Harajuku Stn,
Yamanote line 🕐Treasure Museum and Annex: Closed
for renovation; Nai-en garden: dawn–dusk daily (times
vary seasonally) 🌐meijijingu.or.jp/english

For Tokyo's residents, the lush 170-acre (69-ha)
grounds of the Meiji Shrine (Meiji Jingū) are a welcome
green lung in the heart of this hectic city. As the capital's
most important Shinto shrine, it offers visitors a
tantalizing glimpse of an older Japan. Take a stroll
through its beautiful grounds, stocked with some
120,000 trees, learn more about the imperial family
through the artifacts on display in the museums,
and soak up traditional temple life.

Originally built in 1920, the Meiji Shrine was
destroyed during the Tokyo air raids, but
was rebuilt in 1958. Controversially, the shrine
was rededicated to Emperor Meiji (1852–1912),
rather than a *kami* (spirit), contravening the
imperial family's renunciation of divinity
following World War II. At the Treasure Museum
and its annexe, visitors can see items belonging
to the imperial family, including gorgeous
kimonos, lacquerware, and furniture. Don't miss
the Nai-en garden, said to have been designed
by the emperor for his wife. Here, a teahouse
overlooks a pond stocked with water lilies and
carp. To the right of the pond, a path leads to
the beautiful Minami-ike Shobuda (iris garden),
which contains over 150 species.

Guiding Spirit
One of the most striking sights at the Meiji
Shrine is the huge wall of sake barrels. While
the barrels on display are empty, they are
loaded with meaning. Sake is supposed to
facilitate the connection with the gods and in
the oldest Japanese texts "miki," the old word
for sake, is written with the characters for "god"
and "wine." Shinto shrines pray for the brewers'
prosperity and, in turn, the breweries donate
sake for the shrines' rituals and ceremonies.

📷 PICTURE PERFECT
Here Comes the Bride
Fortunate visitors may catch a glimpse
of a traditional Shinto wedding taking
place at the shrine. Take a picture of the
bride in her magnificent wedding kimono
(from a respectful distance), as she
shelters under a red parasol accompanied by a procession of priests.

THE MEIJI EMPEROR
Having succeeded to
the throne in 1868 at
just 14 years of age,
the Meiji Emperor set
out to modernize Japan.
During his reign, the
Diet was founded, the
industrial revolution
took place, and the
country emerged
victorious from con-
flicts with China, Korea,
and Russia.

← Devotees performing *harai* (ritual cleansing) before approaching the shrine

→ Admiring the huge wall of empty sake barrels, marked with the name of the breweries they were made in, at the entrance to the shrine

↑ Visitors at the Minami-shin Mon, the gate to Meiji Shrine's inner sanctuary

②

WEST SHINJUKU

西新宿

🅱B5 🆂Shinjuku Stn, Toei Shinjukum Hibiya &
Toei Oedo lines

Most of Tokyo's skyscraper office blocks (and some of its most expensive land) are clustered just to the west of Shinjuku Station. About 250,000 people work here each day, creating endless bustle. Many of West Shinjuku's hotels, and some office blocks, have top-floor restaurants with views of the city.

In 1960 the government designated Shinjuku a *fukutoshin* ("secondary heart of the city"), and in 1991, when the city government moved into architect Kenzo Tange's massive 48-story Metropolitan Government Offices, many started calling it *shin toshin* (the new capital). Tange's building was dubbed "tax tower" by those outraged at its US$1 billion cost. Between the skyscrapers, the streets pulsate with people shopping, heading to restaurants, and seeking evening entertainment, including *pachinko* parlours, nightclubs, and love hotels.

↑ The towering Tokyo Metropolitan Government Offices

Did You Know?

Shoppers spend over ¥1.1 trillion in Shinjuku's stores every year.

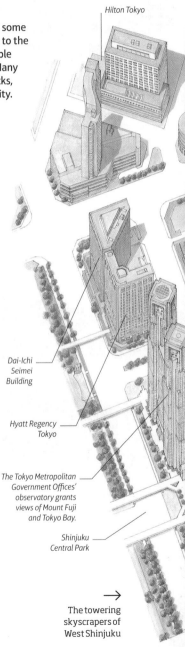

Hilton Tokyo

Dai-Ichi Seimei Building

Hyatt Regency Tokyo

The Tokyo Metropolitan Government Offices' observatory grants views of Mount Fuji and Tokyo Bay.

Shinjuku Central Park

→ The towering skyscrapers of West Shinjuku

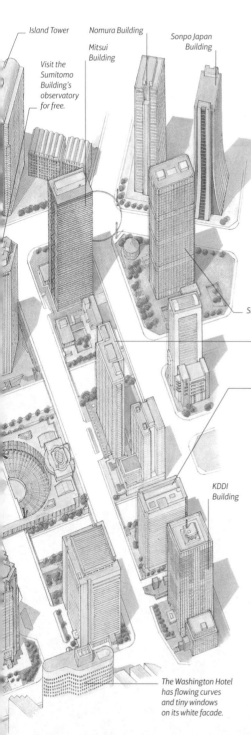

Island Tower

Nomura Building

Mitsui
Building

Sonpo Japan
Building

Visit the
Sumitomo
Building's
observatory
for free.

Shinjuku Center Building

Keio Plaza Hotel

The Monolith Building
has a pleasant courtyard
garden on the north side.

KDDI
Building

The Washington Hotel
has flowing curves
and tiny windows
on its white facade.

DRINK

New York Bar
The Park Hyatt Tokyo
hotel will be forever
linked to Sofia Coppola's
2003 film *Lost in
Translation*. There is no
better spot in Tokyo
than this iconic bar to
order a whisky soda,
while gazing out at
Tokyo's twinkling lights.

📍A6 🏢52 Fl, Park Hyatt
Tokyo, 3-7-1-2,
Nishishinjuku ⏰5pm–
1am Thu–Sat, 5pm–
midnight Sun–Wed
🌐tokyo.park.
hyatt.co.jp

↑ The distinctive Sonpo
Japan Building, with its
graceful curving base

❸
ROPPONGI DISTRICT

六本木地区

📍E9 🚇Roppongi Stn, Hibiya & Toei-Oedo lines 🏛Mori Art Museum: 6-10-1 Roppongi; National Art Center, Tokyo: 7-22-2 Roppongi; Suntory Museum of Art: 9-7-4 Akasaka ⏰Hours vary, check website 🌐Mori Art Museum: mori.art.museum; National Art Center, Tokyo: nact.jp/english; Suntory Museum of Art: suntory.com/sma

Once harboring a sleazy reputation, the buzzing neighborhood of Roppongi is where Tokyo's grown-ups now come to play. With three ground-breaking art galleries, boundless high-end stores, and a relentless nightlife, upmarket Roppongi has it all.

Huge redevelopment projects, such as iconic Roppongi Hills, have transformed the district into a shopping powerhouse. Here you'll find the Mori Art Museum, housing groundbreaking modern art. Together with the National Art Center, Tokyo – presenting innovative temporary exhibitions – and the Suntory Museum of Art, which displays the whisky dynasty's private collection, Mori forms part of the Roppongi Art Triangle. After visiting one of the museums, the ATRo Saving ticket grants discounted entry to the other two

museums. Alongside these cultural colossi, there are smaller art spaces, such as Ota Fine Arts, Zen Foto Gallery, and complex665. The renowned 21_21 Design Sight museum – the brainchild of architect Tadao Ando and fashion designer Issey Miyake – is a must for any design aficionado.

As the center of Tokyo's nightlife, you can find just about any music you want in Roppongi: jazz, blues, ska, hip-hop, classic disco, country and western, and soul. Night-clubs, such as V2 TOKYO, Esprit Tokyo, and Cat's Tokyo, all boast rosters of superstar DJs.

→ Louise Bourgeois's *Maman* outside the Mori Art Museum

 PICTURE PERFECT
Not so Itsy Bitsy

Head to the Mori Art Museum to see Louise Bourgeois's spider-like *Maman*. At a terrifying 30 ft (9 m) tall and 33 ft (10 m) wide, the bronze statue is the stuff of nightmares. Pose next to one of the sculpture's towering legs to show the perspective.

MORI ART MUSEUM

With a focus on contemporary pieces and the postwar avant-garde, the Mori Art Museum is an influential presence within Japan's art scene. This private museum's program of temporary exhibitions always hits the mark when it comes to showing the hottest artists, such as Takashi Murakami and Leandro Erlich. Located on the 53rd floor of the Mori Tower, the museum also grants access to Tokyo City View. This indoor-outdoor viewing platform offers panoramas over the capital.

↑ The gleaming exterior of Mori Tower, home to the Mori Art Museum

←

People walking across a busy crossing in the Roppongi District

←

Overlooking the city from Tokyo City View at the top of Mori Tower

↑ Commuters on the platform
at Shinjuku, the busiest
train station in the world

EXPERIENCE MORE

4

Shinjuku Station
新宿駅

📍 B5 🚇 Shinjuku Stn, Toei
Shinjuku, Hibiya & Toei
Oedo lines

With over two million people
passing through each day, this
is the world's busiest train
station. A major stop on both
the JR and metropolitan
subway systems, Shinjuku
Station is also the starting
point for trains and buses into
the suburbs. On the Yamanote
and Chuo line platforms during
the morning rush hour (about
7:30–9am) staff are employed
to push those last few commuters on to the train.

It's easy to lose your way in
this maze of seemingly identical passages between the
lines. For a time in the 1980s
and early 1990s, a substantial
number of homeless people
built cardboard villages in the
station's corridors. In a contro-
versial move, the municipal
government forcibly removed
them; they settled in new
places, including Ueno Park.

the wide street running
through it, is a renowned
center for boutiques.

On Gaien-Nishi-dori, a
fashionable street nicknamed
"Killer-dori," is the **Watari-um,**
also known as the Watari
Museum of Contemporary Art.
Exhibits are by international
and Japanese artists, and
change regularly.

Back on Aoyama-dori, turn
left at the Omotesando junction for the **Nezu Museum,**
which houses a collection of
Japanese, Chinese, and Korean
art and is situated in landscaped gardens containing
traditional teahouses. A very
different museum is found a
few blocks away. The **Taro
Okamoto Memorial Museum**
houses the peculiar works
of this post-war sculptor. The
towering figures have crudely
realized faces and tapering
plant-like tendrils.

> ### COMMUTER
> ### CULTURE
>
> Commuters packed into
> trains are a common
> sight in Tokyo. High
> house prices force peo-
> ple farther out of the
> city, and a commute of
> at least an hour is stan-
> dard. An entire indus-
> try has come up around
> commuters, including
> stand-up eateries
> serving meals to those
> with a long ride ahead.

5

Minami-Aoyama
District
南青山地区

📍 C8 🚇 Gaienmae Stn,
Ginza line

Favored by artists, writers,
and young entrepreneurs, this
bustling district lies between
the large Aoyama Cemetery
and Shibuya. Aoyama-dori,

Did You Know?

Tokyo's crows know
how to use tools and
can recognize
human faces.

A short walk from here is Kotto-dori, another fashionable street, which is full of antique shops selling scrolls, paintings, and porcelain. This street is one of the hottest in Tokyo, with notable boutiques, cafés, and shops springing up. The area is pleasant for an afternoon shopping or browsing.

Return to Aoyama-dori, near the Omotesando junction toward Shibuya, and the next landmark is the white, geometric Spiral Building, which owes its name to the large, spiral ramp inside. Designed by Fumihiko Maki in 1985, and one of the most popular places in Minami-Aoyama, this building is the figurative definition of cool. There is nothing in it that can't be described as hip and trendy (*torendi* in Japanese), and that includes most of the people. Attractions inside comprise an exhibition and performance space, the Spiral Hall, also used for exhibitions and performances, an Italian café, a French restaurant, a stationery and housewares boutique, and a beauty salon.

Head eastward toward the Nogizaka subway station for the **Aoyama Cemetery**, Japan's first public necropolis, and probably its most

exclusive. A number of high-profile people are buried here, including former prime minister Shigeru Yoshida and famed novelist Yukio Mishima. This tranquil, green spot is also a popular, though somber, place to view cherry blossoms.

Watari-Um
⊛ 🕙 🏠 3-7-6 Jingūmae
🕙 11am-7pm Tue-Sun (to 9pm Wed) 🆆 watarium.co.jp

Nezu Museum
⊛ 🏠 6-5-1 Minato 🕙 10am-5pm Tue-Sun 🆆 nezu-muse.or.jp/en

Taro Okamato Memorial Museum
⊛ 🏠 6-1-19 Minamiaoyama
🕙 10am-6pm Wed-Mon
🆆 taro-okamoto.or.jp/en

Aoyama Cemetery
⊛ 🏠 2-32-2 Minato 🅲 (03) 3401-3652 🕙 24 hours daily

→
An upscale boutique near Omotesando, in the Minami-Aoyama District

 6

Harajuku District
原宿地区

◻B7 S Meiji-jingumae "Harajuku" Stn, Chiyoda & Fukutoshin lines **◻**Harajuku Stn, Yamanote line

Harajuku Station was the main station for the 1964 Tokyo Olympic village and that concentration of international culture had a great impact on the area, attracting the young and innovative of Tokyo. Today Harajuku remains a center for fashion from high-end international stores to bargain boutiques.

Takeshita-dori, a narrow alley between Meiji-dori and Harajuku Station, is the place to find what's hot in teen fashion and culture. Sundays bring the biggest crowds. Prices range from cheap to outrageous, as do the fashions.

Starting from the Harajuku Station end, about 200 m (220 yards) down, a left turn leads up some stairs to Togo Shrine, founded for Admiral Togo, the commander who defeated the Russian fleet in the Battle of Tsushima, which was part of the Russo-Japanese War. It was a huge naval victory, the first of an Asian country over a Western one. Admiral Togo remains a hero in Japan, and his shrine has a beautiful garden and pond. Located a few blocks east of the shrine is **Design Festa Gallery**. This Postmodern, bohemian gallery focuses on future-generation artists and has a design-themed café-bar.

Running parallel to, and south of, Takeshita-dori is the more sophisticated Omotesando. With its wide, tree-shaded sidewalks and dozens of boutiques showcasing top fashion designers and brands such as Celine, Fendi, and Dior, this is one of the best places to stroll in Tokyo.

As you walk from Harajuku Station, just before the intersection with Meiji-dori, off to the left you will see a small street leading to the **Ukiyo-e Ota Memorial Museum of Art**, which houses one of the best collections of ukiyo-e prints (p131) in Japan. A vivid image of a Kabuki actor portraying a superhero in the classic *aragoto* style by Sharaku and a masterful program of a memorial Kabuki performance by Hiroshige are among many familiar works. There is a small restaurant and a shop selling prints and other ukiyo-e-related souvenirs.

Just to the left down Meiji-dori is LaForet, a fashion mecca, with more than 150 boutiques. Leading off Omotesando, just before the pedestrian bridge, a

---

 PICTURE PERFECT
Japan in the Mirror

Quirky Tokyu Plaza Omotesando Harajuku, a multistory shopping complex in the heart of the district, is accessed via a mirror-encased ecalator (p82). Snap a kaleidoscope-like image from the top as you exit.

> **Takeshita-dori, a narrow alley between Meiji-dori and Harajuku Station, is the place to find what's hot in teen fashion and culture. Sundays bring the biggest crowds.**

← Crowds on neon-lit Takeshita-dori, in the Harajuku District

narrow lane to the left is lined with boutiques of up-and-coming designers and gives a good idea of residential life in this upscale area. Farther up the hill from the footbridge on the left is Omotesando Hills. This huge complex is home to boutiques such as Jimmy Choo, and specialist luxury-goods stores, as well as dozens of brand stores such as UGG Australia and Catimini. Over the pedestrian bridge to the right is the Oak Omotesando Building. This two-story shopping zone has an impressive glass facade and houses several luxury brands, such as Coach and Emporio Armani, as well as Japan's first Nespresso boutique. Just before the Oak Omotesando Building is the vermilion-and-white Oriental Bazaar, a collection of shops full of real and fake antiques and good handicrafts, ideal for souvenirs.

Design Festa Gallery

3-20-18 Jingūmae, Shibuya
11am–8pm daily designfestagallery.com

Ukiyo-e Ota Memorial Museum of Art

1-10-10 Jingūmae, Shibuya 10:30am–5:30pm Tue–Sun 27th–end of each month

Tokyo Opera City
東京オペラシティー

A6 3-20-2 Nishi-Shinjuku, Shinjuku-ku Hatsudai Stn, Keio line operacity.jp

This towering skyscraper is home to Tokyo's impressive music and theater complex. On the first floor of the building, you'll find two main halls. One of these is primarily used for Japanese classical music and theater, while a vast opera hall with a soaring vaulted roof stages large-scale opera recitals. Performances are frequent – phone for details (03 5353-0770) or pick up a leaflet from the foyer information counter for a list of upcoming shows.

On top of the two halls, there are 54 floors, mostly housing offices of companies, including Apple. The first three floors are accessible to the public, however, and house an art gallery, shops, and restaurants, which are worth investigating before or after the opera. The expansive NTT Intercommunication Center occupies the fourth floor. This is one of Tokyo's primary centers for modern interactive art. The 53rd and 54th floors of the buildings hold a dozen restaurants and bars, some of which boast great city views.

HARAJUKU GIRLS

Harajuku has been a mecca for Tokyo teens since at least the mid-1990s, when disparate fashion sub-cultures would gather near the former Olympic Park to shop and show off. Around that time, a magazine called *FRUiTS* would feature portraits of young people in zany outfits, popularizing the idea of Tokyo as a hub for teen fashion. A number of mainstream brands, such as Uniqlo, moved into the district, transforming it into a tourist hot spot. In 2017, the print edition of *FRUiTS* ceased publication. Nevertheless, one Sunday a month, devotees gather for the Harajuku Fashion Walk to relive the glory days.

Elaborate samurai armor on display in the Samurai Museum in Kabukicho

Olympics, when they will be used as handball venues, as well as for wheelchair rugby and badminton in the Paralympics. The impressive curves of the shell-like structures are achieved with the use of steel suspension cables.

Samurai Museum

📍B5 🏠2-25-6 Kabukicho, Shinjuku 🚉Shinjuku Stn, Yamanote line 🕐10:30am–9pm daily 🌐samurai museum.jp

Geared toward international visitors and conveniently located in Kabukicho, this museum displays samurai swords, armor, and a plethora of other fearsome-looking weapons. Its beautifully laid-out displays put the rise of the samurai in context and explain the history of this uniquely Japanese style of warfare, as well as what happened when the Japanese warriors came up against the Mongols in the 13th century.

EATING IN GOLDEN GAI

Just around the corner from the Samurai Museum, the Golden Gai area retains a shabby charm that is fast disappearing in the increasingly slick and tidy modern city. In this labyrinth of dark alleys and backlit acrylic signs, there are more than 200 tiny bars and restaurants to choose from. But don't head over too early – nothing opens before 9pm. Plus, there's no rush, as the fun goes on all night.

Visitors can indulge in some Japanese-style cosplay, try on lacquered armor, and handle a reproduction *katana* sword. Enthusiastic English-speaking guides give regular tours that include demonstrations of sword moves and terrifying battle cries. Exhibition fights are also regularly staged.

To see more amazing suits of armor, head to the Tokyo National Museum in Ueno Park *(p128)*.

Yoyogi Park
歌舞伎座

📍A7 🚉Harajuku Stn, Yamanote line

For almost three decades the park filled with a fantastic array of performers and bands every Sunday. These events were stopped by the authorities in the mid-1990s, supposedly due to worries about the rise in criminal activities and maintaining public order. Sundays are still a good time to visit, though, for the weekly flea market. At the entrance to the park you can still see members of the *zoku* (tribes) who used to perform here, from punks and goths to hippies and break-dancers.

Kenzo Tange's two Olympic stadiums, the landmark structures in Yoyogi Park, were completed in 1964 for the Tokyo Olympics. They are currently being renovated for the upcoming 2020 Tokyo

Akasaka District
歌舞伎座

📍E7 🚉Akasaka-Mitsuke Stn, Ginza & Marunouchi lines; Nagatacho Stn, Yurakucho, Namboku & Hanzomon lines

With the Diet Building *(p116)* and many government offices just to the east, Akasaka is a favorite place for politicians to socialize. Limousines carry

---

TOP 5 TYPES OF JAPANESE BAR

Snack
Usually run by a "mama-san" who will chat and sing karaoke with patrons.

Yokocho
Concentrated in Golden Gai, these drinking dens rarely accommodate more than ten people.

Izakaya
The Japanese equivalent of a pub, *izakaya* are great for socializing and unpretentious food.

Jazz
Japan has a vibrant, thriving jazz scene.

Tachi-nomi
These standing bars usually have friendly and quick service.

dark-blue-suited men to the many exclusive establishments lining the streets here.

About 200 m (220 yards) along Aoyama-dori from Akasaka-Mitsuke Station is Toyokawa Inari Shrine (also called Myogon-ji). With its red lanterns and flags, and dozens of statues of foxes (the traditional messengers of Inari, a Shinto rice deity), this is a pleasant place to linger for a while.

Back past the station and over the moat, you will see a large building up ahead that you may recognize from the James Bond film *You Only Live Twice* (1967), in which it featured. This is the huge, luxurious Hotel New Otani.

On the 17th floor is THE SKY revolving restaurant, which serves Chinese, Japanese, and Western cuisine (diners can choose the ingredients and the chefs will prepare it on the spot), and offers stunning 360-degree views across central Tokyo and the Imperial Palace. In the grounds and open to all is the 400-year-old garden of Kato Kiyomasa, lord of Kyushu's Kumamoto area.

South of Akasaka-Mitsuke Station is the shrine of Hie Jinja, which was erected in 1478. Shogun Ietsuna moved it here in the 17th century to buffer his castle; the present-day buildings are all modern. Each year in mid-June the Sanno Matsuri is celebrated here with a grand procession of 50 *mikoshi* (portable shrines) and people in Heian-era costumes.

The approach to Toyokawa Inari Shrine in the Akasaka District, lined by dozens of fox statues *(inset)*

EAT

Maruhachi
The food served at this friendly *izakaya* can be washed down with *shochu* (sweet potato and rice liquor) or *awamori* (made from long-grain rice).

🗺B9 🏠2-10-12 Dogenzaka, Shibuya 📞(03) 3476-5739

¥ ¥ ¥

Den
Chef Zaiyu Hasegawa crafts beautiful dishes. Order the "Dentucky Fried Chicken."

🗺C7 🏠2-3-18 Jingumae, Shibuya 🕐L & Sun 🌐jim bochoden.com

¥ ¥ ¥

A SHORT WALK
EAST SHINJUKU

Distance 1.5 miles (2.5 km) **Time** 35 minutes
Nearest subway Shinjuku Station

East Shinjuku is where Tokyoites come to play. The area has been a nightlife center as early as the Edo Period, when it was the first stop on the old Tokaido road to Kyoto. Since Shinjuku Station opened in the 1880s, the area's entertainments have been targeted at commuters (mainly men) en route back to the suburbs. Amusements are focused in the tiny bars of Golden Gai, and in the red-light district of Kabukicho. Daytime attractions include several art galleries, a tranquil shrine, and some of Tokyo's best department stores. A late-afternoon stroll as the neon starts to light up will take in both the highbrow and dark sides of this fascinating, bustling area.

Did You Know?

Despite its name, a *kabuki* theater was never built in Kabukicho.

Instantly recognizable by its huge TV screen, **Studio Alta** *is a popular place for meeting up or just hanging out.*

Blue Bottle Coffee *is a convenient stop.*

OTAKIBASHI-DORI

Seibu-shinjuku

CINECITY SQUARE

GINZA-DORI

KABUKICHO

CHUO-DO...

START

MOA 2ND ST

MOA C...

Studio Alta

FINISH

Shinjuku Station

Blue Bottle Coffee

0 meters 150
0 yards 150
N

↑ Flashing advertisements on the exterior of Studio Alta shopping complex

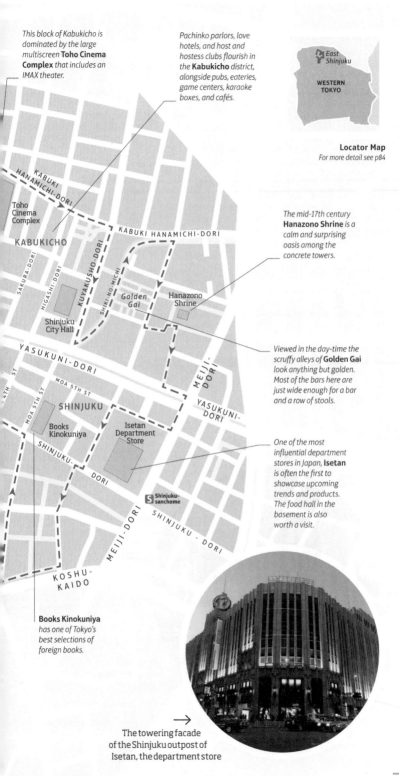

This block of Kabukicho is dominated by the large multiscreen **Toho Cinema Complex** that includes an IMAX theater.

Pachinko parlors, love hotels, and host and hostess clubs flourish in the **Kabukicho** district, alongside pubs, eateries, game centers, karaoke boxes, and cafés.

East Shinjuku

WESTERN TOKYO

Locator Map
For more detail see p84

KABUKI HANAMICHI-DORI

Toho Cinema Complex

KABUKICHO

KABUKI HANAMICHI-DORI

SAKURA-DORI

HIGASHI-DORI

KUYAKUSHO-DORI

SHIKI-NO-MICHI

Golden Gai

Hanazono Shrine

Shinjuku City Hall

YASUKUNI-DORI

MEIJI-DORI

MOA 5TH ST

4TH ST

MOA 5TH ST

SHINJUKU

Books Kinokuniya

Isetan Department Store

SHINJUKU-DORI

S Shinjuku-sanchome

YASUKUNI-DORI

MEIJI-DORI

SHINJUKU-DORI

KOSHU-KAIDO

The mid-17th century **Hanazono Shrine** is a calm and surprising oasis among the concrete towers.

Viewed in the day-time the scruffy alleys of **Golden Gai** look anything but golden. Most of the bars here are just wide enough for a bar and a row of stools.

One of the most influential department stores in Japan, **Isetan** is often the first to showcase upcoming trends and products. The food hall in the basement is also worth a visit.

Books Kinokuniya has one of Tokyo's best selections of foreign books.

→ The towering facade of the Shinjuku outpost of Isetan, the department store

A SHORT WALK
SHIBUYA

Distance 2 miles (3 km) **Time** 45 minutes
Nearest subway Shibuya Station

Shibuya has been the *sakariba* (party town) for Tokyo's youth since the 1930s, when the Tokyu Toyoko Line made the area a key terminal between the capital and Yokohama, and the first facades featured rockets streaking across the sky. Today, it still feels out of this world – this is the place to see the latest in fashion, food, music, and gadgets, both in the stores and on the streets. Shibuya's continuing expansion has been spurred by the appetites of the increasingly affluent youth of the world's third-biggest economy. Due to their demands, the area, which lies to the northwest of Shibuya Station and south of Yoyogi Park, is a mix of trendy boutiques, fashionable department stores, and record shops. On top of these commercial enterprises, a stroll through the area will also take you past a couple of interesting museums, as well as the multifaceted Bunkamura cultural center. Once you've explored Shibuya, head into the adjoining area of Dogen-zaka, where you'll find a jumble of sloping streets and alleyways lined with nightclubs, bars, and love hotels.

Did You Know?

Shibuya translates as "Bitter Valley", but it is now called "Bit Valley" because of its electronic shops.

Bunkamura is a popular site for rock and classical concerts, but also shows movies, and houses an art gallery and theater.

INOKASHIRA DORI

SHOTO

Bunkamura

Live musicians perform at Tsutaya O-East every night.

Tsutaya O-East

Yosano Akiko Monument

The Yosano Akiko Monument immortalizes the female poet.

← Nighttime traffic on an expressway in Shibuya

This purple clock tower stands in front of the Shibuya Ward Office and is overlooked by Yoyogi Park and the NHK Studios.

The **Humax Pavilion**, resembling a cartoon rocket, is one of the more fanciful buildings in the area.

Locator Map
For more detail see p84

WESTERN TOKYO

Shibuya

Tower Records has a good stock of Japanese and international music at prices among the best in Tokyo.

Marui Jam Department Store is a paradise for clothes – the place for fashionable under 25s.

Center Gai is lined with shops, pachinko parlors, restaurants, and karaoke bars full of students.

The **Statue of Hachiko** has stood here since 1934, commemorating the dog who waited for his master at the station every night for more than a decade after his death.

Though **Dogen-zaka** (named after a bandit who retired here as a monk) is a nighttime destination, it also has several art galleries.

Clock Tower

UDAGAWACHO

JINNAN

KOEN-DORI

ORGAN-ZAKA

Tokyu Hands

PENGUIN ST

KOEN-DORI

Humax Pavilion

INOKASHIRA-DORI

SHIBUYA CENTER GAI

BUNKAMURA-DORI

Shibuya 109 Building

DOGEN-ZAKA

Statue of Hachiko

Shibuya Mark City

DOGENZAKA

TAMAGAWA-DORI

Jingu-dori Park

Miyashita Park

Tower Records

Marui Jam

PARK ST

MEIJI-DORI

START/ FINISH

SHIBUYA

Shibuya Station

Shibuya bus station

0 meters 200
0 yards 200
N ↑

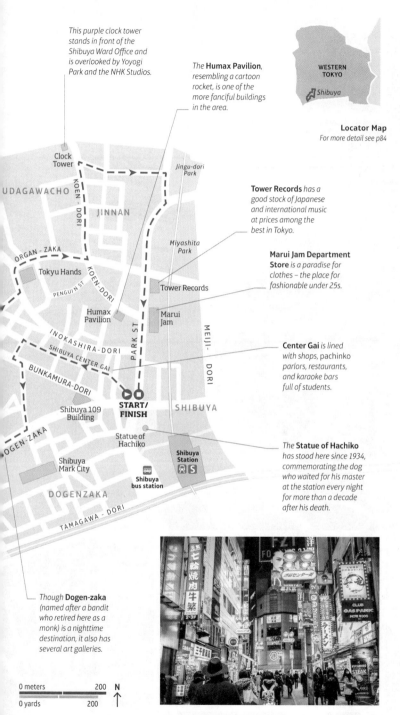

↑ Strolling Shibuya's busy central shopping street, neon-lit Center Gai

CENTRAL TOKYO

Situated to the north and west of the Sumida River, this area has been at the heart of Tokyo since the shogun Tokugawa Ieyasu built his castle and capital where the Imperial Palace still stands today. When Ieyasu moved his military center here in 1590, it was surrounded by swamp and marshland. Once filled in, the area that became Ginza – "the silver place" – attracted tradesman and merchants. Destroyed by a series of disasters, including a devastating fire in 872, the Great Kanto Earthquake of 1923, and the Allied bombing in World War II, the area has reinvented itself several times over, but has always remained true to its history as the center of Tokyo.

The presence of the Hibiya business district and cosmopolitan Marunouchi, home to the Tokyo International Forum, means that Central Tokyo is still politically important, despite the decline of the Imperial Palace. Ginza and Nihonbashi remain as thriving and prosperous today as they have been since the Edo period, offering a mix of department stores and affluent side-street boutiques.

TAITO-KU

KOTOBUKI

MISUJI

KURAMAE

Suehirocho

KURAMAEBASHI-DORI

Akihabara Electronics District

Akihabara

Akihabara

ASAKUSA-BASHI

Asakusa-bashi

Yanagibashi

Kanda River

River

Yanagi Bridge

Iwamotocho

IWAMOTOCHO

Shin-nihonbashi

Bakurocho

Bakuro-yokoyama

Higashi-nihombashi

Kodenmacho

Hamacho

Ryogoku

RYOGOKU

MIDORI

TATEKAWA

CENTRAL TOKYO

CHUO-KU

Ningyocho

NIHONBASHI-NINGYOCHO

Mitsukoshimae

Nihonbashi District

Tokyo Stock Exchange

NIHONBASHI

Suitengumae

Kayabacho

SHINKAWA

Eital Bridge

Takaracho

Hatchobori

SHINTOMI

MINATO

Shintomicho

CHUO-KU

Tsukiji

AKASHICHO

Hongan-ji Temple

TSUKIJI

Namiyoke Inari Shrine

Tsukuda Bridge

Sumiyoshi Shrine

TSUKUDA

Tsukishima

Kachidoki

KACHIDOKI

TSUKISHIMA

HAMACHO

HARUMI

0 meters   750   N
0 yards   750

CENTRAL TOKYO

Must Sees
1 Ginza
2 Nihonbashi District
3 Imperial Palace

Experience More
4 Jinbocho Booksellers' District
5 Tokyo International Forum
6 Kabuki-za Theater
7 Hama-rikyu Gardens
8 The Diet Building
9 Marunouchi District
10 Shiba Park and Tokyo Tower
11 Akihabara Electronics District
12 Kitanomaru Park
13 Koishikawa Korakuen Garden
14 Yasukuni Shrine
15 Kanda Myojin Shrine

Eat
1 Takashimaya
2 Sushi Sora
3 Chuka Soba Inoue

Stay
4 Aman Hotel
5 The Tokyo Station Hotel
6 Tokyo Prince Hotel

Shop
7 Ginza Six
8 Ginza Wako

❶
GINZA
銀座

📍 H7 🚇 Ginza Stn, Ginza, Hibiya & Marunouchi lines

Tokyo must count as the single greatest city to shop in the world, and Ginza is its Mayfair, Fifth Avenue, and Avenue Montaigne rolled into one. Tiny shops selling traditional crafts mix with trendy galleries and sprawling department stores for an unrivaled shopping experience.

The sophisticated neighborhood of Ginza, with its tree-lined avenues and broad pedestrianized streets, can feel a world away from the frenetic pace of the rest of Toyko. The area was destroyed by a devastating fire in 1872 and the newly restored imperial government commissioned Irish architect Thomas Waters to rebuild Ginza in red brick – the height of fashion at the time. The area has never looked back and its leafy streets are now home to some of the smartest boutiques and chicest restaurants that the capital has to offer. These include the gargantuan Ginza Six, which focuses on the latest fashion trends, and Ginza Wako, a traditional department store dating from the 1940s. Known as Brand Street, Chuo-dori is home to some of Japan's most prestigious shopping, ranging from department stores such as Matsuya to international fashion boutiques, including Dior, Gucci, Louis Vuitton, and Prada.

←
Fashion-forward retail concessions in the foyer of Ginza Six

PICTURE PERFECT
Capsule Capture

Completed in just 30 days in 1972, the Nakagin Capsule Tower is a rare example of Japanese Metabolism (p37). Take a picture of this modular building, seemingly built out of washing machines, from across the street.

↑ Walking past the stylish window displays of Chanel on Chuo-dori

Did You Know?

The irregular windows on the Mikimoto building aim to mimic the ocean's surface.

The striking exterior of Mikimoto, a jewelry store on Chuo-dori ↑

A SHORT WALK
GINZA

Distance 1 mile (2 km) **Time** 30 minutes
Nearest subway Yarakucho Station

Ever since Thomas Waters rebuilt the area in red brick back in the 19th century, Ginza *(p106)* has been Japan's epicenter of Western influences and all things modern, and it is still one of Tokyo's great commercial centers. Tiny shops selling traditional crafts mix with galleries and landmark department stores for an unrivaled shopping experience. Wander Ginza's leafy streets, and take a moment to pop into the many department stores to check out glitzy food halls, where gleaming cabinets display delicious delectables. Some of these mammoth stores even house their own art galleries.

Did You Know?

On Sundays and public holidays, Chuo-Dori Street is closed to traffic.

The second floor of the **Gallery Center Building** *houses exclusive galleries showcasing Japanese and Western art. There is an auction house on the fifth floor.*

Hankyu and Seibu department stores focus on fashions, with a mix of Japanese and international labels.

Yurakucho Station

Hankyu and Seibu

START/ FINISH

TOKYO EXPRESSWAY

Sukiyabashi Park

Sony Showroom

SONY-DORI

Gallery Center Building

SUKIYA-DORI

KOJUNSHA-DORI

SOTOBORI-DORI

MIYUKI-DORI

Asahi Building

NAMIKI-DORI

NISHI-GOBANGAI-DORI

The **Asahi Building** *contains a traditional kimono shop, silversmiths, and several boutiques.*

Known as Brand Street, **Namiki-Dori** *and* **Chuo-Dori** *are lined with boutiques such as Gucci, Dior, Louis Vuitton, and Cartier.*

0 meters	150
0 yards	150

N ↑

↑ The facade of the Bulgari store on Chuo-Dori

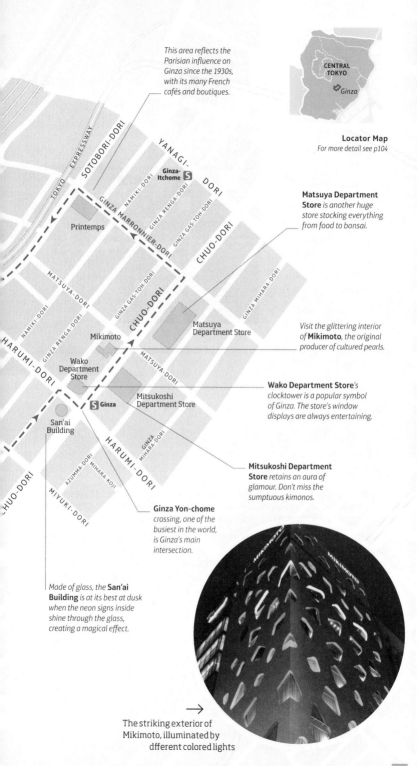

This area reflects the Parisian influence on Ginza since the 1930s, with its many French cafés and boutiques.

Locator Map
For more detail see p104

CENTRAL TOKYO

Ginza

Ginza-Itchome Ⓢ

SOTOBORI-DORI

TOKYO EXPRESSWAY

GINZA MARRONNIER-DORI

YANAGI-DORI

NAMIKI-DORI

GINZA RENGA-DORI

GINZA GAS-TOH-DORI

CHUO-DORI

Printemps

MATSUYA-DORI

CHUO-DORI

GINZA GAS-TOH-DORI

NAMIKI-DORI

GINZA RENGA-DORI

HARUMI-DORI

Mikimoto

Wako Department Store

Ⓢ Ginza

San'ai Building

MATSUYA-DORI

Mitsukoshi Department Store

HARUMI-DORI

AZUMMA-DORI

MIHARA-KOJI

GINZA MIHARA-DORI

MIYUKI-DORI

CHUO-DORI

Matsuya Department Store

GINZA MIHARA-DORI

Matsuya Department Store is another huge store stocking everything from food to bonsai.

Visit the glittering interior of **Mikimoto**, the original producer of cultured pearls.

Wako Department Store's clocktower is a popular symbol of Ginza. The store's window displays are always entertaining.

Mitsukoshi Department Store retains an aura of glamour. Don't miss the sumptuous kimonos.

Ginza Yon-chome crossing, one of the busiest in the world, is Ginza's main intersection.

Made of glass, the **San'ai Building** is at its best at dusk when the neon signs inside shine through the glass, creating a magical effect.

→
The striking exterior of Mikimoto, illuminated by different colored lights

---

EAT

Takashimaya

The recipe for the sauce used at Takashimya eel shop has not been altered since the eatery opened in 1875. What's more, this venerable restaurant doesn't just serve up any old eel to its discerning clientele. Only the Kyosui *unagi*, a slow-growing and richer flavored sub-species of the fish, will be found in the kitchen here. A bento option for takeout is available.

📍J6 🏠11-11-15 Nihonbashikobunachō, Chūō-ku 🕐Sun 🌐takashimaya.info

¥¥¥

→

An illuminated street lined with stores in the Nihonbashi District

2

NIHONBASHI DISTRICT

日本橋地区

📍J6 Ⓢ Tokyo Stn, Marunouchi line; Nihonbashi Stn, Ginza, Tozai & Toei Asakusa lines; Mitsukoshimae Stn, Ginza & Hanzomon lines 🚉Tokyo Stn, many lines 🕐Tokyo Stock Exchange: 9am–4:30pm Mon–Fri 🌐Tokyo Stock Exchange: jpx.co.jp/english

The mercantile and entrepreneurial center of Edo and Meiji Tokyo, Nihonbashi has been the city's traditional commercial hub for centuries. It is here, amid the ultramodern streets and buildings, that you will find some of the oldest continuously operating businesses in the world, including dozens of bank headquarters, huge department stores, and smaller traditional stores.

Home to both the Bank of Japan and the Tokyo Stock Exchange, which has an observation deck, Nihonbashi feels as if it is at the center of the city. The district is named after the famous bridge, immortalized in Hokusai's prints of great processions passing over on their way into the shogun's city. The Edo era still feels within touching distance in this densely packed district and, to this day, Nihonbashi remains the center for traditional Japanese small-scale crafts in the city. Kimono-makers, embroiderers, and even toothpick whittlers still sell their wares here. One former kimono shop is Mitsukoshi. Founded in 1673, this labyrinthine complex was Japan's first department store, and serves as a monument to consumption. A newer addition to the neighborhood is Coredo Nihonbash, an upmarket shopping mall focusing on women's fashion, near the station.

Although trading in the Tokyo Stock Exchange was computerized in 1999, this is still a great place to see the importance of commerce in the capital. The visitors' observation deck overlooks the trading floor.

Did You Know?

In Japan, distances are measured from Nihonbashi bridge.

1. Nihonbashi bridge is decorated with statues of symbolically powerful animals, including lions and dragons.

2. The main hall of Mitsukoshi is crowned with a statue of the Goddess of Sincerity.

3. Although cherry trees can only be found along Edo Sakura-dori, Nihonbashi celebrates the flowering of sakura with many events, including light shows.

3 Ⓜ️

IMPERIAL PALACE

皇居

📍G6 Ⓢ Nijubashimae Stn, Chiyoda line; Otemachi Stn, many lines
🚃 Tokyo Stn, many lines 🕐 Imperial Palace: Jan 2, Dec 23; East Gardens
of the Imperial Palace: 9am–4pm Tue–Thu, Sat & Sun (to 4:30pm May–
mid-Apr, Sep & Oct; to 5pm mid-Apr–Aug) 🌐 kunaicho.go.jp

The residence of the emperor of Japan, the Imperial Palace is a modern,
working castle at the heart of Tokyo. In a city where everything can
feel to be in a permanent state of flux, the palace and its grounds
form a green thread of continuity with the capital and Japan's past.

Following the Meiji Restoration in 1868, Japan's imperial family
moved from Kyoto to Tokyo. Edo Castle, the former home of the
Tokugawa shoguns, was commandeered for the emperor and
rechristened the Imperial Palace. None of the main buildings
from this period remain today, but the moats, walls, entrance
gates, and guardhouses bear testament to this martial past.
Most of the palace was destroyed during World War II, but it was
rebuilt in the same style. Popular sights include Nijubashi – two
bridges that form an entrance to the inner palace grounds – and
the East Gardens of the Imperial Palace. The grounds feature
Japanese- and Western-style gardens and the foundations of
the castle's former keep. Visitors are only able to
enter the Imperial Palace on two days each
year, but guided tours of the grounds are
available throughout the rest of
the year at 10am and 1:30pm.

> **In a city where
> everything can feel
> to be in a permanent
> state of flux, the
> palace and its
> grounds form a green
> thread of continuity.**

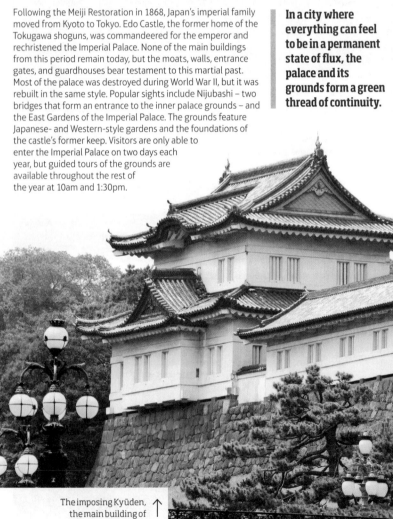

The imposing Kyūden,
the main building of
the Imperial Palace

An entrance to the East Gardens of the Imperial Palace

Browsing through stalls selling secondhand books in Jinbocho Booksellers' District

EXPERIENCE MORE

❹
Jinbocho Booksellers' District
神保町古本屋街

📍 G4 Ⓢ Jinbocho Stn, Toei Mita, Hanzomon & Toei Shinjuku lines

Three of the country's great universities – Meiji, Chuo, and Nihon – started out in this area in the 1870s and 1880s, and soon booksellers sprang up selling both new and used books. At one time as many as 50 percent of Japan's publishers were based in this district.

Although only Meiji University and Nihon University are still in the area, dozens of bookshops, including several selling ukiyo-e prints, remain, all clustered around the junction of Yasukuni-dori and Hakusan-dori. For English books on Eastern subjects, try Issei-do or Kitazawa Books; for ukiyo-e prints, visit Oya Shobo – all are on the south side of Yasukuni-dori, walking away from Hakusan-dori.

The change in the economic status (as well as pastimes and priorities) of Tokyo's university students is evident in Jinbocho Booksellers' District. Shops selling surf- and snowboards are now everywhere, and music shops selling electric guitars seem as numerous as the bookshops.

Did You Know?

The Japanese word *"tsundoku"* means "to buy more books than you can ever read."

INSIDER TIP
Market Days

The best time to visit the Tokyo International Forum is on the first or third Sunday of the month when the Oedo Antique Market – the largest in Japan – takes over the forecourt with overflowing stalls.

6

Kabuki-za Theater
歌舞伎座

◆H8 ◆4-12-15 Ginza
Ⓢ Higashi-Ginza Stn, Toei Asakusa & Hibiya lines
ⓦ kabukiweb.net/ theatres/kabukiza/ information/index.html

Tokyo's principal theater for Kabuki opened in 1889 during the reign of Emperor Meiji as part of Kabuki's shift from daytime entertainment for the masses in Asakusa to a more high-brow art form.

Despite facing destruction multiple times, the building is one of the oldest surviving examples of a Japanese-style structure built using Western materials and techniques. It was almost destroyed by the Allied bombing of 1945, and was rebuilt in 1951, only to be demolished again in 2010. The theater reopened in 2013 and enchanting performances take place here most days.

The enormous, sleek interior of the Tokyo International Forum ↑

 5

Tokyo International Forum
東京国際フォーラム

◆H7 Ⓢ Yurakucho Stn, Yurakucho line; Tokyo & Ginza Stns, Marunouchi line ◆Tokyo and Yurakucho Stns, many lines ◆7am–11:30pm daily ⓦ t-i-forum.co.jp/en

Designed by the American-based architect Rafael Viñoly, and completed in 1996, the International Forum is one of downtown Tokyo's most distinctive and enjoyable buildings. A bustling cultural center, it is made up of two buildings: a curved, glass atrium soaring 200 ft (60 m), and a white, cube-like structure housing four halls (the largest seating 5,012).

A tree-shaded courtyard separates the two, while glass walkways provide an overhead link.

The interior of the huge atrium is filled with light and has a ceiling resembling a ship's hull. There are shops, cafés, and restaurants, as well as conference rooms, all supported by state-of-the-art facilities including high-speed internet access available in the lobby.

→
The entrance to the much-reconstructed Kabuki-za Theater

↑ The hero of a Noh
performance fighting
a masked demon

JAPANESE TRADITIONAL THEATER

Four major types of traditional theater are still performed regularly in Japan: Noh, Kyogen, Kabuki, and Bunraku. Originating in Shinto rites, Noh became more ritualistic and ceremonial, before splintering into different forms designed to entertain the masses.

NOH

First performed by Kan'ami Kiyotsugu (1333–84), Noh is a restrained but powerful theatrical form. One or two masked characters appear on the bare stage at a time, and perform slow, choreographed actions *(kata)* to music.

KYOGEN

This form evolved from comic interludes devised as relief from the demanding nature of Noh. A down-to-earth, colloquial form, its characters highlight human foibles. Rather than masks, the actors wear distinctive yellow *tabi* socks.

↑ Elaborately dressed Kabuki
performers on stage

KABUKI

If Noh is stark, Kabuki is flamboyant and colorful. Elaborate make-up replaced Noh masks, and a curtain allowed set changes. Although Kabuki was founded by a woman, all actors are now male, and female roles are played by highly skilled *onnagata*.

BUNRAKU

Elaborately dressed 4-ft- (1.2-m-) high puppets are manipulated by a puppeteer and his two assistants. *Shamisen* music accompanies the action, and a narrator both tells the story and speaks all the parts.

↑ A Bunraku puppet striking
a ceremonial bell

A stream running through the charming, tree-filled Hama-rikyu Gardens

8

The Diet Building
日比谷地区と国会議事堂

📍F7 **🚇**Nagatacho Stn, Hanzomon, Namboku & Yurakucho lines; Kokkai-Gijidomae Stn, Chiyoda & Marunouchi lines; Hibiya Stn, Toei Mita, Chiyoda & Hibiya lines **🕐**8am–5pm Mon–Fri (by reservation) **🌐**sangiin.go.jp/eng/index.htm

Completed in 1936, the Diet Building houses the legislature of the Japanese government, originally established as the Imperial Diet in the Meiji era. Tours (in Japanese only) cover the well-worn inside, including the Diet chamber, where you can see the deliberations of Diet members, and the extravagantly decorated rooms formerly used by the emperor for official functions.

Nearby, you'll find Central Tokyo's only Western-style park, Hibiya Park. Its

7

Hama-rikyu Gardens
浜離宮庭園

📍H9 **📞**(03) 3541-0200 **🚇**Shiodome Stn, Oedo line **🚉**Shinbashi Stn, Yamanote line **🕐**9am–5pm daily

Situated where the Sumida River empties into Tokyo Bay, this 62-acre (25-hectare) garden dotted with colorful and fragrant plants like camellia and azalea was built in 1654 as a retreat for the shogun's family, who also hunted duck here. The garden has had an illustrious history. The US president Ulysses S. Grant stayed in a villa in the gardens during his visit in 1879 and sipped green tea in Nakajima teahouse.

The garden grounds surrounding the duck ponds are still a pleasant, uncrowded place to stroll and unwind, although all of the original teahouses and villas, trees, and vegetation burned down after a devastating bombing raid on November 29, 1944. But Nakajima teahouse has been faithfully rebuilt, appearing to float over the large pond. Green tea and Japanese sweets are available here.

> **INSIDER TIP**
> ### All Aboard!
>
> A cruise on the Sumida River from Hama-rikyu Gardens to Asakusa in Northern Tokyo offers a little-seen view of the city. In a space-ship-like boat, you'll pass under colorful bridges, take in the city's soaring sky-scrapers, and see people relaxing in the parks by the water. Near Asakusa there are long, low boats that take out groups for lantern-lit evening cruises (www. suijo bus.co.jp/en).

→ The imposing entrance to Tokyo Station, in Marunouchi District

location, close to the political centers of Kasumigaseki and the Diet Building, makes it a favorite place for public protests, especially on May Day. The large bandstand in the center is also occasionally used for concerts.

 9

Marunouchi District
丸の内地区

📍H6 **S** Tokyo Stn, Marunouchi line
🚃 Tokyo Stn, many lines

During the Edo era, this district earned the name "Gambler's Meadow" as its isolation made it an ideal place to gamble secretly. In the Meiji period the army used it, selling it in 1890 to Mitsubishi. The arrival of the railway increased the desirability of this barren wasteland as a business site, and after the 1923 earthquake, many other firms moved here.

Tokyo Station, designed by Kingo Tatsuno and completed in 1914, is supposedly based on the design of Amsterdam's Centraal Station. Its dome was damaged in the 1945 air raids and subsequently replaced by the polyhedron there today. The original reliefs adorning the domes above the north and south exits are worth a look. Opposite the station's south gate is the shopping mall KITTE, with the **Tokyo City-i** information center on the first floor. The English-speaking staff here, including Pepper the robot, offer advice and help to visitors.

A short walk west of the station up Miyuki-dori and over the moat via the Wadakura bridge leads to the Wadakura Fountain Park, which contains some interesting water features. Returning over the Wadakura bridge, cross Hibiya-dori and turn right. About 500 m (550 yds) away is the Meiji Seimei Kan Building (1934), with its huge Corinthian columns. Hiroshige, the wood-block print artist, was born on this site in 1797.

Tokyo City-i
🏠 2-7-2 Marunouchi, Chiyoda
🕐 8am–8pm daily
🌐 en.tokyocity-i.jp

Did You Know?

During the Edo Period, some of Japan's most powerful feudal lords resided in Marunouchi.

STAY

Aman Hotel
A glamorous high-rise hotel, with a hot tub in each room.

📍H6 🏠 1-5-6 Otemachi, Chiyoda 🌐 aman.com

¥¥¥

The Tokyo Station Hotel
Next to Tokyo Station, this luxury hotel is an oasis of calm and peace.

📍H6 🏠 1-9-1 Marunouchi, Chiyoda 🌐 thetokyostation hotel.jp/en

¥¥¥

Tokyo Prince Hotel
Although it's slightly dated, this hotel makes a great base from which to explore the city.

📍F9 🏠 3-3-1 Shibakoen, Minato 🌐 prince hotels.co.jp

¥¥¥

10

Shiba Park and Tokyo Tower
芝公園と東京タワー

♀F9 Ⓢ Shibakoen Stn, Toei Mita line

Shiba Park used to be the Tokugawa family's graveyard, and you'll find Zojo-ji – their temple – at its center. Founded in 1393, it was moved here in 1598 to protect the new capital spiritually from a southeasterly direction. The present building dates from 1974; nearby are the Daimon (big gate) and the Sanmon (great gate, 1622).

To the west of the park is **Tokyo Tower**. Completed in 1958, at 1,093 ft (333 m) tall, it is higher than the Eiffel Tower in Paris, on which it is based. You can visit two viewpoints – the main one at 492 ft (150 m) and a higher one at 820 ft (250 m), with more spectacular views. In 2012 Tokyo Tower was usurped by the 2,080 ft (634 m) Tokyo Sky Tree (p135).

Tokyo Tower

⊛ 🅐 4-2-8 Shibakoen, Minato Ⓢ Akabanebashi stn, Oedo line 🕘 9am-11pm daily 🅦 tokyotower.co.jp

---

> **JAPAN'S OTAKU (GEEK) CULTURE**
>
> *Otaku* is the Japanese term for people with obsessive interests, particularly in anime and manga, but also cameras, cars, pop stars, or electronics. Although originally a pejorative, like the English word "geek," an increasing number of people now self-identify as *otaku*. The subculture began in the 1980s, coinciding with the anime boom, as changing social mentalities led a section of Japanese society to consider themselves outcasts.

Did You Know?

Zojo-ji temple in Shiba Park is home to a 5th-century grave mound, untouched by time.

11

Akihabara Electronics District
秋葉原電気街

♀H4 Ⓢ Akihabara Stn, Hibiya line 🄰 Akihabara Stn, Yamanote, Chuo & Sobu lines

The city's electronics district surrounds Akihabara Station. Directly under the station is a bazaar of tiny shops selling any electronic device, from Christmas-tree lights to the latest microchip. The market grew out of the ruins of World War II, when the Japanese army had surplus equipment it wanted to dispose of. Students from the nearby universities would buy the army parts and made radios to sell on road-sides or in tiny shops here. Akihabara and electronics have been synonymous ever since. Later, as the economy improved, the focus changed to televisions, washing machines, and refrigerators. You can still see these, but increasingly the emphasis is on computers, cell phones, and video games.

Brand-name goods are available at a 3 to 10 percent discount – sometimes more. On Chuo-dori, Laox is a famous source of tax-free goods for tourists.

12

Kitanomaru Park
北の丸公園

♀F5 Ⓢ Kudanshita Stn, Hanzomon, Toei Shinjuku & Tozai lines; Takebashi Stn, Tozai line

A former ground for the Imperial Palace Guard, this area became a park in 1969. Before entering, walk past with Tayasumon gate on the left to reach Chidorigafuchi (the west moat), one of Tokyo's most beautiful cherry-blossom viewing spots. Row-boats can be rented here.

Within Kitanomaru's grounds are a number of buildings. Near Tayasumon is the Nippon Budokan. Built for the 1964 Olympics martial arts competition, it is now used mostly for rock concerts. A short walk on is the **Science and Technology Museum**.

↑ Vibrantly colored neon signs lighting up the streets of Akihabara Electronics District

The fun interactive exhibits include virtual bike rides and electricity demonstrations (explanations are in Japanese).

Five minutes beyond, over a main road and left down the hill, is the **National Museum of Modern Art**. The permanent collection comprises Japanese works from the 1868 Meiji Restoration to the present day; visiting exhibits are often excellent. Nearby is the National Museum of Modern Art's **Crafts Gallery**. Inside this 1910 Neo-Gothic brick building is an exquisite collection of modern workings of traditional Japanese crafts – pottery, lacquerware, and damascene (etched metal artifacts). Some pieces are for sale.

Science and Technology Museum
 2-1 Kitanomaru Koen, Chiyoda ⏰9:30am–4:50pm Thu–Tue 🌐jsf.or.jp/eng

National Museum of Modern Art
 3-1 Kitanomaru Koen, Chiyoda ⏰10am–5pm Tue–Sun (to 8pm Fri & Sat) 🌐momat.go.jp/english

Crafts Gallery
 1-1 Kitanomaru Koen, Chiyoda 📞(03) 5777-8600 ⏰10am–5pm Tue–Sun

People rowing on a lake and *(inset)* strolling in Kitanomaru Park during cherry-blossom season →

13. ⟨⟩

Koishikawa Korakuen Garden
小石川後楽園

📍F4 📞(03) 3811-3015 🚇Korakuen Stn, Marunouchi & Namboku lines ⏰9am–5pm daily

Korakuen, meaning "garden of delayed pleasure," is one of Tokyo's best traditional stroll gardens. Construction started in 1629 and finished 30 years later. Exiled Chinese scholar Zhu Shunsui helped design the Engetsukyo (full-moon) bridge, a stone arch with a reflection resembling a full moon. Tsukenkyo bridge, a copy of a bridge in Kyoto, is striking for the contrast between its vermilion with the surrounding deep-green forest.

The garden recreates larger landscapes in miniature, including Rozan, a famous Chinese mountain, and Kyoto's Oikawa River. In the middle of the large pond is Horai island, a beautiful composition of stone and pine trees.

EAT

Sushi Sora
One of Tokyo's best-kept secrets, this sushi restaurant at the Mandarin Oriental has the best view in the capital.

📍H6 🏠2-1-1 Nihonbashimuromachi, Chūō 🌐mandarin oriental.com

¥¥¥

Chuka Soba Inoue
The ramen served here is legendary among Tokyo's noodle soup aficionados – and well worth the inevitable queue for a table.

📍H8 🏠4-9-16 Tsukiji, Chūō 📞(03) 3542-0620

¥¥¥

Yasukuni Shrine
靖国神社

⑨ F5 ⑤ Kudanshita Stn, Hanzomon, Tozai & Toei Shinjuku lines ⊙ 6am-6pm daily ⓦ yasukuni.or.jp/english

The 2.5 million Japanese, soldiers and civilians who have died in war since the Meiji Restoration are enshrined at Yasukuni Jinja (Shrine of Peace for the Nation), which was dedicated in 1879. It is a sobering place to visit.

Until the end of World War II Shinto was the official state religion, and the ashes of all who died in war were brought here regardless of the families' wishes. Controversially, the planners and leaders of Japan during World War II and the colonization of China and Korea are also enshrined here, including wartime prime minister Hideki Tojo.

Beside the shrine is the **Yushukan**, a museum dedicated to the war dead. Many exhibits put a human face on Japan at war: under a photo of a smiling young officer is a copy of his last letter home, and there are

mementos of a nurse who died from overwork. Still, romanticized paintings of Japanese soldiers in Manchuria and displays of guns, planes, and even a locomotive from the Thai-Burma Railway may be troubling to some.

Yushukan
 ⊙ 9am-4:30pm daily

Kanda Myojin Shrine
神田明神

⑨ H4 ⓒ (03) 3254-0753 ⑤ Ochanomizu Stn, Marunouchi line ⓡ Ochanomizu stn, Chuo & Sobu lines ⊙ 24 hours daily

Myojin is more than 1,200 years old, although the

present structure is a reproduction built after the 1923 earthquake. The gate's guardian figures are tight-lipped archers: Udaijin on the right and Sadaijin on the left. Just inside the compound on the left is a big stone statue of Daikoku, one of the *shichi-fuku-jin* (seven lucky gods). Here, as always, he is sitting on top of two huge rice bales.

The vermilion shrine itself and its beautiful interior, all lacquer and gold, are very impressive. Early morning is the best time to glimpse the Shinto priests performing rituals. The Kanda Matsuri is one of the greatest and grandest of Tokyo's festivals – come early and be prepared for crowds.

Behind the main shrine is a **museum** containing relics from the long history of Myojin.

Museum
 ⊙ 9am-4pm daily

The distinctive vermilion exterior of Kanda Myojin Shrine ↑

↑ The brightly colored main hall of Kanda Shinto
Shrine in Tokyo's Chiyoda district

SHINTO

Japan's oldest religion, Shinto's core concept
is that deities, *kami*, preside over all things
in nature, be they living, dead, or inanimate.
Today, there are few pure Shintoists, but *jinja*
(shrines) still line waysides and Shinto rituals
are observed alongside Buddhist practices.

SACRED GATES

The approach to the *jinja* transports
worshippers from the secular to the sacred
world. Vermilion torii often line the path,
symbolizing gateways, and red-bibbed stone
foxes stand guard at Inari Shrines. Inside the
shrine's main complex, *shimenawa*, a rope
made of twisted rice straw, hangs over
entrances to ward off evil and sickness.

HAIDEN AND HONDEN

At the *haiden*, or hall of worship, devotees
pull on a bell rope, toss money into a box,
clap three times to summon the resident
kami, then stand in silent prayer for a few
moments. The *kami* is believed to live in
the shrine's *honden* (main sanctuary), but
usually only the head priests are permitted
to enter this hallowed space.

KANNUSHI

The Shinto priesthood *(kannushi)* tended to
be passed down through families, and some
of these dynasties *(shake)* are still connected
with certain shrines. Usually dressed in white
and orange robes, the *kannushi* perform
purification ceremonies and other rituals.

CHARMS AND VOTIVE TABLETS

Good-luck charms, called
omamori, are sold at shrines
across Japan. Common themes
relate to fertility, luck in
examinations, general health,
or safety while driving. The
charm itself might be written on
a piece of paper or thin wooden
board and tucked into a cloth
bag, which can be worn next to
the body or placed somewhere
relevant. Do not open the bag to
read the charm or it will not
work! Prayers or wishes can
also be written on *ema*
boards *(above)* and
hung at the shrine.

→
A cloth bag
containing a
paper *omamori*

121

NORTHERN TOKYO

The northern districts of Ueno and Asakusa contain what remains of Tokyo's old Shitamachi (low city). Once the heart and soul of culture in Edo, Shitamachi became the subject of countless ukiyo-e woodblock prints. Merchants and artisans thrived here, as did Kabuki theater. As a consequence of this liberal atmosphere, the Yoshiwara red-light district moved to near Asakusa in the 17th century after the Great Fire of Meireki in 1657. By 1893, there were over 9,000 women living and working in this raucous area.

One of the last great battles in Japan took place in Ueno in 1868 when Emperor Meiji's forces defeated the Tokugawa shogunate. In 1872, Dr Anthonius Baudin, a Dutch miliary doctor, observed the area's natural beauty and petitioned for it to be turned into a park, rather than the proposed army hospital and cemetery. In 1876, Ueno Park was registed as Japan's oldest park. The park became a haven for art and thought, hosting the first and second National Industrial Exhibitions in 1887 and 1881 respectively, and becoming home to the Tokyo National Museum in 1882.

NORTHERN TOKYO

Must Sees
1. Ueno Park
2. Tokyo National Museum
3. Senso-ji

Experience More
4. Shitamachi Museum
5. Ameyoko Market
6. Yanaka District
7. Tokyo Skytree
8. Inaricho District and Kappabashi-dori

Eat
① Yamabe Okachimachi

Shop
② Kamata

❶

UENO PARK

上野公園

◎ J3 **Ⓢ** Ueno Stn, Hibiya & Ginza lines **Ⓡ** Uguisudani & Ueno Stns, many lines **◷** Hours vary, check websites for details **Ⓦ** Ueno Zoo: tokyo-zoo.net; Tokyo Metropolitan Art Museum: tobikan.jp; National Museum of Nature and Science: kahaku.go.jp; National Museum of Western Art: nmwa.go.jp

Erupting in a riot of pink cherry blossoms every spring, it is little wonder that Ueno Park, one of Tokyo's most beautiful green spaces, has figured in so many woodblock prints and stories.

Ieyasu, the first Tokugawa shogun, built the Kan'ei-ji temple and subtemples in Ueno in the 1600s to negate evil spirits from the northeast. Judging by how long the Tokugawas lasted, it was a wise move, and parts of the temple still stand. In 1873, five years after the Battle of Ueno, when the last supporters of the shogun were crushed by imperial forces, the government designated Ueno a public park. It has been a popular spot ever since for Tokyo locals to relax. As well as its tranquil tree-lined paths,

Shinobazu Pond (actually three ponds) is an annual stop for thousands of migrating birds. Ueno Park is home to the Tosho-gu Shrine and Japan's oldest zoo, as well as a whole host of museums. There's the Tokyo Metropolitan Art Museum, displaying contemporary Japanese art, the extensive National Museum of Western Art, and the National Museum of Nature and Science, with its jaw-dropping dinosaur skeletons. Topping them all is the vast Tokyo National Museum (p128).

> **💬 INSIDER TIP**
> **Sakura Spotting**
>
> More than 1,200 cherry trees grow on the 133 acres (54 ha) that make up Ueno Park. Over two weeks every year, more than 2 million people visit the park for *hanami* (cherry-blossom-viewing) picnics. To find out the best time to sit beneath the flowers in the park, check with the Japan Weather Association (*www.jwa.or.jp/english*).

> **Did You Know?**
>
> Before *hanami*, *umemi* (plum-viewing) was enjoyed during the Nara period.

People enjoying *hanami* picnics under the cherry blossoms in Ueno Park ↑

← Skeletons on display in the dinosaur gallery of the family-friendly National Museum of Nature and Science

→ One of the ornate Edo-era halls that make up the Tosho-gu Shrine, where Ieyasu was first enshrined

→ Statue of Saigo Takamori, the leader of the victorious Meiji forces, located near the site of the old Kan'ei-ji temple

Heiseikan

Gallery of
Horyu-ji
Treasures

Honkan

Hyokeikan

*Ueno
Park*

Toyokan

Locator Map
For more detail see p124

EAT

**Yamabe
Okachimachi**
Instead of having lunch
at one of the museum's
pricey restaurants,
head here for tasty
tonkatsu (breaded pork).

◌ J3 ◌ 4-5-1 Ueno
◌ 03-5817-7045

¥¥¥

① The Western-style works
of Kuroda Seiki, including
Lakeside (1897), are displayed
in the Kuroda Memorial Hall.

② The Honkan gallery has
examples of ukiyo-e (woodblock prints), including these
14th-century portraits of the
36 Immortals of Poetry.

③ The Gallery of Horyu-ji
Treasures displays a collection of items from the
temple, including rare
statues dating from the
7th to 8th centuries.

↑ The exterior of Honkan, the main building of the Tokyo National Museum

2

TOKYO NATIONAL MUSEUM

東京国立博物館

📍 J2　Ⓢ Ueno Stn, Hibiya & Ginza lines　🚇 Ueno Stn, many lines; Uguisudani Stn, Yamanote line　🕐 9:30am–5pm Tue–Sun (to 9pm Fri & Sat)　🌐 tnm.jp

Five buildings in the northeast corner of Ueno Park make up one of Tokyo's finest museums. Displaying everything from kimonos to archaeological finds, it provides an intriguing insight into Japan's history and culture.

More than 110,000 items make up the Tokyo National Museum's collection – the best assembly of Japanese art in the world – and the displays change frequently, with about 4,000 of these exhibits on public view at any one time. The museum also stages temporary exhibitions, covering art from around the world. If you only have a couple of hours to spare, stick to the second floor of the Honkan gallery. With audio guides, tours, and good signage in English, it's a great introduction to Japanese heritage. Those with the luxury of more time can explore the museum's other buildings, admiring ancient statues, Chinese ceramics and Impressionist paintings at their leisure.

Did You Know?

The Tokyo National Museum is the oldest museum in Japan.

A wooden statue of a
Shinto deity on display ↑
in the Honkan gallery

Exploring the Galleries

The Honkan is the museum's main building, housing Japanese
art from ancient finds to modern masters. To its east is the
Toyokan, housing non-Japanese Eastern art. The 1909 Beaux-
Arts Hyokeikan is usually closed to the public and opens only
for special exhibitions. Behind it is the Gallery of Horyu-ji
Treasures, containing stunning objects from Horyu-ji Temple,
near Nara, and the Heiseikan, which hosts exhibitions of
archaeology. Access to all of the museum's buildings is included
in the cost of one admission ticket, so set out to explore
as much of this expansive museum as possible.

Did You Know?

Ukiyo-e translates
as "pictures of the
floating world."

A folding screen by ↑
Okamoto Shuki on display
in the Honkan gallery

Must See

TOP 4 UNMISSABLE EXHIBITS

Ukiyo-e
Honkan is home to poetic woodblock prints, dating from the 17th to 19th centuries.

Gilt Bronze Buddhas
Don't miss the collection of statues, all 30 to 40 cm (12 to 16 inches) tall, in the Gallery of Horyu-ji Treasures.

Korean Art
Ancient Korean pieces, some dating from the Bronze Age (100 BC to AD 300), are displayed in Toyokan.

Haniwa Figures
From warriors to horses, you'll find charming examples of these clay figures in Heiseikan.

Museum Galleries

Honkan

▷ Spanning two floors, this gallery is arranged chronologically to show the development of Japanese art from Jomon-era (from 10,000 BC) clay figures to 19th-century ukiyo-e woodblock prints showing everything from landscapes to scenes from pleasure houses *(right)*. In between is everything from calligraphy and tea utensils to armor, as well as textiles used in Noh and Kabuki. The first floor is themed, with stunning exhibits of sculpture, lacquer-ware, swords, and Western-influenced modern art. The gallery is best navigated by working your way counterclockwise.

Toyokan

Opened in 1968, Toyokan displays an excellent and eclectic collection of Asian art that ranges from textiles to ceramics. Many of the exhibits are from China and Korea - a consequence of these countries' historic ties with Japan. On the first floor, you'll find beautiful Buddhist statues, while the second floor houses sculptures from India, as well as artifacts from Egypt and the Middle East. A collection of Chinese art spans the third and fourth floors, and the final floor is dedicated to the history of Korea, including the rise and fall of the country's kings.

Heiseikan

Built in 1993 to commemorate the Crown Prince's wedding - its name translates as "to express congratulations" - the Heiseikan houses major temporary exhibitions and a superb collection of Japanese archaeological artifacts, with items from 10,000 to 7,000 BC onward. The highlight of this collection is undoubtedly the Haniwa figures. Literally meaning "clay ring," Haniwa is used to describe earthenware sculptures that were made for 4th- to 7th-century tombs and were thought to protect the dead. The gallery also houses Jomon-period (14,500-300 BC) finds, including *dogu*, ceramic figures with bulging eyes.

Gallery of Horyu-Ji Treasures

◁ When the estates of Horyu-ji Temple *(p232)* near Nara were damaged during the Meiji reforms, the impoverished temple gave a number of its treasures to the imperial family in exchange for money to finance its repairs. Over 300 of those priceless treasures *(left)*, including rare and early Buddhist statues, masks used for Gigaku dances, and beautifully painted screens, are housed in this modern gallery, designed by Yoshio Taniguchi.

Koruda Memorial Hall

Dedicated to Kuroda Seiki (1866-1924), this building displays the Western-style artist's oil paintings, sketches and other works. There is also a collection of letters from the painter, giving a greater insight into Kuroda's life and times.

3 🏛

SENSO-JI

浅草寺

📍L3 📞(03) 3842-5566 (information) 🚇Asakusa Stn, Ginza, Tobu Skytree & Toei-Asakusa lines 🚆Tobu-Asakusa Stn, Tobu Skytree line; Asakusa Stn, Asakusa Express line 🕐Temple: 6am-5pm daily (from 6:30am Oct–Mar); Nakamise-dori: 9:30am-7pm daily (individual hours vary)

Popularly known as Asakusa Kannon, this is Tokyo's most sacred and spectacular temple, as well as the city's oldest. Although the buildings are impressive, it is the people following their daily rituals that make this place so special.

In AD 628, two fishermen pulled a small gold statue of Kannon, the Buddhist goddess of mercy, from the Sumida River. First, their master built a shrine to Kannon, then, in 645, the holy man Shokai built a temple to her. Senso-ji's fame, wealth, and size grew until Tokugawa Ieyasu bestowed upon it a large stipend of land. When the Yoshiwara pleasure quarter moved nearby in 1657, the temple became even more popular. Senso-ji survived the 1923 earthquake but not World War II bombing. Its main buildings are therefore relatively new, but follow the original Edo-era layout. Today, incense still wafts through the air and people teem in Nakamise-dori's shops.

The Garden

① The Five-Story Pagoda, containing the ashes of the Buddha, is a 1973 replica of the original structure.

② Built of reinforced concrete in 1964, the two-story Hozomon Gate has a treasure house upstairs holding a number of 14th-century Chinese sutras.

③ The shops lining the expansive Nakamise-dori sell obi sashes, haircombs, fans, dolls, and kimonos.

The Kaminarimon Gate, or "Thunder Gate," is topped by guardian statues of Fujin (right) and Raijin (left), which have elderly heads and young bodies.

Awashima-do Hall

Yogodo Hall houses eight Buddha statues.

Five-Story Pagoda

The main hall, which is decorated with paintings, houses the original Kannon image in a gold-plated shrine.

Asakusa Jinja, built in 1649, is dedicated to the fishermen who found the Kannon statue.

Niten-mon gate was built in 1618.

Incense burner

Hozo-mon Gate

The bell in the Benten-yama Shoro belfry used to ring on the hour in Edo.

←

Senso-ji's vast complex, reached by the long Nakamise-dori

Nakamise-dori is a treasure trove of traditional wares.

↑ Looking down Nakamise-dori towards the Hozo-mon Gate

Must See

💬 **INSIDER TIP**
Backstreet Boys

Senso-ji sits at the heart of Asakusa, where the atmosphere of postwar Tokyo survives. After visiting the temple, explore the backstreets of this rough and tumble neighborhood, heading for one of its streetside eateries, where crates serve as tables.

EXPERIENCE MORE

4

Shitamachi Museum
下町風俗資料館

📍 J3 🏠 2-1 Ueno-koen, Taito-ku 📞 (03) 3823-7451 🚇 Ueno Stn, Hibiya & Ginza lines 🚉 Keisei-Ueno Stn, Keisei line; Ueno Stn, many lines 🕐 9:30am–4:30pm Tue–Sun

This museum is dedicated to preserving the spirit and artifacts of Shitamachi. The 50,000 exhibits include recreations of Edo-era shops, traditional toys, tools, and photographs, all donated by Shitamachi residents.

5

Ameyoko Market
アメ横

📍 J3 🚇 Ueno Stn, Hibiya & Ginza lines; Ueno-Okachimachi Stn, Oedo line 🚉 Okachimachi Stn, Yamanote & Keihin-Tohoku lines; Ueno Stn, many lines

One of the great bazaars in Asia, Ameyoko is a place where almost anything is available – and almost always at a discount. In Edo times,

---

SHOP

Kamata

Made in Kappabashi, Kamata's famous knives are crafted from the same metal and to the same principles as samurai swords. A must for all keen chefs.

📍 K3 🏠 2-12-6 Matsugaya, Taitō-ku 🌐 kap-kam.com

---

this was the place to come and buy *ame* (candy). After World War II, black-market goods – such as liquor, cigarettes, chocolates, and nylons – started appearing here, and *ame* acquired its second meaning as an abbreviation for American (*yoko* means "alley"). An area of tiny shops packed under the elevated train tracks, Ameyoko is no longer a black market, but still the place for bargain foreign brands, including Chanel and Rolex. Clothes and accessories are concentrated under the tracks, while foods, including a huge range of seafood, line the street that follows the tracks.

6

Yanaka District
谷中地区

📍 H2 🚉 Nippori Stn, many lines

This quiet area is rewarding to wander through because it survived the 1923 earthquake and bombing of World War II. It preserves something of the feel of old Shitamachi, with tightly packed houses in narrow alleys, and traditional food stalls selling rice crackers and old-fashioned candy.

The large Yanaka Cemetery is a must-see in cherry-blossom season. Inside is Tenno-ji, a temple with a large bronze Buddha dating from 1690. To the west of Tenno-ji is the **Asakura Museum of Sculpture**, home of sculptor Fumio Asakura (1883–1964). On the second floor is a delightful room full of his small statues of one of his favorite subjects – cats – but the garden is the real highlight, with its traditional composition of water and stone. Sansaki-zaka, the area's main street, has some traditional shops. The

---

JAPANESE FUNERAL CUSTOMS

When a Japanese person dies, the body is brought back home to spend one final night on his or her own futon. The next morning, it is taken to the service. At the wake, guests offer gifts of money and, after the cremation, the family use a special pair of chopsticks to pick the bones out and transfer them to an urn. Remembrance ceremonies are held in the following years on the anniversary of the death.

---

understated **Daimyo Clock Museum** has 100 Edo-era clocks lovingly presented.

Asakura Museum of Sculpture

📍 🏠 7-18-10 Yanaka, Taito 📞 (03) 3821-4549 🕐 9:30am–4:30pm Tue–Wed & Fri–Sun

Daimyo Clock Museum

📍 🏠 2-1-27 Yanaka, Taito 📞 (03) 3821-6913 🕐 Jan 15–Jun 30 & Oct 1–Dec 24: 10am–4pm Tue–Sun

↑ Unassuming entrance to the Asakura Museum of Sculpture

7

Tokyo Skytree
東京スカイツリー

M3 **1-1-2 Oshiage, Sumida** **S** **Tokyo Skytree Stn & Oshiage Stn, Tobu Skytree line** **8am–10pm** **tokyo-skytree.jp/en/**

At 2,080 ft (634 m), this is the tallest building in Japan. While its main function is broadcasting, the Skytree also hosts a large mall, aquarium, planetarium, and restaurants. The Tembo Deck, at 1,150 ft (350 m) above ground level, offers 360-degree views across Tokyo. Another viewing deck, Tembo Galleria, is the highest observation deck in Japan at 1,475 ft (450 m). On a clear day you can see as far as Mount Fuji.

8

Inaricho District and Kappabashi-dori
稲荷町地区とかっぱ橋通り

K3 **S Inaricho & Tawaramachi Stns, Ginza line**

Inaricho District is the Tokyo headquarters for wholesale religious goods. Small wooden boxes to hold Buddhas and family photos, paper lanterns, bouquets of brass flowers (*jouka*), Shinto household shrines, and even prayer beads can be found here.

Kappabashi-dori, named after the mythical water imp (*kappa*) who supposedly helped build a bridge (*bashi*) here, is Tokyo's center for kitchenware and the source of the plastic food displayed in almost every restaurant window. Although the "food" is for sale, prices are much higher than for the real thing.

→

Slender silhouette of the Tokyo Skytree, towering above the city's skyline

BEYOND THE CENTER

Must See

1 Toyosu Fish Market

Experience More

2 Gotoh Museum
3 Japan Folk Crafts Museum
4 Ikebukuro District
5 Arakawa Tram Line
6 Ebisu District
7 Sengaku-ji
8 Ghibli Museum
9 Rikugi-en Garden
10 Ryogoku District
11 Odaiba

Greater Tokyo, home to an astonishing 35 million people, is by far the biggest urban area on the planet. The districts beyond the center of Tokyo are some of its most characteristic – whether it is the new pop cultural hotspot of Ikebukuro, the manmade islands of Tokyo bay, or the hip neighborhoods of Ebisu, Daikanyama, and Meguro on the west side. Here, too, you'll find some of the city's most exciting developments, such as Toyosu, the location of one of Tokyo's largest shopping malls, and the vast fish market. Nearby, futuristic Odaiba and its surrounds are a breath of fresh air from the frenetic inner city.

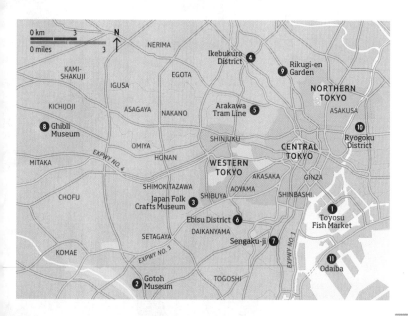

❶

TOYOSU FISH MARKET

東京都中央卸売市場豊洲市場

🏠 6-6-2 Toyosu, Koto-ku 🚉 Shijo-mae Stn, Yurikamome line

The largest market of its kind in the world and the beating heart of Japan's gastronomic culture, the Toyosu fish market turns over some 1,200 tons of seafood every single day. Most visitors come here not to buy fish, but to soak up vibrant market life and to eat the freshest sushi.

After years of delays, this state-of-the-art fish market opened in 2018 in Toyosu, just 1 mile (2 km) away from the previous site at Tsukiji. Sleeker and less chaotic than its predecessor, Toyosu's purpose-designed layout eliminates previous tensions between tourists and market traders. Head to the observation deck to watch the daily tuna auction below (book in advance).

This takes place from 4:30am, and lasts up to an hour, with huge fish laid out in long rows for buyers. While visitors are not able to purchase directly from the market, many sushi vendors that plied their trade in the shadow of the old Tsukiji market have also made the move over to Toyosu, providing hungry visitors with some of the freshest sushi imaginable.

TUNA FISH SUPPLIES

Toyosu specializes in *maguro* (tuna) from as far away as New Zealand and the North Atlantic. The Japanese consume about 30 per cent of the annual global 1.7 million-ton tuna catch, and eat 80 per cent of tuna raw, as sashimi, which requires the best cuts of fish. The Pacific Ocean's South Blue Fin tuna, a favorite for sashimi, is declining steadily in spite of efforts to manage numbers. The Japanese fishing industry has come under a great deal of scrutiny, with other governments exerting pressure on Japan to keep an eye on its activities.

→

Bustling stalls laden with fresh fish in the Toyosu Fish Market

1 Market traders can be seen slicing fish using a huge knife requiring two people. Cutting the fish in this way serves to demonstrate its freshness to potential buyers.

2 Buyers browse tuna fish before bidding on them.

3 As well as fish, Toyosu's traders sell fruit and vegetables, such as wasabi, in a designated area.

Did You Know?

The tuna auction area is cooled down to almost 0° C (32° F) - bring a sweater!

↑ A skilled chef preparing different kinds of sushi at a restaurant in Tokyo

SUSHI AND SASHIMI

Newcomers to Japan are often both fascinated and intimidated by these ubiquitous dishes. While sashimi denotes sliced fillets of raw fish served without rice, there are several different types of sushi (usually written with the suffix "-zushi") in which cold, lightly sweetened, and vinegared rice is topped or wrapped up with raw fish or other items, such as pickles or cooked meat.

NIGIRI-ZUSHI

Thin slices of raw fish are laid over molded fingers of rice with a thin layer of wasabi in between. Dip it in soy sauce, and consume in one mouthful.

CHIRASHI-ZUSHI

The "scattered" style involves a colorful combination of toppings, including fish, chunks of omelet, and vegetables, artfully arranged on a deep bed of cold rice.

MAKI-ZUSHI

"Rolled" sushi is very familiar outside Japan. Rice is combined with slivers of fish and other morsels, and rolled up in a sheet of toasted seaweed (nori).

SASHIMI

Sliced fillets of the freshest uncooked fish may be served alone. Sashimi is delicate and creamy, and the only accompaniments should be soy sauce, wasabi, daikon, and maybe a shiso leaf.

POPULAR FISH IN JAPAN

Of the 3,000 or so varieties of fish eaten in Japan, the most common are *maguro* (tuna), *tai* (sea bream), *haze* (gobies), *buri* (yellowtail), *saba* (mackerel), crustaceans such as *ebi* (shrimp) and *kani* (crab), and fish that are usually salted such as *sake* (salmon) and *tara* (cod). You'll find these fish on menus and market stalls all year round, but some fish are seasonal treats. In spring, the *ayu* (sweet-fish) – a river fish traditionally caught by trained cormorants – is enjoyed. *Katsuo* (skipjack tuna) is available in spring and summer, *unagi* (eel) in midsummer, and *sanma* (saury) in the fall. Winter, meanwhile, is the time for *dojo* (loach), *anko* (angler fish), and *fugu* (blowfish), prized for its delicate flavor but also feared for deadly toxins in its liver and ovaries.

EXPERIENCE MORE

2

Gotoh Museum
五島美術館

📍 3-9-25 Kaminoge, Setagaya-ku 📞 (03) 5777-8600 🚉 Tokyu Denentoshi line from Shibuya Stn to Futago-Tamagawa, then Tokyu Oimachi line to Kaminoge Stn 🕐 10am–5pm Tue–Sun

Set in a pleasant hillside garden, this museum showcases the private collection of the late chairman of the Tokyu Corporation, Keita Gotoh. He was originally attracted to Buddhist calligraphy, particularly that of 16th-century priests. His collection contains many examples of this work, called *bokuseki*. Also included are ceramics, calligraphy, paintings, and metalwork mirrors; items are changed several times a year. The museum's most famous works, however, are scenes

Did You Know?

The *Tale of Genji*, written in the 11th century, is thought to be the world's oldest novel.

from 12th-century scrolls of the *Tale of Genji*, painted by Fujiwara Takayoshi, which have been designated National Treasures. They are shown once a year, usually in "Golden Week" (April 29–May 5). The museum is closed during summer maintenance, when exhibitions change over, and on New Year's Day.

3

Japan Folk Crafts Museum
日本民芸館

📍 4-3-33 Komaba, Meguro-ku 📞 (03) 3467-4527 🚉 Komaba-Todaimae Stn, Keio Inokashira line 🕐 10am–4:30pm Tue–Sun

Known to the Japanese as Mingeikan, this small but excellent museum was set up by art historian Muneyoshi Yanagi. The museum building, designed by Yanagi and completed in 1936, uses black tiles and white stucco outside. The criteria for inclusion in the museum's collection are that the object should be the work of an anonymous maker, produced for daily use, and representative of the region from which it comes.

Items ranging from woven baskets to ax sheaths, iron

kettles, pottery, and kimonos present a fascinating view of rural life. There are also themed exhibits, such as 20th-century ceramics or Japanese textiles, and a room dedicated to Korean Yi-dynasty work. A small gift shop sells fine crafts and some books.

DRINK

Belg Aube Toyosu
A café with a good range of Belgian beers and European dishes such as Iberico ham, duck confit, and, of course, mussels.

📍 LaLaport Toyosu 1F, 2-4-9 Toyosu, Koto 📞 (03) 6910-1275

Tawaragi
This bar serves up mojitos, and other drinks, made with Ron Zacapa – a Guatemalan brand of rum, which is aged at an altitude of 7,546 ft (2,300 m).

📍 3-6-7 Tsukishima, Chuo-ku 📞 (03) 3531-0799

Towers Craft Beer Bar
Japanese microbrews Yona Yona Real Ale and Baird's Rising Sun Pale Ale have a regular spot here, with other guest beers available on tap.

📍 Lim Tsukishima 2F, 4-18-2 Tsukishima, Chuo-ku

←

Exterior of the Japan Folk Crafts Museum, designed by its art-historian founder

4 Ikebukuro District
池袋地区

🇸 **Ikebukuro Stn, Fukutoshin, Marunouchi & Yurachuko lines**
🇯 **Ikebukuro Stn, Yamanote & many other lines**

With the third-busiest train station in Japan (after Shinjuku and Shibuya), Ikebukuro is a designated *fukutoshin* (subcenter) of Tokyo. By the station's south entrance is the flagship store of Seibu, perhaps the country's most innovative department store, with boutiques of up-and-coming designers and a large basement food market. To the west of the station is the large Tobu department store with a similar set-up.

The Sunshine City complex, including the Sunshine 60 tower, is a short walk east of the station. It is built on top of what was Sugamo Prison, where seven Class-A World War II war criminals, including the prime minister, Hideki Tojo, were convicted and hanged. The Ancient Orient Museum, on the 7th floor of Sunshine City's Bunka Kaikan Building, has collections from Egypt, Iran, and Pakistan. In Sunshine 60 there is also a planetarium, an aquarium, and a rooftop viewing platform.

5 Arakawa Tram Line
荒川都電

🇸 **Edogawabashi Stn, Yurakucho line**

In 1955, 600,000 people a day were riding the dozens of tram lines that crisscrossed the city. Now the 8-mile (13-km-) Arakawa line is one of only two that remain. The others were eliminated as old-fashioned in the modernization for the 1964 Olympics.

The Arakawa tram line runs from Waseda in the west to Minowabashi in the east and costs ¥170 for each trip, short or long. Near the Waseda end of the line is the quiet stroll garden of Higo-Hosokawa Teien. There are few outstanding sights en route, but the pleasure of this tram ride lies in seeing a quieter, residential side to Tokyo. A short walk from Arakawa Yuenchimae stop, past tightly packed, tiny houses, is a modest amusement park, Arakawa Yuen Park. The Sumida River boat *(p116)* leaves from here for special tours – not the usual water-bus service – several times a month. Check ticket availability and book online. Opposite the Arakawa Nanachome stop is Arakawa Nature Park.

↑ A tram trundling along the Arakawa Tram Line at night

6 Ebisu District
恵比寿地区

🇸 **Ebisu Stn, Hibiya line**
🇯 **Ebisu Stn, Yamanote line**

The completion in the mid-1990s of Yebisu Garden Place, a commercial and residential center, brought this area to life. The **Tokyo Photographic Art Museum**, to the right of the entrance, has a permanent collection of work by Japanese and foreign photographers. In the center are a Mitsukoshi store, boutiques, two cinemas, a theater, and restaurants. To the left of Mitsukoshi is the small **Yebisu Beer Museum** with exhibits and videos about beer worldwide and in Japan, plus free samples.

Tokyo Photographic Art Museum
🔶 📍 1-13-3 Mita, Meguro
🇼 topmuseum.jp

Did You Know?

Ikebukuro translates as "pond bag" and there were once lots of lakes in this area.

↑ Admiring rays and other fish in the aquarium of the Sunshine City complex in Ikebukuro District

Yebisu Beer Museum

 📍 4-20-1 Ebisu, Shibuya 📞 (03) 5423-7255 ⏰ 11am-7pm Tue-Sun (last adm for tours till 5:10pm)

---

❼

Sengaku-ji
泉岳寺

📍 2-11-1 Takanawa, Minato Ⓢ Sengaku-ji Stn, Toei Asakusa line ⏰ Museum: 9am-4:30pm (to 4pm Oct-Mar) 🌐 sengakuji.or.jp

This is the site of the climax of Japan's favorite tale of loyalty and revenge, retold in the play *Chushingura* and many movies. Lord Asano was sentenced to death by *seppuku* (ritual disembowlment) for drawing his sword when goaded by Lord Kira. Denied the right to seek revenge, 47 of Asano's retainers (or ronin), led by Oishi Kuranosuke, plotted in secret. In 1702, they attacked Kira's house and beheaded him, presenting the head to Asano's grave at Sengaku-ji. They in turn were sentenced to *seppuku* and are buried here. Inside the temple gate and up the steps is the well where the ronin washed Kira's head. Farther ahead on the right are the retainers' graves. Back at the base of the steps is a museum with artifacts from the incident, which you can visit for a fee.

→ Statue of ronin leader Oishi Kuranosuke at Sengaku-ji

---

❽

Ghibli Museum
三鷹の森ジブリ美術館

📍 1-1-83 Shimoren-jaku, Mitaka 🚉 Mitaka Stn, Chūō line ⏰ 10am-6pm Wed-Mon 🚫 Dec 28-Jan 2 🌐 ghibli-museum.jp

Japanese animation company Studio Ghibli is known throughout the world for its Oscar-winning anime. The studio's founder Hayao Miyazaki personally designed this museum with the aim of making fans feel as if they have stepped straight into the sets of *Princess Mononoke* (1997), *Spirited Away* (2001), and many more of his films. The museum features a whimsical children's playground, a cinema showing short films, and collections of original drawings from the famous films, as well as charming cafés and shops.

Tickets must be booked in advance online as none are available at the gate.

EAT

TY Harbor

Serving up burgers, steaks, and crab cakes on the waterfront, Ty Harbor also brews its own beer.

📍 2-1-3 Higashi-shinagawa, Shinagawa 📞 (03) 5479-4555

¥ ¥ ¥

Tokyo Rāmen Kokugi-kan

Six ramen shops offering Sapporo-style miso ramen, Hakata-style *tonkotsu* (pork bone) ramen, and more.

📍 Aqua City Odaiba 5F, 1-7-1 Daiba, Minato 📞 (03) 3599-4700

¥ ¥ ¥

Odaiba Takoyaki Museum

Seven different stalls dish up variations on the classic fried batter and octopus balls.

📍 Decks Tokyo Beach, 1-6-1 Daiba, Minato 📞 (03) 3599-6500

¥ ¥ ¥

 9

Rikugi-en Garden
六義園

S Komagome Stn, Namboku line **R** Komagome Stn, Yamanote line **C** (03) 3941-2222 **O** 9am–5pm daily

Yanagisawa Yoshiyasu, grand chamberlain of the fifth shogun, built this, one of the finest Edo-era stroll gardens, from 1695. The fine design recreates 88 landscapes in miniature from famous *waka* (31-syllable poems), so the view changes every few steps. Sit on one of the many seats and enjoy the views while listening to songbirds overhead.

LIFE IN A SUMO STABLE

At the age of about 15, boys are accepted into a *beya*. Sumo society is supremely hierarchical, with newcomers serving senior wrestlers as well as cleaning and cooking for the entire *beya*. Junior practices may start at 4am. The day's single meal of *chanko-nabe*, a large stew, comes about noon, with juniors getting what the seniors leave. After, more work follows.

10

Ryogoku District
両国地区

S Ryogoku Stn, Toei-Oedo line **R** Ryogoku Stn, JR Sobu line

A great entertainment and commerce center in Edo's Shitamachi, Ryogoku is now a quiet place, but it still has its most famous residents: sumo wrestlers. Many *beya* (sumo stables) are here, and it is not unusual to see huge young men walking the streets in *yukata* (light cotton kimonos) and *geta* (wooden sandals).

The Ryogoku Sumo Hall has been here since 1945; the current building dates from 1985. Inside the stadium, the **Sumo Museum** is lined with portraits of all the *yokozuna* (grand champions).

Beside the stadium is the **Edo-Tokyo Museum**, one of Tokyo's most imaginative museums. Two zones trace life in Edo and then Tokyo, as Edo was renamed in 1868. The exhibits have explanations in Japanese and English. The route around the museum starts by crossing a traditional arched wooden bridge, a replica of Nihonbashi. There are life-sized reconstructed buildings, plus scale-model dioramas showing everything from the house of a daimyo (feudal lord) to a section of

Shitamachi. Beside a scale model of Tokyo's first skyscraper is rubble from the 1923 earthquake. Models of the boats that once plied the Sumida River give an idea of just how important the river was to Edo life. In the media section is a step-by-step example of how ukiyo-e woodblock prints *(p130)* were produced.

The **Sword Museum** is full of fine Japanese swords, some dating back to the 12th century. There is also a display of decorated hilts and old Japanese texts, illustrated with beautiful drawings, explaining the finer points of sword-making.

Sumo Museum

A 1-3-28 Yokoami, Sumida-ku **O** 10am–4:30pm Mon–Fri **C** Public hols **W** sumo.or.jp

Edo-Tokyo Museum

 A 1-4-1 Yokoami, Sumida-ku **O** 9:30am–5:30pm Tue–Sun (to 7:30pm Sat) **W** edo-tokyo-museum.or.jp

Sword Museum

A 1-12-9 Yokoami, Sumida-ku **O** 9:30am–5pm Tue–Sun **C** New Year hols **W** touken.or.jp/english

→

The distinctive bulk of the Tokyo Big Sight building, in Odaiba

↑ A bridge crossing a pond in the verdant Rikugi-en Garden

 Odaiba
お台場

 Yurikamome monorail from Shinbashi Stn to Odaiba-kaihinkoen Stn; Rinkai line to Tokyo Teleport 🚢 **From Hinode Pier 11:25am–6pm, every 40–50 mins**

When the West began to force Japan to open up in the 1850s, the shogunate constructed a series of *daiba* (obstructions) across Tokyo harbor to keep the foreign ships out. Odaiba (sometimes known as Daiba), an island almost blocking the mouth of Tokyo Bay, takes its name from these. The spectacular route to Odaiba is via the Yurikamome monorail, which climbs a loop before joining Rainbow Bridge high over Tokyo Harbor.

The first station, Odaiba-Kaihin-Koen, leads to Tokyo's only beach. Nearby is the Daisan Daiba Historic Park, with the remains of the original obstructions. A short walk west is Decks Tokyo Beach, which has six floors of restaurants and shops, plus Joypolis, a huge Sega center full of the latest electronic games. In front of Decks is the station for water buses from Hinode Pier. Located in Aomi, the **National Museum of Emerging Science and Innovation**, better known as Miraikan, has interactive robots, biotechnology, and ecological exhibits. The Fuji TV building dominates the area.

At Aomi station is the Palette Town development, including Venus Fort, a shopping mall whose interior recreates an 18th-century Italian town at twilight. Palette Town also includes Mega Web's Toyota City Showcase, with a massive display area, and state-of-the-art driving simulators. The Wanza Ariake building has shops and restaurants and is connected to Kokusai-Tenjijo Seimon station, as is Tokyo Big Sight (or Tokyo International Exhibition Hall).

National Museum of Emerging Science and Innovation
🏠 2-3-6 Aomi, Koto 📞 (03) 3570-9151 🕙 10am–5pm Wed–Mon 🚫 Dec 28–Jan 1

STAY

Hotel Metropolitan Tokyo Ikebukuro
Located at the center of the bustling Ikebukuro neighborhood, this is a relaxed and welcoming luxury hotel at an affordable price. Some rooms boast views of Mount Fuji.

🏠 1-6-1 Nishiikebukuro, Toshima 🌐 metro politan.jp

¥¥¥

Samurais Hostel Ikebukuro
At this kitsch hostel, guests can enjoy classical Japanese art on the walls, as well as glow-in-the-dark samurai murals. Private rooms are also available if you don't want to share a dorm.

🏠 3-52-12 Ikebukuro, Toshima 🌐 hiromas.net

¥¥¥

EXPERIENCE JAPAN

Central Honshu..148

Kyoto City...180

Western Honshu..210

Shikoku..246

Kyushu...260

Okinawa...282

Northern Honshu......................................294

Hokkaido..314

CENTRAL HONSHU

Lying between Kyoto and Tokyo's sprawling suburbs, Central Honshu epitomizes the contrasts of Japan today. Its densely populated coastal belt includes Yokohama and Nagoya, the country's second- and fourth-largest cities, while the interior contains its highest, wildest mountains, with Mount Fuji as well as the North and South Japan Alps, with many peaks over 10,000 ft (3,000 m).

During the Edo period five post roads crossed the region, two of which linked Edo (Tokyo) and Kyoto. Feudal lords were required to spend half their time in Edo, so long processions traveled the roads, and checkpoints and post towns grew up along the route. Most heavily used were the Tokaido via Yokohama, and Hakone, Shizuoka, and the Nakasendo through the Kiso Valley, which can still be walked. The settlements en route are relatively accessible, yet remote enough to remain unspoiled. The post towns of Kiso and the thatched villages of Shokawa offer Edo-period architecture, while Takayama and Chichibu attract thousands to their historic festivals, which originated in the 16th and 18th centuries respectively. The region's roots are also evident in the traditional crafts produced here: lacquerware in Takayama, Noto, and Kiso; carving in Kamakura; and *yosegi-zaiku* (Japanese marquetry) in Hakone. Until the 1970s, silkworms were raised in Shokawa and Chichibu, and silk is still dyed in Kanazawa.

CENTRAL HONSHU

Must Sees

1 Yokohama
2 Kamakura
3 Mount Fuji and the Fuji Five Lakes
4 Takayama
5 Kanazawa

Experience More

6 Narita
7 Kawagoe
8 Hakone
9 Izu Peninsula

10 Nagoya
11 Shizuoka
12 Inuyama
13 Shokawa Valley
14 Gifu
15 Matsumoto
16 Nagano
17 Kamikochi
18 Chichibu-Tama-Kai National Park
19 Eihei-ji
20 Noto Peninsula

↑ The modern skyline of Yokohama's Minato Mirai 21 district

1

YOKOHAMA

横浜

🅰F5 🚉Kanagawa Prefecture 🚃🚌 🛈In Yokohama Stn by west exit; www.yokohamajapan.com

Japan's second-largest city, Yokohama has been a center for shipping, trade, foreign contact, and modern ideas since the mid-19th century. Formerly a small fishing village on the Tokaido road, it was made a treaty port in 1859; there followed an influx of foreign traders, making it the biggest port in Asia by the early 1900s.

①

Landmark Tower

🅰2-2-1 Minato Mirai
⏰10am–9pm daily
🌐yokohama-landmark.jp

Landmark Tower is the focal point of the futuristic Minato Mirai 21 district, an area of redeveloped docks that is particularly lively at the weekend. Built in 1993, the tower is Japan's second-tallest building at 971 ft (296 m). Reached by the world's fastest elevator, traveling at 2,500 ft (750 m) per minute, the 69th-floor public lounge has a spectacular 360-degree view. Within the tower is the enormous Landmark Plaza shopping mall, which houses a number of luxury brands. It is also home to the Pokémon Center, which stocks a huge array of franchise-related merchandise.

②

Yokohama Museum of Art

🅰3-4-1 Minato Mirai
⏰10am–6pm Fri–Wed
🌐yokohama.art.museum

Yokohama's role as a meeting point between East and West means that it has long been a hub for the exchange of ideas. The Yokohama Museum of Art, designed by Kenzo Tange, celebrates this legacy with its impressive collection of modern art and photography. The museum is highly engaged with Yokohama itself, and focuses on Japanese artists with connections to the city, including Imamura Shiko, Kanzan Shimomura, and Chizuko Yoshida.

③

NYK Maritime Museum

🅰3-9 Kaigandōri ⏰10am–5pm Tue–Sun 🌐nyk.com

Founded in the 1880s, Nippon Yusen Kaisha (NYK) is one of the world's largest shipping companies. The quirky NYK Maritime Museum – with its exquisitely detailed model ships – celebrates the company's history and Yokohama's connection to the sea, showing how maritime commerce has revolutionized marine technology, trade, and politics. Visitors are also provided with a free tea ceremony.

> 🔍 HIDDEN GEM
> **Oodles of Noodles**
>
> True ramen obsessives should make a stop at Yokohama's cup noodle museum *(www.cup noodles-museum.jp)*, where visitors can fry their own ramen and design their own cup.

④ Hikawa Maru

🏠 Yamashita Park ⏰ 10am-5pm Tue-Sun 🌐 nyk.com

Originally built in 1930 as a cruise liner and light cargo ship, the Hikawa Maru spent World War II operating as a floating hospital and in its 30 years of service crossed the Pacific 254 times, carrying some 25,000 passengers. The restored liner is now permanently docked in Yokohama, where visitors can stroll the decks, inspect the elegant wood-panelled cabins and soak up the Art Deco glamour of the lounge. Those who are technically minded will enjoy the opportunity to get close to the vessel's mighty engines.

Did You Know?

Japan's first railroad was constructed in 1872, connecting Yokohama to Tokyo.

⑤ Kantei-byo Temple

🏠 140 Yamashitacho ⏰ 9am-7pm daily 🌐 yokohama-kanteibyo.com

Few sites better evoke Yokohama's cosmopolitan roots than Kantei-byo, the temple that has served as the heart of the city's Chinese community – the largest in Japan – for the past 150 years. This popular temple functions as a spiritual, cultural, and social hub, and is particularly atmospheric during Chinese New Year.

⑥ Foreigners' Cemetery

🏠 96 Yamatecho ⏰ 10am-5pm Tue-Sun 🌐 yfgc-japan.com

Yokohama Foreign General Cemetery was founded in 1854 following the death of an American marine. Among the 4,500 tombs in the early 20th-century Foreigners' Cemetery graveyard is that of Edmund Morel, the English engineer who helped build Japan's first railroads, which has an unusual tombstone shaped like a railroad ticket.

⑦ Sankai-en Garden

🏠 58 Honmokusannotani ⏰ 9am-5pm daily 🌐 sankeien.or.jp

With its ponds, bamboo groves, rivers, and meandering trails, this hideaway transports visitors back to ancient Japan. Among the garden's architectural treasures is a 15th-century pagoda. Constructed in Kyoto, it was relocated to Sankei-en in 1914.

Opened to the public in 1906, the entire garden was once the private home of Tomitaro "Sankei" Hara (1868-1939), an extremely wealthy silk merchant. His personal lodgings – a sprawling complex featuring dozens of airy traditional tatami rooms, overlooking a private lawn – can be toured at the site.

↑ Visitors, under the cover of umbrellas, paying their respects to the Great Buddha

❷

KAMAKURA

鎌倉

🅰F5 🚉Kanagawa Prefecture 🚋JR, Odakyu and Enoden lines 🛈At Kamakura Stn; www.city.kamakura.kanagawa.jp/kamakura-kankou/en

A seaside town of temples and wooded hills, Kamakura was Japan's administrative capital from 1192 until 1333. Favored by artists and writers, Kamakura has numerous antique and crafts shops, and in cherry-blossom season and on summer weekends, it teems with visitors.

①

Great Buddha

🏠2-2-8 Hase 🚉Hase Stn 🚌 🕐8am–6pm daily 🌐kotoku-in.jp

The Great Buddha (Daibutsu) is Kamakura's most famous sight. Cast in 1252, the bronze statue of the Amida Buddha is 44 ft (13.5 m) tall. Its proportions are distorted so that it seems balanced to those in front of it – this use of perspective may show Greek influence (via the Silk Road).

---

②

Hase-dera Temple

🏠3-11-2 Hase 🚉Hase Stn 🚌 🕐8am–5:30pm daily (to 5pm Oct–Feb) 🌐hasedera.jp/en

Simple and elegant, Hase-dera is home to a superb 11-faced Kannon, bodhisattva of mercy. The Treasure House displays characterful Muromachi-era carvings of the 33 incarnations of Kannon. There is also a sutra repository; rotating the sutras is said to earn as much merit as reading them.

The 1264 bell is the town's oldest. Below it is a hall dedicated to Jizo, guardian of children, surrounded by countless statues to children who have died or been aborted.

---

③

Myohon-ji

🏠1-15-1 Omachi 📞(0467) 22-0777 🚉Kamakura Stn 🕐9am–5pm daily

On a hillside of soaring trees, this temple, with its unusually steep, extended roof, is the town's largest that belongs to the Nichiren sect. It was established in 1260, in memory of a 1203 massacre.

> **INSIDER TIP**
> **Getting Around**
>
> Some parts of the town are best explored on foot but, with so many hills, it's worth buying a one-day bus pass from Kamakura station. The energetic can also rent a bicycle from here.

> **Did You Know?**
>
> The Great Buddha has shock absorbers in its base to protect it from earthquakes.

④

Tsurugaoka Hachiman-gu Shrine

🏠 2-1-31 Yukinoshita
📞 (0467) 22-0753
🚃 Kamakura Stn
🕐 Shrine: 5am-9pm daily; Museum: 9am-4:30pm Tue-Sun

Japan's Hachiman shrines are dedicated to the god of war; this one is also a guardian shrine of the Minamoto (or Genji) clan. Built in 1063 beside the sea, it was moved here in 1191. The approach runs between two lotus ponds: the Genji Pond has three islands (in Japanese *san* means both three and life) while the Heike Pond, named for a rival clan, has four (*shi* means both four and death).

The main shrine was reconstructed in 1828 in Edo style. To the east, the Kamakura National Treasure House Museum contains a wealth of temple treasures.

---

⑤

Zuisen-ji

🏠 710 Nikaido   📞 (0467) 22-1191 🚃 🕐 9am-5pm daily

This secluded temple is known for its naturalistic garden. Created in 1327 by the monk Muso Soseki, it features a waterfall-fed lake, rocks, and sand; a Zen meditation cave is cut into the cliff. Decorative narcissi also bloom here in January, and Japanese plum trees blossom in February, making it an idyllic natural oasis even before the cherry trees bloom.

→

The *hongu* (main hall) of the ornate Tsurugaoka Hachiman-gu Shrine

Kita-Kamakura Station ⑪ Engaku-ji
Tokei-ji ⑩   ⑨ Meigetsu-in Temple
YAMANOUCHI   Hansobo Shrine
Jochi-ji Temple
⑧ Kencho-ji
Choju-ji Temple   Kakuon-ji Temple
KAJIWARA   KAMAKURA-KAIDO
Enno-ji Temple   Tsurugaoka Hachiman-gu Shrine
OGIGAYATSU   ④   Kamakura-gu Shrine   Zuisen-ji ⑤
Zeni-Arai Benten Shrine ⑫   National Treasure House Museum   YUKINOSHITA   NIKAIDO
Sasuke-no Inari Shrine   Sugimoto-dera Temple ⑥   Jomio-ji Temple
SASUKE   KANAZAWA-KAIDO
SHIYAKUSHO-DORI   Hokai-ji Temple   JOMYOJI
KOMACHI-DORI   WAKAMIYA-OJI   ⑦ Hokoku-ji
IWAKOJI
Kamakura Station   Oimo Café Kanaria
KOMACHI
① Great Buddha   ③ Myohon-ji
SASAMEMACHI
② Hase-dera Temple   Wadazuka   Myoho-ji Temple
HASE   Yuigahama   OMACHI   HISAGI
Hase   WAKAMIYA-OJI   Ankokuron-ji Temple
YUIGAHAMA   YUIGAHAMA-DORI
NATIONAL HIGHWAY   Nameri River   ZAIMOKUZA   Chosho-ji Temple
Yuigahama Beach   134   Kuhon-ji Temple

0 meters 800
0 yards 800
N

6

Sugimoto-dera Temple

🏠 903 Nikaido 📞 (0467) 22-3463 🚍 ⏰ 8am–4:30pm daily

Founded in 734, this is the oldest temple in Kamakura and pleasantly informal. The softly thatched hall contains three wooden statues of 11-faced Kannon, protected by ferocious guardian figures at the temple gateway.

7

Hokoku-ji

🏠 2-7-4 Jomyoji 📞 (0467) 22-0762 🚍 ⏰ 9am–4pm daily

This Rinzai Zen temple was founded in 1334 and boasts a lovely bamboo grove, which you can visit for a fee, as well as a pleasant rock garden. The temple's Sunday-morning *zazen* (meditation) sessions are open to all.

> **Kencho-ji's beautiful rear garden is constructed around a pond supposedly in the shape of the kanji character for heart or mind.**

8

Kencho-ji

🏠 8 Yamanouchi 📞 (0467) 22-0981 🚉 Kamakura Stn ⏰ 8:30am–4:30pm daily

Kencho-ji is the foremost of Kamkura's "five great" Zen temples and the oldest Zen training monastery in Japan. Founded in 1253, the temple originally had seven main buildings and 49 subtemples; many were destroyed in fires, but ten subtemples remain. Beside the impressive Sanmon Gate is the bell, cast in 1255, which has a Zen inscription by the temple's founder. The Buddha Hall contains a Jizo bodhisattva, savior of souls of the dead. Behind the hall is the Hatto, where public ceremonies are performed. The Karamon (Chinese gate) leads to the Hojo, used for services. Kencho-ji's beautiful rear garden is constructed around a pond supposedly in the shape of the kanji character for heart or mind. To the side of the temple, a tree-lined lane leads to subtemples and up steps to Hanso-bo – the temple's shrine.

9

Meigetsu-in Temple

🏠 1-8-9 Yamanouchi 📞 (0467) 24-3437 🚉 Kamakura Stn ⏰ 9am–4pm daily

Known as the "hydrangea temple," Meigetsu-in is a small Zen temple with pretty gardens. As well as

hydrangeas – which are at their peak in June – there are irises; these bloom in late May, when the rear garden, usually only tantalizingly glimpsed through a round window, is opened to the public.

Must See

Inside the grand Butsunichian, the mausoleum of the founder of Engaku-ji

⑩
Tokei-ji

🏠 1367 Yamanouchi
📞 (0467) 22-1663
🚉 Kamakura Stn
🕐 8:30am–4:30pm daily

This quiet little temple was set up as a convent in 1285, at a time when only men were allowed to petition for divorce. If a woman spent three years in a convent she could divorce her husband. Thus Tokei-ji was nicknamed the "divorce temple." In 1873 the law was changed to allow women to initiate divorce, and in 1902 Tokei-ji became a monastery. It is still refuge-like, with gardens stretching back to the wooded hillside.

⑪
Engaku-ji

🏠 409 Yamanouchi
📞 (0467) 22-0478
🚉 Kita Kamakura Stn
🕐 8am–4:30pm daily

The largest of Kamakura's "five great" Zen temples, and set deep in trees, Engaku-ji was founded by the Hojo regent Tokimune in 1282. An influential *zazen* (meditation) center since the Meiji era, it now runs public courses.

Although much of Engaku-ji was destroyed by the 1923 Kanto Earthquake, 17 of its more than 40 subtemples remain, and careful rebuilding has ensured that it retains its characteristic Zen layout (p177). One of its highlights, in the Shozoku-in subtemple, is the Shariden, which houses the relics of the Buddha. Japan's finest example of Chinese Sung-style Zen architecture, it is open only at New Year but can be seen through a gate at other times. Farther on, the Butsunichian – the mausoleum of Engaku-ji's founder – serves *matcha* tea to visitors. This was the setting for Kawabata Yasunari's 1949 novel *Senbazuru* (Thousand Cranes).

←
The main gate to Hokoku-ji, surrounded by bamboo forest

⑫
Zeni-Arai Benten Shrine

🏠 2-25-16 Sasuke 📞 (0467) 25-1081 🚉 Kamakura Stn
🕐 8:30am–4:30pm daily

This popular shrine to Benten, goddess of music, eloquence, and the arts, is one of the "seven lucky gods" of folk religion. Hidden in a niche in the cliffs, it is approached through a small tunnel and a row of torii. These lead to a cave spring where visitors wash coins in the hope of doubling their value.

EAT

Oimo Café Kanaria
This eatery near Kamakura station serves up *kakigori* (shaved ice with syrup). Try one of the traditional flavors, such as green tea or adzuki bean.

🏠 1F Enomoto Bldg, 2-10-10 Komachi, Kamakura-shi, Kanagawa 248-0006 🕐 D, Wed
🌐 oimocafe.exblog.jp

Mount Fuji, framed by blossom and reflected in Lake Kawaguchi

3

MOUNT FUJI AND THE FUJI FIVE LAKES

富士山と富士五湖

🅰F5 🏠 Shizuoka & Yamanashi Prefecture 🚊 Fuji-san, Kawaguchi-ko, Gotenba, Mishima (Tokaido Shinkansen), or Fujinomiya 🚌 Summer only, from all stations to the nearest 5th stage, also direct from Tokyo (Shinjuku Stn west side or Hamamatsu-cho) to Kawaguchi-ko, Gotenba, and Lake Yamanaka 🅹 Fuji-Yoshida; city.fujiyoshida.yamanashi.jp

At 12,390 ft (3,776 m), Mount Fuji (or Fuji-san) is Japan's highest peak by far, its near-perfect cone floating lilac-gray or snowcapped above hilltops and low cloud. A true Japanese icon, its silhouette is famed the world over.

Dormant since 1707, this volcano first erupted 8,000–10,000 years ago and its upper slopes are formed of loose volcanic ash, devoid of greenery. Until 150 years ago, Mount Fuji was considered so sacred that it was climbed only by pilgrims; women were not allowed until 1868. Today, the hiking trails, which are divided into ten stages, are traversed by a host of climbers. The Fuji Five Lakes, at the foot of the mountain, offer sports facilities and various attractions, including the Itchiku Kubota Art Museum.

> 💬 INSIDER TIP
> **Tips for Walkers**
>
> You can only climb from July to mid-September. To catch the sunrise, start at the 5th stage in the afternoon, sleep in a hut at the 7th or 8th stage, and rise early to finish the climb. Watch out for altitude sickness above the 8th stage.

MOUNT FUJI IN ART

With its graceful, almost symmetrical form, its changing appearance with the seasons, and its dominance over the landscape, Mount Fuji has always been a popular subject for artists. The mountain features in various ukiyo-e, including Katsushika Hokusai's *Thirty-Six Views of Mount Fuji* (1830–32), and *Fifty-Three Stages of the Tokaido* (1833–4), by Hiroshige. In other arts, Mount Fuji is echoed in decorative motifs, for instance on kimonos, in wood carvings, and even in the shape of window frames.

→ Climbers around the torii (gate) at the mountain's summit

↑ The Shiraito waterfalls on the Fujinomiya trail, a five-hour trek from the 5th stage

4

TAKAYAMA

高山

🅰E4 🅐Gifu Prefecture 🚃JR Takayama line 🛈In front of
JR Stn; www.hida.jp/english/index.html

Agriculturally poor but rich in timber, characterful
Takayama has a centuries-long tradition of producing
skilled carpenters. The city's isolated mountain
location has meant the survival of its unspoiled
Edo-period streets – today lined with tiny shops,
museums, and eating places – while the pure water
is ideal for brewing sake.

Takayama Festival Floats Exhibition Hall

🏠178 Sakuramachi
📞(0577) 32-5100
🕘9am-4:30pm daily

Takayama Festival dates from
about 1690 and takes place
twice a year: in spring, coin-
ciding with planting, and in
fall at harvest time. Both
of these festivals involve
processions of 11 tall, lavishly
decorated floats, guided by
townspeople dressed
in traditional costume.

Four floats also feature
karakuri marionettes.
This form of puppetry
was invented in Edo
(Tokyo) in 1617, and
features mechanized
dolls that perform
traditional actions,
such as pouring tea or bowing
to the audience. These early
robots feature in festivals all
over Japan.

Between Takayama's two
festivals, four of the floats are
displayed in this hall next to
the Sakurayama Hachiman
Shrine, along with photo-
graphs of the others. Intricately
carved, they serve as evidence
of Takayama's legendary
craftsmanship. Once you've
admired the floats, pop into
the gallery next door, which
displays exquisite scale
models of Nikko Tosho-gu
Shrine (*p300*).

→

A float on display at
the Takayama Festival
Floats Exhibition Hall

↑ Walking through the attractive historic center of Takayama

are the kitchens and living quarters of the governor's family. To one side is a jail, with a small array of torture instruments. The storehouses contain items relating to the rice-tax system.

---

④

Hida Folk Village

🏠 1-590 Kamiokamotomachi
☎ (0577) 34-4711
🕐 8:30am–5pm daily

Just outside Takayama is Hida Folk Village, which contains over 30 examples of rural houses from the surrounding area, including a *gassho-zukuri* house from the Shokawa Valley. There are also reconstructed storehouses and a festival stage to explore here, and plenty of traditional crafts are on display. The buildings, located on a hillside that offers views of the Japanese Alps, are interesting both architecturally and for the human details that they reveal – such as the demands of a snowy climate or the life of a village headman.

💬 INSIDER TIP
Cycling Tours

A bicycle tour with Hida Satoyama *(www.satoyama-experience.com)* through the lush rice fields and charming avenues of Takayama gives a rare insight into rural Japan. Stopping off at natural hot springs, wooden farmhouses, orchards and farms, the three-hour Takayama cycling tour travels along 14 miles (22 km).

②

Lion Dance Ceremony Exhibition Hall

🏠 53-1 Sakuramachi
☎ (0577) 32-0881
🕐 9:05am–4:25pm daily

Lion dances, to drive away wild animals and evil spirits, are integral to festivals such as Takayama's. This exhibition hall contains over 800 lion masks from all over Japan, as well as armor, screens, pottery, and coins. The highlight of any visit to the museum is catching a performance by the *karakuri* marionettes.

---

③

Takayama Jinya

🏠 1-5 Hachikenmachi
☎ (0577) 32-0643
🕐 8:45am–5pm daily

This government office was built in 1615 for Takayama's lord, but in 1692 it was made the provincial office of the shogunate – the only one still in existence. The front of the building comprises waiting and meeting rooms; behind

> Lion dances, to drive away wild animals and evil spirits, are integral to festivals such as Takayama's. This exhibition hall contains over 800 lion masks.

A SHORT WALK
TAKAYAMA

Distance 1 mile (2 km) **Time** 30 minutes **Nearest train station** JR Takayama line

With its unspoiled pedestrianized streets, Takayama's Sannomachi Quarter is the perfect place to explore on foot. From 1692 to 1868 this area was under direct shogunate control as a source of timber, and the quality of the surrounding forests, as well as the famed skills of the town's carpenters, are reflected in the charming wooden buildings that line the streets. These old merchant houses reveal high, skylighted ceilings, wooden beams, and fireproof storage rooms. Many of them are still shops selling local crafts, making them the perfect spots to pause. There are several fascinating museums in this part of town, too.

START

SHIMO NINOMACHI

SHIMO SANNOMACHI

YAYOI-BASHI BRIDGE

Once a sake merchant's house, the **Yoshijima Heritage House** *has retained its wooden beamed interior, lit by high windows.*

MIYA RIVER

Rebuilt of Japanese cypress in 1879 after a fire, this house is a well-preserved money-lender's dwelling. It now houses the **Kusakabe Folk Museum**, *displaying folkcraft items.*

Morning market

| 0 meters | 50 |
| 0 yards | 50 |

N

←
A merchant presenting his wares at Takayama's morning market

↑ Strolling through a charming street in the Sannomachi Quarter

*The **Sannomachi Quarter** is an unusually large, intact area of Edo-period merchants' shops and houses, which are now home to specialty shops and sake brewers.*

*In a former candle and pomade shop, the **Hirata Folk Art Museum**'s collection includes Edo-period clothing and toys.*

Takayama City Museum *chronicles the town's history.*

KAMI ICHINOMACHI

YASUGAWA-DORI

KAMI NINOMACHI

SAN-MACHI-DORI

KAMI SANNOMACHI

YANAGI-BASHI BRIDGE

BASHI BRIDGE

*The **Archaeological Museum** displays local finds and crafts.*

IKEDA-BASHI BRIDGE

🏁 FINISH

*Some of the old houses of the Sannomachi Quarter overlook the fast-flowing **Miya River.***

163

↑ A street lined with wooden buildings in the Nagamachi Samurai Quarter

5

KANAZAWA

金沢

🅰E4 🄰Ishikawa Prefecture ✈Komatsu 🚆JR lines (Hokuriku Shinkasen) 🌐kanazawa-kankoukyoukai.or.jp

Wealth encouraged cultural development in this city. In 1583 the area, known as Kaga, passed from an egalitarian government under the Ikko Buddhist sect to the firm rule of the Maeda lords; while much of Japan was still unstable, Kaga had three centuries of peace and became the richest domain in the land. As a result, artists from Kyoto came and developed new styles here.

①

Nagamachi Samurai Quarter

Bisected by the picturesque Onosho Canal, this historic area of Kanazawa was once home to the city's samurai. Retaining its traditional earthen walled streets, this atmospheric neighborhood of waterways and winding lanes is located at the foot of Kanazawa castle. Some of the former samurai houses and their gardens are open for public viewing.

At the end of the Edo Era, many samurai were ruined by the collapse of the financial system. One such family was the Nomuras who were forced to sell their home. While many others were simply torn down, one samurai house was bought by Kubo Hikobei, a wealthy businessman, who restored it. With its intricate woodwork, costly window-panes, and serene garden, **Nomura Family Samurai House** grants a rare insight into the day-to-day lives of the samurai. Visitors can even partake in a traditional tea ceremony for an extra charge.

Nomura Family Samurai House

 🄰1-3-2 Nagamachi ⏰8:30am–4:30pm daily 🌐nomurake.com

②

Seisonkaku Villa

🄰1-2 Kenrokumachi ⏰9am–5pm Thu–Tue 🌐seisonkaku.com

The exquisite two-story Seisonkaku Villa adjoining Kenroku-en Garden was built in 1863 by Maeda Nariyasu, 13th lord, for his mother. Its lower floor houses formal receiving rooms, with walls coated in gold dust, and *shoji* paper doors with rare Dutch stained-glass insets. Upstairs is more informal and colorful. The house also features a famed 65-ft- (20-m-) long covered walkway known as the "horsetail corridor", which was engineered in such a way that no supporting beams hold up the roof.

 HIDDEN GEM
Kimono Time

The Nagamachi Kaga Yuzen Silk Center exhibits this intricate material, which necessitates an 18-step dyeing process. For a fee, you can try your hand at silk painting and try on a kimono for size (kagayuzen-club.co.jp).

③ Ishikawa Museum of Traditional Arts and Crafts

📍 1-1 Kenrokumachi
🕐 9am–5pm daily 🚫 Apr–Nov: 3rd Thu of month; Dec–Mar: Thu 🌐 ishikawa-densankan.jp

At this tastefully laid-out museum, visitors can immerse themselves in the traditional crafts that the Ishikawa prefecture is renowned for, including the gorgeous Kutani pottery, silk painting, lacquerware, metalwork, gold leaf details, Japanese paper, and fireworks. Visitors are encouraged to interact with

↑ The beautiful and serene Kenroku-en Garden, its features blanketed in snow

the objects by making them themselves, and the museum hosts regular demonstrations by experience traditional craftsmen. The shop on the ground floor offers an assortment of pieces, all produced by local artisans and at reasonable prices.

For information about the demonstrations and hands-on experiences led by the experts, check the museum website for details.

Did You Know?

In winter, the city's mud walls are covered with straw mats to protect them from harsh weather.

④ Kenroku-en Garden

📍 Kenrokumachi 🕐 Daily
🌐 pref.ishikawa.jp

Created by the Maeda family, Kenroku-en is one of Japan's "great three" gardens. It name means "garden of six qualities": spaciousness, seclusion, an air of antiquity, ingenuity, flowing water, and views, which are desired in a Chinese garden.

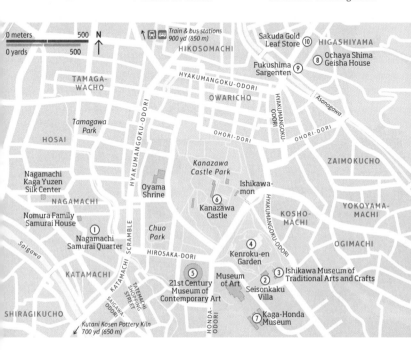

5
21st Century Museum of Contemporary Art

⌂1-2-1 Hirosaka
🕐10am–6pm Tue–Sun 🌐kanazawa21.jp

This experimental museum was created by the famous architectural duo SANAA (Kazuyo Sejima and Ryue Nishikawa), who won the Pritzker Prize in 2010. The museum explores emerging new work in visual arts, design, craft, fashion, architecture, and film, particularly in relation to multiculturalism and transportation, technology, gender issues, and identity. The art on display encourages physical interaction from visitors and, as a result, it is particularly popular with families.

→
Olafur Eliasson's *Colour activity house* (2010) at the 21st Century Museum of Contemporary Art

6
Kanazawa Castle

⌂Marunouchi 📞(076 234-3800 🕐9am–4:30pm daily 🌐pref.ishikawa.jp

The size of Kanazawa Castle, one of the largest in feudal Japan, reflects the importance of its former residents, who were said to be the second most powerful family in Japan. The Maeda clan began building their castle here in 1583, and the family resided within its walls for fourteen generations,

only leaving in 1869. The fortification was almost entirely destroyed by fire in 1881, and only the armory and rear gate, Ishikawa-mon, survived. Since then, a major restoration project has been underway, recreating the structures using original construction techniques. In the centre of the castle's park, visitors can access three large-scale reconstructions of the original buildings. Inside these structures are intricate models of the castle, as well as displays, showing the various architectural techniques used in the restoration.

7
Kaga-Honda Museum

⌂3-1 Dewamachi 🕐9am–5pm daily 🌐honda-museum.jp

Gain a glimpse into the history of feudal Japan through these artifacts belonging to the descendants of Honda Masanobu, an advisor to the Tokugawa Shogun and the lord of Maeda's highest vassal. This unique exhibition showcases a rare collection of military hardware, including exquisite armor and weaponry. Look out for the the items connected to the samurai's mount, including a delicately lacquered saddle, stirrups with elaborate gold inlay, and imposing horse armor, which are said to be some of the finest examples in Japan. Also on display are curiosities such as fire-fighting attire, as well as wedding trousseaux belonging to women from the Maeda clan who married into the Honda family.

←
The reconstructed exterior of Kanazawa Castle, with its fortified walls

⑩ 👜

Sakuda Gold Leaf Store

🏠 1-3-27 Higashiyama
🕐 9am–6pm daily
🌐 goldleaf-sakuda.jp

Despite Japan's reputation as the home of minimalism, gold leaf decorates everything from folding screens to chopsticks. For over 400 years, Kanazawa has been the center for gold leaf production, and the city still crafts over 98 percent of the country's output. The city's humid climate is perfect for production because it minimizes the build-up of static electricity, which can tear the delicate sheets. At the Sakuda Gold Leaf Store, master craftsmen demonstrate how gold leaf is applied to all manner of traditional crafts. Here, you can take a tour of the factory, view the production process, and even try applying some of the gold leaf to an object of your choice.

Did You Know?

At Sakuda Gold Leaf Store, visitors can try a cup of tea with shimmering flecks of gold in it.

⑧

Ochaya Shima Geisha House

🏠 1-13-21 Higashiyama
🕐 9am–6pm daily
🌐 ochaya-shima.com

This museum is dedicated to preserving the history of Higashi Chaya-gai. Established in 1820, this was the grandest pleasure district outside Kyoto and Edo, and was frequented by rich merchants and nobility. The area is still full of atmosphere, with old-fashioned street lamps and wooden-lattice windows, but these now hide elegant restaurants and crafts galleries.

At the center of the area, the Ochaya Shima Geisha House is still much the same as it was in the Edo era. On the upper floor are guest rooms with small stages where the geisha sang and danced for their customers, while downstairs are modest living quarters. The museum's collection displays items once used by the geisha who lived here, including tea ceremony utensils and musical instruments. After exploring the collection, you can relax with a cup of matcha here.

⑨

Fukushima Sargenten

🏠 1-1-8 Higashiyama
📞 (076) 252-3703
🕐 8:30am–6pm Mon–Sat
🚫 2nd & 4th Sat of month; public hols

For those interested in traditional Japanese music, a visit to this shop where the Fukushima family have been hand-crafting three-stringed *shamisen* since the early 20th century is a must. All geisha must master this instrument during their training and the haunting sound of the *shamisen* is one of the most evocative experiences in Japan, conjuring up cold winter evenings. At Fukushima Sargenten, for a small fee, visitors can learn to play one of these instruments and learn how they were made. But this tutorial is not for everyone – the most traditional *shamisen* are crafted from cat and dog skin.

SHOP

Kutani Kosen Pottery Kiln

The only surviving kiln in Kanazawa has been producing porcelain since the mid-19th century. All pieces sold here are handmade. Old Kutani-ware uses deep, over-glazed blues, greens, reds, and ochers, while modern work has more delicate and varied designs. You can design your own piece at the Kutani Kosen Pottery Kiln, which can be shipped to you once it is fired.

🏠 5-3-3 Nomachi
🕐 9am–5pm daily
🌐 kutanikosen.com

EXPERIENCE MORE

 6

Narita
成田

🅰️G4 🄰Chiba Prefecture ❌🚉 🛈In front of JR Stn; www.nrtk.jp

A quiet little town, Narita is worlds away from its nearby bustling airport. The town's main attraction is Narita-san Shinsho-ji, an interesting Esoteric Shingon-sect temple founded in 940 and dedicated to Fudo Myo-o, Deity of Immovable Wisdom. Several times daily, the priests burn wooden sticks to symbolize extinguishing of earthly passions. The streets are full of traditional shops for the 12 million temple visitors a year.

Near Narita are over 1,000 ancient burial mounds (kofun); the best are in the open-air museum, **Boso no Mura**.

Did You Know?

Narita is famous for its eel restaurants, which once served Edo lords en route to Tokyo.

The **National Museum of Japanese History** offers a good survey of Japan.

Boso no Mura
🄰8 mins by taxi from Ajiki Stn 🄲(0476) 95-3333 🄾Tue-Sun

National Museum of Japanese History
🄰15-min walk from Keiseisakura Stn 🄲(043) 486-0123 🄾Tue-Sun

7

Kawagoe
川越

🅰️F4 🄰Saitama Prefecture 🚉 🛈At JR Stn; (049) 222-5556

Nicknamed "Little Edo," Kawagoe preserves the atmosphere of 19th-century Edo (Tokyo) because of its kura buildings. These clay-walled structures have double doors, and heavy shutters. About 30 kura remain and are a ten minute walk north of Hon-Kawagoe station. The **Kura-Zukuri Shiryokan**, formerly a kura tobacconist, is now a museum and gives visitors the opportunity to peak inside one of these old-fashioned buildings. It also

displays historic machines. Nearby, Toki-no-kane wooden bell tower was built in 1624 to tell the time and warn of fires. East of the kura streets is Kita-in, a Tendai-sect temple which includes the only extant rooms from Edo Castle.

At one time, Kawagoe possessed its own castle, which was the dominant structure in the area. Part of that castle remains in the shape of **Honmaru Goten**, the former residence of the lord, with many commodious rooms.

Kura-Zukuri Shiryokan
🄰7-9 Saiwachō 🄲(049) 222-5399 🄾Tue-Sun 🄲4th Fri of month

Honmaru Goten
🄰2-13-1 Kurawa-machi 🄲(049) 222-5399 🄾9am-4:30pm Tue-Sun

8

Hakone
箱根

🅰️F4 🄰Kanagawa Prefecture 🚉 🛈706-35 Yumoto, Hakone; www.hakone.or.jp/en/

Popular since the 9th century, Hakone is a hilly hot-spring town, with scattered

YOSEGI-ZAIKU MARQUETRY

Originating in the 9th century, this type of marquetry looks like inlaid mosaic but in fact employs a very different technique. Strips are cut from planks of up to 40 varieties of woods and glued together to form patterned blocks, which are in turn glued into larger blocks. These are then either shaped with a lathe into objects like bowls, or shaved into sheets, and used to coat boxes and purses.

↑ Wandering past steaming sulphur vents in Owakudani valley, Hakone

cultural and natural attractions. The Hakone area extends across the collapsed remains of a huge volcano, which was active until 3,000–4,000 years ago, leaving a legacy today of hot springs and steam vents.

Although Hakone can be visited as a long day trip from Tokyo, it is worth an overnight stay. Two- or three-day public-transportation passes are available on the Odakyu line from Shinjuku, Tokyo. A convenient circuit of the main sights starts from the *onsen* town of Hakone-Yumoto, taking the Tozan switchback train up the hillside to **Hakone Open-Air Museum**, with its modern sculptures. Continue via funicular to **Hakone Art Museum**, which has an excellent Japanese ceramic collection and garden. Via the funicular and then a ropeway over the crest of the hill is the fascinating Owaku-dani ("valley of great boiling"), an area of sulfurous steam vents. This is an active volcanic zone, so sometimes the ropeway or sections of this area are closed to visitors for safety reasons. The ropeway continues to

←

Old-fashioned street in Kawagoe, with *kura* buildings and a wooden clock tower

Lake Ashi, where replicas of historical Western-style boats run to Hakone-machi and Moto-Hakone. In clear weather there are stunning views of Mount Fuji. At Hakone-machi is an interesting reconstruction of the **Seki-sho Barrier Gate**, a checkpoint that used to control passage on the Edo-period Tokaido road between Tokyo and Kyoto.

From Hakone-machi it is a short walk to Moto-Hakone. Located on a hilltop overlooking Lake Ashi, **Narukawa Art Museum** exhibits 1,500 artworks by modern Japanese masters, and has spectacular views of the surrounding mountains. Over a pass beyond Moto-Hakone is the Amazake-chaya teahouse, and Hatajuku village, known for *yosegi-zaiku*, a form of decorative marquetry.

Hakone Open-Air Museum
⊛ ⌂1121 Ninotaira
☏(0460) 82-1161
🕒9am–5pm daily

Hakone Art Museum
⊛ ⌂1300 Gora ☏(0460) 82-2623 🕒9am–4:30pm Fri-Wed

Seki-sho Barrier Gate
⊛ ☏(0460) 83-6635 🕒Daily

Narukawa Art Museum
⊛ ⌂570 Motohakone
☏(0460) 83-6828 🕒9am–5pm daily

STAY

Hakone Kowakien Ten-yu
A luxurious spa resort with an open-air *onsen* in each room.

⌂F4 ⌂1297 Ninotaira, Hakone, Ashigara-shimogun, Kanagawa 250-0407 🆆ten-yu.com

---

Narita Hotel Blan Chapel Christmas
With trees and tinsel, it's Christmas year-round at this adults-only hotel.

⌂G4 ⌂239-1 Yoshikura, Narita, Chiba-ken 286-0133 🆆chapel-hotel.co.jp

---

Ryokan Hakone Ginyu
Enjoy views over the Hakone mountains at this traditional *ryokan*.

⌂F4 ⌂100-1 Miyanoshita, Hakone, Ashigara-shimogun, Kanagawa 250-0404 🆆hakoneginyu.co.jp

↑ Sunset over the harbor at Shimoda, on the Izu Peninsula

 9

Izu Peninsula
伊豆半島

⚑F5 **🏯Shizuoka Prefecture** **🚉** **ℹ️Atami, Ito, and Shuzenji Stns**

A hilly peninsula with a benign climate, Izu is popular for its many hot springs. A place of exile during the Middle Ages, in the early 1600s it was home to the shipwrecked Englishman William Adams, whose story was the basis of the James Clavell novel *Shogun*. Shimoda, on the southern tip, became a coaling station for foreign ships in 1854, then opened to US traders. Today Shimoda has little of interest besides pretty gray-and-white walls, reinforced against typhoons with crisscross plasterwork.

Izu's east coast is quite developed, but the west has charming coves and fishing villages, such as Toi and Heda, offering delicious long-legged crabs and other seafood. The center is also relatively unspoiled, with wooded mountains and rustic hot springs, including Shuzenji *onsen* and a chain of villages from Amagi Yugashima to Kawazu. These latter were the setting for Yasunari Kawabata's short story *The Izu Dancer*, commemorated across Izu.

 10

Nagoya
名古屋

⚑E5 **🏯Aichi Prefecture** **✈🚉** **ℹ️At Nagoya JR Stn; www.nagoya-info.jp/en**

A major transportation hub for the region, Nagoya is a pleasant and convenient, if unexciting, base. It rose to prominence in the 17th century as a Tokaido castle town, birthplace of feudal lords Oda Nobunaga and Toyotomi Hideyoshi. Japan's fourth-largest city and an industrial center, it was heavily bombed in World War II.

The city's Me-guru one-day sightseeing bus pass, or a bus-and-subway pass are good

↑ Autumn leaves framing the elegant architecture of Nagoya Castle

for exploring. **Nagoya Castle**, built in 1610–12 and one of the largest, most sophisticated of the Edo period, was destroyed in a bombing raid in 1945; today's concrete reconstruction has a top-floor observatory and exhibitions about the castle. The main keep will be closed until 2022.

A short bus ride east is the **Tokugawa Art Museum**, with superb Edo-period treasures, as well as a 12th-century illustrated handscroll of the *Tale of Genji*, part of which is exhibited each November. Reproductions of the scrolls are on permanent display.

Nagoya Castle
⊕ 🏯1-1 Hommaru 📞(052) 231-1700 🚇Shiyakusho Stn 🚌Nagoya-jo Seimon-mae stop 🕘9am–4:30pm daily

Tokugawa Art Museum
⊕ 🏯1017 Tokugawa-cho 🚌Shindeki stop 🕘10am–5pm Tue–Sun 🌐tokugawa-art-museum.jp/en

Did You Know?

Nagoya is the birthplace of *pachinko* – the pinball machine.

11

Shizuoka
静岡

F5 🏠Shizuoka & Yamanashi Prefecture 🚉 🛈 In JR Stn; www.visit-shizuoka.com/en

Settlement in this area goes back to AD 200–300. Later the retirement home of Tokugawa Ieyasu, Shizuoka is today a sprawling urban center, the city in Japan at greatest risk of a major earthquake – and probably the only place that is fully prepared.

The **Toro ruins** near the port have reconstructions of ancient buildings and an excellent interactive museum. The view from Nihondaira plateau, in the east of the city, to Mount Fuji and Izu is superb. Nearby is Kunozan Tosho-gu, one of the three top Tosho-gu shrines.

West of Shizuoka, Kanaya has one of Japan's largest tea plantations. Fields can be visited, and the elegant **Ocha no Sato** museum portrays tea lore. Nearby, the Oigawa steam railroad takes you right into the untamed South Alps.

Toro ruins
⊛ 🏠5-10-5 Toro 📞(054) 285-0476 🕘9am–4:30pm Tue–Sun

Ocha no Sato
⊛ 🏠3053-2 Kanaya Fujimicho 📞(0547) 46-5588 🕘9am–5pm Wed–Mon

12

Inuyama
犬山

E5 🏠Aichi Prefecture ✈🚉 🛈 In front of W side of station; (0568) 61-6000

This quiet town sits on the Kiso River. The small, simple **Inuyama Castle**, built in 1537, is the oldest in Japan. It places more emphasis on defense than show, but is still quite graceful, with views across the river far below.

Outside Inuyama is **Meiji Mura**, a theme park with over 60 Meiji-era (1868–1912) buildings. Yaotsu, where Chiune Sugihara was born, is a train ride away. Japan's consul in Lithuania in World War II, Sugihara saved around 6,000 Jews using transit visas via Japan. He is commemorated by a monument and museum at the Hill of Humanity Park.

Inuyama Castle
⊛ 🏠65-2 Inuyama Kitakoken 📞(0568) 61-1711 🕘9am–4:30pm daily

Meiji Mura
⊛ 🏠20 mins by bus from Inuyama Stn 📞(0568) 67-0314 🕘9:30am–5pm Tue–Sun (from 10am Aug; to 4pm Nov–Feb) 🚫Jan 21–Feb 25

DRINK

ID Café
This vast nightclub in Nagoya's raucous Sakae district packs as many as 5,000 people on to its six dance floors.

E5 🏠3-1-15 Sakae, Naka-ku, Nagoya-shi, Aichi 460-0008 🌐idcafe.info

---

Shooters
With seating for 130, Shooters is Nagoya's largest sports bar, with over a dozen screens.

E5 🏠2-9-26 Sakae, Naka-ku, Nagoya-shi, Aichi 460-0008 📞(052) 202-7077

---

7 Days Brew
Close to Nagoya station, this bar dispenses an excellent range of craft beer on draft.

E5 🏠4-42-1 Meieki, Nakamura-ku, Nagoya-shi, Aichi 450-0002 🌐7daysbrew.business.site

---

A tourist boat on the Kiso River, overlooked by the charming Inuyama Castle

Gassho-Zukuri houses in the pretty village of Ogimachi, in the Shokawa Valley

Shokawa Valley
庄川渓谷

E4 **Gifu and Toyama Prefectures** **From Nagoya, Takayama, Toyama, Shin-Takaoka, Kanazawa** **ml. shirakawa-go.org/en**

A remote mountain region with unique thatched houses, the Shokawa Valley comprises two areas: Shirakawa-go (including Ogimachi) to the south and the five hamlets of Gokayama to the north. Under deep snow from December to March, the region was historically a refuge for the defeated and persecuted. Until the 1970s most families here produced silk, raising silkworms in *gassho-zukuri* thatched houses.

Of the original 1,800, fewer than 150 *gassho* houses remain. Three settlements – Ogimachi, Suganuma, and Ainokura – are World Heritage Sites. Every April–May, a few houses are re-thatched, one roof taking 200 villagers and volunteers two days. Ogimachi is the largest village, with 59 *gassho* houses and an **Open-Air Museum**.

Suganuma has nine *gassho* buildings. Ainokura is a hillside hamlet of 20 *gassho* houses (two open to visitors).

Open-Air Museum

 Across the river from Ogimachi (05769) 6-1231 Apr-Nov: 8:40am-5pm daily; Dec-Mar: 9am-4pm Fri-Wed

Gifu
岐阜

E5 **Gifu Prefecture** **At Gifu JR Stn; www. travel.kankou-gifu.jp**

This rather garish spa town is known for *ukai*, a tradition that involves using trained cormorants to catch fish. Nightly from mid-May to mid-October, except at full moon or when stormy, fishermen and their cormorants go out on torchlit boats; the birds dive for *ayu* (sweetfish) and trout, which they are prevented from swallowing by a ring around their necks.

On dry land, the town is known for the largest lacquer Buddha in Japan, at Shoho-ji temple. Dating from 1832, it comprises a woven bamboo frame covered with sutra-inscribed paper, then coated in clay and lacquered.

Gifu is also known for its unique cuisine, the result of its history as a center for trade.

TOP 5 GIFU FOODS

Ayu
This fish is grilled over an open flame and served with just a sprinkling of salt.

Fuyu persimmons
A winter treat that tastes of dates, brown sugar, and cinnamon.

Hida beef
This high-quality beef is known for its marbling and a layer of fat.

Kuri kinton
Symbolizing wealth and usually eaten at New Year, this is a dish of candied chestnuts with mashed sweet potatoes.

Keichan
Chicken thighs stir-fried with cabbage and garlic soy sauce.

GASSHO-ZUKURI HOUSES

These houses are named for their steep thatched roofs, shaped like *gassho* ("praying hands"). Formed of a series of triangular frames on a rectangular base, the roofs are able to withstand heavy snow and shed rain quickly so that the straw does not rot. Generally three or four stories tall, the first floor of *gassho-zukuri* houses traditionally accommodated extended families of 20–30 people, who were all involved in silkworm cultivation. The upper floors housed the silkworms, permitting variations in light, heat, and air at different stages. To maximize ventilation and light, windows at both ends were opened to allow the wind through. Architectural details vary from village to village.

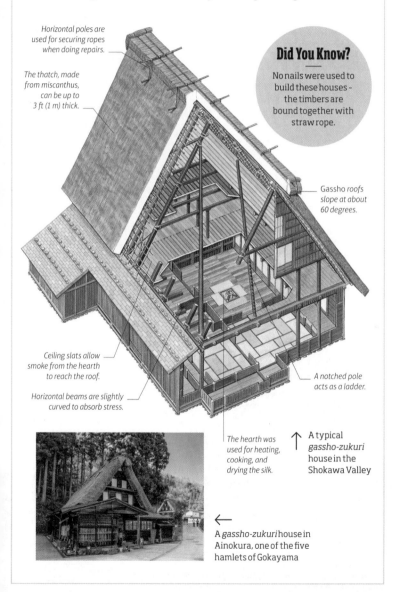

Horizontal poles are used for securing ropes when doing repairs.

Did You Know?

No nails were used to build these houses – the timbers are bound together with straw rope.

The thatch, made from miscanthus, can be up to 3 ft (1 m) thick.

Gassho roofs slope at about 60 degrees.

Ceiling slats allow smoke from the hearth to reach the roof.

A notched pole acts as a ladder.

Horizontal beams are slightly curved to absorb stress.

The hearth was used for heating, cooking, and drying the silk.

↑ A typical *gassho-zukuri* house in the Shokawa Valley

← A *gassho-zukuri* house in Ainokura, one of the five hamlets of Gokayama

15

Matsumoto
松本

E4 Nagano Prefecture
🚄🚌 🛈 At Matsumoto JR
Stn; www.visitmatsumoto.
com/en

Despite being the gateway to the Japanese Alps, this city's main attraction is **Matsumoto Castle**. It has the oldest five-tiered keep in Japan (1593) and its walls and moat date from 1504. Defensive devices include niches for archers, guns, and dropping stones. The top floor holds a shrine to the goddess of the 26th night who was thought to protect against fire and invasion.

Beside the keep stands the Moon-Viewing Turret, added in the 1630s for aesthetic purposes. The castle admission includes entry to the Matsumoto City Museum in the grounds, which features local geography, wildlife, history, dolls, and tools.

Also in Matsumoto are the **Japan Ukiyo-e Museum**, an excellent collection of woodblock prints, and **Matsumoto Folkcraft Museum**, with folk art from Japan and across Asia; on the edge of the city, Utsukushigahara and Asama have pleasant hot springs.

North of Matsumoto, Hotaka is home to Japan's largest wasabi (horseradish) farm.

Matsumoto Castle
⊘ 🏯 20-min walk from
Stn 📞 (0263) 32-2902
🕙 8:30am–4:30pm daily

Japan Ukiyo-e Museum
⊘ 🏯 7-min drive from Stn
📞 (0263) 47-4440 🕙 10am–
5pm Tue–Sun

Matsumoto Folkcraft Museum
⊘ 🏯 15 mins by bus from
Stn, Mingeikan-mae stop
📞 (0263) 33-1569 🕙 9am–
5pm Tue–Sun

16

Nagano
長野

E4 🏯 Nagano Prefecture
🚌 🛈 At Nagano JR Stn;
www.go-nagano.net

Surrounded by low mountains, Nagano is a skiing center and was the main venue for the 1998 Winter Olympics. In the town, the prime attraction is Zenko-ji, a non-sect temple that has, unusually, always been open to women as well as men. Established in 670, it enshrines what is thought to be Japan's oldest Buddhist image, an Amida triad brought from Korea in the 6th century. This is kept

DOSOJIN STONES

These two jaunty stone figures are guardian deities of travelers. They are found at many roadsides in northern Nagano Prefecture, as well as at village boundaries. The pair are often depicted holding hands.

hidden, and a copy shown every six years. The temple also has a pitch-dark underground passage containing a "key to paradise": touching the key, positioned on the right-hand wall, is said to bring happiness in the afterlife.

In nearby Obuse, the **Hokusai Museum** is devoted to artist Katsushika Hokusai (1760–1849), who stayed in the town as an old man. Farther into the mountains Jigokudani Monkey Park, reached by bus from Kanbayashi *onsen*, is famous for the wild macaques living around its hot pools.

→ Walking over the Kappabashi bridge to cross the Azusa River, in Kamikochi

Hokusai Museum

 ⚐ 10-min walk from Obuse Stn ☎ (026) 247-5206 ⏱ 9am–5pm daily

---

 17

Kamikochi
上高地

🅰 E4 ⚐ Nagano Prefecture 🚉 To Shin-Shimashima, then bus 🚌 From Hirayu *onsen* or Shin-Shimashima ℹ Next to Kamikochi bus terminal; (0263) 95-2433

An alpine valley with a handful of hotels and campsites, Kamikochi lies in the southern part of the Chubu Sangaku (North Japan Alps) National Park, at an altitude of 4,900 ft (1,500 m) and is a good hiking and climbing base. The valley is reached by a tunnel (open late April–early November); in July, August, Golden Week, and on some weekends, private cars are banned. Japan's highest (after Fuji) and wildest mountains are in the South Alps, but the North Alps have more snow and more impressive scenery. Plentiful mountain refuges allow hikes of several days from hut to hut, often via a hot spring.

The most spectacular climb is a three-day route from Kamikochi taking in Mount Yari and Mount Hotaka – at 10,470 ft (3,190 m), the highest peak in the North Alps. Short hikes include the rocky scree of Mount Yake, the only active volcano in the North Alps. In bad weather, walks are restricted to the valley floor by the rushing river.

← The moat surrounding Matsumoto Castle, built in the early 16th century

---

 18

Chichibu-Tama-Kai National Park
秩父多摩甲斐国立公園

🅰 F4 ⚐ Tokyo, Saitama, Nagano, and Yamanashi Prefectures 🚉 Seibu-Chichibu Stn, Seibu-Chichibu line; Chichibu Stn, Chichibu line; Okutama or Mitake Stns, JR line ℹ Seibu-Chichibu Stn; (0494) 21 2277

Chichibu-Tama-Kai National Park is a remote region of low mountains, stretching from the narrow valleys of Okutama in the south to the basin around Chichibu city in the north. The two parts of the park are separated by mountains, crossed only by a few hiking trails. Within the park, railroads reach a few spots, but travel is mostly by bus.

A silk-producing area until the early 1900s, Chichibu is now known for a pilgrim route linking 34 Kannon temples. To the north, at Nagatoro, the Arakawa River runs past rare schist rock formations.

In the Okutama area, Mount Mitake has a mountaintop shrine village, and the **Nippara Caves** are worth visiting.

Nippara Caves

 ⚐ 30 mins by bus from Okutamaeki stop ☎ (0428) 83-8491 ⏱ 8am–5pm daily

---

EAT

Kobayashi
Matsumoto is famous for soba noodles, and this is one of the best places to enjoy them.

🅰 E4 ⚐ 3-3-20 Ote, Matsumoto-shi, Nagano 390-0874 ☎ (0263) 32-1298

 ¥ ¥ ¥

Alps Gohan
This cult restaurant offers patrons two daily-changing options.

🅰 E4 ⚐ 3-7-5 Fukashi, Matsumoto-shi, Nagano 390-0815 🌐 alpsgohan.com

 ¥ ¥ ¥

Fureai Yamabekan
Learn to make soba noodles for yourself with the help of experienced teachers.

🅰 E4 ⚐ 85-1 Satoya-mabe, Matsumoto-shi, Nagano 390-0221 ☎ (0263) 35-9076

 ¥ ¥ ¥

19

Eihei-ji
永平寺

🅐 D4 🅐 Fukui Prefecture
📞 (0776) 63-3188 (bookings
and Zen training) 🅐

Established in 1244, Eihei-ji
is one of the Soto Zen sect's
two head temples and has
been Japan's most active
Zen meditation monastery
since the late 16th century.
In a classic rectilinear plan, its
halls and covered corridors
climb up the wooded moun-
tainside. Soto Zen pursues
gradual enlightenment by
practicing meditation away
from the real world; the
monastery has about 50
elders and 250 trainees. The
atmosphere is cheerful, yet
life is austere, with no heating
and a simple diet. In the Sodo
Hall (to the left), each trainee
has just one tatami mat for
eating, sleeping, and *zazen*
(meditation). Silence must
be observed in the hall, as
well as in the bath building
and toilet. Laypeople wishing
to experience the rigorous
Soto Zen regime must book
well ahead.

↑ The Jouyoumon gate of the Eihei-ji Temple,
an important Soto Zen monastery

SHOP

Wajima Market

Each morning, the
streets of Wajima ring
out with the cries of the
vendors at this market,
which is said to be over
1,000 years old. Stalls
sell fish brought in from
the port, vegetables
from the nearby
farmland, and handi-
crafts like the famous
Wajima lacquerware.

🅐 E3 🅐 1-115 Kawai-
machi, Honmachidori,
Wajima 928-0001
🕗 8am-noon, except
2nd & 4th Wed of month

20

Noto Peninsula
能登半島

🅐 E3-4 🅐 Ishikawa
Prefecture 🚌🚆 🛈 In
the old Wajima train stn;
(0768) 22-1503

Projecting 45 miles (70 km)
into the Japan Sea, Noto is
a quiet region of fishing
villages known for seafood
and untouched traditions.
The east coast and the sandy
west near Kanazawa are quite
developed, but the north
and northwest are rocky
and picturesque. Public
transportation around Noto
is limited; bus and train are
similar in time and cost, but
the bus network is wider.

Wajima, a weathered
fishing town, produces top-
quality, durable lacquerware
with at least 70 layers of lacquer. Nearby Hegura island
is a stopping-off point for
migratory birds. Located just
east of Wajima, Senmaida is
so famed for its "1,000" narrow
rice terraces by the sea that
it has been awarded heri-
tage status by the Food &
Agriculture Organization of
the UN, while Sosogi's coast
has unusual rock formations.
Many summer festivals here
feature demon-masked drum-
mers and *kiriko* lanterns,

 PICTURE PERFECT
Sun Rice, Sunset

Shiroyone Senmaida
comprises over 1,000
small rice paddies on
the steep slopes leading
down to the Noto
Peninsula's rocky
shoreline. Head here
at sunrise or sunset for
an atmospheric shot.

standing up to 50 ft (15 m) tall.
Between events, drums are
played at Wajima and Sosogi.

To the west, Monzen has
the major Soji-ji Zen temple
(partially open while undergoing restoration). In Hakui
are the important shrine of
Keta Taisha and a 2,000-year-
old sumo ring – Japan's oldest,
still used each September.
Senmaida, Sosogi, and Monzen
can be reached by bus from
Wajima, Hakui by bus or train
from Kanazawa.

Did You Know?

Wajima lacquerware
is created by applying
nunokise (cloth)
onto the objects
to be glazed.

THE LAYOUT OF A ZEN BUDDHIST TEMPLE

Designed to facilitate the path to englightenment, Zen Buddhist temples transport worshippers from the earthly world to that of the Buddha.

Based on Chinese Sung-dynasty structures, Japanese Zen temples are usually set out in a straight line. The entrance is marked by a bridge over a water, symbolizing the overcoming of earthly obstacles. The main buildings, including the Sanmon (main gate), Hatto lecture hall, Butsuden (Buddha Hall), meditation or study hall, and the abbot's and monks' quarters, are beautiful but natural looking. Often made of unpainted wood, they are intended to be conducive to emptying the mind of worldly illusions, facilitating enlightenment.

↑ Kinkaku-ji (Golden Pavilion), a Zen Buddhist temple in Kyoto

↑ A serene statue of the Buddha in Engaku-ji, Kamakura

TOP 5 ZEN BUDDHIST TEMPLES

Eihei-ji
The "temple of eternal peace" is a *daihonzan* (head temple) of the Soto Zen sect.

Kinkaku-ji
The Golden Pavilion is reflected in the pond at this Kyoto temple *(p199)*.

Engaku-ji
The most beautiful of Kamakura's five great Zen temples *(p157)*.

Ginkaku-ji
Despite its name, Kyoto's Silver Pavilion was never covered in silver foil *(p195)*.

Soji-ji
This *daihonzan* is one of the largest and busiest temples in Japan.

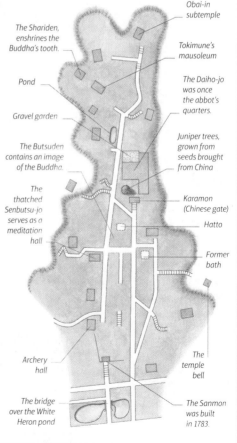

Obai-in subtemple

The Shariden, enshrines the Buddha's tooth.

Tokimune's mausoleum

Pond

The Daiho-jo was once the abbot's quarters.

Gravel garden

The Butsuden contains an image of the Buddha.

Juniper trees, grown from seeds brought from China

The thatched Senbutsu-jo serves as a meditation hall

Karamon (Chinese gate)

Hatto

Former bath

Archery hall

The temple bell

→
The layout of Engaku-ji, a Zen Buddhist temple in Kamakura

The bridge over the White Heron pond

The Sanmon was built in 1783.

Standing on one of ↑
the boulders in the
Nezame-no-toko gorge

A DRIVING AND WALKING TOUR
KISO VALLEY TOUR

Distance 37 miles (60 km) **Stopping-off points** Narai, Magome,
Tsumango **Difficulty** Trails and roads are well-maintained

The Kiso River runs through a picturesque mountain valley
that was the route of the Nakasendo, one of the Edo-
period post roads. Take a drive along this ancient route,
stopping at the 11 charming post towns en route.
Tsumago, Narai, and Magome, in particular, still retain
much of that atmosphere, their narrow streets lined
with wooden inns and stores. Parts of the old
Nakasendo walking trail, especially between
Tsumago and Magome, are as they were
in the Edo days and can be followed past
woods, farms, and milestones. More
challenging hiking is found on
nearby mountains such as Ontake.

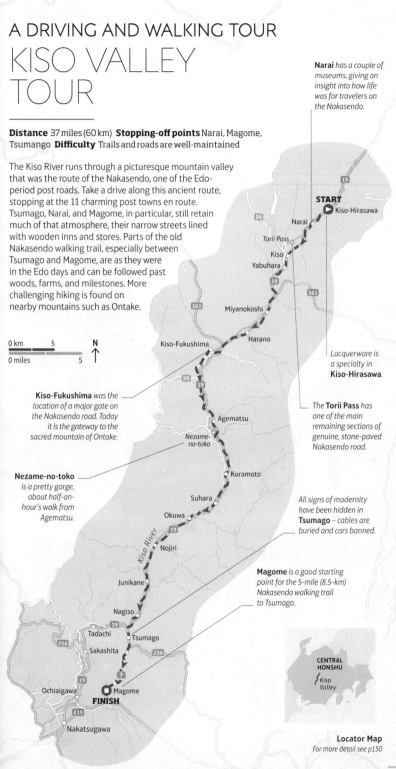

Narai *has a couple of
museums, giving an
insight into how life
was for travelers on
the Nakasendo.*

START
Kiso-Hirasawa

*Lacquerware is
a specialty in*
Kiso-Hirasawa.

The **Torii Pass** *has
one of the main
remaining sections of
genuine, stone-paved
Nakasendo road.*

Kiso-Fukushima *was the
location of a major gate on
the Nakasendo road. Today
it is the gateway to the
sacred mountain of Ontake.*

Nezame-no-toko
*is a pretty gorge,
about half-an-
hour's walk from
Agematsu.*

*All signs of modernity
have been hidden in*
Tsumago *– cables are
buried and cars banned.*

Magome *is a good starting
point for the 5-mile (8.5-km)
Nakasendo walking trail
to Tsumago.*

FINISH
Magome

**CENTRAL
HONSHU**
*Kiso
Valley*

Locator Map
For more detail see p150

179

KYOTO CITY

Founded in 794 as Heian-kyo (capital of peace and tranquility), the city was modeled on the Tang Chinese city of Chang-an. Bounded on three sides by mountains and bisected by a river flowing north to south, the site was considered ideal by Emperor Kanmu's geomancers (people who practiced the art of divination by interpreting markings in the earth). As the population grew, however, hygiene was a problem, especially when the Kamo River flooded. A series of rituals and festivals came into being to placate the spirits responsible for plagues and other catastrophes, resulting in a tightly knit fabric of ritual and custom, mostly still observed.

Kyoto culture became an amalgam of several influences, of which the imperial court and nobility were the first and most important. Later came the samurai, patrons of Zen Buddhism, and the tea ceremony. Merchants were also influential, especially the silk weavers of Nishijin. The city was reduced to ashes at various times by earthquakes, fires, and the ten-year period of civil strife known as the Onin War (1467–77). During the Edo period (1603–1868), the balance of power shifted from Kyoto to Edo (Tokyo), and Kyoto eventually lost its status as capital in 1869. Despite this, Kyoto retains its refined, imperial air, while at the same time embracing all that comes with being a cosmopolitan 21st-century city.

Around Kyoto

Kurama District ㉝

Ohara District ㉟

Hieizan Enryaku-ji ㊲

Takao District ㉜

Sagano District ㉘

Kamoeka

Arashiyama District ㉚

Area of main Kyoto map

KYOTO

Otsu

Yamashina

Muko

Fushimi

Fushimi Inari-taisha ②

Daigo-ji ㉟

0 km 5
0 miles 5

N

Kyoto Golf Club Kamigamo course

KITA-KU

KAMIGAMO

KAMOKAIDO

SHICHIKU

Kitayama

Kyoto Botanical Garden

IMAMIYA DORI

Kita-Oji

KOYAMA

Kamo Ki

SHIMEI-DORI

Kuramaguchi

KARASUMA-DORI

Imadegawa

Daitoku-ji ⑲

KITAOJI-BASHI

Kinkaku-ji (Golden Pavilion) ㉒

HIRANO

KURAMAGUCHI-DORI

Suika Tenman-gu shrine

Insho Domoto Museum ㉗

Ryoan-ji ㉔

KINU-KAKE-NO-MICHI

NISHIOJI-DORI

Kitamo Tenman-gu Shrine ㉑

IMADEGAWA-DORI

Kongo Noh Theater ⑭

Kyoto Imperia Palace ⑮

Ninna-ji ㉓

SHIJAN-KAIDO

Utano

Omuro-Ninnaji

Ryoanji

Toji-in

Myoshin-ji

KITANO

NISHIJIN

NAKADACHIURI-DORI

Sento Imperial Palace

Kitano-Hakubaicho

SENBON-DORI

Imperial Park

3 miles (5 km) ⑤

Narutaki

Myoshin-ji ㉕

KAMIGYO-KU

SAWARAGICHO-DORI

MARUTAMACHI-DORI

Marutamachi

Tokiwa

HANAZONO

Hanazono

Emmachi

HORIKAWA-DORI

Koryu-ji ㉖

Uzumasa-Koryuji

Kaikonoyashiro

Uzumasa-Tenjingawa

Yamanouchi

KADONONAKA-DORI

KADONOOJI

YAMANOUCHI

SAIIN

Nishioji-Oike

OIKE-DORI

Nishioji Sanjo

SANJO-DORI

Saiin

Sai

SHIJO-DORI

MATSUBARA-DORI

Nijo-jo ①

Nijo

Nijojo-mae

Kyo Shiyakusho-m

Karasuma Oike

NAKAGYO-KU

Shijo-Omiya

Omiya

OMIYA-DORI

HORIKAWA-DORI

KARASUMA-DORI

Karasuma

Shijo

KEIHAN SANJO

④

Kyc

Kawarama

KAWARAMACHI-DORI

NISHI-GOJO-DORI

Nishikyogoku Sports Park

Katsura River

NISHIOJI

Nishi-kyogoku

HANAYA-MACHI-DORI

GOJO-DORI

Tanbaguchi

SHIMOGYO-KU

Kiyomizu-G

Gojo

Shosei-e Garden

NISHI-NANAJO

Nishi Hongan-ji ⑧

Higashi Hongan-ji ⑨

SHICHIJO-DORI

UMEKOJI

Kyoto ⑥

Kyoto Station

Shichi

NISHI-KYOGOKU

Katsura Imperial Villa ㉛

0 kilometers 1
0 miles 1

N

Nishioji

Toji Temple ③

Toji

KUJO-DORI

Kujo

MINAMI-KU

KYOTO CITY

Must Sees
1 Nijo-jo
2 Fushimi Inari-taisha

Experience More
3 Toji Temple
4 Kyoto National Museum
5 Sanjusangen-do Temple
6 Kyoto Station
7 Chion-in Temple
8 Nishi Hongan-ji
9 Higashi Hongan-ji
10 Pontocho Alley
11 Kiyomizu-dera Temple
12 Gion District
13 Nanzen-ji
14 Kongo Noh Theater
15 Kyoto Imperial Palace
16 Ginkaku-ji (Silver Pavilion)
17 Shoren-in Temple
18 Okazaki Area
19 Daitoku-ji
20 Kamo Shrines
21 Kitano Tenman-gu Shrine
22 Kinkaku-ji (Golden Pavilion)
23 Ninna-ji
24 Ryoan-ji
25 Myoshin-ji
26 Koryu-ji
27 Insho Domoto Museum
28 Sagano District
29 Shisen-do Temple
30 Arashiyama District
31 Katsura Imperial Villa
32 Takao District
33 Kurama District
34 Manshu-in Temple
35 Daigo-ji
36 Shugaku-in Imperial Villa
37 Hieizan Enryaku-ji
38 Ohara District

Eat
1 Kichikichi
2 Gyoza Shop Gion

Drink
3 Jam Sake Bar

Stay
4 Tawaraya Ryokan
5 Hoshinoya Kyoto
6 Jam Hostel

Shop
7 Kasagen

❶ 🖊️ 🗺️

NIJO-JO

二条城

📍C3 🏯Entrance on Horikawa-dori 📞(075) 841-0096
🚇Nijojo-mae Stn 🚌9, 50, 101 🕐Feb-Jun & Sep-Nov:
8:45am–5pm daily; Jan, Jul, Aug & Dec: 8:45am–5pm
Wed-Mon (to 6:10pm Jul & Aug) 🚫Dec 26–Jan 3

Although it might not look like an impressive stronghold
from the outside, the interior of Nijo-jo will not disappoint.
Full of innovative defences, and undeniably beautiful,
it's a fascinating place to explore.

With few of the grand fortifications of other castles in Japan,
Nijo-jo is instead best known for its unusually ornate interiors
and "nightingale floors." This ingenious flooring is so called
because it was designed to make bird-like squeaking sounds
when walked upon, a warning of possible intruders. The
complex was created by shogun Tokugawa Ieyasu (1543–1616), and
symbolized the power and riches of the newly established Edo-
based shogunate. Ieyasu's grandson Iemitsu commissioned the
best Kano School painters for the reception halls, in preparation
for an imperial visit. Ironically, in 1867 the last Tokugawa shogun
resigned at Nijo-jo, in the presence of Emperor Meiji.

PAINTERS OF THE KANO SCHOOL

Kano artists came from a low-ranking samurai family, but grew to prominence in the 15th century for their Chinese-style landscapes, figures, and bird and flower scenes. Nijo-jo has the largest Kano pieces ever executed. Among the motifs are life-size tigers crouching among bamboo groves, wild herons in winter, and frolicking peacocks.

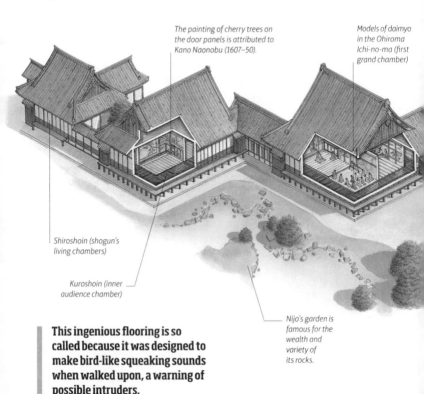

The painting of cherry trees on the door panels is attributed to Kano Naonobu (1607–50).

Models of daimyo in the Ohiroma Ichi-no-ma (first grand chamber)

Shiroshoin (shogun's living chambers)

Kuroshoin (inner audience chamber)

Nijo's garden is famous for the wealth and variety of its rocks.

> This ingenious flooring is so
> called because it was designed to
> make bird-like squeaking sounds
> when walked upon, a warning of
> possible intruders.

1 The Momoyama-period Karamon Gate has a Chinese-style gable and gold-plated fixtures.

2 In the teahouse, visitors can take part in a traditional ceremony.

3 The castle's grounds are planted with a huge variety of cherry trees, which flower at different times between late March and mid-April.

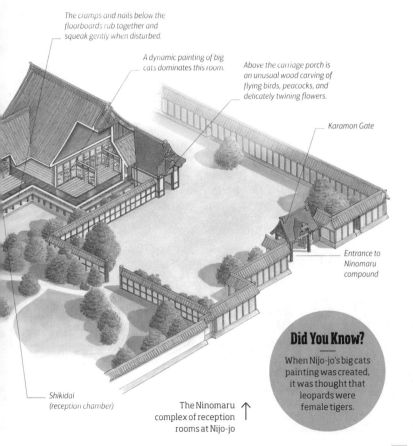

The cramps and nails below the floorboards rub together and squeak gently when disturbed.

A dynamic painting of big cats dominates this room.

Above the carriage porch is an unusual wood carving of flying birds, peacocks, and delicately twining flowers.

Karamon Gate

Entrance to Ninomaru compound

Shikidai (reception chamber)

The Ninomaru complex of reception rooms at Nijo-jo ↑

Did You Know?

When Nijo-jo's big cats painting was created, it was thought that leopards were female tigers.

② FUSHIMI INARI-TAISHA

伏見稲荷大社

📍 B2 🏠 68 Yabunouchi, Fukakusa, Fushimi-ku 📞 (075) 641-7331
🚉 Fushimi-Inari Stn, Keihan line; JR Inari Stn, Nara line 🚌 Minami 5
to Inari Taisha mae 🕐 24 hours daily

This vast sprawling mountainside shrine complex with its thousands of bright red gates, meandering up the hills to the south of Kyoto City, is one of Japan's most striking sites.

Said to predate the founding of Kyoto, Fushimi Inari Shrine is an ancient wonder. Located in the ward of Fushimi – meaning "hidden water" – it is dedicated to Inari, the Shinto god of rice and sake (appropriate given that the area is Japan's second-largest producer of sake).

The thousands of vermilion torii that line the 2.5-mile- (4-km-) long trail from the main to the inner shrine were donated by individuals and companies, and their name and the date of donation is inscribed on the back of each gate. Larger gates can cost as much as a million yen to dedicate. The most impressive of these is the gargantuan Romon Gate, which stands before the main shrine. It was donated in 1589 by Toyotomi Hideyoshi, the warlord responsible for the unification of the country.

> 💬 INSIDER TIP
> **Hit the Streets**
>
> The streets around the shrine are worth exploring for their intriguing traditional architecture and bustling atmosphere. Keep an eye out for vendors selling roast sparrows on skewers. This traditional snack might not be for everyone as the bird is still very recognizable.

→ The stage, used for dance performances during yearly rituals at the shrine

← A red-collared statue of a fox - believed to be one of Inari's messengers - in the expansive grounds of the Fushimi Inari-taisha

Did You Know?

The function of a torii is to mark the boundary between the everyday and the sacred.

↑ Walking along the torii-lined path at the Fushimi Inari-taisha

EXPERIENCE MORE

3

Toji Temple
東寺

📍 B5 🏛 1 Kujyomachi, Minami-ku 📞 (075) 691-3325 🚌 42 to Toji Higashimon-mae; 19 & 78 to Toji Minamimon-mae; 16 to Toji Nishimon-mae 🕐 8am–5pm daily (to 4:30pm winter)

Although it lacks the mossy beauty of many Kyoto temples, dusty Toji (actual name Kyo-o-gokoku-ji) impresses with the sheer weight of its history. Its Buddhas have been watching over the city ever since Kukai founded the temple in 794. The city's religious foundations were laid here, and echoes of bygone rituals seem to linger in Toji's hallowed halls.

Kukai turned Toji into the main headquarters of Shingon Buddhism. The sect's rituals relied heavily on mandalas, and in the Kodo (lecture hall), 21 statues form a mandala, at the center of which is Dainichi Nyorai, the cosmic Buddha who first expounded the esoteric teachings. About 1,200 years old, these and other major images were carved from single blocks of wood.

Statues of Yakushi Nyorai, the Buddha of healing, and

his attendants Gakko and Nikko, are enshrined in the two-story Kondo (main hall). First built in 796, the present structure dates from 1603 and is considered a masterpiece. Rebuilt in 1644, Toji's magnificent five-story pagoda – at 180 ft (55 m) the tallest wooden pagoda in Japan – has become a symbol of Kyoto. Inside are images of four Buddhas and their followers.

Northwest of the Kodo is the Miei-do or Taishi-do (great teacher's hall) where Kukai lived. It houses a Secret Buddha, a Fudo Myo-o image, shown on rare occasions, as well as an image of Kukai. A National Treasure, the graceful structure dates from 1380.

THE BENTO BOX

A bento is a take-home meal in a compartmentalized box: office workers buy them for lunch, schoolchildren eat from them at their desk, and business travelers buy them at stations, such as Kyoto's, to enjoy with a beer on the bullet train. In its compartments there will invariably be a portion of rice, a main serving of meat or fish, pieces of omelet, some vegetables, and pickles. But part of the charm of the bento is that anything goes. You may open a bento and find a small octopus or a tiny whole fish gazing up at you.

Kukai is remembered on the 21st of each month, when a flea market is held in the temple precincts. Many shoppers take time out for a brief pilgrimage to the Miei-do, where they offer money and incense, some rubbing the smoke onto whatever body part is troubling them.

4

Kyoto National Museum
京都国立博物館

📍 D5 🏛 527 Chayamachi, Higashiyama-ku 🚌 100, 206 & 208 to Hakubutsukan Sanjusangendo-mae 🕐 9:30am–6pm Tue–Sun (to 8pm Fri & Sat) 🌐 kyohaku.go.jp/eng/indextop.html

The city's National Museum was established in 1895 and is noted for its pictorial works, including Buddhist and ink paintings, textiles, and Heian-period sculptures. Special exhibitions are held in the Meiji-era brick building to the right of the entrance.

←

The five-story wooden pagoda in the grounds of Toji Temple

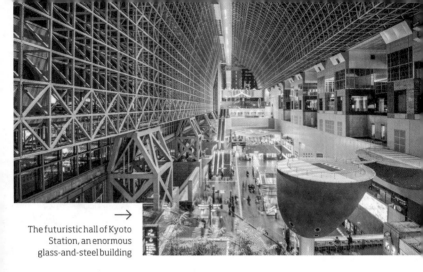

→ The futuristic hall of Kyoto Station, an enormous glass-and-steel building

 5

Sanjusangen-do Temple
三十三間堂

📍 D5 🏠 657 Sanjusangen-domawari, Higashiyama-ku ☎ (075) 561-0467 🚉 Keihan Nanajo Stn 🚌 100, 206, 208 to Hakubutsukan Sanjusangen-do-mae 🕐 Apr–mid-Nov: 8am–5pm daily; mid-Nov–Mar: 9am–4pm daily

Rengeo-in, more commonly known as Sanjusangen-do, induces an almost hallucinatory effect on its visitors who, once inside its elongated main hall, find themselves face to face with ranks of nearly identical Kannon (goddess of mercy) images – 1,001 of them, to be precise – all glimmering in the dark. Sanjusangen-do dates from 1164 and is the longest wooden structure in the world. Its name derives from the 33 (*sanjusan*) spaces between the building's pillars. The temple's main image of a 1,000-armed Kannon was carved in 1254 by Tankei at the age of 82. Upon its head are ten other heads, including a miniature image of the Amida Buddha. Stretching out on either side are 1,000 smaller images. Kannon was believed to have 33 manifestations, so the faithful would have invoked the mercy of 33,033 Kannons.

On the first Sunday in January the temple hosts an archery contest for young women, who shoot arrows from one end of the veranda of the main hall to the other.

 6

Kyoto Station
京都駅

📍 C5 ℹ️ 2nd flr main concourse, left from escalator; (075) 361-4401/(075) 343-0548

A sleek complex of soaring spaces, glass surfaces, and bleacher-like staircases, Kyoto's JR train station provides a futuristic entry to Japan's old imperial capital. Completed in 1997, the structure is the work of architect Hiroshi Hara, a former Tokyo University professor whose design triumphed in an international competition. Although it has been criticized for its refusal to incorporate traditional Japanese motifs in its design, the station is undeniably eye-catching. Thanks to its open-air spaces it also, ironically, resembles a traditional wooden Kyoto house: pleasant in summer, but drafty and cold in winter.

Within the station is a shopping area called The Cube, specializing in Kyoto craft items and food products.

STAY

Tawaraya Ryokan
Each room at this old *ryokan* is traditionally decorated, with its own private garden.

📍 C4 🏠 278 Nakahakusancho, Nakagyo ☎ (075) 211-5566

¥¥¥

Hoshinoya Kyoto
On the Hozugawa River, this luxury hotel is accessible only by boat. Soak in a deep cedar tub at the end of a long day.

📍 A3 🏠 11-2 Genrokuzancho, Nishikyo-ku 🌐 hoshinoya.com

¥¥¥

Jam Hostel
A no-frills affair, this hostel offers communal dormitories with bunk beds, as well as a few private rooms.

📍 D4 🏠 170 Tokiwachō, Higashiyama-ku 🌐 sakebar.jp

¥¥¥

Did You Know?

Chion-in Temple's Sanmon is the largest gate in Japan.

7

Chion-in Temple
知恩院

📍 D4 🏠 400 Rinkacho, Higashiyama-ku 🚇 Higashiyama Stn, Tozai line 🚌 206 to Chion-in-mae 🕐 9am–4:30pm daily 🌐 chion-in.or.jp/en

The colossal Sanmon was built to proclaim the supremacy of Jodo-sect Buddhism, of which Chion-in is the headquarters. It also emphasized the authority of the Tokugawa shogunate, which funded the temple's restoration.

The well-endowed complex occupies the site where Honen, the founder of the Jodo sect, started to preach in 1175. It boasts a lavish founder's hall, a smaller hall enshrining an image of Amida Buddha, and elegant reception halls decorated with Kano School paintings. The Gongen-do

mausoleum enshrines the spirits of Tokugawa Ieyasu, his son Hidetada, and grandson Iemitsu. The temple also possesses a huge bell that is solemnly rung 108 times (once for each sin man is prone to commit) on New Year's Eve.

8

Nishi Hongan-ji
西本願寺

📍 C5 🏠 60 Horikawa-dori Hanaya-chō, Shimogyo-ku 🚌 9, 28, 75 to Nishi Honganji-mae 🕐 5:30am– 5pm daily 🌐 hongwanji. or.jp/english

With their ornately carved transoms (panels above doors), massive flower-decked altars, and shimmering expanses of tatami matting, Kyoto's cavernous Hongan-ji temples, with their huge Goei-do (founder's halls) and smaller Amida-do, testify to the power and popularity of the Jodo-Shinshu sect.

Nishi Hongan-ji is rich in national treasures, but not all are always on view. They include the Shoin (study hall), with its lavishly decorated Shiroshoin and Kuroshoin compartments; Kokei no Niwa, a garden featuring cycad palms; two Noh stages,

one of which is thought to be the oldest Noh stage in existence; Hiunkaku, a large tea pavilion; and the Karamon, or Chinese gate. The Shoin is open twice a month, but dates vary (the Kuroshoin, however, is never shown). Hiunkaku can only be visited if a booking is made at least a day in advance, although this is not required on days when special events are held. A large donation is required if attending a tea ceremony or a Noh event at Hiunkaku.

9

Higashi Hongan-ji
東本願寺

📍 C5 🏠 754 Tokiwacho, Karasumadori Shichijo-agaru 🚉 JR Kyoto Stn 🕐 Mar–Oct: 5:50am–5:30pm daily; Nov–Feb: 6:20am– 4:30pm daily 🌐 higashi honganji.or.jp

Higashi Hongan-ji's immense and lavish Goei-do gate is one of the first traditional structures visitors to Kyoto see as they head north out of Kyoto Station. The temple's Goei-do (founder's hall) dates

↑ Worshippers lighting incense sticks and praying at Kyoto's Chion-in Temple

↑ The hilltop Kiyomizu-dera Temple, where visitors of all sects leave prayers (inset)

from 1895 and claims to be the largest wooden structure in the world. The striking white plaster and gray-tile walls on the temple's northern side belong to the temple *kura*, or storehouse. Inside, there are many treasures.

Two blocks east of Higashi Hongan-ji proper is Shosei-en (nicknamed Kikoku-tei), a spacious garden owned by the temple. Poet-scholar Ishikawa Jozan (1583–1672) and landscape architect Kobori Enshu (1579–1647) are said to have had a hand in its design. Herons, ducks, and other wildlife find refuge here.

 ⑩

Pontocho Alley
先斗町通り

◎D4 🚃Kawaramachi stn, Hankyu Kyoto line 🚌5, 17, 205 to Shijo-Kawaramachi

This charming alleyway is best appreciated after dusk, when it is reminiscent of an ukiyo-e print (p130). Formerly a sandbar, the stretch of land began to be developed in 1670. The area flourished as an entertainment district

and was licensed as a geisha quarter, a role it continues to play. Although neon and concrete are encroaching, the street largely remains the preserve of the traditional wooden *ochaya* – the type of teahouse where geisha entertain clients.

Pontocho is also home to the tiny Tanuki Shrine. In 1978 a fire broke out in Pontocho, taking the life of a geisha. Where it stopped, a ceramic *tanuki* (raccoon dog) was found shattered by the heat. Believing that the raccoon had sacrificed itself on their behalf, the residents built this little shrine to house its remains. Throw in a coin and a recorded message imparts such pearls of wisdom as "beware of fire." *Tanuki* statues have big testicles, symbolising sacks of gold.

From the beginning of June to mid-September, many of Pontocho's riverside restaurants erect platforms, called *yuka*, over the canal running parallel to the Kamo River.

⑪ 🐾

Kiyomizu-dera Temple
清水寺

◎D4 🏠1-294 Kiyomizu, Higashiyama-ku 🚌100, 206, 207 to Gojyozaka ◷6am-5:30pm, 6pm, or 6:30pm daily 🌐kiyomizu dera.or.jp/en

While many other famous temples are the preserves of certain sects, Kiyomizu-dera seems to belong to everyone. For over 1,000 years, pilgrims have prayed to the temple's 11-headed Kannon image and drunk from its sacred spring. The main hall's veranda, a nail-less miracle of Japanese joinery, offers wonderful views of Kyoto. To see the temple itself, walk to the pagoda across the ravine, and you'll see why "to jump off Kiyomizu's stage" is the Japanese equivalent of the English "to take the plunge."

Gion District
祇園地区

D4 **Gion-shijo Stn, Keihan line** 46, 201, 203, 207 to Gion

By turns tawdry and sublime, the Gion is Kyoto's best-known geisha quarter where Japanese men come to revel in the company of professional geishas at private inns and teahouses found on the streets north and south of Shijo-dori, beside the Kamo River. Its history started in feudal times, with stalls catering to the needs of pilgrims and other visitors. These evolved into teahouses, or *ochaya*, fulfilling a variety of appetites. In the late 16th century, Kabuki theater moved from the Kamo riverbank, where it had started, into several venues just east of the river, furthering the Gion's reputation as a play-boy's paradise. One of these, Minami-za, still exists.

The Yasaka Shrine, whose striking two-story vermilion gate rises above the eastern end of Shijo-dori, was estab-lished in around 656 and originally called Gion Shrine.

Its deities protect from illness and, in 869, were paraded through the streets to stop an epidemic – the beginning of the famous Gion Matsuri. On New Year's Day, thousands flock here to pray for health and prosperity, while in early April crowds stream through its gates on their way to Maruyama Park, a cherry-blossom viewing site.

Gion's main shopping area is the stretch of Shijo between Yasaka Shrine and Shijo Bridge, which includes shops with expensive kimono accessories. On the southeast corner of Shijo and Hanamikoji is the Gion's most famous *ochaya*, Ichiriki. Easily identified by its distinctive red walls, this teahouse is the setting of a scene in the Kabuki play *Chushingura*. Hanamikoji itself, a historically preserved zone, shows the Gion at its classic, and classy, best. The restaurants and *ochaya* here are the haunts of politicians and com-pany presidents, and are likely to turn a cold shoulder to people without a proper intro-duction. More accessible to tourists are the nearby Gion Corner and the Gion Kobu Kaburenjo venues.

Running east from Hanami-koji, north of Shijo, is Shinba-shi, a street lined with discreet *ochaya*, and nary a neon sign to be seen. The average Gion-goer, however, is more likely to partake in karaoke with their colleagues in one of the gaudy, neon-lit buildings that populate the cluttered streets that make up the north-eastern part of the district, than to engage in geisha play at a prestigious *ochaya*.

DRINK

Jam Sake Bar
This bar boasts more than 30 different types of sake, organized by region, including many Kyoto specialties. Flights (tasters of different sakes) are available, and the staff speak English.

D4 **170 Tokiwachō, Higashiyama-ku** sakebar.jp

← A kimono-wearing woman in Gion District, with the Yasaka Shrine in the background

EXPERIENCE Kyoto City

GEISHA, GEIKO, AND MAIKO

Despite the fact that the profession, dating from the 17th century, is in decline and blurred by the activities of so-called *onsen* geisha and others who offer more sexual than classical arts, geisha still tread the streets of Kyoto. Known as *geiko* (child of the arts), their enclaves are Gion-kobu, Pontocho, Miyagawa-cho, and Kamishichi-ken.

GEIKO AND MAIKO COSTUME

Less polished than their *geiko* "sisters," *maiko*, apprentice geisha, are a Kyoto-only phenomenon. They wear their hair in a distinctive style, with ornamental hairpins, and sport a unique costume featuring a long, hanging *obi* (sash), tall *koppori* clogs, and an under-kimono with an embroidered collar. When becoming a fully fledged *geiko*, they exchange the embroidered collar for a white one in a transition known as *eri-kae*.

PERFECT PERFORMANCES

Geishas' knowledge of traditional arts, skill at verbal repartee, and ability to keep a secret win them the respect, and sometimes love, of their well-heeled male clients. The geisha world moves to the rhythm of the *shamisen*, a three-stringed instrument that originated in Okinawa. Poised and posture-perfect, the geisha dance to this eery sound, sometimes using a fan as a prop. Geisha who choose not to specialize in dance will instead master the *shamisen* or another instrument, and play throughout their life.

A maiko's *hair is her own, not a wig.*

The white face and red lips are classic Japanese ideals of beauty.

Under-kimono

Tabi *socks*

Koppori *clogs*

→

A maiko wearing her traditional costume before she becomes an accomplished geiko

 INSIDER TIP
When to Visit

If you want to see geisha, the best time to visit Kyoto is April. Every day of this month, geisha in Gion-kobu stage performances, and the Miyagawa-cho district holds the Kyō Odori dance. For small-scale shows, head to Kamishichiken in the last two weeks of April for Kitano Odori.

↑ A geisha playing a *shamisen* with her teacher as another looks on

13 Nanzen-ji
南禅寺

E4 **86 Nanzenji
Fukuchicho, Sakyo-ku**
Keage Stn, Tozai line
**5 to Nanzen-ji-Eikan-
do-michi** **8:40am-5pm
daily (to 4:30pm Dec-Feb)**
nanzenji.com

From its pine-studded outer
precincts to the inner recesses
of its subtemples, this quintessential Zen temple exudes
an air of serenity. Since 1386,
Nanzen-ji has been the center
of Kyoto's Gozan, or "five great
Zen temples."

The Hojo (abbot's quarters)
includes a small but exquisite
dry garden attributed to
Kobori Enshu (1579–1647),
and Momoyama-period
paintings, including the Kano
Tanyu masterpiece *Tiger
Drinking Water*. Nearby is a
room overlooking a waterfall
and garden, where a bowl
of *matcha* (ceremonial tea)
and a sweet can be enjoyed
for a small fee.

The temple's colossal Sanmon,
a two-story gate built in 1628
to console the souls of those
killed in the Summer Siege of
Osaka Castle, is said to have
been the hideout of Ishikawa
Goemon, a legendary outlaw
hero who was later boiled
alive in an iron cauldron.

Three of Nanzen-ji's twelve
subtemples are open to
the public year-round. The
most impressive, Konchi-in,
boasts work by Kobori Enshu,
featuring pines and boulders
arranged in a tortoise-and-
crane motif. Tenju-an has a
dry garden and a small, lush
stroll garden. Nanzen-in
occupies the original site of
Emperor Kameyama's villa.
Restored in 1703, it faces a
pond-centered garden backed
by a wooded mountainside.

The red-brick aqueduct in
front of Nanzen-ji may seem
incongruous, but for Japanese
tourists this structure is one
of Nanzen-ji's greatest
attractions. Built in 1890, it
formed part of an ambitious
canal project to bring water
and goods from neighboring
Shiga Prefecture into the city.
It was one of Meiji Japan's
first feats of engineering.

Nanzen-ji is synonymous
with *yudofu*, boiled tofu, a
delicacy best enjoyed during
cold months. Specialty restaurants are located within
the temple precincts.

TOP 5 KYOTO SPECIALTIES

Yudofu
Kyoto is said to produce
some of Japan's best
tofu. *Yudofu* is soft tofu
gently cooked in broth.

Kyo Tsukemono
Pickles made with just
vinegar and salt.

Kyoto-style Sushi
Featuring preserved
fish and vinegary rice.

Yatsuhashi
A soft, chewy, sweet
cinnamon delicacy.

Yuba
The skin that forms on
the surface of boiling
soy milk is served with
soy sauce, wasabi, and
ponzu (citrus dressing).

14 Kongo Noh Theater
金剛能楽堂

C3 **Nakadachiuri-
agaru, Karasuma-dori,
Kamigyo-ku** **Imadegawa
Stn, Karasuma line** **(075)
441-7222** **Tue-Sun**

The Kongo Noh Theater
across from the Imperial
Palace grounds opened
in June 2003, following its
relocation from a site in Shijo
Muromachi. During the Edo
period (1603–1868) Noh was
adopted as the official art
of the warrior class, and
the Kongo Theater has the
longest history of regular use
as a Noh stage in Japan; its
players are particularly known
for their agility and acrobatic
feats. The theater incor-
porates several features

←
The aqueduct in front of
Nanzen-ji, whose grounds
offer opportunities for
peaceful walks *(inset)*

The bucolic setting of Ginkaku-ji, also known as the Silver Pavilion

from the earlier design, including the outdoor stage, pillars, and large acoustic earthenware jars. Regular performances are held at the theater, usually on the last Sunday of the month. Look out for exhibitions of Noh costumes and masks in the lobby.

Kyoto Imperial Palace
京都御所

📍 C3 🏠 3 Kyoto-Gyoen Kamigyo-ku 🚇 Imadegawa Stn, Karasuma line 📞 (075) 211-1215 🕐 9am-5pm Tue-Sun (to 4:30pm Mar & Sep; to 4pm Oct-Feb) 🚫 Dec 28-Jan 4, public hols

With its stately pines and vistas of the Higashiyama, the Kyoto Imperial Palace Park (Kyoto Gyoen) is a spacious oasis in the heart of the city. On its grounds are the Imperial Palace (Kyoto Gosho) and Sento Imperial Palace (Sento Gosho), whose impressive stroll garden was built in 1630. The Imperial Household Agency (Kunaicho), where tickets are issued for the imperial structures as well as to Shugaku-in (p204) and Katsura villas (p203), is in the northwest corner. Remember to bring your passport.

At the southern end of the park is a delightful pond with an arched bridge. This is all that remains of one of several noble families' estates that occupied much of what is now parkland. From the bridge is an unobstructed view all the way north to the Kenreimon, the majestic gate in the middle of the south wall, which may be used only by the emperor.

Ginkaku-ji (Silver Pavilion)
銀閣寺

📍 E3 🏠 2 Ginkakuji-cho Sakyo-ku 📞 (075) 771-5725 🚌 100 to Ginkaku-ji-mae 🕐 Mar-Nov: 8:30am-5pm daily; Dec-Feb: 9am-4:30pm daily

Ginkaku-ji – actual name, Jisho-ji; English nickname, Silver Pavilion – is considered by some to be an unequaled masterpiece of garden design; others find it overrated. But the important role the temple has played in Japanese culture is indisputable. Within its walls the tea ceremony, flower arrangement, and ink painting found new levels of refinement.

The temple was originally the mountain retreat of shogun Yoshimasa (1436–1490), who is remembered for an artistic renaissance now referred to as Higashiyama culture. In tribute to his grandfather, who covered Kinkaku-ji in gold leaf (p199), Yoshimasa had intended to finish his pavilion in silver. However, the ruinous Onin War thwarted that ambition. Minus its final coating, the graceful Silver Pavilion now shines with the patina of age.

EAT

Kichikichi
Enjoy chef Motokichi Yukimura's *omurice* (omelet on top of fried rice).

📍 D4 🏠 185-4 Zaimokucho, Sanjo Pontocho-dori Kudaru, Nagoya-ku 🌐 kichi2.net

---

Gyoza Shop Gion
This gem specializes in *gyoza*, fried dumplings.

📍 D4 🏠 373-3 Kiyomotocho, Higashiyama-ku 📞 (075) 533-7133

Shoren-in Temple
青蓮院

Q D4 **A** 69-1 Awataguchi Sanjobocho, Higashiyama-ku **S** Higashiyama Stn, Tozai line **E** 5, 46, 100 to Jingu-michi **O** 9am–5pm daily (see website for late openings) **W** shorenin.com

This aristocratic temple's symbol is its ancient camphor trees whose 800-year-old gnarled limbs spread majestically on either side of the front gate. Shoren-in grounds are beautifully landscaped, with a bright pond garden on one side and a mysterious, camphor-tree-shaded expanse of moss on the other. The teahouse in the garden has been rebuilt, the original having been burned in April 1993 by left-wing radicals protesting the Emperor's visit to Okinawa.

> Shoren-in's grounds are landscaped, with a bright pond garden on one side and a mysterious, camphor-tree-shaded expanse of moss on the other.

18

Okazaki Area
岡崎公園一帯

Q D3 **E** 5 or 100 to Kyoto Kaikan Bijutsukan-mae

Okazaki is home to museums, galleries, sports grounds, the municipal zoo, and Heian-Jingu, one of Kyoto's largest and newest shrines. Built in 1895, the shrine was intended to help boost the city's morale and economy – both of which were at a low ebb after Tokyo was made capital in 1868. With its vermilion pillars and green tiles, the shrine harks back to Tang Dynasty China. Its pond garden is famous for irises and a Chinese-style covered bridge.

The **National Museum of Modern Art** houses a superb collection of paintings by a school of Kyoto artists active during the Meiji and Taisho eras. Across the street is the venerable **Kyoto Municipal Museum of Art**, which hosts exhibitions of European and American works. The **Kyoto International Exhibition Hall (Miyako Messe)**, hosts a variety of shows, while its basement museum presents scores of Kyoto crafts, including Kiyomizu-*yaki* porcelain.

National Museum of Modern Art

A 26-1 Okazaki Enshoji-cho, Sakyo-ku **C** (075) 761-4111 **O** 9:30am–5pm Tue–Thu & Sun; 9:30am–8pm Fri & Sat (to 9pm Jul–Oct)

Kyoto Municipal Museum of Art

A 124 Okazaki Enshoji-cho, Sakyo-ku **C** (075) 771-4107 **O** 9am–5pm Tue–Sun

International Exhibition Hall (Miyako Messe)

A 9-1 Okazaki Enshoji-cho, Sakyo-ku **C** (075) 762-2630 **O** 7am–10:30pm daily

↑ Admiring works in the National Museum of Modern Art

The beautiful gardens of Shoren-in Temple as seen from the teahouse ↑

THE TEA CEREMONY

The point of the *chaji* (ritual), in which a light meal and whisked powdered *matcha* (tea) are served by a host to a few invited guests, is summed up by the samurai notion "one lifetime, one meeting" *(ichigo, ichie)*. In other words, this is a moment to be treasured.

TAKING THE TEA

Valued for its medicinal qualities, tea was imported from China in the 8th century. The nobility took to drinking it at lavish parties, and Murata Shuko (1422–1502) later developed the custom's spiritual aspects, which appealed to the samurai.

 Preparing the ancient tea utensils for a *chaji* ceremony

The tea ceremony is a well-orchestrated series of events. First, you meet your fellow guests, before walking through the grounds of the teahouse, performing ablutions en route. Once you are inside the cell-like room, you should compliment the features of the room, and the quality of the utensils, as you watch the tea being prepared. Only after bowing, can you consume the *wagashi* (sweet) and tea.

In Kyoto, where the tea ceremony was developed, special rituals are put on for tourists, with commentary about the complex etiquette and Zen ideals.

↑ A host presenting a decorated bowl of matcha to one of their guests

> **INSIDER TIP**
> **The Perfect Matcha**
>
> To drink matcha, sit *seiza* (kneeling) on the tatami mat, bow to your host when offered a steaming bowl, then hold the tea with your right hand, and place it in the palm of your left. Turn the bowl clockwise about 90 degrees, raise it with both hands, and then empty the *matcha* in three gulps.

↑ Buddha statue in the Butsuden Hall of Daitoku-ji Temple

 19

Daitoku-ji
大徳寺

🚩B2 🏠53 Murasakino Daitoku-ji-cho, Kita-ku 📞(075) 491-0019 🚇Kita-Oji Stn, Karasuma line 🚌1, 12, 102, 204, 205, 206 to Daitoku-ji-mae 🕐9am–4:30pm daily

An air of eloquent restraint pervades the grounds of Daitoku-ji. Founded in 1325, the temple prospered in the latter half of the 16th century, when it came under the patronage of warlords (and tea ceremony aficionados) Oda Nobunaga and Hideyoshi. Today, Daitoku-ji's subtemples, many with famous tearooms and jewel-like gardens promote the ways of Zen and Tea.

Daisen-in, a subtemple, is famous for its Muromachi-period garden, while Koto-in features a grove of slender maples and a *roji* (tea garden). Zuiho-in, built in 1535 for a Christian daimyo (feudal lord), has a modern garden by Shigemori Mirei, with a crucifix made out of rocks. Ryogen-in, founded in 1502, has five gardens in different styles.

 20

Kamo Shrines
上賀茂・下賀茂神社

🚩D2 🚌4, 46, 67 to Kamigamo-jinja-mae; 4, 205 to Shimogamo-jinja-mae

At the northern reaches of the Kamo River, **Kamigamo Shrine** has probably existed since the 7th century, while **Shimogamo**, its southern counterpart, is a century older. Both are dedicated to the thunder deity. Set in sylvan Tadasu no Mori, Shimogamo has long played a role in ensuring the success of the rice harvest. The Aoi Festival features a procession between the shrines, horse races, and archery. Kamigamo Shrine is noted for its Haiden hall, rebuilt in 1628. In the vicinity are several *shake*, priests' residences. Of these, **Nishimura House** is open to the public.

DAISEN-IN GARDEN AT DAITOKU-JI

Mankind's relationship with nature, fate, and our place in the universe are all expressed in this masterpiece of dry-landscape design. For example, the "river of life" reemerges wider and deeper after being temporarily dammed, and the Takarabune ("treasure ship") stone glides serenely down, while the "turtle" stone tries vainly to swim upstream.

Kamigamo Shrine
🏠339 Kamigamo-Motoyama, Kita-ku 📞(075) 781-0011 🕐5:30am–5pm daily

Shimogamo Shrine
🏠59 Shimogamo Izumigawa-cho, Sakyo-ku 📞(075) 781-0010 🕐6:30am–5pm daily

Nishimura House
🏠1 Kamigamo Nakaojicho, Kita-ku 📞(075) 781-0666 🕐Mar 15–Dec 8: 9:30am–4:30pm daily

 21

Kitano Tenman-gu Shrine
北野天満宮

🚩B3 🏠931 Bakuro-cho, Kita-ku 🚌10, 50, 51, 55, 101, 102, 203 to Kitano Tenman-gu-mae 🕐Feb–Sep: 5am–6pm daily; Oct–Mar: 5:30am–5:30pm 🌐kitanotenmangu.or.jp

Always thronged with students praying for success in exams, Kitano Tenman-gu enshrines

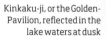
→ Kinkaku-ji, or the Golden-Pavilion, reflected in the lake waters at dusk

Heian statesman Sugawara no Michizane, or Tenjin-san, the deity of learning. Michizane's favorite tree, the plum (ume), is found throughout the grounds. On the 25th of each month, the shrine is the site of a bustling flea market, selling everything from Imari porcelains to nylon stockings.

Kamishichi-ken, an ochaya (teahouse) and bar-lined street running from Kitano Tenman-gu to Imadegawa-dori, is Kyoto's smallest, but oldest geiko (geisha) district. On February 25 the geiko conduct a tea ceremony in the shrine's orchard, and perform dances for the public every spring and fall at the local theater.

Kinkaku-ji (Golden Pavilion)
金閣寺

◊ B2 ⌂ 1 Kinkakujicho, Kita-ku ℂ (075) 461-0013 🚌 12 or 59 to Kinkaku-ji-mae; 101, 102, 204, 205 to Kinkaku-ji-michi ◷ 9am–5pm daily

A glimmering legacy of medieval Japan, Kinkaku-ji (formal name Rokuon-ji) is known as the Golden Pavilion. It was built by the third Ashikaga shogun, Yoshimitsu (1358–1408), who, relinquishing his official duties (but not his hold on power), entered the priesthood at the age of 37. The temple originally served as his retirement villa. A fervent follower of the Zen priest Soseki, Yoshimitsu directed that the finished complex become a temple after his death, with Soseki as its superior.

The approach to the temple is along a tree-shaded path, which emerges into a bright garden facing the fabled pavilion. An exact replica of the original, which was destroyed by arson in 1950 (an event dramatized in Yukio Mishima's novel *The Temple of the Golden Pavilion*), the three-story structure is covered in gold leaf and topped by a bronze phoenix.

Mount Kinugasa serves as a backdrop to the stroll-type garden. The harmonious inter-play of its various components makes it a superb example of Muromachi-period land-scaping. Both pavilion and garden are especially exquisite after a snowfall.

📷 PICTURE PERFECT
Going for Gold

Arrive at the Golden Pavilion as soon as it opens and head straight to the pond to get a shot of its golden silhouette reflected in the water. Use the surrounding maple trees to frame your shot.

23

Ninna-ji
仁和寺

A3 33 Omuro Ouchi, Ukyo-ku (075) 461-1155 Omuro-Nina-ji Stn, Keifuku Kitano line 10, 26, 59 to Omuro Nina-ji 9am–5pm daily (to 4:30pm Dec–Feb)

Ninna-ji's colossal front gate serves as a reminder that this Shingon-sect temple used to be, until fires devastated it, a huge complex numbering up to 60 subtemples.

Completed by Emperor Uda in 888, until the Meiji Restoration (1868) Ninna-ji was always headed by an imperial prince. The Kondo (main hall) and its wooden Amida image are National Treasures. Other sights include a five-story pagoda and a stand of dwarf cherry trees – the last of Kyoto's many sakura (cherry trees) to bloom.

Situated in the southwest of the precincts is the Omuro Gosho, a compound with a lovely Edo-period garden. On the mountain behind is the Omuro 88-Temple Pilgrimage, which reproduces in miniature the temples on Shikoku's 88-Temple Pilgrimage (p258). It takes about 2 hours to complete the full circuit.

↑ Visitors contemplating the rock garden and cherry trees in bloom at Ryoan-ji

24

Ryoan-ji
龍安寺

A2 13 Ryoan-ji Goryonoshitacho (075) 463-2216 Ryoan-ji Stn, Keifuku Kitano line (10-min walk) 59 to Ryoan-ji-mae Mar–Nov: 8am–5pm daily; Dec–Feb: 8:30am–4:30pm daily

Founded in 1450, Ryoan-ji is famous for its rock garden, a composition of white gravel and stones thought to be the ultimate expression of Zen Buddhism. Its riddles can be unraveled only by silent contemplation, something that the hordes of high-school students, not to mention the temple's recorded explanations, do little to facilitate. To avoid both, try to arrive just as the gates open.

The temple's lower pond garden should not be overlooked. Created before Zen arrived in Japan in the 12th century, its soft contours are in contrast to the spiritual rigors of the rock garden.

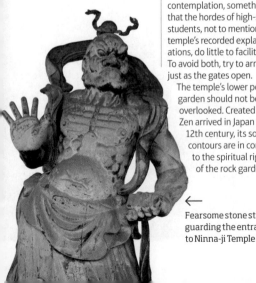

←

Fearsome stone statue guarding the entrance to Ninna-ji Temple

25

Myoshin-ji
妙心寺

A3 64 Hanazono Myoshijicho, Ukyo-ku (075) 463-3121 Myoshin-ji Stn, Keifuku Kitano line; Hanazono Stn, JR Sagano line 10, 26 to Myoshin-ji Kitamon-mae 9:10am–4:40pm daily (to 3:40pm Nov–Feb)

Founded at the behest of retired Emperor Hanazono in 1337, destroyed during the Onin War, and rebuilt on a grand scale, this Rinzai-sect Zen temple complex boasts some 47 subtemples rich in Kano School paintings and other art objects. The main structures, aligned in a row in typically Zen fashion, include the Hatto (lecture hall), famous for a huge dragon painted by Kano Tanyu on its ceiling, and its bell, the oldest in Japan.

Subtemples normally open to the public include Keishun-in, with its four gardens and famous tea arbor, and Taizo-in, which has both a dry garden by Kano Motonobu (1476–1559) and a modern one by Nakane Kinsaku (1917–95). Taizo-in's prize possession is a famous example of Zen ink painting, Josetsu's *Catching a Catfish with a Gourd* (1413).

Daishin-in has three gardens. Subtemples Reiun-in, which houses many Kano Motonobu works, and Tenkyu-in, noted for paintings by Kano Sanraku, are open on special days.

26

Koryu-ji
広隆寺

📍 A3 🏠 32 Uzumasa Hachiokacho, Ukyo-ku
📞 (075) 861-1461
🚉 Uzumasa-Koryuji stn, Keifuku Arashiyama line
🚌 11, 63, 66, 72, 73, 76 to Uzumasa Koryu-ji mae
🕐 9am–5pm daily (to 4:30pm Dec–Feb)

Koryu-ji was founded in 603 by Korean immigrants. Among the impressive images in its Reihoden (treasure hall), is a Miroku Bosatsu (Buddha of the future) believed to have been brought to Japan from Korea in the 7th century. Kyoto's oldest image, the seated figure is known throughout the nation for its beatific smile. The temple's oldest structure, the Kodo, houses a 9th-century statue of the Amida Buddha.

27

Insho Domoto Museum
堂本印象美術館

📍 B2 🏠 26-3 Kamiyanagi-cho, Hirano Kita-ku 📞 (075) 463-0007 🚌 12, 15, 50, 51, 52, 55, 59, 202, 205 to Ritsumeikan University-mae 🕐 9:30am–5pm Tue–Sun 🔒 Dec 28–Jan 4

Along the road skirting the base of Mount Kinugasa lies the Insho Domoto Museum. It houses the impressive works of 20th-century *nihonga* master, Insho Domoto (1891–1975). Often translated as "Japanese-style painting," *nihonga* is a fresco-like painting technique that utilizes mineral pigments.

SHOP

Kasagen

Located in the atmospheric Gion District, Kasagen is the oldest umbrella maker in Japan. This tiny traditional shop sells beautiful *wagasa* umbrellas favored by *maiko* (apprentice geisha). Completely handmade, each umbrella is a work of art. The handle and scaffold are made from bamboo from Kameoka, a city to the west of Kyoto, while the umbrella skin is made from Gifu's Meinong paper, which is brushed with sesame oil and tied with fine strings.

📍 D4 🏠 284 Giommachi Kitagawa, Higashiyama-ku
🕐 10am–7pm daily
🌐 gion.or.jp

↑ Works by the artist Insho Domoto in the Kyoto museum dedicated to him

28

Sagano District
嵯峨野地区

📍A1 🚉JR Saga-Arashiyama Stn, Sagano line 🚌28 or 91 to Daikaku-ji

Sagano's varied sights are by turn pastoral and poignant. Start exploring at Torii Moto, where a vermilion shrine gateway (torii) marks the beginning of a trail leading up to Mount Atago, abode of the fire divinity. Two thatched teahouses near the torii have been offering refreshment to pilgrims for centuries.

From the torii, head south to Adashino Nenbutsu-ji. From the Heian to Edo periods, Adashino was a remote place where corpses were often disposed of. Established to offer solace for the souls of these forgotten dead, the temple gathered together their grave markers – rocks on which a likeness of the Buddha had been carved. The sight of row after row of these stone figures is strangely moving.

To the south is Gio-ji, a tiny thatched nunnery. Known for the beauty of its fall foliage, the temple is bounded on one side by a magnificent stand of bamboo, while, to the front, slender maples rise from an emerald carpet of moss.

In central Sagano, Jodo-sect temple Seiryo-ji houses an image of the Shakamuni Buddha reportedly brought

The pond in the garden of Tenryu-ji, Arashiyama District ↑

to Japan in 987. Nison-in has standing images of Amida and Shakamuni. The many maple trees on the temple's grounds attract large numbers of visitors in the fall. Charming Rakushi-sha (hut of the fallen persimmons) was the humble home of haiku poet Mukai Kyorai (1651–1704).

Secluded Nichiren-sect temple Jojakko-ji is on Ogura-yama mountain. A steep flight of stone steps leads to the temple from where there are great views of Kyoto and Mount Hiei.

29

Shisen-do Temple
詩仙堂

📍E2 📍27 Monguchi-cho, Ichijo-ji, Sakyo-ku 📞(075) 781-2954 🚌5 or 8 to Ichijo-ji Sagarimatsu-cho 🕘9am-5pm daily

A samurai who had fallen out of favor with the shogunate, Ishikawa Jozan constructed this retirement villa below the Higashiyama mountains in 1641. A nearly perfect blend of building and garden, the hermitage (now a Soto-sect

Zen temple) retains the feel of a home. The garden is divided into two levels. The upper, best viewed from the main building's veranda, features a broad expanse of packed sand bordered by clipped azalea bushes. The lower level, which also makes use of areas of sand to add light and space, offers a fine view of the villa's tile-and-thatch roof and moon-viewing chamber.

30

Arashiyama District
嵐山地区

📍A1 🚉Arashiyama Stn, Hankyu line; Hankyu Arashiyama Stn 🚌11, 28 or 93 to Arashiyama Tenryu-ji-mae

Arashiyama has long held a special place in the hearts of the Japanese. At its center

 GREAT VIEW
Bamboo Grove

Behind Tenryu-ji is the fairy-tale-like Arashiyama Bamboo Grove, with its towering stalks. Visit during the Arashiyama Hanatoro in December, when the forest is bathed in an otherworldly green light every evening.

←

Standing among the tall bamboo trees of Adashino Nenbutsu-ji, Sagano District

is timeless Togetsu-kyo, the graceful "moon-crossing" bridge. North of the bridge, mountainsides thickly forested with cherries and pines drop steeply to the river, which in summer becomes the stage for *ukai*, fishing done by firelight with trained cormorants. The narrow-gauge Torokko Train provides a different way of viewing the scenery.

Rinzai-sect temple Tenryu-ji was founded by the first Ashikaga shogun, Takauji, in 1339. The serene garden features a pond in the shape of the Chinese character *kokoro*, or "enlightened heart."

Katsura Imperial Villa
桂離宮

📍**A5** 🚃**Katsura-Misono** 📞**(075) 211-1215** 🚉**Katsura Stn, Hankyu line** 🚌**33 to Katsura Rikyu-mae** ⏰**By appt only Tue–Sun; apply at Imperial Household Agency, (075) 211-1215**

Katsura Imperial Villa was built in 1620 by Hachijo no Miya Toshihito, an imperial prince, and later added to by his son. A sumptuous stroll garden *(p49)*, Katsura is famous for the way in which its paths and stepping stones control the visitor's line of

sight, resulting in a series of ingeniously planned vistas. The scenic view from the Shokin-tei (pine zither) tea arbor, replicates the scenery of Amanohashidate *(p238)*. Many of the garden's scenic allusions are to places mentioned in the Chinese and Japanese classics. The tour includes the Shoka-tei (flower-viewing teahouse), then past the Shoi-ken (sense-of-humor teahouse), and on to the main villa, a set of halls poetically described as resembling a flock of geese in flight.

Takao District
高雄地区

📍**A1** 🚌**Takao bus or 8 to Takao**

Esoteric mountain temples and pristine mountain scenery are Takao's main attractions. Jingo-ji, founded in the 9th century, houses a wealth of national treasures including the Yakushi Nyorai (Buddha of healing). Set in an ancient cryptomeria forest, Kozan-ji, founded in 774, has the look of an elegant estate.

Copies of the handscroll *Choju-Jinbutsu-giga* (frolicking birds and animals) are displayed in the Sekisui-in, a brilliant example of Kamakura residential architecture.

TOP 4 QUIRKY KYOTO MUSEUMS

Kyoto International Manga Museum
Home to about 300,000 manga and comic books *(www.kyotomm.jp)*.

Gekkeikan Okura Sake Museum
This museum explores the history of sake brewing in Japan *(www.gekkeikan.co.jp)*.

Nishijin Textile Center
Focuses on the history of fabrics in the city. You can also try on kimonos *(www.nishijin.or.jp)*.

Costume Museum
The place to see life-sized dolls dressed in beautiful traditional Japanese costumes *(www.iz2.or.jp)*.

Kurama District
鞍馬地区

📍**B1** 🚉**Kurama Stn, Eizan line** 🚌**32 from Demachiyanagi Stn**

Famous as the abode of gods, demons, and superheroes, Kurama was once an isolated village of foresters. Now a Kyoto suburb, it still retains an untamed feeling, a quality fully in evidence on the night of October 22, when the town celebrates its Fire Festival.

Kurama-dera, a Buddhist temple, was built in 770 to provide refuge for meditation. A gate marks the beginning of a mountain trail to the main temple buildings; the main hall offers splendid views of the Kitayama mountains. From the Reihokan (treasure hall) a path winds beneath towering cryptomeria trees to the village of Kibune, a collection of inns and tea-houses alongside a stream.

34

Manshu-in Temple
曼殊院

Q E2 **A** 42 Takenouchi-cho, Ichijo-ji, Sakyo-ku **C** (075) 781-5010 **🚌** 5, 8, 31 to Ichijoji-Shimizu-cho **◷** 9am–5pm daily

Even in spring and fall when its cherries and maples draw the crowds, Manshu-in maintains an atmosphere of repose. This Tendai-sect temple was restored in 1656 by the son of the prince who designed Katsura Imperial Villa *(p203)*, and its elegant buildings call to mind those of the villa. The garden is composed of islands of rock and vegetation amid swaths of raked gravel, with the Higashiyama mountains forming a backdrop.

35

Daigo-ji
醍醐寺

Q B2 **A** 22 Higashioji-cho, Daigo, Fushimi-ku **S** Daigo Stn, Tozai line

The main draw at Daigo-ji is subtemple **Sanpo-in**. Because Toyotomi Hideyoshi took a personal interest in restoring this after a visit in 1598, it contains some of the most representative works of art of the Momoyama period.

Did You Know?

Emperor Go-Mizunoo had 27 healthy children by six different women.

The lavish garden is noted for its many magnificent rocks, which were gifts to Hideyoshi from his daimyo (feudal lords).

The rest of Daigo-ji is older and the graceful five-story pagoda, built in 951, is one of only two Heian-era pagodas in existence.

Sanpo-in
C (075) 571-0002 **◷** 9am–4:30pm daily (to 5pm Mar–Dec)

36

Shugaku-in Imperial Villa
修学院離宮

Q E1 **A** Yabuzoe, Shugaku-in **R** Shugaku-in Stn, Eizan line **🚌** 5, 31, 65 to Shugaku-in Michi **◷** By appt only Tue–Sun; apply at Imperial Household Agency, (075) 211-1215

If Katsura Villa *(p203)* could be said to be yin, then Shugaku-in could only be described as yang. While the former's garden, layered with literary and poetic allusions, is characterized by an inward-looking sensibility, spacious Shugaku-in might strike the viewer as extroverted.

Created by retired emperor Go-Mizunoo (1596–1680), the garden was a lifetime labor of love. Divided into three levels, each with a teahouse, the complex is imbued with a spirit of understated simplicity. Yet, a surprise awaits: the approach to the uppermost teahouse is designed so that the visitor is kept unaware until the very last minute of the panorama from the top of the Kitayama mountains, spread out as if an extension of the garden.

37

Hieizan Enryaku-ji
比叡山延暦寺

Q B1 **A** 4220 Sakamoto Honmachi, Otsu, Shiga Prefecture **C** (077) 578-0001 **R** Yase-Hieizan-guchi Stn, Eizan line, then cable car; or Hieizan Sakamoto Stn, Kosei line, then cable car **🚌** Enryaku-ji bus from Kyoto, Keihan Sanjo or Keihan Demachiyanagi Stns

A once mighty monastery fortress with 3,000 subtemples

> 💬 **INSIDER TIP**
> **Blossom Hunting**
>
> To have the cherry blooms to yourself during sakura season, try to get out and about before 8am, to beat the crowds, or after 6pm, when the tour buses leave the city.

← Autumnal maple trees framing a graceful pagoda at Daigo-ji

Lush gardens with fish-filled ponds *(inset)*, the serene setting for the Jakko-in nunnery, Ohara

and thousands of *sohei*, or warrior monks, Hieizan today is but a shadow of its former self. Still, the solemnity of its isolated mountaintop setting and the grandeur of its remaining buildings make the trek here worthwhile.

Founded by the monk Saicho in 792, Hieizan became the main monastery of the Tendai sect. Although initially entrusted to protect the city from evil forces, the area itself became the bane of the capital. Emperor Go-Shirakawa (1127–92) once lamented that there were only three things beyond his control: the flooding of the Kamo River, the roll of the dice, and the warrior monks of Hieizan. In 1571, however, warlord Oda Nobunaga, angered by the temple's resistance to his authority, sent his army to attack the mountain. The complex was burned to the ground, and every man, woman, and child massacred.

The temple is divided into three precincts, connected by shuttle bus. The Kokuho-den, a museum of treasures, is in the **east precinct** (Todo). Here, too, is the famous Konpon Chu-do, the inner sanctum, which enshrines a Healing Buddha image said to have been carved by Saicho himself. Nearby Jodo-in (Pure Land Hall) is the site of Saicho's tomb.

In the Jogyo-do hall in the **west precinct** (Saito) monks chant an invocation called the *nembutsu*, while in the Hokke-do hall they meditate upon the Lotus Sutra, a central tenet of Tendai belief. Beyond these two buildings is the Shaka-do, the main hall of the west precinct.

Shuttle buses operate between these precincts, as well as to the lesser-known Yokawa precinct to the north.

East Precinct

⏰ Mar–Nov: 8:30am–4:30pm daily; Dec: 9am–4pm daily; Jan & Feb: 9am–4:30pm daily

West Precinct

⏰ Mar–Nov: 9am–4pm daily; Dec: 9:30am–3:30pm daily; Jan & Feb: 9:30am–4pm daily

38

Ohara District
大原地区

📍 B1 🚌 17 from Kyoto Stn

Known for its thatched farmhouses, delicious pickles, and other rustic charms, Ohara is also home to two famous temples. Set in an incomparably beautiful setting, Sanzen-in's Amida Hall dates from 1148 and houses a meditating Amida Buddha. Its approach is lined with shops selling such local products as *shiba-zuke*, a pickle dyed purple with the leaf of the beefsteak plant. Across the valley is tiny Jakko-in, a nunnery where Kenreimon-in (1155–1213) lived. The sole survivor of the Taira clan, she prayed here for the souls of her son and kin killed by the Genji.

A SHORT WALK
EASTERN GION AND THE HIGASHIYAMA

Distance 1 mile (1.6 km) **Time** 20 minutes
Nearest station Gion-Shijo

For most of Kyoto's history, the area comprising the Higashiyama (Eastern Mountains) district lay outside capital's official boundaries. As a result, it was always more secluded. Furthermore, being separated from the main city by the Kamo River, it was spared the fires that often ravaged Kyoto. Consequently, Higashiyama remains one of the city's most charming and unspoiled districts, making it a lovely place for a walk.

The pleasant **Ishibe-Koji Lane**, *with its discreet inns and teahouses, is an extension of the Gion entertainment district (p192). The exquisite wooden buildings with tiny gardens reflect the peaceful atmosphere of old Kyoto.*

The elegant, five-story **Yasaka Pagoda** *is all that remains of a Buddhist temple that once stood here.*

The **Yasaka Shrine** *(p192) oversees the religious rites of the city's main festival, the Gion Matsuri, in July.*

KACHO-MICH

HIGASHIOJI-DORI

GIONMACHI KITAGAWA

Yasaka Shrine

START

GIONMACHI MINAMIGAWA

NE-NE-NO MICHI

ISHIBE-KOJI LANE

HIGASHIOJI-DORI

Yasaka Pagoda

HOSHINOCHO

MATSUBARA DORI

GOJO-ZAKA

SHIMIZU NEW WAY

← The iconic levels of Yasaka Pagoda rising above the rustic streetscape of Higashiyama

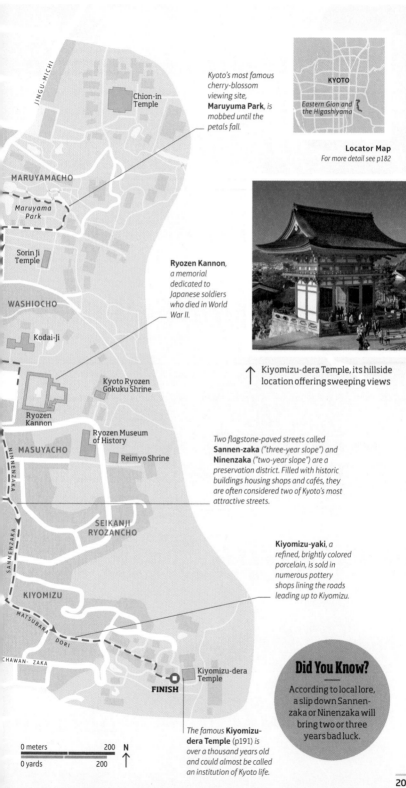

Kyoto's most famous cherry-blossom viewing site, **Maruyama Park**, is mobbed until the petals fall.

Chion-in Temple

JINGU-MICHI

MARUYAMACHO

Maruyama Park

Sorin Ji Temple

WASHIOCHO

Kodai-Ji

Ryozen Kannon, a memorial dedicated to Japanese soldiers who died in World War II.

Kyoto Ryozen Gokuku Shrine

Ryozen Kannon

Ryozen Museum of History

Reimyo Shrine

MASUYACHO

NINENZAKA

SANNENZAKA

SEIKANJI RYOZANCHO

KIYOMIZU

MATSUBARA DORI

CHAWAN-ZAKA

FINISH

Kiyomizu-dera Temple

↑ Kiyomizu-dera Temple, its hillside location offering sweeping views

Two flagstone-paved streets called **Sannen-zaka** ("three-year slope") and **Ninenzaka** ("two-year slope") are a preservation district. Filled with historic buildings housing shops and cafés, they are often considered two of Kyoto's most attractive streets.

Kiyomizu-yaki, a refined, brightly colored porcelain, is sold in numerous pottery shops lining the roads leading up to Kiyomizu.

Did You Know?

According to local lore, a slip down Sannen-zaka or Ninenzaka will bring two or three years bad luck.

The famous **Kiyomizu-dera Temple** (p191) is over a thousand years old and could almost be called an institution of Kyoto life.

0 meters 200 N

0 yards 200

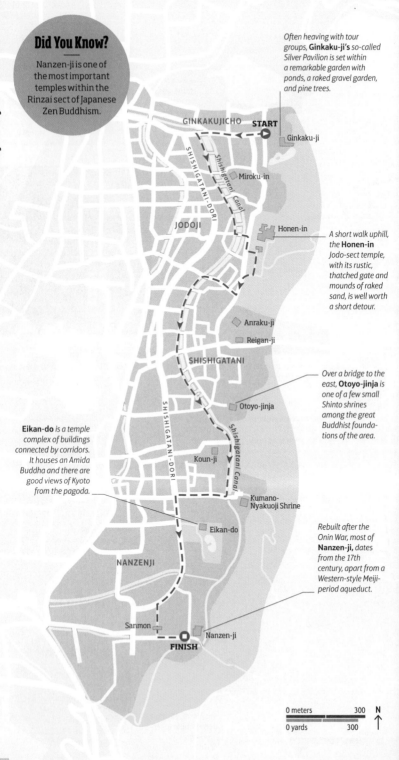

Did You Know?

Nanzen-ji is one of the most important temples within the Rinzai sect of Japanese Zen Buddhism.

Often heaving with tour groups, **Ginkaku-ji's** *so-called Silver Pavilion is set within a remarkable garden with ponds, a raked gravel garden, and pine trees.*

GINKAKUJICHO **START**

Ginkaku-ji

Miroku-in

SHISHIGATANI-DORI

Shishigatani Canal

JODOJI

Honen-in

A short walk uphill, the **Honen-in** *Jodo-sect temple, with its rustic, thatched gate and mounds of raked sand, is well worth a short detour.*

Anraku-ji

Reigan-ji

SHISHIGATANI

Over a bridge to the east, **Otoyo-jinja** *is one of a few small Shinto shrines among the great Buddhist foundations of the area.*

Otoyo-jinja

SHISHIGATANI-DORI

Shishigatani Canal

Eikan-do *is a temple complex of buildings connected by corridors. It houses an Amida Buddha and there are good views of Kyoto from the pagoda.*

Koun-ji

Kumano-Nyakuoji Shrine

Eikan-do

Rebuilt after the Onin War, most of **Nanzen-ji,** *dates from the 17th century, apart from a Western-style Meiji-period aqueduct.*

NANZENJI

Sanmon

Nanzen-ji

FINISH

0 meters 300

0 yards 300

N

A SHORT WALK
THE PHILOSOPHER'S WALK

KYOTO

The Philosopher's Walk

Locator Map
For more detail see p182

Distance 1.2 miles (2 km) **Time** 25 minutes
Nearest station Mototanaka

One of Kyoto's best-loved spots, the Philosopher's Walk follows a cherry-tree-lined canal meandering along the base of the scenic Higashiyama (Eastern Mountains) between Ginkaku-ji south to Kumano-Nyakuoji Shrine, and connects with roads leading to the precincts of Nanzen-ji. The pedestrian path is so-named because a Kyoto University philosophy professor, Nishida Kitaro (1870–1945), used it for his daily constitutional. A range of relaxed cafés, art and craft shops, restaurants, and boutiques are scattered along the scenic route. The path becomes a veritable promenade during the cherry and maple seasons, as couples from all over the Kansai region flock to enjoy its unspoiled nature blossoming before their eyes.

> INSIDER TIP
> **A Tranquil Path**
>
> For perfect harmony of peace and natural beauty, try an early morning walk among the petals. You'll find it easier to imagine Kitaro meditating along the canal without the crowds.

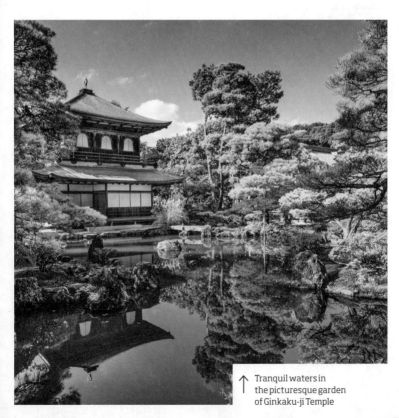

↑ Tranquil waters in the picturesque garden of Ginkaku-ji Temple

WESTERN HONSHU

The cultural heartland of the country, Western Honshu is where Japan's first imperial courts held sway, in an area called Yamato. The name Yamato refers to where heaven and earth divide, and also to the land founded by the mythical son of the gods, emperor Jimmu. In the Japanese mind, Yamato is a holy place, a homeland, as the legendary emperor Keiko expressed it in verse form almost two millennia ago, "whose trees and rocks, streams, and mountains house the gods."

Legend solidified into fact in the 4th century AD when a clan called Yamato expanded its kingdom in the region. Japan's first emperors, the Yamato rulers set up court on the Yamato Plain, the site of present-day Nara Prefecture, home to the graceful ancient city of Nara, with its quiet stroll gardens, the smell of lingering incense, and the reflections of winged pagodas in green ponds.

Despite this mystical history, this is not just a land of antiquity. Hiroshima, reborn after the devastating 1945 atomic bomb, the international port of Kobe, and Osaka are Western Honshu's great metropolitan centers.

WESTERN HONSHU

Must Sees

1. Nara
2. Osaka
3. Kobe
4. Himeji-jo
5. Hiroshima Peace Memorial Park
6. Miyajima Island
7. Horyu-ji

Experience More

8. Asuka Plain
9. Koka Ninja Village
10. Yoshino
11. Mount Koya
12. Kii Peninsula
13. Iga-Ueno
14. Okayama
15. Inbe
16. Kurashiki
17. Tottori Sand Dunes
18. Fukiya
19. Amanohashidate Sandbar
20. Lake Biwa
21. Uji City
22. Matsue
23. Yamaguchi
24. Akiyoshi-dai Tablelands
25. Izumo
26. Iwakuni
27. Hagi
28. Tsuwano

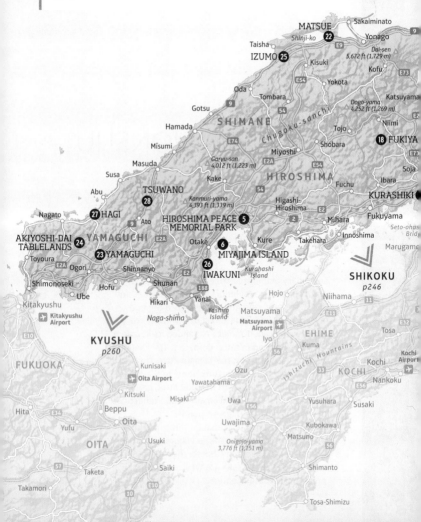

↑ Children playing by a pond in the expansive Nara Park

NARA

奈良

🅐 D5 🅐 Nara Prefecture 🚃 JR line from Kyoto, Kintetsu line from Kyoto ℹ️ At Kintetsu Nara Stn; www.visitnara.jp

Founded in 710, Nara, then known as Heijo-kyo (citadel of peace), became one of Asia's most splendid cities. Avidly absorbing ideas from the mainland, the city became the grand diocese of Buddhism and the Far Eastern destination of the Silk Road. Having retained its natural beauty, Nara remains a symbol of tranquility.

① Nara Park

This 1,300-acre (502 ha) park is the cultural heart of the city, and it's where most of Nara's temples are located. Over 1,200 tame deer, regarded as messengers of the gods, roam the park.

② Kofuku-ji

🅐 48 Noboriojicho 📞 (0742) 22-7755 🕐 9am–5pm daily

Few of the 175 buildings in this temple's original 669 complex remain. But even the reconstructions can lay claim to antiquity – the current five-story pagoda, burned to the ground five times, dates from 1426. The Treasure House has one of Japan's foremost collections of Buddhist art.

 PICTURE PERFECT
Oh Deer!

These hooved nomads have wandered Nara Park for centuries, nagging passersby for food. Grab your camera and stroll through the park to snap a shot or two of these beautifully photogenic critters.

---

③ Nara National Museum

🅐 50 Noboriojicho 🕐 9:30am–5pm Tue–Sun 🌐 narahaku.go.jp

Most of the exhibits in the Nara National Museum's collection, including Buddhist sculptures, paintings, and calligraphy, date from the Nara and Heian periods. The museum holds an annual exhibition in October and early November of treasures from the Shoso-in Treasure Repository, a storehouse in the Todai-ji complex (p216) that was built to preserve Emperor Shomu's private collection of precious objects from all along the Silk Road.

---

④ Isui-en Garden

🅐 74 Suimoncho 🕐 9:30am–4:30pm Wed–Mon (daily in Apr, May, Oct & Nov) 🌐 isuien.or.jp/en

This Meiji-era garden, with its many teahouses, is popular in spring for its plum, cherry, and azalea blooms, and in autumn for red maples.

⑤ Kasuga Taisha Shrine

🏠 160 Kasuganocho
☎ (0742) 22-7788 ⏰ Apr–
Sep: 6am–6pm daily; Oct–
Mar: 6:30am–5pm

Originally built as the tutelary
shrine of the Fujiwaras, who
helped to establish Nara,
Kasuga Taisha is one of the
best-known Shinto sites.
The original building was
completed in 768 but, due to
the strictures of purity and
renewal governing Shinto
beliefs, the structure has been
rebuilt every 20 years. The
temple's astounding number
of lanterns are lit during festivals in February and August.

⑥ Shin-Yakushi-ji

🏠 1352 Takabatakecho
☎ (0742) 22-3736 ⏰ 9am–
5pm daily

This temple was built by
Empress Komyo (701–60) as
an offering to the gods to help
her husband recover from an
eye disease. Some structures
were rebuilt in the 13th century,
but the main hall, the clay
figures of the Healing Buddha,
and the Twelve Heavenly
Generals are originals.

---

⑦ Toshodai-ji

🏠 13-46 Gojocho ⏰ 8:30am–
5pm daily 🌐 toshodaiji.jp

Founded in 759 by the blind
Chinese sage and priest Ganjin,
Toshodai-ji is home to a
stunning 18-ft- (5.5-m-)
high Senju Kannon statue.

⑧ Yakushi-ji

🏠 457 Nishinokyocho
⏰ 8:30am–5pm daily

Emperor Tenmu had this
temple built for his wife's
health, a gesture that seems
to have worked as she outlived
him. The temple's masterpiece
is its east pagoda. Built in 730,
it appears to have six levels,
but three are roofs placed
between the floors, creating
an appealing optical effect.

↑ The grand Golden Hall, the spectacular
main hall of Shin-Yakushi-ji Temple

⑨ ✍

TODAI-JI

東大寺

📍 406-1 Zoshicho 🚌 Daibutsuden Kasuga-Taisha-mae stop ⏰ Mar: 8am–5pm daily; Apr–Sep: 7:30am–5:30pm daily; Oct: 7:30am–5pm daily; Nov–Feb: 8am–4:30pm daily 🌐 todaiji.or.jp

The construction of Todai-ji was ordered by Emperor Shomu ostensibly to house Nara's Great Buddha image but also to consolidate the position of the city as the capital and a powerful center of Buddhism.

This temple is the headquarters of the Kegon school of Buddhism. A World Heritage Site, Todai-ji consists of the Great Buddha hall (Daibutsuden), and sub-temples, halls, pagodas, and gates of exceptional historical and architectural interest. The most impressive building is undoubtedly the Great Buddha Hall. It was rebuilt twice and the current structure, completed in 1709, is only two-thirds of the original size. Despite this fact, it is still reputedly the largest wooden building in the world. Natural disasters have also failed to diminish the scale of the seated figure inside. At 53-ft (16-m) high, it is the world's largest bronze image of the Buddha. Behind the Buddha is a small hole bored into a large wooden pillar. A popular belief holds that if you can squeeze through the hole you will be protected from bad things happening to you in the future.

Entrance

> **Natural disasters have also failed to diminish the scale of the seated figure inside. At 53-ft (16-m) high, it is the world's largest bronze image of the Buddha.**

The Great Buddha Hall with the towering statue inside, at Todai-ji ↑

Timeline

752
△ The construction of the temple is ordered by Emperor Shomu and the first incarnation of the Great Buddha is cast.

1692
△ After fires and earthquakes dislodged previous versions, the current head of the Great Buddha was cast and has remained in place ever since.

1709
△ The current Great Buddha Hall is constructed.

1994
△ International names, including Bob Dylan, Jon Bon Jovi, INXS, and Joni Mitchell, perform at the temple for four nights in May during the Great Music Experience.

Kokuzo Bosatsu, an Enlightened Being

Komokuten, a guardian

The hall has unusual bracketing and a beam-frame construction.

The striking roof, with its golden "horns," was an 18th-century addition.

Tamonten, a guardian

The legendary small hole in a large wooden pillar behind the Buddha

The casting of the Great Buddha in 752 used hundreds of tons of molten bronze, mercury, and vegetable wax.

Nyoirin Kannon Bosatsu, an Enlightened Being

Covered walkway in compound

↑ Walking towards the striking Great Buddha Hall at Todai-ji

> 💬 **INSIDER TIP**
> ## Spring Clean
>
> Time your visit with Todai-ji Ominugui. Literally translating as "Wiping Down the Great Buddha," this ceremony takes place on the morning of August 7. Up to 120 priests, wearing white robes and straw sandals, abseil down the Buddha's face, dusting as they go.

OSAKA

大阪

🅰 D5 🏠 Osaka Prefecture ✈ Kansai, 22 miles (35 km) S; Itami, 6 miles (10 km) N 🚆 Sanyo & Tokaido Shinkansen, JR, Hankyu, Keihan, Nankai, Hanshin, and Kintetsu lines 🅰 In JR Osaka Stn, Midosuji exit; www.osaka-info.jp

Toyotomi Hideyoshi encouraged traders from all over Japan to settle in Osaka in the 16th century, and by the early 1900s it was an industrial powerhouse. Nowadays, the nondescript skyline is being replaced with galleries, futuristic living spaces, and exciting Postmodernist architecture, while the city's nightlife and culinary predilections attract fans from far and wide.

①

Osaka Museum of History

🏠 4-1-32 Otemae 🚇 Tanimachi-Yon-Chome Stn, Chuo or Tanimachi lines ⏰ 9:30am–5pm Wed-Mon 🌐 mus-his.city.osaka.jp

This modern museum uses life-size reconstructions, miniature models, and video presentations to bring alive the history of Osaka from ancient times to the modern day. Its most notable exhibits are objects excavated from the 7th-century Naniwa Palace, which once stood on this site. On the 10th floor there is a model of the Daikokuden, the main building of the palace, and excavations in the base-ment and on the adjacent archaeological site reveal the remains of warehouses and palace walls.

Of special interest to young children is the Resource Center on the eighth floor. Here, kids can complete a jigsaw puzzle using ancient pottery pieces or play with Bunraku puppets.

②

Osaka Castle

🏠 1-1 Osakajo 🚇 Osakajo-koen Stn, JR Kanjo line 🚇 Tanimachi-Yonchome Stn, Chuo or Tanimachi lines ⏰ 9am–5pm daily 🌐 osakacastle.net/english

The present main donjon, dating from 1931, is smaller than the castle completed by Hideyoshi in 1586 but still gives some idea of the power and majesty of the original. The largest castle in the country at the time, Osaka-jo's turbulent history began when it was besieged and destroyed by the Tokugawa shogunate in 1615. The castle was rebuilt only to be struck by lightning a few years later, and then the remains were burned down in a fire in 1868. Some ancillary buildings, including the Tamon tower and the impressive Otemon Gate, have survived from the Tokugawa period.

The modernized lower floors of the main keep displays a collection of armor and memorabilia connected with Hideyoshi. Make sure you ride the elevator up to the eighth floor of the donjon – you'll be rewarded with great views over the city below.

↑ Beautiful Osaka Castle, framed by golden fall foliage

③

Museum of Oriental Ceramics

🏠 1-1-26 Nakanoshima
🚉 Naniwabashi Stn, Keihan Nakanoshima line 🅂 Yodo-yabashi Stn, Midosuji line
🕙 9:30am–5pm Tue–Sun (to 8pm Fri & Sat) 🌐 moco.or.jp

With over 1,000 items of mostly Chinese and Korean origin, this museum houses one of the world's finest collections of Oriental ceramics. The display comes from the Ataka Collection. Computer-regulated, light-sensitive rooms highlight the surfaces of the items. A few of the Japanese pieces are National Treasures.

④

National Museum of Art

🏠 4-2-55 Nakanoshima
🚉 Watanabebashi Stn, Keihan Nakanoshima line
🕙 10am–5pm Tue–Sun (to 7pm Fri) 🌐 nmao.go.jp

The entrance of the National Museum of Art, made from curved steel and extending high above the building itself, was designed to invoke both the strength and the flexibility of bamboo. The collection inside is equally awe-inspiring, with works by Western artists such as Picasso, Cézanne, Miró, and Warhol, as well as ancient Chinese treasures and modern Japanese art. Check out the museum's website for a list of upcoming exhibitions.

↑ The futuristic curved exterior of the National Museum of Art

Must See

> 💬 INSIDER TIP
> **Hot Ticket**
>
> The city center is served by a user-friendly loop system called the JR Kanjo line. Visitors who intend to cover a lot of sightseeing ground will benefit from buying a one-day pass that offers unlimited travel on subways, trams, and local train lines.

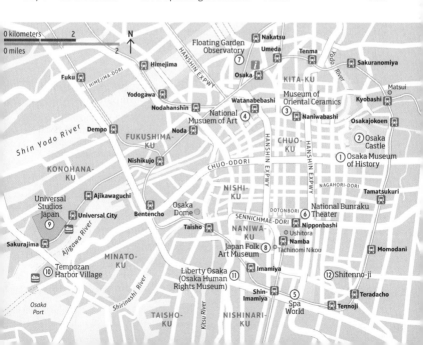

⑤
Spa World

🏠 3-4-24 Ebisuhigashi
🚉 Shin-imamiya Stn, JR
Kanjo and Nankai lines
Ⓢ Osakajo-koen Stn, JR
Kanjo Dobutsuenmae Stn,
Midosuji line ⏰ 10am-
8:45am daily 🌐 spaworld.
co.jp/english

Built to cater for up to 5,000
people at any time, Spa World
offers an amazing bathing
experience, with the water
coming from springs almost
3,000 ft (900 m) underground.
The complex is divided into
zones representing bathing
customs of various countries
around the world, including
China and Turkey.

⑥
National Bunraku Theater

🏠 1-12-10 Nippon-bashi
🚉 Nipponbashi Stn, Kintetsu
line Ⓢ Nipponbashi Stn,
Sennichi-mae & Sakaisuji
lines 🌐 ntj.jac.go.jp.co.jp

Japan's main venue for Bunraku
puppet dramas can be spotted
by the colorful banners hanging outside. Shows take place
every January, April, June, July,
August, and November, and
headsets are available for
foreign visitors.

⑦
Floating Garden Observatory

🏠 1-1-88 Oyodonaka 🚉 JR
Osaka Stn, JR Kanjo line
Ⓢ JR Osaka Stn, JR Kanjo
line ⏰ 9:30am-10:30pm
daily 🌐 kuchu-teien.com

This futuristic structure,
reached by taking an exposed
glass escalator to the 39th
floor, is not for those who
suffer from vertigo or fear of
being caught in high places in
earthquake-prone regions.
The observatory, 576 ft (173 m)

Walking toward the twin
towers housing the Floating
Garden Observatory ↑

above ground, straddles the
twin towers of Hara Hiroshi's
Umeda Sky Building. Views of
Osaka from the top are
incredible. High-tech displays
and a virtual-reality game
center also occupy the observatory, but neither can really
compete with the panoramas.

⑧
Japan Folk Art Museum

🏠 3-7-6 Nambanaka
📞 (06) 6641-6309
🚉 Namba Stn, Nankai and
Kintetsu lines Ⓢ Namba
Stn, Midosuji line Nihon-
teien-mae ⏰ Closed for
restoration work until 2020

An outstanding collection of
traditional folk arts and crafts
is housed in this museum. It
offers a superb introduction

to regional handicrafts
centering on textiles and
fabrics, ceramic ware, bamboo, toys, and more.

⑨
Universal Studios Japan

🏠 2-1-33 Sakurajima
🚉 Universal Studio City
Stn, JR Yumesaki line
⏰ Hours vary, check
website for details
🌐 usj.co.jp/e

This theme park aims to attract
people of all ages and is fast
becoming a major landmark
of Osaka. There are nine
themed areas, as well as live
entertainment throughout
the site. Among the attractions are the Hollywood
Premiere Parade, Hollywood
Magic, and, in the "New York"

area, a St. Patrick's Day Celebration. The Wizarding World of Harry Potter, meanwhile, features a state-of-the-art Harry Potter and the Forbidden Journey™ ride. The latest addition is Minion Park, inspired by *Despicable Me*.

⑩ Tempozan Harbor Village

🏠 1-1-0 Kaigandori
Ⓢ Osaka-ko stn, Chuo line
⏰ Daily

Begun as a reclamation program in the 1830s, this waterfront project in Osaka Port is the new face of an older, Edo-period landfill. The enormous Tempozan Ferris Wheel, once the world's tallest at 371 ft (113 m), offers passengers panoramic views of the entire city of Osaka, the ocean, and mountains. The ferris wheel can hold up to 480 passengers in its 60 cars. At night the illuminated wheel is a popular date venue for the locals.

As well as the mammoth Osaka Aquarium Kaiyukan, the village is also home to the Tempozan Marketplace – a large center for restaurants and shopping.

⑪ Liberty Osaka (Osaka Human Rights Museum)

🏠 3-6-36 Naniwanishi
📞 (06) 6561-5891
🚇 Ashiharabashi or Imamiya Stns, JR Kanjo line ⏰ 10am–4pm Wed-Fri, 1–5pm Sat 🚫 4th Fri of month

This museum provides a sobering insight into the dark side of Japan, examining subjects rarely discussed such as the Burakumin – a discriminated group descended from leather-workers, who disposed of the dead and did other "unclean" jobs. Environmental issues, and discrimination against ethnic minorities are also covered.

⑫ Shitenno-ji

🏠 1-11-18 Shitennoji
Ⓢ Shitenno-ji Stn, Tanimachi line 📞 (06) 6771-0066 ⏰ Daily

Prince Shotoku ordered the construction of the original temple here in 593, and the

complex is considered to be the birthplace of Japanese Buddhism. The temple was destroyed many times by fire and the current concrete buildings date from 1965. As exact copies of the originals, however, they are of interest to visitors wishing to know more about early Buddhist architecture. The best time to visit the temple is on the 21st of every month, when an excellent flea market is held on the site.

←

The vermilion Saidaimon (West Gate) at the entrance to Shitenno-ji

❸

KOBE
神戸

🅰D5 🏔Hyogo Prefecture ✈Kobe, 5 miles (8 km) SE; Kansai 43 miles (70 km) S 🚉JR Shin-Kobe Stn, Sanyo Shinkansen line; Sannomiya Stn, JR Tokkaido, Hankyu, & Hanshin lines 🛈In front of JR Sannomiya Stn; www.feel-kobe.jp

Kobe has been a center of international trade since the 8th century and is today home to a large expatriate community. The city hit the headlines in 1995 when a huge earthquake struck, but there is little evidence of the disaster now, so effectively has the city been rebuilt. The downtown area is famous for its nightlife, while Kobe beef is renowned around the world.

①
Chinatown

🏠5-min walk S of Motomachi Stn

The city's 14,000 or more Chinese residents have turned this quarter (Nankin-machi) into a lively and colorful slice of Kobe life. Approached via four large gateways, the central plaza, Nankin Park, is bordered by Chinese restaurants and trinket shops, and is filled with street vendors. The park has statues representing the 12 animals of the Chinese astrological calendar.

②
Kobe City Museum

🏠10-min walk S of Motomachi Stn ⏰Hours vary, check website 🌐city. kobe.lg.jp/culture/culture/institution/museum

This museum covers the history of the city from its origins to its reconstruction after the 1995 earthquake. There is an intriguing display of objects retrieved from the Old Foreign Settlement and a scale model of the area. The museum also has the world's top collection of 16th-century

Did You Know?

Kobe beef only comes from the black wagyu cows of Hyogo Prefecture.

Nanban art. The word Nanban ("southern barbarian") was at first applied to foreigners who arrived from the south, mainly the Portuguese. Later it was applied to all Europeans.

③
Kitano-cho

🏠12-min walk N of Sannomiya Stn

Wealthy foreign traders and diplomats built homes in this area after Kobe became one of Japan's major international ports at the start of the Meiji period. Over 20 of these beautifully preserved homes, many in the Gothic Victorian style, are open to the public. The area, which suggests fin de siècle European elegance to many Japanese people, is considered one of Kobe's more fashionable districts.

↑ Cosmopolitan Kobe's eye-catching skyline at sunset

THE GREAT HANSHIN EARTHQUAKE

At 5:46am on January 17, 1995, the Great Hanshin Earthquake struck Japan, its epi-center 10 miles (16 km) beneath the Akashi Strait near Kobe. The tremor lasted almost a minute and measured 6.9 on the Moment Magnitude scale. The quake and aftershocks killed over 6,000 inhab-itants and destroyed over 100,000 buildings.

④ Meriken Park

⌂ 10-min walk S of Motomachi Stn ⊙ Museum and Port Tower: daily

Meriken Park's name comes from the Meiji-era rendition of "American." From the park you will see the distinctive outline of the Kobe Maritime Museum, which has a roof designed like the sails of a ship and houses displays on the city's role as a port. For a good overview of the area climb the Kobe Port Tower on Naka Pier.

⑤ Kikumasamune Shuzo Kinenkan

⌂ 5-min walk N of Minami Uozaki Stn ⊙ 9:30am–4:30pm daily

Although most of the best breweries were razed during the earthquake, reconstruction and preservation of the few that were left has been going on at a furious pace, and it is possible once again to visit some of Kobe's best-known brand-name producers. The Kikumasamune Shuzo Kinenkan museum offers an insight into the art of making sake. Although the brewery's storehouses perished in the quake, the water-mill cottage survived and now houses a small but interesting display of brewing utensils.

DRINK

Hamafukutsuru Ginjo Brewery

At this brewery and shop, visitors can take a tour to watch the fermenting process and also try a selection of sakes in a tasting.

⌂ 5-min walk from Hanshin Uozaki Stn
☎ (078) 411-8339
⊙ 10am–5pm Tue–Sun

4

HIMEJI-JO
姫路城

D5 ⌂ Half a mile (1 km) N of Himeji Stn, Hyogo Prefecture ⬛ Himeji Stn, Shinkansen line ⏰ 9am–4pm daily (to 5pm May–Aug) 🌐 himeji-kanko.jp

Better known as Shirasagi-jo, the "white egret castle," Himeji-jo resembles a bird taking flight, with its plastered walls stretching either side of the main donjon. For many people its military architecture, ameliorated by these graceful aesthetic lines, qualifies Himeji-jo as the ultimate samurai castle.

The castle's main donjon was developed by Ikeda Terumasa in 1609, transforming a modest military stronghold into a symbol of the Tokugawa shogunate's newly consolidated power. With its undulating dormer and Chinese gables, the tower is undeniably beautiful, but it was also built to withstand attack. Angled chutes set at numerous points in the walls enabled stones, boiling oil, and water to be dropped on the heads of any invaders. On the roof, dolphin-like *shachi-gawara* motifs were thought to protect the donjon from fire, while the portholes, in the shape of circles, triangles, and rectangles, were used by musketeers and archers.

Originally an armaments store, the interior remains largely unadorned and houses exhibits relating to castle life. The Museum of Weaponry displays samurai arms and armor, as well as guns and pouches of gun powder, introduced to Japan by the Portuguese in the 16th century. The uppermost chamber offers panoramas on four sides over Himeji, but the main donjon's exterior is far more awe-inspiring than its stark interior.

↑ Admiring samurai armor in the Museum of Weaponry

↑ A *shachi-gawara* statue on the roof of the main donjon

> Better known as Shirasagi-jo, the "white egret castle," Himeji-jo resembles a bird taking flight, with its plastered walls stretching either side of the main donjon.

Timeline

1333
△ Norimura Akamatsu builds a fort in a strategic location on top of a hillock at Himeji.

1600
△ Battle of Sekigahara, after which Ikeda Terumasa is rewarded with Himeji-jo.

1609
△ The five-story donjon is completed.

1749
△ Sakai Tadasumi and descendants live in the castle until the Meiji Restoration of 1867.

Did You Know?

The main donjon appears to have five floors, but it actually has six.

The main donjon of Himeji-jo standing on a hill high above the city ↑

Exploring the Complex

Built on a high bluff, Himeji-jo, the grandest of Japan's 12 remaining feudal castles, dominates the city of Himeji, and is a designated UNESCO World Heritage Site. Its cinematic potential was exploited by Akira Kurosawa in his 1985 film *Ran*, a Japanese retelling of Shakespeare's *King Lear*. But the tranquil grounds and graceful buildings seem a world away from both the castle's feudal past and the modern city that it overlooks. The verdant complex is crowned by its famed donjon, but it is also blessed with undulating walls, moats, and baileys. Although these aspects were once defensive, they now serve as the perfect setting for taking a stroll, spotting cherry blossoms, or even practicing tai chi.

Vanity Tower – the abode of Princess Sen (1597–1667) and other women – was locked each night under guard.

West bailey (nishi-nomaru)

Entrance

Sangoku moat

Though never put to the test, the castle's labyrinth of passageways and gateways in the outer zones were designed to confuse enemies.

> **INSIDER TIP**
> ### Castle of Light
>
> Every May, during the Himeji Castle Festival, the main donjon is illuminated by a dazzling light show. Time your visit to the castle complex for the week after Golden Week – usually at the middle of the month – to view this nighttime extravaganza, where the old and new world seem to collide in a riot of color.

↑ Himeji-jo covered in blush-pink blooms during cherry-blossom season

↑ Practicing tai chi in a park in the city overlooked by Himeji-jo

Second bailey (ninomaru)

Main bailey (honmaru)

Main donjon

The waist quarter (koshi-kurawa), behind the main tower, is the weakest point of the stronghold.

Graceful fan-shaped stone walls were very difficult for enemies to scale.

Despite its name, the suicide quarter was probably used only for its water supply.

↑ The expansive complex of Himeji-jo, with its huge walls and moats

5

HIROSHIMA PEACE MEMORIAL PARK

広島平和記念公園

A B5 **A** Hiroshima Prefecture **B** Hiroshima Airport 25 miles (40 km) E
R Shinkansen line **G** Genbaku-Domu-mae **O** Peace Memorial Museum:
8:30am–6pm daily (to 5pm Dec–Feb; to 7pm Aug) **W** visithiroshima.net

For the worst of reasons, Hiroshima needs no introduction. Each year
millions of visitors are drawn to the city where so many people were
wiped out in one instance of apocalyptic destruction. Built in the 1950s,
this poignant park remembers this earth-shattering event.

The half-melted wreckage of the A-Bomb Dome – the former
Industrial Promotion Hall – stands at the hypercenter of the blast.
By the northern entrance to the park is the Peace Bell and the
Memorial Mound, which contains the ashes of tens of thousands
of people cremated here. Farther into the park is the Children's
Peace Monument, depicting a girl with a crane. A victim of the
bomb, this girl believed that she would recover if she made
1,000 paper cranes. She did not survive, but fresh paper cranes
sent by school children adorn the memorial. Across the road is
the Flame of Peace, which will only be extinguished when nuclear
weapons have been eliminated, and the Cenotaph. Designed by
Kenzo Tange for the victims of the bomb, this chest contains
the names of all those who died, together with an inscription
that reads "Rest in peace. We will never repeat the error." The
centerpiece of the park is the Peace Memorial Museum. Poignant
exhibits include a half-melted bronze Buddha, a mangled
tricycle, and the imprint of a dark shadow on the granite steps
of the Sumitomo Bank building – the sole remains of someone.

THE BOMBING OF HIROSHIMA

As World War II dragged
on into the summer of
1945, the US decided to
deploy an entirely new
weapon to force Japan
to surrender. On August
6 a B-29 bomber sent
the first atomic bomb
down on Hiroshima, a
city that had seen little
conventional bombing.
It exploded at 8:15am,
1,900 ft (580 m) above
the city center. Tens of
thousands of people
were killed instantly by
the blast, and the death
toll rose to 200,000 over
the following years as
after-effects took hold.
Nagasaki (p266) suf-
fered a similar fate
three days later.

Paying respect to
the victims at the
curved Cenotaph ↑

→

Strings of paper cranes hanging on
the Children's Peace Monument

297,684

Names contained in the chest of the Cenotaph.

↑ Cherry blossom blooms in front of the haunting twisted girders of the A-Bomb Dome

6 ✿

MIYAJIMA ISLAND

宮島

🅰B5 🏠Hiroshima Prefecture 🚃From Hiroshima to Miyajima-guchi, then ferry
🚢From Hiroshima Port or Miyajima-guchi Stn 🅸At ferry terminal; www.visit-miyajima-japan.com/en

Miyajima, as this sacred place is commonly known, means shrine island, although its official name is Itsukushima. A UNESCO World Heritage Site, it is symbolized by Itsukushima Shrine's prominent vermilion Otorii (Grand Gate) rising from the sea during low tide, and enchanting visitors for centuries.

The shrine sits in a beautiful setting. Felling trees is forbidden so the island has maintained its virgin forest and provides a home to a variety of flora and fauna, while tame deer roam freely. Nature trails snake up Momijidani Park, which towers behind Itsukushima Shrine.

Acclaimed as one of Japan's three most scenic views, the torii of Itsukushima Shrine appears to float in the water. To maintain the island's purity, pilgrims were not allowed to set foot on its ground. Instead, their boats would pass through this gate to reach the shrine, which had a pier into the water. The warlord Taira no Kiyomori, who funded the shrine, built the first Otorii in the 12th century, but the present 50-ft- (16-m-) high structure dates from 1875.

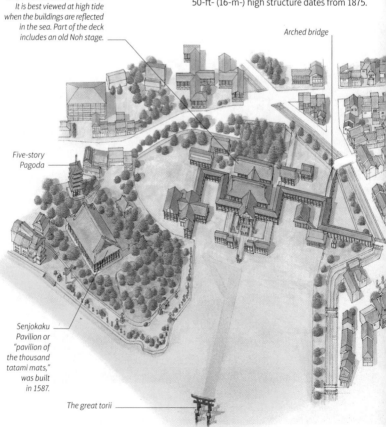

Itsukushima Shrine, founded in 593, is built on stilts over a cove. It is best viewed at high tide when the buildings are reflected in the sea. Part of the deck includes an old Noh stage.

Arched bridge

Five-story Pagoda

Senjokaku Pavilion or "pavilion of the thousand tatami mats," was built in 1587.

The great torii

EXPERIENCE Western Honshu

1 The Otorii's four-legged *(yo-tsuashi)* construction grants it stability.

2 On a bluff overlooking the Itsukushima Shrine is the Goju-no-to, a five-story pagoda built in 1407.

3 *Komainu*, or "lion-dogs," often guard the entrance or *honden* of Shinto shrines.

Did You Know?

To maintain the island's sacredness, no births or burials are permitted here.

Daisho-in Temple is a delightful complex with an eclectic mix of Buddhist statuary. It is blissfully peaceful, away from the crowds of the waterfront and Itsukushima Shrine.

The Treasure House, completed in 1934, houses a valuable collection of gifts presented to the Itsukushima Shrine by the Taira clan and other patrons over the centuries.

Two-story Tahoto Pagoda

Housed in a beautiful mid-19th-century mansion, the Municipal History and Folklore Museum houses a collection of artworks, household utensils, and furniture.

← The area around Itsukushima Shrine, with its famous floating Otorii

 PICTURE PERFECT
Tidal Pull

The best time to take a photograph of the great torii of Miyajima is at high tide, when the gate appears to float above the waves. At low tide, you can walk to the foot of the Otorii, which is said to mark the boundary between the spirit and the human worlds.

7

HORYU-JI

法隆寺

D5 **Nara Prefecture** **JR Yamatoji line from Nara, then 20-min walk** **From Kintetsu Nara Stn or Kintetsu Tsutsui Stn to Horyu-ji-mae stop** **Feb 22–Nov 3: 8am–5pm daily; Nov 4–Feb 21: 8am–4:30pm daily** **horyuji.or.jp/en**

Regarded as the cradle of Japanese Buddhism, the Horyu-ji complex is also thought to contain some of the world's oldest surviving wooden structures, dating from the early 7th century.

The temple was erected by Prince Shotoku (573–621) in his effort to entrench Buddhism alongside Shinto as a pillar of the Japanese belief system. Some exceptional works of art, including ancient images of the Buddha, are housed here. Horyu-ji's star attraction, is the 105-ft- (32-m-) high five-story pagoda, which is the oldest one of its kind in Japan. Japanese pagodas originated in China, where they had developed from the Buddhist stupa in ancient India. The symbolism of such buildings is subject to debate. Some say that a five-story pagoda represents the elements, as shown; others disagree and say that pagodas have an odd number of floors because Chinese numerology claims that this make them lucky.

The nine rings (kurin) of the finial are made of bronze.

Four scythes, a feature unique to Horyu-ji's pagoda, are said to stop it from being destroyed by lightning.

Ornamental roof clays are made of bronze.

Wind chime

A fragment of the Buddha's bone is enshrined in the central pillar's base.

The central column is fashioned from a single cypress tree. Columns at Horyu-ji are almost Greek in style, a legacy of the Silk Route.

↑ A golden bodhisattva sitting beside the Buddha at Horyu-ji

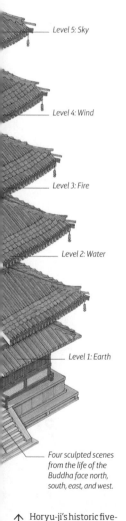

🔍 HIDDEN GEM
Temple Treasures

Although many of Horyu-ji's artifacts are housed in the Tokyo National Museum (*p128*), the Gallery of Temple Treasures still houses Kudara Kannon, a slender Buddha.

Level 5: Sky

Level 4: Wind

Level 3: Fire

Level 2: Water

Level 1: Earth

Four sculpted scenes from the life of the Buddha face north, south, east, and west.

↑ Horyu-ji's historic five-story pagoda, with its symbolic floors

8
Asuka Plain
飛鳥地方

🅐 D5 🄰 Nara Prefecture
🄰 Asuka 🄵 (0744) 54-3624

The Asuka Plain is scattered with excavation sites from the proto-capital Asukakyo, which flourished in the 5th to 7th centuries. The best way to explore the various tombs and temples is by bicycle.

One of the best-known sites, Takamatsuzuka Kofun contains vivid murals of stars and mythological animals. Notable images elsewhere include Sakabune Ishi, a concentric stone that may have been used to make sake; Kame and Saru Ishi, turtle and monkey-shaped statues; and Nimen Seki, a stone with faces carved on each side.

Asuka-dera was Japan's first Buddhist temple. The Asuka-Daibutsu statues are influenced by various East Asian cultures.

9
Koka Ninja Village
甲賀の里忍術村

🅐 D5 🄰 394 Kokacho Oki, Koka, Shiga Prefecture
🄰 Koka, then free shuttle from north entrance
🄼 10am–4pm daily
🅦 koka.ninpou.jp

Shiga prefecture once hosted one of Japan's most secretive sects – the ninja (*p235*). Today, visitors can learn the arts of espionage, sabotage, and infiltration at this ninja village. In the grounds are a museum dedicated to ninja techniques, a house full of traps and secret panels, and a *shuriken* throwing-star dojo, as well as the Mizugomo Water Spider Pond, where you can attempt to get across the water using two floating rings and a rope. Visitors can also experience ninja training for themselves and can even dress up to better understand the ways of these stealthy assassins.

↑ Delicate paintings on the ceiling of Asuka-dera temple, in Asuka village

Yoshino
吉野

D5 **Nara Prefecture**
(0746) 32-3081

This attractive village, its multistoried houses built on the side of a remote mountain, is one of Japan's most popular cherry-blossom-viewing spots. The Yoshinoyama area boasts 100,000 trees planted at different altitudes. Each level blooms in succession, extending the viewing period to almost three weeks.

The Yoshinoyama area stretches from the south banks of the Kii River to the north end of the Omine mountain range. A UNESCO World Heritage Site, the region is dotted with many temples, including Kinpu-Senji Temple, Kinpu Shrine, Yoshimizu Shrine, and Yoshino Mikumari Shrine. There is also a pilgrimage route across the mountains. Chikurin-in Temple is known for its stroll garden designed by the tea master Sen no Rikyu. Visitors can take advantage of the perfect vistas afforded by Mount Yoshino-yama to view cherry blossom trees, as well as hot springs that are present in the area.

Mount Koya
高野山

D5 **Wakayama Prefecture** **Nankai line from Osaka, then cable car from Gokurakubashi Stn** **Nr Senjuinbashi bus stop; www.eng.shukubo.net**

Set amid clumps of black cedar at an altitude of 3,000 ft (900 m) in the heart of the Kii Peninsula, Mount Koya, or Koya-san, is Japan's most venerated Shingon-Buddhist site. Saint Kukai (774–835) established a monastic retreat here in 816. There were almost 1,000 temples on the mountain by the Edo period, but typhoons and fire have since reduced the number to 117.

The western part of Koya-san contains the grandest and most revered structures. Kongobu-ji, built in 1593 by Toyotomi Hideyoshi, is Koya-san's chief temple. Its rhododendrons and the sliding doors of its inner chambers, painted in the 16th century by artists of the Kano school, are among its attractions. The nearby Danjogaran complex includes the Fu-do (Fudo Hall), built in 1197, and the Konpon Dai-to, a two-story vermilion-and-white pagoda. Rebuilt in 1937, the pagoda is regarded as the symbol of Koya-san.

The aptly named Reihokan (Treasure House), opposite the complex, displays over 5,000 paintings, statues, and mandalas in two separate buildings. The Daimon (great gate), the traditional main entrance to Koya-san, lies

---

STAY

Ekoin
Sample vegetarian food, or relax in a hot spring at this Mount Koya temple.

D5 **497 Koyasan, Koya-cho, Ito-gun, Wakayama-ken 648-0201** **ekoin.jp/en/**

Shojoshin-in
This temple offers simple rooms, as well as more luxurious quarters.

D5 **566 Koyasan, Koya-cho, Ito-gun, Wakayama-ken 648-0211** **shojoshinin.jp**

↑ A pagoda in front of the Nachi-no-taki waterfall, on the Kii Peninsula

a little west of here on the edge of the plateau. It affords matchless views.

In the eastern half of Koya-san are a vast necropolis and the Okuno-in (inner sanctum), Kukai's mausoleum. The stone-paved approach to Okuno-in is flanked with statues and tombs housing the remains of Japan's most illustrious families. In front of Kukai's mausoleum is the Toro-do (Lantern Hall). Day and night 11,000 lanterns burn here, including two that are said to have remained lit since the 11th century.

12

Kii Peninsula
紀伊半島

▲D6 ◻Wakayama, Mie, and Nara Prefectures ✈Nanki-Shirahama ◻JR Kinokuni line

The Kii Peninsula, with densely forested mountains at its center and craggy headlands, pine-covered islands, and coves along its shoreline, has

←

Cherry trees at various stages of blossoming in the hills around Yoshino

largely avoided the industrial development that scars much of Japan's Pacific coastline.

From the small port town of Shingu, on the east coast, you can take a bus to Shiko, then a 50-minute boat trip along the Kumano River to Doro Valley, a spectacular gorge. From May to June rhododendrons and azaleas bloom on the river's banks.

A 20-minute bus ride inland from Shingu lies Nachi-no-taki, Japan's highest waterfall. A stone path parallel to the falls leads to the ancient Nachi Taisha shrine. The next port south of Shingu is Katsuura, a pine-studded bay with several picturesque islets. Visitors interested in the Japanese perspective on whaling should go to the **Whale Museum** in nearby Taiji, a whaling community since the 17th century.

Farther south, the resort of Kushimoto is known for Hashi-gui-iwa, a chain of 30 rocks that seem to march out to sea, connecting the town to the island of Oshima. The peninsula's southernmost point is marked by Shio-no-misaki, a headland with a white lighthouse dating from 1863. One of the three oldest hot springs in Japan, Shirahama Onsen, on the west coast, also has one of the area's finest beaches.

Taiji Whale Museum

⊘ ◻2934-2 Taiji ◻(0735) 59-2400 ◻8:30am–5pm daily

13

Iga-Ueno
伊賀上野

▲D5 ◻Mie Prefecture ✈ ◻1st Floor, Haito-Pia bldg, in front of Ueno-shi Stn; (0595) 24-0270

This castle town was the birthplace of Japan's revered haiku poet Matsuo Basho and home to the Iga ninja, the most inventive and feared spies of Japan's feudal era. The main attraction for most visitors is the **Iga Ninja Museum**, a clan farmhouse that served as the secret headquarters of these spies and assassins. The well-restored building retains hidden panels, spy holes, secret escape routes, and trapdoors intended to repel night attacks from enemy warlords and rival ninja groups. Ninja methods are demonstrated by guides in pink day-glo ninja outfits.

Iga Ninja Museum

⊘ ◻117 Ueno Marunochi ◻9am–5pm daily ◻iga ninja.jp/en

THE NINJA

Ninjutsu, the "art of stealth," was developed during the bloody clan warfare of Japan's feudal era. The ninja elevated their profession of spying and assassination into a sophisticated discipline by practicing mountain asceticism and studying such subjects as astronomy, herbalism, medicine, and nutrition. They developed ingenious devices to outwit enemies, including lock picks, collapsible floats for crossing water, clothing designed to conceal swords and knives, and over 30 different kinds of *shuriken*, deadly throwing stars made of metal.

14

Okayama
岡山

🅰C5 🚉Okayama Prefecture ✈🚌 ℹ️Outside JR Stn; www.okayama-kanko.net/sightseeing/en

The former center of a domain ruled by the feudal Ikeda family, Okayama today is a vibrant modern city. Japanese tourists come to marvel at the Seto Ohashi Bridge, linking Okayama with Shikoku, which is over 8 miles (13 km) long.

The **Koraku-en Garden**, one of Japan's "famous three" gardens, was commissioned by Lord Ikeda and completed in 1700. Though a classic stroll garden, it was the first in Japan to have large expanses of lawn. The garden is divided into three sections and features bamboo, pine, plum, and cherry trees, along with tea bushes. The nearby castle is incorporated into the design.

Okayama Castle is called the "Crow's Castle" due to its black walls. Destroyed in World War II, the exterior of the 16th-century castle was rebuilt in 1966. The interior displays samurai helmets, swords, and the like. More items owned by the Ikeda clan are on view at the **Hayashibara Museum of Art**, just south of the castle.

To the northeast, the **Orient Museum** traces how Near-Eastern art reached Japan via the Silk Route. The **Okayama Prefectural Museum of Art** has a collection of mostly 20th-century Japanese paintings and a few works by older artists.

Koraku-en Garden
⊗ 🏠1-5 Korakuen 🚌Koraku-en-mae stop ⏱7:30am-6pm daily

Okayama Castle
⊗ 🏠2-3-1 Marunouchi ⏱9am-5:30pm daily

Hayashibara Museum of Art
⊗ 🏠2-7-15 Marunouchi ⏱10am-5pm Tue-Sun

Orient Museum
⊗ 🏠9-31 Tenjincho 📞(086) 232-3636 ⏱9am-5pm Tue-Sun

Okayama Prefectural Museum of Art
⊗ 🏠8-48 Tenjincho 📞(086) 225-4800 ⏱9am-5pm Tue-Sun

___

15

Inbe
伊部

🅰C5 🚉Okayama Prefecture 🚌 ℹ️in Inbe JR Stn; (0869) 64-1100

The home of Bizen pottery, Inbe is full of shops, galleries, and kilns. Originating in the Kamakura period, Bizen-ware is earthy, unglazed, and prized by tea-ceremony enthusiasts. The **Bizen Pottery Traditional and Contemporary Art Museum** displays superb examples from the Muromachi, Momoyama, and Edo periods.

Bizen Pottery Traditional and Contemporary Art Museum
⊗ 🏠1659-6 Inbe 📞(0869) 64-1400 ⏱9:30am-5:30pm Tue-Sun

→ Sailing along a peaceful canal in the well-preserved Edo-era town of Kurashiki

16

Kurashiki
倉敷

🅰C5 🅰Okayama Prefecture 🚊 ℹ️North building, 2nd Floor; www.kurashiki-tabi.jp/tourist-information-center

The Edo-period mercantile town of Kurashiki is beautifully preserved. Kurashiki means "storehouse village," a reference to the dozens of granaries (kura) with mortar and black-tiled walls that dot the town. In the heart of the old city, the Bikan Historical Area just south of the station, 200-year-old kura flank a tranquil canal lined with willows. Many of the kura have been converted into galleries, restaurants, inns, and tasteful shops and boutiques.

In the old district the finest museum is the **Ohara Museum of Art**. The collection was commissioned by industrialist Ohara Magosaburo in 1930 on the premise that great art should be accessible – even to the people of a relative backwater such as Kurashiki. It includes rare works by the likes of Matisse, Renoir, Picasso, Degas, and Gauguin, and genuine masterpieces, like El Greco's *The Annunciation*. The annex houses an outstanding collection of works from Japan's *mingei* (or folk craft) scene.

The small **Kurashiki Archaeological Museum** occupies an old *kura* and includes items excavated in the region. In the **Kurashiki Folk Art Museum** you'll find folk crafts housed in connecting *kura*. The **Japan Rural Toy Museum** has an extensive display of traditional old toys from around the world.

Ohara Museum of Art
🔷 🅰1-1-15 Chuo 📞(086) 422-0005 🕘9am-5pm Tue-Sun

Kurashiki Archaeological Museum
🔷 🅰1-3-13 Chuo 📞(086) 422-1542 🕘9am-5pm Wed-Sun

Kurashiki Folk Art Museum
🔷 🅰1-4-11 Chuo 🕘9am-5pm Tue-Sun

Japan Rural Toy Museum
🔷 🅰1-4-16 Chuo 🕘9am-5pm daily (from 10am Dec-Feb)

← Koraku-en Garden in Okayama, featuring vast stretches of lawn

→ The Sahara-like landscape of the Tottori Sand Dunes along the San-in coast

 17

Tottori Sand Dunes
鳥取砂丘

🅰C4 🏯Tottori Prefecture 🚉Tottori 🚌From Stn 🛈At Tottori Stn; (0857) 22-3318

A huge expanse of brown and yellow undulations, the Tottori sand dunes stretch for 10 miles (16 km) along the San-in coast. To the Japanese, the towering dunes, some rising to 300 ft (90 m), and the shifting patterns and shadows formed across the sand, are lyrical reminders of the human condition. Abe Kobo's powerful existential novel *The Woman in the Dunes* (1962) is set here. Commercialization has inevitably hit the area – head east across the dunes or rent a bike for a quieter experience.

 18

Fukiya
吹屋

🅰C5 🏯Okayama Prefecture, Takahashi city 🚌From Bitchu Takahashi

A prosperous boom town at the center of the 19th-century copper and red-ocher mining industry, Fukiya is now a rustic hamlet tucked into beautiful mountain countryside. Well-to-do merchants and mine owners built grand houses here. Characterized by white plaster walls and red-ocher-colored latticework windows

and doors, these distinctive buildings are the village's main cultural asset.

Several are open to the public, including the former house of the Katayama family, now Fukiya's **Local History Museum**, and an old plaster-and-tile schoolhouse.

Just outside the village is a copper and ocher mine, which can be visited. The **Hirokane-tei**, an unusual Edo-period home resembling a fortified chateau, is about 2 miles (4 km) outside the town.

Local History Museum
🔯 🏠699 Nariwachō 🕘9am–5pm Wed–Mon

Hirokane-tei
🔯 🏠2710 Nakano 🕘9am–5pm daily

→ Cherry trees framing Hikone Castle, whose keep *(inset)* offers views of Lake Biwa

 19

Amanohashidate Sandbar
天橋立

🅰D4 🏯Kyoto Prefecture 🚉Amanohashidate 🛈At Amanohashidate Stn; (0772) 22-8030

One of the highlights of Miyatsu Bay, along the San-in coast, is Amanohashidate, the "bridge of heaven." The 2-mile (4-km) pine-studded sandbar separates the bay from Asokai lagoon. According to Japanese mythology, this is the spot where the gods conceived the Japanese islands. Visitors usually take the boat across the lagoon from the pier near the station, then a cable car

It is easy to see how Amanohashidate got its heavenly name when you bend over and look at the sandbar upside down from the summit of Kasamatsu. From here, the sand spit appears to be literally reaching into the sky from the sea.

from the base of Kasamatsu Park to its hilltop summit, which is the best viewing point of the sandbar.

20

Lake Biwa
琵琶湖

D5 Shiga Prefecture
 Outside Otsu Stn; (077) 522-3830

With a total mass of 263 sq miles (674 sq km), Biwa-ko, Japan's largest lake, covers an area greater than Tokyo. The lake is named after the *biwa*, a musical instrument whose outline it is said to resemble. In the 15th century the highlights of Lake Biwa were named Omi Hakkei, "the eight views of Omi." Development has changed some of these views radically, but the lake remains a beautiful place, its shore fringed with shrines, temples, and modest pensions. **Lake Biwa Museum** gives visitors a chance to learn more about this ancient lake.

Otsu, on the southwest edge, is the lake shore's largest city. Visitors come here to see Onjo Temple, with its huge gates, and Ishiyama-dera Temple, which has some 8th-century buildings. Murasaki Shikibu, author of the *Tale of Genji*, is believed to have used one of the chambers of the Main Hall in which to write her 11th-century masterpiece.

Hikone, on the lake's eastern shore, is home to the 17th-century **Hikone Castle**. From the top floor of the keep is a superb view of Lake Biwa.

Lake Biwa Museum
 1091 Oroshimocho, Kusatsu 9:30am–5pm Tue–Sun

Hikone Castle
 1-1 Konkicho, Hikone 8:30am–5pm daily

DRINK

Kaya
Matsue's only reggae bar, this vibrant haunt offers Jamaican classics such as jerk chicken and meat pies, plus Red Stripe beer.

C5 199-1 Teramachi, Matsue-shi, Shimane 690-0063
 m.me/kaya.diningbar

Oideyasu Okiniya
One of the best *izakayas* in Matsue, with a great selection of beer and sake, as well as tasty snacks. Try the *maitake* (mushroom) tempura.

C5 13 Suetsugu Hon-machi, Matsue-shi, Shimane 690-0843
 (0852) 24-8839

Bar E.A.D.
This cool riverside hangout offers a stylish space to enjoy a drink while taking in the view of the city at sunset. In summer, the rooftop is open and live bands keep the crowd going well into the night.

C5 36 Suetsugu Hon-machi, Matsue-shi, Shimane 690-0843
 (0852) 28-3130

Uji City
宇治市

D5 **Uji Stn, Keihan-Uji or Nara lines**

In addition to some of the best green tea grown in Japan, the small city of Uji boasts **Byodo-in**, which is featured on the 10-yen coin. The temple's Phoenix Hall and Amida Nyorai image inside are marvelous remnants of one of Japan's greatest epochs.

Manpuku-ji was established in 1661 by Ingen, a priest who fled China after the fall of the Ming dynasty. Ingen introduced the *sencha*, or leaf tea, ceremony.

Close by, in Shigaraki, the **Miho Museum** has some fine Japanese treasures such as Buddha statues and handscrolls, as well as treasures from Egypt and Persia.

Byodo-in
116 Uji Renge 8:30am–5:30pm daily

Manpuku-ji
34 Gokasho Sanban-wari 9am–4:30pm daily

Miho Museum
300 Tashiro Momodani, Shigaraki-cho, Shiga (074) 882-3411 10am–5pm Tue–Sun miho.or.jp

LAFCADIO HEARN

Lafcadio Hearn (1850–1904) arrived in Japan in 1890. He published several books, such as *Glimpses of Unfamiliar Japan* and *In Ghostly Japan*, which allowed the Japanese to view their culture through the eyes of a foreigner for the first time. Hearn's first Japanese home was Matsue. He married the daughter of a local samurai family and later acquired Japanese citizenship, changing his name to Koizumi Yakumo.

Matsue
松江

C5 **Shimane Prefecture** **Yonago and Izumo** **At Matsue JR Stn; www.visit-matsue.com**

Situated at the intersection of Lake Shinji with Miho bay and Nakaumi lagoon, Matsue is also known as the "water city" and is rarely explored by international visitors.

Matsue is referred to at length in *Glimpses of Unfamiliar Japan* (1894) by Lafcadio Hearn, a journalist of Irish-Greek descent who spent 15 months in the town. Hearn described **Matsue Castle** as "a veritable architectural dragon, made up of magnificent monstrosities." One of the few in Japan to remain intact, it was built in 1611 of pine and stone, then partially reconstructed 31 years later. Its five-story keep is Japan's tallest.

Within a short walk of the castle are two more modest architectural gems. The **Buke Yashiki** is a mansion built in 1730 by the Shiomi family, who were chief retainers at the castle, and the **Meimei-an Teahouse** (1779) is one of Japan's oldest and best preserved. Along the same street is the **Tanabe Art Museum**, with a refined collection of tea bowls and other tea-related objects.

Just north of the castle, the **Lafcadio Hearn Residence** is

↑ The interior of Uji City's Miho Museum, designed by I. M. Pei with Pei Cobb Freed & Partners

beautifully preserved, and the **Lafcadio Hearn Memorial Hall** displays Hearn's manuscripts, desk, and pipes.

Matsue Castle
 🏠 1-5 Tonomachi 🚋 Kencho-mae stop 📞 (0852) 21-4030 🕐 8:30am-6pm daily

Buke Yashiki
 🏠 305 Kitahoricho 📞 (0852) 22-2243 🕐 8:30am-6:30pm daily (to 5pm Oct-Mar)

Meimei-an Teahouse
 🏠 278 Kitahoricho 📞 (0852) 21-9863 🕐 8:30am-5pm daily

Tanabe Art Museum
 🏠 310-5 Kitahoricho 📞 (0852) 26-2211 🕐 9am-5pm Tue-Sun

Lafcadio Hearn Residence
 🏠 315 Kitahoricho 📞 (0852) 23-0714 🕐 8:30am-6:30pm daily

Lafcadio Hearn Memorial Hall
 🏠 322 Okudanicho 📞 (0852) 21-2147 🕐 8:30am-5pm daily (to 6:30pm Apr-Sep)

㉓
Yamaguchi
山口

🅰B5 🏠 Yamaguchi Prefecture 🚆 ℹ️ Yamaguchi Stn, 1st floor; www.yamaguchi-city.jp/w/en/index.html

Laid out in the 14th century, Yamaguchi was modeled on Kyoto. When the Jesuit Francis Xavier visited here in 1550 he found a city of great wealth and sophistication; the Xavier Memorial Chapel, built in 1952, marks the 400th anniversary of the priest's stay. The painter Sesshu (1420–1506) designed a garden for the temple of Joei-ji's, while Ruriko-ji has a Japanese cypress-wood, five-story pagoda. Nearby is a set of tombs belonging to the influential Mori clan.

↑ Rock formations in the Akiyoshido Cave in the Akiyoshi-dai Tablelands

㉔
Akiyoshi-dai Tablelands
秋吉台

🅰B5 🏠 Yamaguchi Prefecture 🚌 From Yamaguchi ℹ️ At bus stn; (0837) 62-0305

Akiyoshi-dai is a plateau of grassland and rocky outcrops, which tour buses pass on their way to **Akiyoshido Cave**, one of the largest limestone grottos in Asia. The cave is 6 miles (10 km) deep, only half a mile (1 km) of which is open to the public. Passageways are well lit, and a clear map is provided.

Akiyoshido Cave
 📞 (0837) 62-0115 🕐 8:30am-5:30pm daily

㉕
Izumo
出雲

🅰C5 🏠 Shimane Prefecture 🚆🚌 ℹ️ At Taisha-mae Stn; (0853) 53-2298

Alive with myths, legends, and tales of the supernatural, Izumo, known until the 3rd century as the "eightfold-towering-thunderhead land," has an enthralling heritage. The town is well known throughout Japan for the

Izumo Taisha Grand Shrine, one of the most revered and oldest Shinto shrines in the country. It is dedicated to Okuninushi-no-Mikoto, a deity who is closely associated with agriculture and medicine, as well as marriage – the latter explaining the popularity of the shrine for wedding ceremonies. The entrance to the shrine, through 11 torii (gates), is impressive. Unusually tall, the Honden (Main Hall) is not open to the public, although the Treasure House can be visited. The shrine's environs are sacred and therefore ecologically pristine, with towering cryptomeria trees surrounding the main compound. Just east of the shrine are a number of old houses occupied by priests who serve here. Note the traditional clay and stone walls.

Just past the shrine, on Route 431 to Okuni, there is a monument to a nun who is said to have danced on the banks of the Kamo River in Kyoto to raise money for the shrine. The dance was developed into the Kabuki theatrical form (p115).

Izumo Taisha Grand Shrine
 🏠 195 Taishacho Kizukihigashi 📞 (0853) 53-3100 🕐 Daily

26

Iwakuni
岩国

B5 🏯Yamaguchi Prefecture 🚄Sanyo Shinkansen line to Shin-Iwakuni, JR Sanyo line to Iwakuni 🛈At 2F bus terminal near Iwakuni Stn; (082) 721-6050

This city's main draw is the elegant Kintai-kyo, or "brocade sash" bridge, named for the rippling effect created by its five linked arches. The original structure, built in 1673, was destroyed by a typhoon in 1950. This almost exact replica depends on first-rate joinery and an invisible quantity of reinforced steel.

Kikko Park is home to samurai houses, including **Mekata House**. **Iwakuni Art Museum** has an impressive display of armor and weapons. A cable car climbs to Iwakuni Castle, a faithful 1962 reconstruction of the 1608 donjon.

Mekata House
🏯2 Yokoyama ⏰9am-4:30pm Tue-Sun

Iwakuni Art Museum
♿ 🏯2-10-27 Yokoyama 📞(0827) 41-0506 ⏰9am-5pm daily

27

Hagi
萩

B5 🏯Yamaguchi Prefecture 🚃🚌 🛈(0838) 25-1750

Hagi was a minor fishing port until Mori Terumoto fortified it in 1604. Mori samurai helped spark off the anti-Tokugawa revolt in the mid-1800s, and many of Meiji Japan's founding fathers came from Hagi. Today it is best known for its pottery-making tradition. Hagi's charm is in the details: its mossy cemeteries, teahouses, and the tiny, purple bloom of bush clover *(hagi)*. The central Teramachi district contains old temples and shrines.

Jonen-ji is noted for its finely carved gate, Hofuku-ji its bibbed Jizo statues, Kyotoku-ji for its garden, and Choju-ji for an atmospheric cemetery. Camellias and *natsu mikan* (summer oranges) hanging over whitewashed mud walls typify the samurai quarters to the west of Teramachi. Several residences are located here, including **Kikuya House**, a merchant villa with a small museum and beautiful garden attached. The **Ishii Tea Bowl Museum** has a superb ceramics collection. Wealthy merchants appointed by the Mori clan once owned the fine collection in the **Kumaya Art Museum** to the north of here. It includes tea-ceremony utensils, paintings, and screens.

HAGI'S CERAMIC ARTS

Hagi's first kilns date from the Heian period, but the town's reputation for refined tea vessels and other wares began in the 16th century with the introduction of apprentice potters from Korea. A distinguishing mark of *hagi-yaki* (Hagi-ware) is its translucent glaze *(right)*. Hagi-yaki improves with age, the muted pinks and pastels of the stoneware softening to beiges as tannin from the tea soaks through the porous glaze.

← The graceful arches of the Kintai-kyo bridge over the Nishiki River in Iwakuni

Kikuya House
◈ 🏠 1-1 Gofukumachi
🕐 9am–5:30pm daily

Ishii Tea Bowl Museum
◈ 🏠 33-3 Minamihuruhagi-cho 🕐 9am–4:30pm Thu-Tue

Kumaya Art Museum
◈ 🏠 47 Imauono tanamachi
🕐 9am–4pm Tue, Thu, Sat & Sun

 28

Tsuwano
津和野

🅐 B5 🏠 Shimane Prefecture 🚉🚌 ℹ️ Next to Tsuwano Stn; (0856) 72-1771

This tiny 700-year-old former castle town, tucked into a river valley deep in the mountains, has a large number of well-preserved samurai houses. Thousands of carp inhabit the town's brooks, outnumbering the residents, it is said, by ten to one. The hillside Taikodani Inari Shrine is one of the most important Inari (fox) shrines in Japan. It is reached through a tunnel of vermilion torii (gates), 1,174 in all. A chairlift goes up the other side of the slope to the scant remains of Tsuwano Castle, and there's a stunning view from the top.

Nishi Amane (1829–97), a Meiji-period statesman and philosopher, was born here. **Nishi House**, now a museum, is on a quiet street in the south of town. Opposite is another notable home – **Mori Ougai House**, a museum to Tsuwano-native Mori Ogai (1862–1922), author of novels such as *The Wild Geese* and *Vita Sexualis*.

→ Ceremony at Tsuwano's Taikodani Inari Shrine, an important fox temple

SHOP

Yoshinaga
This ancient shop is as famous for the koi carp swimming in the pond at the back as it is for the quality of its rice.

🅐 B5 🏠 296 Ushiroda, Tsuwano-cho, Kanoashi-gun, Shimane 699-5605 📞 (0856) 72-0011

Karato Market
After the business trade ends at 7am, vendors here are happy to talk to visitors and explain the different types of fish and marine products on sale at the market.

🅐 B5 🏠 5-50 Karato-cho, Shimonoseki-shi, Yamaguchi-ken 📞 (083) 231-0001

Nishi House
🏠 64-6 Ushiroda 📞 (0856) 72-1771 🕐 9am–5pm daily

Mori Ougai House
◈ 🏠 238 Machida 📞 (0856) 72-3210 🕐 9am–5pm Tue-Sun

The unique Meoto Iwa, or "wedded rocks", at Futamigaura Beach ↑

A TOUR OF
ISE PENINSULA

Distance 70 miles (110 km) **Stopping-off points** Goza Beach, Futamigaura Beach, Kashikojima **Difficulty** The area has excellent bus and train services

On this tour, you'll take in the peninsula's main sites, including the city of Ise, its Grand Shrine – the most sacred in Japan – and the Ise-Shima National Park, as well as off-the-beaten track gems, from the jagged coast, where cultured oyster pearls are grown, to the undulating evergreen-clad hills inland – the habitat of monkeys, wild boars, and flying squirrels.

Locator Map
For more detail see p212

0 kilometers 5

0 miles 5

N

*Female divers can be seen collecting sea-weed and sea urchins at the **Mikimoto Pearl Island,** just offshore from the town of Toba.*

*At **Futamigaura Beach** two rocks called the Meoto Iwa (wedded rocks) are connected by a sacred rope.*

Reconstructed every 20 years in accordance with Shinto principles of purity and renewal, Ise's shrines are in two main groups: the Ge-ku (outer shrine) and Nai-ku (inner shrine)

Ise Shrines
START

Mount Asama
FINISH

*A good route back on a clear day, this road goes over the summit of **Mount Asama**, with views of the peninsula.*

Futamigaura Beach

Futamicho

Funae
Ise
Kurosecho

Uraguchi

Asama

Mikimoto
Pearl Island

Toba

Toshi
Island

Suga
Island

Toba Bay

Iwakuracho

Matsuocho

Gochi

Isobe

Gonkashura

Konsa

Hiyamaji

Nanabari

Hamajima

Shima

Kashikojima

Osatsucho

Matoya Bay

Agocho Kou

Daicho
Nakiri

Daicho
Funakoshi

Ago Bay

Goza

Shimacho
Koshika

INSIDER TIP
Tips for Travelers

Rather than driving, take the train or bus on this tour. Buses and trains run between almost every town on the peninsula. There are also some train links from Fukuoka – allow more time for these.

*The most popular stretch of sand on the peninsula, **Goza Beach** can be reached by road or by boat from Kashikojima.*

Kashikojima *is one of the peninsula's best resort areas. Take a boat trip past scenic islets, and oyster rafts.*

SHIKOKU

Late Paleolithic sites and *kofun* (burial mounds) dating from the 3rd century AD are evidence of early human activity on Shikoku. The Dogo Onsen Honkan in Matsuyama is referred to in the *Kojiki*, Japan's oldest chronicle, written in 712. Despite such ancient sites, however, Shikoku has mainly been on the margin of Japanese history. The island's most famous figure is Kukai, who was born into a poor aristrocratic family in 774. This Buddhist priest, who has been called the Father of Japanese Culture, visited 88 of the island's temples in a pilgrimage that has been imitated by others for more than a thousand years.

In 1183, as chronicled in the *Tale of the Heike*, the war between the Taira and Minamoto clans for dominance of Japan spilled over into the Inland Sea and Shikoku. Some of the defeated Taira went into hiding in a gorge in central Shikoku, where many of their descendants still live.

Farmland and mountains continue to dominate Shikoku's landscape, although agriculture employs only 3 percent of the island's four million residents. Assembly of cars and manufacture of electronic goods, particularly in the ports along the Seto Inland Sea, are the most important industries. Other industries include fruit farming (mandarin oranges in particular), seaweed and pearl cultivation, and food and chemical processing.

SHIKOKU

Must See

❶ Benesse Art Site Naoshima

Experience More

❷ Seto Inland Sea
❸ Kotohira
❹ Takamatsu
❺ Naruto Whirlpools
❻ Kochi
❼ Tokushima
❽ Matsuyama
❾ Ozu
❿ Uchiko
⓫ Uwajima

Katsuyama

Tsuyama

E29

Yamazaki

HYOGO

Niimi

E2A

OKAYAMA

Tatsuno

Ono

E2A

Fukiya

E73

Himeji

E2

Miki

Okayama
Airport

Bizen

Ako

Kakogawa

Akashi

Kobe

Soja

Inbe

Okayama

Osaka

WESTERN HONSHU
p210

Tonosho

*Shodo
Island*

1 BENESSE ART
SITE NAOSHIMA

HYOGO

Awaji

Seto-Ohashi
Bridge

E30

Sakaide

4 TAKAMATSU

Sumoto

Marugame

E11

KAGAWA

Sanuki

*Awaji
Island*

Mitoyo

Takamatsu
Airport

Hiketa

*Naruto
Bridge*

E28

28

Nandan

Wakayama

26

Kan-onji

3 KOTOHIRA

193

Naruto

5 NARUTO
WHIRLPOOLS

Arida

yomishima

11

Waki

Awa

E32

Yoshino-gawa

7 TOKUSHIMA

*Kiisuido
Strait*

Yuasa

wanoe

E32

Higashimiyoshi

193

Yoshinogawa

Komatsushima

Gobo

Miyoshi

Tsurugi Mountains

Kamiyama

Katsuura

Ochiai

TOKUSHIMA

Naka

Otonohiracani

Anan

*Tsurugi-san
6,414 ft m (1,955 m)*

E32

Otoyo

195

Monobecho
Befu

193

Minami

KOCHI

Umaji

Mugi

Tosa

Kainan

6

E32

Nankoku

KOCHI

Aki

Kitagawa

493

Toyo

Kochi
Airport

Yasuda

Nahari

55

Muroto

*Cape
Muroto*

Pacific Ocean

SHIKOKU

1

BENESSE ART SITE NAOSHIMA

ベネッセアートサイト直島

🅰C5 🏯Kagawa Prefecture 🚢Takamatsu or Uno 🕐Hours vary, check website for individual museums 🌐benesse-artsite.jp/en

One of the 3,000 islands dotting the Seto Inland Sea *(p252)*, Naoshima was once a desolate and depopulated industrial outpost of Japan's rustbelt. Now completely reborn, Benesse Art Site Naoshima brings together the best in contemporary Japanese art and architecture.

Naoshima's incredible transformation into an international art destination began in 1987, when Soichiro Fukutake, the chairman of Benesse Holdings – an education and publishing company – purchased the bottom half of the dilapidated island. Working with the leading Japanese architect Tadao Ando, a specialist in cutting-edge concrete buildings, and responsible for the famous Church of Light in Osaka, Benesse turned Naoshima into one of the world's premier art destinations.

In 1992, Benesse House, Ando's first permanent structure, opened on the site. Now formed of four buildings, it encompasses both guest accommodation and a museum housing a collection of contemporary artworks by the likes of Yves Klein, Cy Twombly, Hiroshi Sugimoto, and Jean-Michel Basquiat.

The next museum to open was the Chichu Art Museum in 2004, designed to encourage visitors to reflect on the relationship between mankind and nature. Inside, five paintings

→

George Rickey's *Three Squares Vertical Diagonal* (2007) at Benessee House

TADAO ANDO

Ando's designs are known for their zen-like simplicity, which are said to be as evocative as haiku. On Naoshima, he crafted Benesse House, the Chichu Art Museum, and the Naoshima Contemporary Art out of crude concrete. For his work, the boxer-turned-architect won the prestigious Pritzker Prize in 1995.

←
One of Yayoi
Kusama's iconic
pumpkin sculptures
sitting on a pier

from Monet's *Water Lilies* series are showcased under natural light. Art and the natural environment are in harmony throughout the island, with Yayoi Kusama's dotty pumpkins perched on piers interrupting the horizon.

Every three years, Benesse Art Site Naoshima serves as a venue for the Setouchi Triennale art festival, attracting almost a million extra visitors to the already popular island. The festival also takes place on other islands in the area such as Shodoshima and Ogijima.

↑ Benesse House's light and airy
restaurant, overlooking the beach

> 💬 INSIDER TIP
> ### Guest Privileges
>
> Guests staying at Benesse House benefit from after-hours access to the museums, away from the crowds, until 11pm. The hotel has four buildings: Museum, Oval, Beach, and Park.

EXPERIENCE MORE

❷ Seto Inland Sea
瀬戸内海

🅰C5 🚢**Setonaikai-kisen (Inland Sea cruises); (082) 253-1212**

The Seto Inland Sea, Japan's most beautiful body of water, is not landlocked, as its name suggests, but seems almost so with its serene waters and over 3,000 pine-studded islands. Donald Richie, in his classic travelogue *The Inland Sea* (1971), sets the scene of a boat journey westward through the narrow defiles of water: "On the left are first the sharp and Chinese-looking mountains of the island of Shikoku, so different that it appears another land, and then the flat coasts of Kyushu. This shallow sea is a valley among these mountainous islands."

You can cycle along a path that stretches from Onomichi to Imabari. Bridges, local ferries, and cruise boats provide access to the 750 or so inhabited islands. The remote fishing villages on these islands, with their salt-weathered wooden houses and black ceramic-tiled roofs, seem to hail from a different era. Among the most visited

are Awaji, the largest island, Setoda, Omi, and Shodo, a beautiful island that, with its olive and orange groves, seems to belong more to the Mediterranean than the Orient. But our favorite island is Naoshima, which serves as a haven for ground-breaking art (*p250*).

❸ Kotohira
琴平

🅰C5 🏛**Kagawa Prefecture** 🚉**JR Kotohira & Kotoden-Kotohira Stns** 🌐**my-kagawa.jp/en/art/art01**

Kotohira is the home of the famous shrine complex Kotohira-gu, also affectionately known as Konpira-san, the spiritual guardian of seafarers. The target of pilgrimages for centuries, the shrine now attracts four million visitors per year and is believed to bestow good luck upon fishermen and sailors.

A 785-stair climb (or ride in one of the palanquins

📷 PICTURE PERFECT
For Shore

Head to Chichibuga Beach, 12 miles (20 km) west of Kotohira, to get an Instagram-ready post. Stand on the sand at sunset, strike a pose, and get someone to capture your silhouette reflected in the mirror-like stretch of water.

available) takes visitors up the rugged mountainside to the shrine, set in beautiful grounds. Within the complex, the Asahi Shrine is built of zelkova, a rock-hard wood that forms an excellent medium for carved relief work. The nearby Omote Shoin and Oku Shoin have celebrated screen paintings by Maruyama Okyo. The first presents burly tigers bristling with Zen energy, the second includes a waterfall flowing across a corner of the room.

The oldest Kabuki theater in Japan, the Kanamaru-za, can also be found in the town.

A wooden bridge crossing one of the ponds in the Ritsuin Garden, Takamatsu

④ Takamatsu
高松

C5 🏯 Kagawa Prefecture
✈🚉 ℹ At JR Stn; (087) 826 0170

The capital of the tiny Kagawa prefecture on the Inland Sea, Takamatsu is the main hub between Shikoku and the outside world. Nonetheless, it maintains a local charm with its neighborhood shops and historic landmarks. The town expanded after Ikoma Chikamasa erected Takamatsu Castle in 1588, the remains of which can still be seen. Takamatsu Castle has a unique seawater moat. Instead of the usual koi fish, visitors can see bream, flounders, and sometimes even puffer fish. When the Tokugawa shoguns assumed power in 1600, they granted the town, castle, and surrounding fiefdom to their relatives, the Matsudaira clan.

←

The Akashi Kaikyo Bridge, linking Kobe to the island of Awaji in the Seto Inland Sea

The family devoted nearly a century to landscaping the six ponds and 13 artificial hillocks that make Ritsurin Garden the city's most famous landmark.

Takamatsu's location as an entry port for Shikoku made it the setting for such historic battles as the one between the Minamoto and the Taira clans in 1185. The **Takamatsu Heike Monogatari Wax Museum** offers a surprisingly effective re-creation of the story's high points, which are also the subject matter of the classic Noh play *Yashima*.

At Yashima volcanic plateau, **Shikoku Mura** is a village where immaculately preserved buildings and other artifacts of rural life display Shikoku craftsmanship.

Takamatsu Heike Monogatari Wax Museum
🅭 📍 3-6-38 Asahicho
📞 (087) 823-8400
🕒 9:30am-5:30pm daily

Shikoku Mura
🅭 📍 91 Yashima-naka-machi 📞 (087) 843-3111
🚉 Kotoden Yashima Stn
🕒 8:30am-5pm daily

5

Naruto Whirlpools
鳴門の渦潮

⚊D5 ⌂Tokushima Prefecture ⛾Naruto Stn, then bus to Naruto Park 🚢Uzushio line ferry (088) 687-0613; Aqua Eddy (www.uzusio.com/en/yoyaku)

Where the tip of Awaji Island nearly touches Shikoku, the tidal pull of two distinct bodies of water – the Seto Inland Sea and the Pacific Ocean – creates large disparities spawning powerful currents and whirlpools. Navigating the churning waters of this 1-mile (1.6-km) strait has been a part of local lore for over a millennium.

Sightseeing boats now ply the 13-mph (20-km/h) currents, and provide startling views of the Onaruto suspension bridge, part of a system linking Shikoku and Honshu via Awaji Island. When the northern end of the system was completed in 1998, it had stretched 3 ft (1 m) as a result of ground shifts caused by the Kobe earthquake.

↑ A small shrine overlooking the coast at Katsurahama Park in the town of Kochi

At the Awaji end of the bridge, the **Uzunooka Onarutokyo Memorial Hall** explains the whirlpool phenomenon and offers a fine view of the Onaruto suspension bridge and the swirling whirlpools from its terrace.

Uzunooka Onarutokyo Memorial Hall

🏛 ⌂936-3 Fukura Hei, Minamiawaji ⏰9am-5pm daily 🌐kinen.uzunokuni.com

6

Kochi
高知

⚊C6 ⌂Kochi Prefecture ✈🚄 ℹ At JR Stn; (088) 826-3337

Kochi city offers a rare blend of sandy beaches, mountain views, and well-preserved historic sites.

The Kochi region, formerly called Tosa, is known for its

forging of cutlery, and shops selling knives line the street in front of **Kochi Castle**, built in 1603. However, most of the castle buildings were rebuilt between 1729 and 1753 following a fire. A startlingly long sword, over 5 ft (1.5 m) in length, is among the weapons on display in the castle. Look out of the windows on the top floors for breathtaking views.

At Katsurahama, a white-sand beach area in the southern part of the city, the **Sakamoto Ryoma Museum** is devoted to the Tosa patriot admired for his part in the overthrow of the shogunate and restoration of the emperor in the 1860s. He was assassinated in 1867. Most Japanese visitors make a point of paying homage to a bronze statue of the man looming over the beach.

AWA-ODORI DANCING

Tokushima's celebrations for O-Bon, the festival of the dead on August 12–15, are the liveliest in Japan. Special dances, called Awa-Odori, are meant to welcome ancestral spirits on their yearly visit to the land of the living. Nicknamed "the fool's dance" because the refrain "you're a fool whether you dance or not, so you might as well dance" is sung, the Awa-Odori allegedly originated when rice wine was passed out to the townspeople of Tokushima to celebrate completion of a castle.

Did You Know?

The anime character Naruto Uzumaki, an adolescent ninja, takes his name from the whirlpools.

From Kochi, take a day trip to Cape Muroto at the southeast tip of Shikoku or Cape Ashizuri to the southwest. Both have views of the Pacific Ocean and some unusual rock formations.

Kochi Castle
◈ 🏯1-2-1 Marunouchi
🕘9am–5pm daily
🚫Dec 26–Jan 1

Sakamoto Ryoma Museum
◈ 🏯830 Urado-shiroyama
🕘9am–5pm daily

7

Tokushima
徳島

🅐D5 🚉Tokushima Prefecture 🚌🚆 🛈In front of Tokushima Stn; www.discovertokushima.net/en

The city of Tokushima forms the gateway into the island

←
The churning waters of the Naruto Whirlpools under the Onaruto Suspension Bridge

of Shikoku from the Kansai region of Honshu and is the traditional point of entry for those who set out to duplicate Kukai's pilgrimage *(p258)*. The old name of the province, Awa, gives its name to the town's Awa-Odori celebration in mid-August, a dancing festival that is broadcast nationwide.

South of Tokushima, the Anan Coast is known for its charming fishing villages, pleasant beaches, and the sea turtles that lay and hatch eggs during the summer months (June to August).

🔍 HIDDEN GEM
Chiiori House

Dating from around 1720, this house in Tokushima province is typical of old Iya construction, with its wooden floors and *irori* (floor hearths). The beams and rafters are black from centuries of fires burning in the floor hearths *(www.chiiori.org)*.

8

Matsuyama
松山

🅐C6 🄰Ehime Prefecture
✉🄰 🄸At JR Stn; www.city.
matsuyama.ehime.jp/
lang/en

The capital of Ehime prefecture and a castle town since 1603, Matsuyama has many powerful associations for the Japanese.

The **Dogo Onsen Honkan**, a famous hot-spring spa, has been in use for over a millennium, and has a fine 19th-century bathhouse. Deeper into the mountains behind the historic bathhouse, is Oku-Dogo Onsen, which is a much newer hotel resort area.

Natsume Soseki, an author whose portrait appears on the ¥1,000 bill, moved to the town in 1895 and later wrote about Matsuyama in his autobiographical novel *Botchan* (1906). The **Shiki Masaoka Museum** is devoted to Soseki's friend Shiki (1867–1902), a Matsuyama native held by many to be Japan's greatest modern haiku poet, as well as a fine painter. The collection includes manuscripts, paintings, and photographs of Shiki and Soseki.

Matsuyama Castle is an extensive complex on a bluff overlooking the city and Seto Inland Sea. Plaques offer intelligent commentary on the castle's strategic features.

Dogo Onsen Honkan

⊛ 🄰5-6 Dogoyunomachi
🚉Dogo Stn 🄲(089) 921-5141
🄾6am-11pm daily

> 🔺 GREAT VIEW
> ### Capture the Castle
>
> Matsuyama's castle stands on a hill. A former defensive feature, today it provides a great view out over the Seto Inland Sea. In spring, when the cherry trees are in bloom, the panorama is even more spectacular.

Shiki Masaoka Museum

⊛ 🄰1-30 Dōgo-kōen; 3-min walk from Dogo Onsen Honkan 🄾9am-6pm Wed-Mon (to 5pm Nov-Apr)

Matsuyama Castle

⊛ 🄰1 Marunouchi
🚉Kencho-mae stop, then steep walk, or Okaido stop, then 5-min walk to cable car or lift 🄲(089) 921-4873
🄾9am-4:30pm daily

9

Ozu
大洲

🅐B6 🄰Ehime Prefecture
🄰 🄸Near City Hall (20-min walk from JR Stn); (0893) 24-2664

A castle town built where the Hiji River snakes in an S-curve through a valley rimmed by picturesque bluffs, Ozu is known to insiders as the "little Kyoto" of Ehime prefecture. Whereas it could be argued that Kyoto offers well-preserved relics of Japan's past, Ozu offers a past that is still alive. The riverfront is lined by quaint, narrow streets of tile-roofed bars and restaurants with sliding wood shutters. A riverside villa called **Garyu Sanso**, built in 1907, is one of the most spectacular buildings. On the river itself, shallow-bottomed skiffs shunt

→

Terraced fields overlooking the harbor and mountainous landscape in Uwajima

cormorant fishermen back and forth through the river breezes. Traditional culture is still the norm in Ozu, where raw silk, dairy products, and vegetables form the basis for the local economy. The town's restaurants serve fish and eel caught in nearby rivers.

The panorama of seasonal change is especially vivid in the wooded hillsides of Ozu. August is marked with a festival of fireworks launched from an islet in the river.

Garyu Sanso

⊛ 🄰411-2 Ozu 🄲(089) 324-3759 🄾9am-5pm daily

⑩ Uchiko
内子

 C6 Ehime Prefecture
 Uchiko; www.we-love-uchiko.jp

Located in a small valley where the Oda River splits into three branches, the town of Uchiko is famous for its historic Kabuki theater, the **Uchiko-za**, and its sloping street of two-story wooden buildings with whitewashed walls, tiled roofs, and broad fronts. In 1982 the government moved to ensure the preservation of these structures, which date from the mid-19th century. Several are open to the public, and others function as craft shops and restaurants. The area is often used for locations in historical films and television dramas.

Uchiko-za
 2102 Uchiko
 (089) 344-2840
 9am–4:30pm daily

Rickshaws outside the centuries-old Dogo Onsen Honkan in Matsuyama

⑪ Uwajima
宇和島

 B6 Ehime Prefecture
 5-min walk from Stn; (0895) 22-3934

Uwajima, a harbor town with a castle, old temple district, and mountain setting, is probably best known for its bullfighting, where the bulls are ranked in the same way as Sumo wrestlers. Two curious sites attract visitors. The **Taga-jinja Shrine** houses famously sexually explicit statues and other objects associated with fertility. Next door, the **Taga-jinja Sex Museum** has similarly provocative statues from around the world.

In the mountains northwest of Uwajima, the **Nametoko Gorge** is noted for its waterfall and fine views.

Taga-jinja Shrine
 1340 Fujie Daily

Taga-jinja Sex Museum
  8am–5pm daily

Nametoko Gorge
 From JR Uwajima Stn to Matsumaru stn (Yodo line), then taxi to Nametoko

EAT

Bakushukan
The perfect place for a cold beer and a snack.

 C6 20-13 Dogoyunomachi, Matsuyama-shi, Ehime-ken 790-0842
 Dogobeer.co.jp

¥¥¥

Nikitatsuan
This restaurant uses fresh local produce.

 C6 3-18 Dogokita-machi, Matsuyama-shi, Ehime-ken 790-0848
 (089) 924-6617

¥¥¥

Kappo Kotobuki
Try the abalone at this sushi restaurant.

 C6 1F Kotojingetsukan, 1-3-12 Nibancho, Matsuyama-shi, Ehime-ken
 kappou-kotobuki.net

¥¥¥

A LONG WALK
THE 88-TEMPLE PILGRIMAGE

Distance About 745 miles (1,200 km) **Time** Six–eight weeks
Difficulty Some tricky terrain; signage is mostly in Japanese

When pilgrims retrace the route of Kukai, the founder of Shingon Buddhism who made a pilgrimage of 88 of the island's minor temples in the 9th century, they are honoring a cultural icon. Those who hope to atone for a grave error complete the pilgrimage in reverse order, believing that they will encounter the saint as they walk or in their dreams. About 100,000 pilgrims complete the circuit each year, and countless others follow part of it. Pilgrims can collect a series of stamps as they visit each temple, many of which offer lodgings and meals. If the circuit is too much, you can walk part of it or take a week-long bus tour.

Popular with tour groups, Temple 51, also known as **Ishite-ji**, *is associated with the legend of a very rich man breaking Kukai's begging bowl.*

Did You Know?

In Shingon Buddhism, 88 represents the number of evils that can beset us.

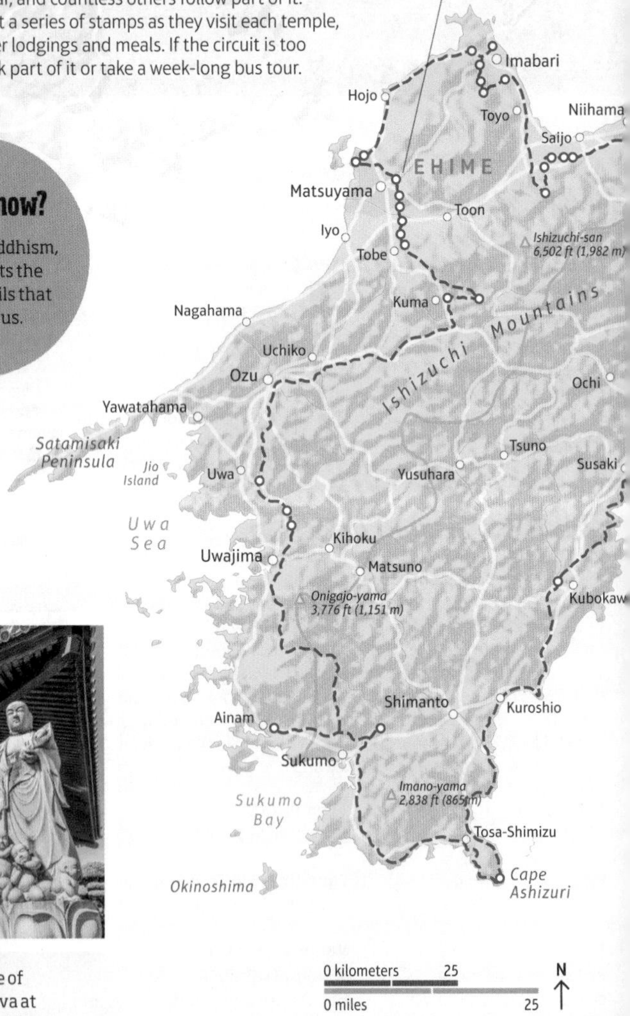

↑ A stone statue of the bodhisattva at Kannon-ji, Temple 16

Imabari
Hojo
Toyo
Niihama
Saijo
EHIME
Matsuyama
Toon
Iyo
Tobe
Ishizuchi-san 6,502 ft (1,982 m)
Kuma
Nagahama
Uchiko
Ishizuchi Mountains
Ozu
Ochi
Yawatahama
Tsuno
Susaki
Satamisaki Peninsula
Jio Island
Uwa
Yusuhara
Uwa Sea
Uwajima
Kihoku
Matsuno
Kubokaw
Onigajo-yama 3,776 ft (1,151 m)
Shimanto
Kuroshio
Ainam
Imano-yama 2,838 ft (865 m)
Sukumo
Tosa-Shimizu
Sukumo Bay
Okinoshima
Cape Ashizuri

0 kilometers   25
0 miles   25
N ↑

Temple 1, **Ryozen-ji**, near Naruto, is the start and end of the pilgrimage, though devout pilgrims will extend the start and end to Mount Koya (p234) on Honshu, the head-quarters of the Shingon sect. Sign the book of completion here.

The birthplace of Kukai is marked by Temple 75, **Zentsu-ji**, one stop from Kotohira.

The name of Temple 2, **Gokuraku-ji**, refers to the Pure Land, or Western Paradise, of the Amida Buddha, a fundamental concept in Shingon Buddhism.

Takamatsu
Sakaide
Sanuki
Marugame
Hiketa
KAGAWA
Mitoyo
Kan-onji
Kotohira
Naruto
Iyomishima
Waki
Awa
Tokushima
Kawanoe
Yoshino-gawa
Komatsushima
Miyoshi
Kamiyama
Tsurugi Mountains
Katsuura
Ochiai
TOKUSHIMA
Anan
Tsurugi-san
6,414 ft m (1,955 m)
Naka
Otoyo
Minami
Tosa
Monobecho
Befu
KOCHI
Umaji
Mugi
Kainan
Kochi
Nankoku
Aki
Kitagawa
Yasuda
Toyo
Nahari
Muroto
Cape
Muroto

Between temples 11 and 12 is an uphill trek notorious as the "pilgrim crusher."

Temple 31, **Chikurin-ji**, was built in 724 by order of Emperor Shomu. Kukai received his training at this temple.

The main hall of **Shinsho-ji**, Temple 25, is home to thousands of small statues of Jizo – the bodhisattva – holding a ship's wheel. Jizo is thought to save sailors caught in storms.

→ A striking golden domed subtemple at Ishite-ji, Temple 51 of the pilgrimage

KYUSHU

Organized communities settled in Kyushu in the Jomon period (14,500–300 BC). According to legend, it was from Kyushu that the first emperor of Japan, Jimmu, set out in the 6th century BC on his campaign to unify the country. And it was through Kyushu in the 4th century AD that Chinese and Korean culture, including Buddhism and the Chinese writing system, first infiltrated Japan. Not all foreign incursions were welcomed, however. The natives of the island repelled several Mongolian invasions, the last and most formidable in 1274 only by the intervention of a powerful storm, the *kamikaze* (divine wind), which scuttled the Mongolian fleet.

In the 16th century, Christianity, firearms, and medicine were introduced through the port cities of Nagasaki and Kumamoto by the merchants and emissaries of Portugal, Spain, and Holland. Later, during the two centuries of Japan's self-imposed isolation, the tiny island of Dejima off the coast of Nagasaki was the country's sole entrepôt for Western trade and learning. The city grew because of this contact with the rest of the world but, four centuries later, Nagasaki was devastated by an atomic bomb detonated by the US in 1945.

Today, the island is characterized by volcanic activity. Kagoshima lies in the shadow of Sakurajima, which daily belches ash; Mount Aso is one of the world's largest calderas; and steaming fissures and fumeroles are found at Beppu, Unzen, and other spa towns.

Map labels:

O-shima

Katsumoto · Iki Island
Gonoura

FUKUOKA ①
Fukuoka Airport

Yobuko · Itoshima
Karatsu

Kasuga
38

Hirado
Matsuura

YOSHINOGARI
RUINS
⑭

Hirado Island

Taku

Imari

SAGA

Saga · Okav

Takeo

Sasebo

NAGASAKI

Kashima · YANAGAWA ⑫

Ariakekai

Nishi-
Sonogihanto

Matsubara

Omuta

207

Arikawa

Goto-
retto

Nakadori
Island

Narao

Omura

Nagasaki Airport

Arao

206

Isahaya

SHIMABARA
PENINSULA ⑬

NAGASAKI ②
E34

Mount Unzen
4,875 ft (1,486 m)

Fukue

Fukue
Island

Kuchinotsu

Misun

251

Nomo-zaki

Hondo

Amakusa
Island

KYUSHU

Must Sees
① Fukuoka
② Nagasaki

Experience More
③ Usa
④ Kokura
⑤ Yufuin
⑥ Beppu
⑦ Usuki Stone Buddhas
⑧ Kurume
⑨ Onta
⑩ Dazaifu
⑪ Kumamoto
⑫ Yanagawa
⑬ Shimabara Peninsula
⑭ Yoshinogari Ruins
⑮ Mount Aso
⑯ Takachiho
⑰ Nichinan Coast
⑱ Kirishima-Kinkowan National Park
⑲ Kagoshima
⑳ Amami Oshima Island
㉑ Chiran

Ushibuka · Minamata

Naga-
shima

Izumi

Akune

Satsur

Sendai

3

Koshiki
Island

Kushikino · Kushikino

Hioki

E3

270

Kaseda

CHIRAN

Satsu
hant

Makurazaki

Amami Oshima Island,
Yakushima Island ↙

WESTERN HONSHU
p210

○ Hofu

0 kilometers 30

0 miles 30

N

KOKURA ❹

Nakama ○ Kitakyushu

✈ Kitakyushu Airport

Suo-nada

Matsuyama

Iizuka ○ Nogata
○ Yukuhashi

FUKUOKA ○ Tagawa

○ Buzen
○ Nakatsu

USA ❸

Kunisaki Peninsula

○ Kunisaki

Onojo ○
322

❿ DAZAIFU
○ Amagi

○ Hiji
○ Kitsuki

✈ Oita Airport

Ozu

Yawatahama

Ogori ○

❾ ONTA
○ Hita

❻ BEPPU
○ Oita

Misaki ○

Uwa

◉ KURUME
○ Kurogi
○ Yame

YUFUIN ❺

210

Uwajima

○ Kusu

Hiko-san 3,937 ft (1,200 m)

○ Minamioguni

OITA

Inukai ○

❼

Tsukumi ○

SHIKOKU
p246

Yamaga ○

Kuju-san 5,876 ft (1,791 m)

USUKI STONE BUDDHAS

Saiki ○

Kikuchi ○

Mt Daikanbo 3,084 ft (940 m)

○ Taketa
○ Bungo-ono

Tamana ○

Koshi ○

✈ Kumamoto Airport

⓯ MOUNT ASO

Sukomo

Uto ○

⓫ KUMAMOTO
○ Takamori

Sobo-san 5,764 ft (1,757 m)

○ Kamae

Uki ○

KUMAMOTO

⓰ TAKACHIHO
○ Hinokage

Misato ○

Kunimi-dake 5,705 ft (1,739 m)

○ Nobeoka

Yatsushiro ○

Kyushu-sanchi

Misato ○

○ Kadogawa

P a c i f i c
O c e a n

shikita ○

Itsuki ○

Kuma ○

Ichifusa-yama 5,666 ft (1,727 m)

○ Hyuga

Yunomae ○

MIYAZAKI

Hitoyoshi ○
○ Taragi

○ Nishimera

○ Tsuno

○ Takanabe

Isa ○

Ebino ○

○ Saito

Islands of Kagoshima Prefecture

○ Ibusuki

○ Kobayashi

MIYAZAKI

⓲

268

○ Miyazaki

✈ Miyazaki Airport

Nishinoomote

Tanega Island

KIRISHIMA-KINKOWAN NATIONAL PARK

○ Kirishima

○ Miyakonojo

Aoshima Island

Kamiyaku

East China Sea

Yaku Island

◉ Kagoshima Airport ✈

Kajiki ○

○ Soo
○ Obi

NICHINAN COAST

⓱

◉ KAGOSHIMA

⓳

Sakurajima Volcano

○ Nichinan

○ Tarumizu
E78

○ Shibushi

Pacific Ocean

KAGOSHIMA
○ Kushima

Kagoshima-wan

○ Kanoya

Shibushi-wan

Naze

26

○ Ibusuki

○ Uchinoura

○ Setouchi

⓴ AMAMI OSHIMA ISLAND

○ Yamagawa

Osumi-hanto

Tokuno Island

○ Tokunoshima

0 km 60

0 miles 60

N

○ Wadomari

Fukuoka's neon-lit buildings reflected in the mirror-like Naka River at nighttime

❶

FUKUOKA

福岡

🅰A6 🏠Fukuoka Prefecture ✈🚆 ℹ️Hakata Stn; 1F Solaria Terminal Bldg, Tenjin; www.city.fukuoka.lg.jp

Strikingly modern, Fukuoka bills itself as the gateway to southern Japan. The closest city to mainland Asia, it has, for at least a millennium, been the country's main port of entry for Chinese and Korean culture. This has lent it an attractive foreign Asian flavor, both culturally and on its restaurant menus.

①
Fukuoka City Museum

🏠3-1-1 Momochihama 🕐9:30am-5:30pm Tue-Sun 🚫Dec 28-Jan 4 🌐museum.city.fukuoka.jp/en

This museum traces the relationship between Fukuoka and its Asian neighbors from the Ice Age to the city's modern waterfront developments. The museum utilizes four generations of a fictitious local family to bring this history to life.

The primary artifact in the collection is a gold 3rd-century Chinese seal, which was discovered on Shika Island, across the bay from the city, in 1784. It is believed to have been gifted to envoys from an early Japanese kingdom by Emperor Guangwu of China.

②
Fukuoka Tower

🏠2-3-26 Momochihama 🕐9:30am-10pm daily 🌐fukuokatower.co.jp/en

The city's tallest structure, at an impressive 768 ft (234 m) tall, dominates the waterfront Momochi district. Resembling a mirrored sail, the tower boasts the highest seaside observation deck in Japan, overlooking the bay and city below, as well as the swanky Sky Lounge & Restaurant.

Fukuoka Tower is also a spectacle from the ground – every evening, on the hour, it is illuminated by a light installation reflecting the time of year.

③
Ohori Park

🕐Fukuoka Art Museum: 9:30am-5:30pm daily 🌐Fukuoka Art Museum: fukuoka-art-museum.jp

Located in the west of the city, Ohori Park is a popular green space, with delightful pathways, lake, pavilions, and islets connected by traditional bridges. The park is also home to the Fukuoka Art Museum, which houses an impressive collection of modern art by artists from around the world.

💬 INSIDER TIP
Use Your Noodle

Fukuoka is celebrated for its *yatai*. These sit-down food stalls are legendary, with their colorful, lamp-lit stands serving steaming bowls of ramen and open-pot stews. Head to Nakasu Island to find them.

---

④

Fukuoka Asian Art Museum

◫ 3-1 Shimokawabatamachi
Ⓢ Nakasu-Kawabata Stn
◷ 10am–8pm Thu–Tue
ⓦ faam.city.fukuoka.lg.jp

An expansive collection of contemporary Asian art is found at this museum. From Pakistan to the Philippines, works from 23 countries are housed here, and the Fukuoka Asian Art Museum can claim to represent all of the distinct cultures found across the continent. Folk art and traditional art are displayed alongside contemporary works to demonstrate the influence of cultural heritage.

⑤

Shofuku-ji

◫ 6-1 Gokushomachi

Despite its modernity, Fukuoka also has sights of impressive antiquity. Shofuku-ji, north-west of Hakata station, is said to be the oldest Zen Buddhist temple in Japan. It was founded in the late 12th century by the priest Yosai, who introduced both Zen and tea to Japan. The Kushida Shrine, just to the west, dates from the 8th century.

---

⑥

Hakata Machiya Folk Museum

◫ 6-10 Reisemmachi
☎ (092) 281-7761 Ⓢ Gion Stn ◷ 10am–6pm daily

The exhibits and dioramas within this traditional building celebrate the heritage of the area. It is also possible to watch local artisans at work here, including demonstrations of Hakata silk weaving.

← Weaving cloth on a loom at the Hakata Machiya Folk Museum

EAT

Hakata Issou

Made from pork from local farms, the rich and silky *tonkotsu* broth served here has been nicknamed the "pork bone cappuccino" by local ramen lovers.

◫ 3-1-6 Hakataekihigashi
☎ (092) 472-7739

¥¥¥

Ganso Hakata Mentaiju

Mentaiko (spiced herring roe), a specialty in this city, is served here with both rice and *tsukemen* (ramen and soup served in two separate bowls). Dip the noodles into the spicy *mentaiko* soup – the result is out of this world.

◫ 6-15 Nishinakasu
☎ (092) 725-7220

¥¥¥

The glowing lights of the buildings lining Nagasaki's historic harbor at dusk ↑

②

NAGASAKI

長崎

🅰A6 🏠Nagasaki Prefecture ✈25 miles (40 km) NE 🚝JR line ℹIn JR Nagasaki Stn; www.travel.at-nagasaki.jp/en

A history of contact and interaction with Europe, even after foreign powers were expelled elsewhere in the country in the 17th century, its tragic fate as victim of the second atomic bomb in 1945, and miraculous resurgence since the war have made Nagasaki one of the most cosmopolitan and eclectic cities in Japan.

①

Shrine to the 26 Martyrs

🏠5-min walk from station 🕐Museum: 9am-5pm daily

Christianity was officially banned in 1597 by the shogun Toyotomi Hideyoshi who feared that conversions would lead to political intrigues and the undermining of the state by foreign powers. In that year, to emphasize the point, 26 defiant Christians were crucified on Nishizaka Hill, the first of over 600 documented martyrdoms in the Nagasaki area alone. A stone relief, a small chapel, and a museum honor the martyrs who, in 1862, were declared saints by the Pope. Without a clergy or a single chapel to worship in, Christianity, astonishingly, managed to survive covertly for another 200 years until the end of Japan's isolationism.

②

Spectacles Bridge

🏠10-min walk from station 🚃Nigiwaibashi, Kokaidomae

One of the most photographed sights in Nagasaki is the curious Megane-bashi, or Spectacles Bridge, a Chinese bequest to the city. Built by the Zen priest Mozi in 1634, it remains the oldest stone bridge in Japan. It earned its name because the curve of the bridge reflected in the Nakashima River resembles a pair of glasses.

③

Dejima

🏠6-1 Dejimamachi 📞(095) 829-1194 🚃Dejima 🕐8am-6pm daily

After the Portuguese were expelled from Japan in 1638, the Dutch, confined to the tiny island of Dejima, were the only foreign power permitted to

→

The simple stone relief depicting the 26 Christian martyrs of Nagasaki

remain in the country. Dejima was once surrounded by mud walls, and the only Japanese people allowed to enter were traders, prostitutes, and monks collecting alms. Dejima Museum, housed in Japan's first Protestant seminary, and Dejima Dutch Factory Historic Site next door contain historical artifacts from excavations on the site.

---

④

Suwa Shrine

🏠 **Kaminishiyama-dori**
🚉 **Suwa Jinjamae**

Located in a wooded hilltop precinct at the top of 277 stone steps, Suwa Shrine affords fine views. The original buildings were destroyed by fire in 1857 but later beautifully restored. The purpose of this popular shrine, home to the city's pantheon of Shinto gods, was to promote Shintoism and eradicate the last vestiges of Christianity from the area. The autumn festival, Kunchi Matsuri, is celebrated here, with blazing floats and dragon dances.

EAT

Kagetsu

Shippoku ryori reflects Nagasaki's historic engagement with other nations. These small sharing dishes combine traditional Japanese flavors with Chinese and European influences. Kagetsu is one of the most historic restaurants in the city to serve this unique meal.

🏠 **2-1 Maruyamamachi**
🌐 **ryoutei-kagetsu.co.jp**

¥ ¥ ¥

---

⑤

Sofuku-ji

🏠 **Sofuku-ji-dori** 🚉 **Sojukuji**

The Chinese provenance of this temple is shown by the entrance gate, which depicts the gateway that, according to legend, is to be seen in the Chinese undersea paradise. The temple also has a second, more illustrious gate known as First Peak Gate, dating from the late Ming period.

Sofuku-ji is one of the three largest Chinese places of worship in Nagasaki. The temple was founded, with the help of local Chinese residents, by a monk in 1629. The gigantic cooking pot that stands in the temple grounds was used to make gruel to feed over 3,000 people each day during one of Nagasaki's worst famines in 1682.

---

⑥

Kofuku-ji

🏠 **Teramachi-dori**
🚉 **Shimenkaikan**

Kofuku-ji, located at the heart of the Teramachi district, was Japan's first Obaku Zen Buddhist temple. Founded by a Chinese priest in 1623, the building is also known as the Nanking Temple and is often visited by residents from that city. The main buildings, including the Buddha hall, are constructed in Chinese style.

⑦
Oura Catholic Church

🏠 5-3 Minami-yamatemachi
🚉 Oura Tenshudo ⏰ 8am–6pm daily

This white church was built in 1864 under the direction of Bernard Petitjean, a French priest who became the first Bishop of Nagasaki. It was erected in order to serve the foreign community that settled in Nagasaki after the new trade treaties were signed but, soon after its foundation, Petitjean was approached by a group of Japanese Christians who had been practicing their faith in secret since it was outlawed.

Classed as a National Treasure, Oura is one of the oldest churches in Japan and the country's earliest Gothic wooden building. A wooden building beside the church contains items connected with the persecution of Nagasaki's early Christians.

⑧
Atomic Bomb Museum

🏠 7-8 Hirano-machi 🚉 Atomic Bomb Museum
⏰ 8:30am–5:30pm daily (to 6:30pm May–Aug)
🌐 nagasakipeace.jp

This museum is a must for anybody

↑ Examining photographs and artifacts at the Atomic Bomb Museum

visiting the city. Displays depict Nagasaki before and after the explosion and also the reconstruction. It traces with great objectivity and fairness the events leading up to the bombing, the history of nuclear weapons, and the evolution of the international peace movement. Photographs, artifacts, videos, and dioramas vividly recreate the tragedy. A clock, frozen at the moment the bomb exploded, is one of the most poignant items.

⑨
Peace Park

🚉 Matsuyama-machi

A black stone pillar marks the spot where the US detonated its second atom bomb at 11:02 on August 9, 1945, three days after the bombing of Hiroshima. The intended target was the nearby shipyards. The blast killed an estimated 75,000, and 75,000 more were injured in its wake. Small wonder that the citizens of Nagasaki have become staunch advocates of world peace, erecting several monuments in the park, including a 30-ft (9-m) tall Peace Statue. A 1959 reconstruction of the Urakami Catholic Church, which stood at the epicenter, stands near the park.

⑩
Confucius Shrine

🏠 10-36 Ouramachi
🚉 Oura Tenshudo
⏰ 8:30am–5pm daily

Vibrant yellow roof tiles and vermilion walls instantly announce this building as a shrine dedicated to the scholar Confucius. Built by the city's Chinese community in 1893, the repairs and extensions accorded the shrine after it was damaged in the atomic bombing included the addition in 1982 of a National Museum of Chinese History. The antiquities on display are on loan from the Chinese National Museum and the prestigious Palace Museum in Beijing.

← Seibo Kitamura's towering Peace Statue in Nagasaki's poignant Peace Park

⑪

Glover Garden

🏠 8-1 Minamiyamatemachi
🚉 Oura Tenshudo Shita
🕐 8am–6pm daily

With the reopening of the port to Westerners in the latter half of the 19th century, Nagasaki flowered as a prosperous international city. Suitable housing was required for the sudden influx of foreigners and many of the comfortable stone and clapboard residencies that were built during this period survive today, preserved in Glover Garden.

The best-known European-style residence here is Glover House. It was built in 1863 for Thomas Glover, an extraordinary British entrepreneur whose ventures included bringing the first steam locomotive to Japan, coal mining, a tea import house, ship repair yards, and the founding of a beer company, the forerunner of today's Kirin Beer.

Other notable buildings in the park include Ringer House, standing on foundation stones brought from Vladivostok, and Walker House, which displays the colorful floats used in the city's annual Kunchi festival. The Old Hong Kong and Shanghai Bank Building houses displays tracing Nagasaki's contact with Western ideas.

---

⑫

Hollander Slope

🚉 Shimin-Byoin-mae

A pleasant cobblestone street built by the Dutch, the Slope was once the center for the city's expatriate community. For a time, all Westerners, irrespective of nationality, were called "Hollanders" by the Japanese. Some of the wooden houses along the Slope are open to the public. One of the most imposing, the 1868 Junibankan, was once the Prussian Legation building.

FOREIGNERS IN NAGASAKI

The Portuguese and Dutch were the first to arrive when Nagasaki's harbor opened to international trade in 1571, followed by Chinese merchants who established their own community. The Portuguese bought Catholicism to the city, but this minority soon faced religious persecution. When Japan became a closed country in 1634, only the Dutch were allowed to trade here. After the port reopened in 1853, British, American, French, German, and Prussian trade missions came to the city. The legacy of this extraordinary foreign contact survives in some of the local festivals and cuisine, like the Portuguese *castella,* an egg-and-flour-based sponge cake.

⑬

Huis ten Bosch

🏠 Near Sasebo 🚉 Huis ten Bosch 🕐 Hours vary, check website 🌐 english.huistenbosch.co.jp

Built in 1992 at the staggering cost of US$1.75 billion, Huis ten Bosch is a reproduction of a traditional Dutch village. Replete with churches, houses, shops, windmills, a farmhouse, and canals, it is one of the largest theme parks in Japan. Replicas of Queen Beatrix's palace and of Holland's tallest church tower are highlights. As you travel through the park by horse-drawn carriage, old-fashioned taxi, or canal boat, you'll soon forget that you aren't in the Netherlands.

A reconstruction of a historic Dutch windmill in Huis ten Bosch

EXPERIENCE MORE

Usa
宇佐

📍 B6 🏛 Oita Prefecture
🚉 🚌 Sightseeing bus tour recommended

The center of Tendai-sect sanctuaries and shrines dedicated to Hachiman, the god of war, the area around Usa and the Kunisaki Peninsula is believed to have been the nucleus of ancient Buddhist sites. These religious places are of Korean inspiration and origin. The most famous site, Usa Jingu, a shrine to the ancient Japanese deities, is also identified with the influential figure of Hachiman.

On the peninsula, to the east of Usa, are stone tombs, Heian-period statues, and, at Kumano Magaibutsu, the largest carved rock-face reliefs in Japan. The ancient ambience of the peninsula can be sensed near the summit of Mount Futago, where stone guardians mark the approach to Futago-ji. Twin avatars of the mountain are enshrined at the temple hall here, built into the side of a cliff. The oldest wooden structure in Kyushu, the main hall of Fuki-ji, dating from the Heian period, has faint, eerily beautiful frescoes of the Buddhist paradise.

Did You Know?

The god of war, Hachiman was held to be the guardian of the samurais.

Kokura
小倉

📍 B5 🏛 Fukuoka Prefecture
🚉 ℹ️ At JR Stn; www.gururich-kitaq.com/en/

The gateway to northern Kyushu, Kokura is a modern city. This is embodied in the designs of architect Arata Isozaki, especially **Chuo Toshokan Kitakyushu** library (1974), a curvaceous building that has been used as a set for many movies. The city and its environs – including Dan no Ura battlefield, where the Taira clan were defeated, and the straits of Shimonoseki – can be seen from Kokura Castle. Next to the castle, the beautifully laid out **Kokura Castle Japanese Garden** surrounds a samurai house.

Chuo Toshokan Kitakyushu

📍 4-1 Jonai 🕐 Tue–Sun

Kokura Castle Japanese Garden

♿ 📍 1-2 Jonai 📞 (093) 582-2747 🕐 9am–5pm daily

Yufuin
湯布院

📍 B6 🏛 Oita Prefecture 🚉 ℹ️ At JR Stn; (0977) 84-2446

Known for picturesque wisps of morning mist rising from its thermally warm lake, Yufuin sits at the foot of Mount Yufudake. The resort prides itself on elegant country inns, boutiques, summer concerts, and a host of museums, including the **Sueda Art Museum** and the **Trick 3D Art Yufuin Museum**.

JR Yufuin station has a sooty, black exterior meant to suggest the boiler of a locomotive. The station, built in 1990 by Arata Isozaki, has art displays in its exhibition hall, and the floors are heated from an underground hot spring.

A walking and cycling path follows the shore of serene Lake Kinrin. Shitan-yu is an old outdoor bath with a thatched roof beside the lake. The bathing here is mixed, as baths often were before the arrival, during the Meiji period, of Americans and Europeans

→ Traditional torii marking the entrance to the famous Usa Jingu

The main shopping street in the spa town of Yufuin, surrounded by mountains

who shamed the Japanese into segregating their baths.

Sueda Art Museum
 1834 Kawakami
(0977) 85-3572
9am–5pm daily

Trick 3D Art Yufuin Museum
3001-8 Yufuincho, Kawakami 9:30am–5pm daily

Beppu
別府

B6 Oita Prefecture
Oita From Tokyo, Osaka, Kobe, and Hiroshima
Beppu Stn; www.city.beppu.oita.jp

If you can accept its brazen commercialism, Beppu, a glitzy, neon-strung hot-spring

> **INSIDER TIP**
> **Be Footloose**
>
> Dotted around Beppu are *ashiyu* - onsen for your feet. Usually found in public places, these small hot water pools are the perfect place to rest weary feet and are often free of charge.

resort, constitutes an amazing thermal and entertainment roller coaster.

The city's porous skin is punctured by a number of vents from which steam continuously rises. Scalding water surfaces at the 3,750 hot springs and 168 public baths, and is also piped into private homes to heat rooms and fuel ovens.

Beppu offers interesting variations on the theme of a hot bath. Visitors can soak in a series of tubs of graded temperatures, plunge into thermal whirlpools, be buried in hot black sand, or sit up to the neck in steaming mud.

The most famous sights are the **Boiling Hells** (Jigoku) – pools of mineral-colored water and bubbling mud. Six of them are within walking distance of each other in the Kannawa district in the north of Beppu. Each has a different function, color, and mineral property. For example, the waters of Ocean Hell (Umi Jigoku) are the color of a tropical sea, while Blood Pond Hell (Chi-no-Ike Jigoku) takes its color from dissolved red clay.

Many baths are attached to hotels but also open to the public. The hugely popular **Suginoi Palace**, a hotel on the western fringes of town, is an irresistible hot-spring fantasy. Built in 1879 just inland from Beppu Bay, **Takegawara**

Bathhouse is one of Beppu's oldest public baths, in which visitors are buried in black sand before plunging into adjacent hot pools. Up in the hills north of Kannawa, **Myoban Hot Spring** is a quieter place to which Japanese people have been coming for well over a thousand years for curative baths. For an overview of Beppu, climb the 410-ft (125-m) Global Tower, between the station and Suginoi Palace.

Boiling Hells
559-1 Kannawa
(0977) 66-1577
8am–5pm daily

Suginoi Palace
Kankaiji 1 (0977) 24-1141 Daily

Takegawara Bathhouse
16-23 Motomachi
(0977) 23-1585 8am–10:30pm daily

Myoban Hot Spring
Myoban 8:30am–5:30pm daily jigoku-prin.com

← A number of carved Usuki Stone Buddhas, about which little is known

7
Usuki Stone Buddhas
臼杵石仏

▲B6 **◗Oita Prefecture** **◻Usuki Stn, then JR bus to Usuki-Sekibutsu**

Despite the dissemination of images of Oita's Seki Butsu (stone Buddhas) throughout Japan, the site itself is only a minor tourist area. Though it is probable that the work was

begun during the late Heian period and completed in the early Kamakura era, there appears to be no consensus regarding the origin of the site, who commissioned or executed the dozens of carvings, or why such a large, relatively remote area was dedicated for the images.

All of this adds a great deal of mystery and charm to the place. Late afternoon is very atmospheric, when sculptured sunlight draws out the earth hues from the faces and torsos of these mysterious and peaceful stone Buddhas.

bus stop. The **Ishibashi Bunka Center**, a five-minute bus ride from the station, has an art museum and Japanese garden.

Many artisans work in the villages of Hirokawa and Yame, a 40-minute bus ride from Kurume. In Hirokawa, visit the **Moriyama Kasuri Workshop**, which employs a 16th-century technique to make paper, using mulberry-tree fibers.

Kurume Regional Industry Promotion Center
◗2F Jibasan Kurume Center, 5-8-5 Higashi Aikawa
☎(0942) 44-3700
◯10am-5pm daily

Ishibashi Bunka Center
◗1015 Nonakamachi
☎(0942) 33-2271
◯9am-5pm Tue-Sun

Moriyama Kasuri Workshop
◗109 Niishiro, Hirokawa-machi ☎(0943) 32-0023 (reservation required)
◯10am-6pm Mon-Sat

SHOP

Head to the town of Arita, in Saga prefecture, to visit ancient pottery studios.

Koransha
▲A6 ◗1-3-8 Kobira, Arita-Cho, Nishimat-suura-Gun, Saga 844-8601 ⬹koransha.co.jp

Fukagawa Seiji
▲A6 ◗1-1-8 Kobira, Arita-Cho, Nishimat-suura-Gun, Saga 844-0005 ☎(0955) 42-5215

Arita Porcelain Lab
▲A6 ◗1-11-3 Kami-Kobira, Arita-Cho, Nishimatsuura-Gun, Saga 844-0022 ⬹aritaware.com

---

8
Kurume
久留米

▲A6 **◗Fukuoka Prefecture** **◻ ℹ(0942) 33-4422**

The sprawling city of Kurume is the center of *kasuri* textiles. These employ a distinctive ikat weaving style, in which the threads have been tie-dyed before weaving; unlike Southeast Asian forms of ikat, both the warp and weft are patterned. The **Kurume Regional Industry Promotion Center** sells these textiles. *Rantai-shikki* is a local basket-weaving style whereby layers of lacquer are applied to bamboo to produce basketware. Examples can be bought at Inoue Rantai-Shikki, opposite the Honmachi-yon-chome

The simple, functional objects are characterized by marked, dribbled glazes in earth colors. The Onta Folk Pottery Festival takes place on the second weekend of October.

10

Dazaifu
大宰府

A6 Fukuoka Prefecture At Dazaifu Stn; (092) 925-1880

Dazaifu was of great military importance under the Yamato government (p211) and an administrative center in the later Nara period. Today, most visitors come for the shrine of **Dazaifu Tenman-gu**. Located in a tranquil district close to the station, the shrine is dedicated to the calligrapher, scholar, and poet Sugawara Michizane. The guardian of learning, Michizane, who died in AD 903, is also known by his divine name of Tenjin. The Treasure House can be visited, and just behind it is a hall displaying curious tableaux of Hakata clay dolls representing scenes from Michizane's life.

PICTURE PERFECT
Time Travel

After going through the torii at Dazaifu Tenman-gu, pause at the pond in the shape of the Japanese character for "heart." Take a picture of the bridges linking the three islands, each representing the past, present, and future.

The **Kyushu National Museum** focuses on the interaction of Japan with other Asian nations. Exhibits include 75 hand-drawn Edo period *Um sum* cards depicting customs.

The **Dazaifu Government Ruins** is a spacious park with a scattering of medieval ruins.

Dazaifu Tenman-gu
4-7-1 Saifu (092) 922-8225 Treasure House: 9am–4:30pm Tue–Sun

Kyushu National Museum
4-7-2 Ishizaka (092) 918-2807 9:30am–5pm Tue–Sun (to 8pm Fri & Sat)

Dazaifu Government Ruins
Mizuki (092) 922-7811 9am–4:30pm daily

9

Onta
小鹿田

B6 Oita Prefecture Hita, then bus to Sarayama (0973) 23-3111

Tucked into a wooded mountain valley, this tiny village has been producing Onta-ware since a group of Korean potters set up their kilns here in 1705. Later luminaries of the *mingei* (folk craft) movement, such as Yanagi Soetsu and Bernard Leach, praised Onta-ware for its unpretentious quality. The kilns, dug into the hillside and water-powered, are still used.

The ornate exterior of Dazaifu Tenman-gu Shrine ↓

Kumamoto
熊本

A6 Kumamoto Prefecture ✕🚉 **ℹ** www.kumamoto-guide.jp/en

Kumamoto was an important seat of power during the Tokugawa shogunate (1603–1868). Its star attraction, one of the largest castles in Japan, dates from this period. The city's main shopping precinct and sights are compressed into an area south of the castle.

The longevity of Kumamoto's residents (the city has several centenarians) is ascribed to a passion for living and a healthy diet. The latter includes *karashi renkon* (deep-fried lotus root stuffed with mustard miso) and various brands of sake made from water supposedly purified by the area's rich volcanic soil.

HIDDEN GEM
World in Miniature

Kumamoto's Suizen-ji Jou-en Garden recreates the 53 post stations – including Mount Fuji and Lake Biwa – of the old Tokaido Highway, the road that connected Edo with Kyoto during the Edo Period *(8-1 Suizenjikoen)*.

Dominating the center of the city from an imposing hill, **Kumamoto Castle** was constructed on the orders of Kato Kiyomasa, a warrior who fought alongside Tokugawa Ieyasu at the decisive Battle of Sekigahara in 1600. He was rewarded for his loyalty with lands encompassing most of present-day Kumamoto. The castle was completed in 1607. Unlike more decorative castles such as Himeji *(p224)*, Kumamoto's citadel is rigorously martial in appearance, with steep, almost impregnable walls. The original structure had 49 towers and 29 gates, but it was almost completely destroyed during the Satsuma Rebellion in 1877. Although the main keep was reconstructed on a smaller scale in 1960, it is a highly effective replica, successfully evoking the fearsome magnificence of the original. Due to damage from the 2016 earthquake, the castle is currently closed, but the imposing structure can still be viewed from the outside, and there is a reconstruction tour route.

Gyobu-tei, an 18th-century residence once owned by the powerful Hosokawa clan, is located a little northwest of the castle grounds. It presents insights into the way the feudal elite lived during the Edo period. This building also suffered serious damage in 2016 and is currently closed.

The family possessions of the powerful Kato and Hosokawa clans can be found near the castle in the **Kumamoto Prefectural Art Museum**, a distinctive modern building with a pleasant tearoom. The museum also has interesting replicas of ancient burial mounds and archaeological finds from the region.

Kumamoto is renowned for its crafts, especially damascene inlay designs, Amakusa pearls, and Yamage lanterns. These lanterns, made from gold paper, are a feature of the city's festival in August. The **Kumamoto Traditional Crafts Center** has a good selection of these local crafts.

Kumamoto Castle

⊘ 🏠1-1 Hommaru ⏰For restoration 🌐kumamoto-guide.jp/kumamoto-castle/en/spot

Gyobu-tei

⊘ 🏠3-1 Furugyocho
📞(096) 352-6522
⏰Until further notice

Kumamoto Prefectural Art Museum

⊘ 🏠2 Ninomaru 📞(096) 352-2111 ⏰9:30am-5:15pm Tue-Sun

Kumamoto Traditional Crafts Center

⊘ 🏠3-35 Chibajomachi
📞(096) 324-4930
⏰9am-5pm Tue-Sun

←

A sightseeing cruise on one of the canals in the town of Yanagawa

Mount Unzen, thought to be dormant until one of its peaks erupted in 1990, can be climbed or partly ascended by ropeway from the Nita Pass.

12

Yanagawa

柳川

A6 Fukuoka Prefecture Okinohatamachi; (0944) 74-0891

The Stone Quays of Yanagawa are not as busy as they used to be, but the canals and old moats that run through this former castle town are still vital to its economy, and eel remains the local delicacy. Visitors can board *donkobune* (gondolas) for a *kawakudari* (river cruise). As you float along the restored canals, you'll glide past old samurai villas and storehouses. The canals are at their best during sakura season in spring.

Other Yanagawa sights include Suiten-gu, a pretty shrine used by the same sect as the shrine in Kurume; Kyu Toshimake Jyutaku, an Edo-period tea garden; and a house-museum, **Hakushu Kinenkan**, the birthplace of Hakushu Kitahara (1885–1942), a prolific writer best known for children's poems.

Hakushu Kinenkan

40-11 Okinohata-machi (0944) 72-6773 9am-5:30pm daily

←

The formidable bulk of Kumamoto Castle, built in the early 17th century

13

Shimabara Peninsula

島原半島

A6 Nagasaki Prefecture Shimabara city From Kumamoto Unzen Spa (0957) 73-3434; Shimabara Peninsula Tourism Association (0957) 62-0656

Ruled by the Christian Lord Arima until 1616, Shimabara Peninsula is known as the site of anti-Christian pogroms ordered by the Tokugawa shogunate. However, in the 1880s, Unzen Spa became a resort for Westerners. At an altitude of 2,300 ft (700 m) and surrounded by pine forests, the spa was an ideal retreat from the summer heat. Thousands of azaleas bloom on the peninsula in spring, and in autumn the maple leaves turn brilliant shades of red. In 1934 the Unzen-Amakusa National Park, one of Japan's first such protected areas, was created.

Most hotels in Unzen Spa have their own hot-spring baths. Away from the resorts, visitors can see the notorious Hells (Jigoku): scalding sulfurous cauldrons in which 30 Christians were boiled alive after the outlawing of Christianity in Japan. As a demonstration of the ferocity of the waters, elderly ladies in smocks lower eggs placed in baskets into the pools and sell them hard-boiled to tourists.

14

Yoshinogari Ruins

吉野ケ里遺跡

A6 Saga Prefecture Yoshinogari-koen or Kanzaki Stns, then 15-min walk or take taxi 9am-5pm daily yoshinogari.jp/en

Pit dwellings and hundreds of burial urns excavated at Yoshinogari point to the existence of a sophisticated Yayoi-period society (300 BC–AD 300) in the region. Smart irrigation systems and rice cultivation were begun in this period, laying the pattern for later Japanese society. The area is believed by some to be the home of Queen Himiko, mentioned in 3rd-century Chinese annals. Watchtowers and Yayoi-period homes have been reconstructed here.

DRINK

Kuma Shochu Museum

Shochu - usually made from sweet potato, rice, or barley - is drunk on the rocks, or mixed with water or juice. At this museum, you can learn about its production and sample the liqueur.

A6 1 Sinmachi, Hitoyoshi, Kumamoto 868-0052 denshogura.jp

↑ Smoke rising from a crater on Mount Aso, Japan's largest active volcano

Mount Aso

阿蘇山

🅰B6 🚗Kumamoto Prefecture 🚆Aso (from Oita only), then bus 🚌Kyushu Odan sightseeing bus from Beppu or Kumamoto 🔗city.aso.kumamoto.jp

Actually a series of five volcanic cones, Mount Aso is one of the world's largest calderas, with a circumference of 80 miles (130 km). Of the five peaks, Mount Takadake, at about 5,220 ft (1,590 m), is the highest. Mount Nakadake is still active, emitting sulfurous fumes and hot gases, earning Kumamoto the epithet *hi-no-kuni* ("the land of fire").

Below these peaks, the caldera is dotted with towns set among forests, grasslands, bamboo groves, and hot

---

💬 INSIDER TIP
Onsen Hopping

Kurokawa, the town at the base of Mount Aso, is considered one of Japan's best *onsen* locations. A pass gives access to several hot springs at a discounted rate *(www.kurokawa onsen.or.jp).*

---

springs. Arriving tour buses pass a curious, grass-covered mountain resembling an inverted rice bowl, aptly named Komezuka (Rice Mound), and often stop at the pretty Kusasenri Meadow.

A cable car (currently suspended and replaced by a bus service) runs to the top of Nakadake, providing, on clear days, awesome views into the depths of the crater and its malodorous green lake. Hikers can follow a path to the summit for a closer look. A popular hiking route starts at the very top of the ropeway, proceeds to Mount Takadake around the crater rim, and descends to Sensui Gorge. Access to the crater is constantly under review depending on volcanic activity, so it is worth checking in advance for an update.

The **Mount Aso Volcanic Museum**, at the base of Nakadake, offers a fascinating preview of the mountain even when the crater is closed due to a high level of dangerous, sulfuric fumes. Two cameras on the crater wall relay continuous images of the cone's volcanic activity.

Mount Aso Volcanic Museum

 🏠1930-1 Akamizu ⏰9am-5pm daily

Takachiho

高千穂

🅰B6 🚗Miyazaki Prefecture

The Takachiho mountain region, a place of homage for those with an affection for Japan's ancient pantheon of gods and goddesses, is alive with the resonances of legend. Most of the sights are connected with Japan's rich mythology. Kagura, a mime-dance said to have been first performed by the Sun Goddess Amaterasu Omikami, is thought to have originated here. The cave into which Amaterasu vanished, casting the world into a contemporary

↑ Rowing boats under a pretty waterfall at Takachiho Gorge

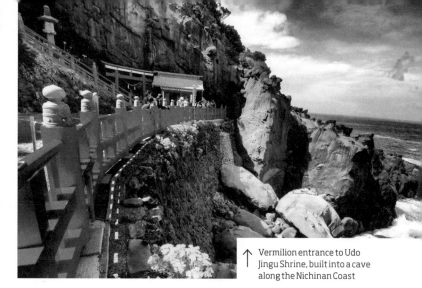

↑ Vermilion entrance to Udo Jingu Shrine, built into a cave along the Nichinan Coast

gloom until she could be lured out, faces Ama no Iwato Shrine, a pavilion-style shrine noted for a sacred tree that stands in its grounds. A short walk from here is Ama no Yasugawara, the grotto where the gods are supposed to have convened in order to devise a way to entice the Sun Goddess from her lair. The entrance to the cavern is next to a clear, pebble-strewn river. Many visitors have placed miniature cairns there in the hope that, by association, some of the wisdom and power of the gods will rub off on them.

The area's main shrine, Takachiho Jinja is famous for its ancient cryptomeria trees, a common feature of Japanese shrines and temple grounds. It was founded by the 11th emperor of Japan around 1,900 years ago. The shrine stages nightly extracts of kagura lasting one hour, providing a rare opportunity to witness a performance in

> **North of Udo Jingu is Sun-Messe Nichinan, where perfectly reproduced statues of Moai, officially approved by Easter Island, are displayed.**

richly atmospheric surroundings. Visitors usually try to factor into their itinerary a rowboat trip along Takachiho Gorge, with its scenic rock formations and waterfalls.

Nichinan Coast
日南海岸

🅰B7 🅼Miyazaki Prefecture 🅽Nichinan line from Miyazaki

The Nichinan coastal landscape is known in Japanese as Onino Sentakuita, the "devil's washboard," an apt description for the eroded, rippled effect presented by the rock shelves.

The gateway to the coast is Aoshima Island, barely a mile in circumference and connected to the mainland by a walkway. An attractive vermilion shrine stands at the center of this densely forested islet, which can get crowded in summertime. Miyazaki city, to the north, is known for its year-round flowers.

Udo Jingu, another striking vermilion-colored shrine about 20 miles (30 km) south of Aoshima, stands in a cave beside the ocean. The shrine is dedicated to Emperor Jimmu's father, who is believed to have been washed there at birth,

and serves as a catalyst for propitious marriages and fertility. The water dripping from breast-shaped rocks is compared to mother's milk, and milk candies are sold at the shrine shop. North of Udo Jingu is Sun-Messe Nichinan, where perfectly reproduced statues of Moai, officially approved by Easter Island, are displayed. One stop farther on the Nichinan line lies Obi, an old castle town, where the ruins of the castle and samurai houses may be visited. Farther south is Ishinami Beach, which is a stretch of fine white sand.

EAT

Iroha
This is one of the best restaurants in Kumamoto *(p274)* to sample *basashi*, a type of horsemeat sashimi and a local delicacy.

🅰A6 🅼4-21 Suizenjikoen, Chūō-ku, Kumamoto-shi, Kumamoto-ken 862-0956

18

Kirishima-Kinkowan National Park
霧島錦江湾国立公園

A7 Miyazaki and Kagoshima Prefectures Kobayashi Stn (JR Kitto line), then Miyazaki Kotsu bus to Ebino Highland

This region, identified with Japanese foundation myths, centers on the volcanic plateau of Ebino-Kogen (Shrimp Meadow), which is surrounded by volcanoes, crater lakes, and hot springs. The Ebino-Kogen Nature Trail is the best of several hiking routes, going past three ponds, two of which are cobalt blue. The climb up to the peak of Mount Karakunidake is popular in summer. There are many steaming hot springs in the area; some of the best are the Iodani, Arayu, Hayashida, and Sakura *onsens*.

This is an active volcanic area, and some parts of the park may be off-limits for safety reasons at any one time. This can also result in closures of roads and hiking trails.

Did You Know?

When it rains, an amazing azure lake forms in Mount Karakunidake's crater.

19

Kagoshima
鹿児島

A7 Kagoshima Prefecture From Tokyo, Nagoya, Osaka, and Nagasaki At Stn; (099) 253-2500

Kagoshima looks out across the broad sweep of a bay to the brooding silhouette of Sakurajima, an active volcano that sometimes showers the city in a blanket of volcanic ash.

Historically, Kagoshima enjoyed an unusual degree of independence. Center of the feudal domain of Satsuma, Kagoshima's Shimazu clan ruled Okinawa for eight centuries, absorbing much of the culture of China and Southeast Asia transmitted through the islands. The legacy of that contact is evident today in a cuisine that relies on sweet potatoes rather than rice, and in its typically Okinawan preference for pork dishes.

Shochu, Kagoshima's liquor made from sweet potatoes, is believed to have passed through Okinawa from China or Korea. There are over 120 *shochu* distilleries in Kagoshima alone. Local craft traditions, particularly ceramics and fine silk brocades, reflect an aesthetic of Asian provenance.

Kagoshima's sultry climate is apparent at **Sengan-en**, where semitropical plants grow alongside plum trees and bamboo groves. The garden's centerpiece is a pond and small waterfall.

 HIDDEN GEM
Sand Baths

A sand bath at Ibusuki, 17 miles (28 km) SE of Chiran, consists of being buried in sand that is naturally heated by rising steam. After staying buried for ten to 20 minutes, guests wash off the sand and enter hot-spring baths.

The waterfront city of Kagoshima, with Sakurajima volcano in the background ↑

↑ Crystal-clear waters at a rock-dotted beach on Amami Oshima Island

On an artificial island in the harbor is the **Kagoshima Aquarium**, with species from local waters and the coral reefs around the Nansei islands, southwest of Kyushu. Also worth seeing is the **City Museum of Art**, with its displays of Satsuma ceramics.

The city is also associated with Saigo Takamori (1827–77), who led the ill-fated Satsuma Rebellion. Japanese visitors

pay their respects to him in a cave on Shiroyama Hill where he committed ritual suicide.

Sengan-en

◈ 🅐 9700-1 Yoshinocho
🅲 (099) 247-1551 🅒 8:30am–5:30pm daily

Kagoshima Aquarium

◈ 🅐 3-1 Honkoshinmachi
🅲 (099) 226-2233 🅒 9:30am–6pm daily

City Museum of Art

◈ 🅐 4-36 Shiroyamacho
🅒 9:30am–6pm Tue–Sun
🆆 city.kagoshima.lg.jp/artmuseum

---

⑳

Amami Oshima Island
奄美大島

🅐 D2 🅐 Kagoshima Prefecture 🛩 From Tokyo, Osaka, Fukuoka, Kagoshima, Naha 🚢 From Kagoshima to Naze 🆆 kagoshima-kankou.com/for/whatsnew/area/amami-island

Subtropical Amami is home to a wealth of flora and fauna. The coral reefs and offshore islets of Setouchi, in the south, are part of a protected marine park offering excellent diving, snorkeling, and boat trips.

The Oshima Tsumugi Mura is an artisan village set aside for the production of *tsumugi*, a delicate handwoven silk fabric used to make kimonos.

㉑

Chiran
知覧

🅐 A7 🅐 Kagoshima Prefecture 🚌 from Kagoshima 🛈 (0993) 83-1120

Tucked into the green folds of tea plantations and wooded hills, exquisite Chiran was one of 113 castle towns built to protect the feudal lords of Satsuma. Seven preserved samurai houses and gardens on Samurai Lane can be visited with a single entrance ticket. Sata combines a dry-landscape garden, an expanse of white raked sand, and mountains used as "borrowed scenery." Hirayama is composed almost entirely of hedges, clipped into the illusion of undulating hills blending seamlessly with a backdrop of mountains. A hill above the village was the site of a World War II training ground for kamikaze pilots. Cherry trees are dedicated to 1,026 men who flew their fatal missions from Chiran.

Selecting porcelain from a laden stall at Arita's ceramics market ↑

A DRIVING TOUR
SAGA POTTERY TOWNS

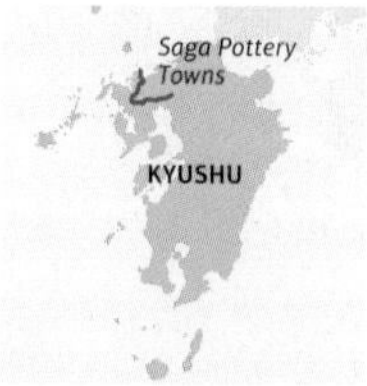

Locator Map
For more detail see p262

Saga Pottery Towns

KYUSHU

Length 50 miles (80 km) **Stopping-off points** Arita, Imari, Karatsu **Difficulty** Easy; roads are in good condition

Ceramics enthusiasts will thoroughly enjoy Saga prefecture, where pottery towns have been producing high-quality wares for at least 500 years. This tour takes in the three main pottery towns – Arita, Imari, and Karatsu – which are all within convenient distances of each other. Stop off at these towns to admire the craftsmanship of the area's potters.

Yobuko's daily produce market includes stalls devoted to reasonably priced ceramics.

Karatsu's wares are often used in tea ceremonies. The Nakazato Taroemon Kiln is run by descendants of the town's first Korean potters.

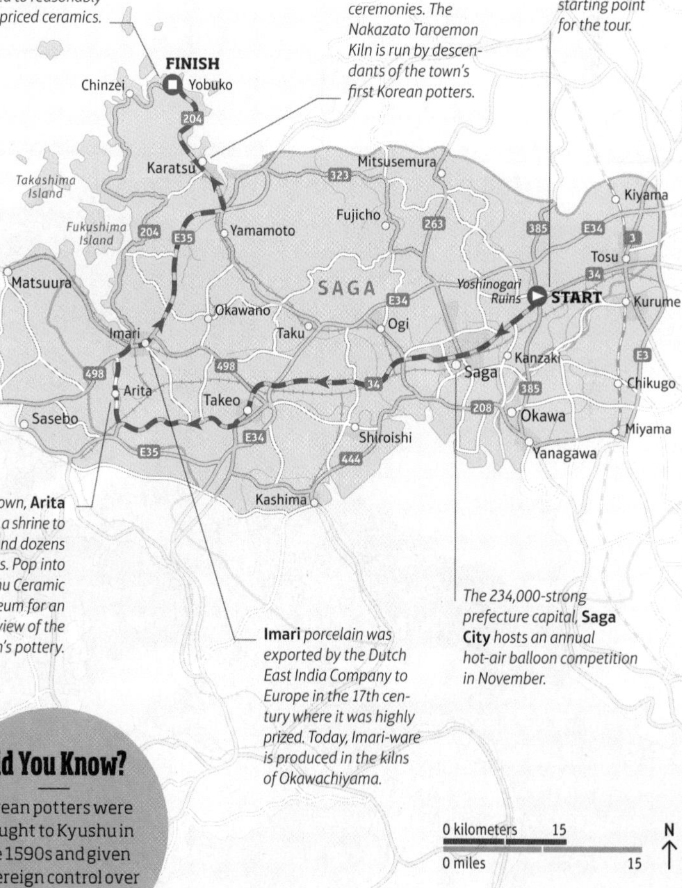

With its 2,500-year-old ceramics, the **Yoshinogari Ruins** is a good starting point for the tour.

FINISH
Chinzei Yobuko
204
Takashima Island
Karatsu
Mitsusemura
323
Kiyama
Fukushima Island
204 E35 Yamamoto
Fujicho
263
385 E34
Matsuura
SAGA
Yoshinogari Ruins
Tosu
34
Kurume
Okawano
E34
START
Imari
Taku
Ogi
Kanzaki
E3
498
498
Saga
385
Chikugo
Arita
Takeo
34
Okawa
Sasebo
E35 E34
Shiroishi
208
Yanagawa
Miyama
444
Kashima

A small town, **Arita** has a shrine to potters and dozens of kilns. Pop into the Kyushu Ceramic Museum for an overview of the region's pottery.

Imari porcelain was exported by the Dutch East India Company to Europe in the 17th century where it was highly prized. Today, Imari-ware is produced in the kilns of Okawachiyama.

The 234,000-strong prefecture capital, **Saga City** hosts an annual hot-air balloon competition in November.

Did You Know?
Korean potters were brought to Kyushu in the 1590s and given sovereign control over the kilns.

0 kilometers   15
0 miles   15

N ↑

OKINAWA

An exotic coral bar slicing through the Pacific Ocean and East China Sea, the Okinawa archipelago was a vassal of China from the 14th century; its masters named it Liu-chiu (Ryukyu in Japanese). Under the Chinese, and later under the suzerainty of the Satsuma domain, the islands assimilated diverse influences, creating a unique, exotic culture that still sets them apart from mainland Japan.

Okinawa, the largest and busiest island in the group, gives its name to the prefecture, which united these 160 islands into one administrative group in 1879. In the closing stages of World War II, during the Battle of Okinawa this was the scene of fierce fighting and the mass suicide of thousands of civilians. Naha, the main city, was damaged in the battle but has since become a heady mix of refined civilization and neon glitz. Art galleries and teahouses stand alongside red-light bars, snake restaurants, and karaoke cabins. Ceramic *shisa* lions, topping the red-tiled roofs of traditional Okinawan houses, add to the eclectic mix of war memorials, sacred groves, flower-covered coral walls, craft shops, luxury hotels, and discos.

OKINAWA

Experience

1 Naha City
2 The Former Japanese Navy
   Underground HQ
3 Okinawa Battle Sites
4 Gyokusendo Cave
5 Nakagusuku Castle Ruin
6 Nakamura House
7 Ie Island
8 Ocean Expo Park
9 Kume Island
10 Kijoka Village
11 Nakijin Castle Ruin
12 Cape Hedo
13 Miyako Islands
14 Yaeyama Islands

Amami Island, Kyushu

IE ISLAND
7

NAKIJIN CASTLE RUIN
11

OCEAN EXPO PARK
8

Motobu

Na

Minnashima

84

72

Sesoko Island

Yae-take
1,486 ft (453 m)

449

58

East China Sea

Nago

Nago Bay

Inbu Beach

E58

58

Moon Beach

Onna

329

Gir

E58

Kin

Zanpamisaki Cape

Nakadomari

58

Ishikawa

Kin Bay

Ikei Islan

Yomitan

329

Miyagi Island

Uruma

Kadena

58

Gushikawa

E58

10

Katsurenzaki Cape

Chatan

330

Okinawa

Ukibaru Islan

6 NAKAMURA HOUSE

Ginowan

5 NAKAGUSUKU CASTLE RUIN

Tsuken Island

Urasoe

58

Nishihara

330

329

NAHA CITY
1

Yonabaru

Kume Island

Naha Airport ✈

Haebaru

Azama

Tomigusuku

E58

331

Chinen

Kudaka Island

THE FORMER JAPANESE NAVY UNDERGROUND HQ
2

77

507

4

Nanjo

331

GYOKUSENDO CAVE

Itoman

Yaese

Himeyuri Peace Museum

Mabuni Hill

3 OKINAWA BATTLE SITES

Cape Kyan

0 kilometers   8

0 miles   8

N

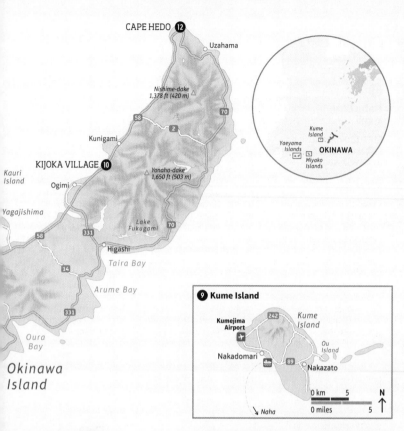

CAPE HEDO 12

Uzahama

Nishime-dake
1,378 ft (420 m)

58
2
70

Kunigami

KIJOKA VILLAGE 10

Ogimi

Kauri
Island

Yagajishima

Yonaha-dake
1,650 ft (503 m)

Lake
Fukugami

70

58

331

14

Higashi

Taira Bay

Arume Bay

331

Oura
Bay

Okinawa
Island

Kume
Island

Yaeyama
Islands

OKINAWA

Miyako
Islands

9 Kume Island

242
Kume
Island

Kumejima
Airport

Ou
Island

Nakadomari

89

Nakazato

0 km   5

0 miles   5

N

↓ *Naha*

13 Miyako Islands   *Ikema*
Island

0 km   6

0 miles   6

N

Irabu
Island

83

Shimoji
Island

Hirara

Miyako
Island

Miyako
Airport

78

Shimoji

Higashi
Henna

Kurima
Island

390

← *Tarama Island*

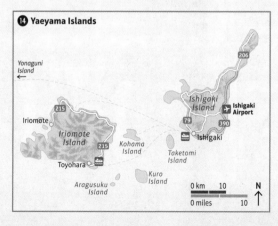

14 Yaeyama Islands

Yonaguni
Island

206

215

Iriomote

Ishigaki
Island

Ishigaki
Airport

Iriomote
Island

79

390

215

Kohama
Island

Ishigaki

Toyohara

Taketomi
Island

Kuro
Island

Aragusuku
Island

0 km   10

0 miles   10

N

EXPERIENCE

Naha City

那覇市

F7 **Okinawa Island**
Naha **Airport 1F;**
(098) 857-6884

Shuri, the most historical settlement in Okinawa, was its capital until the islands became part of Japan in 1879, after which Naha was declared the capital. The two cities have since expanded and merged. Naha prospered through its seaborne trade with other parts of Asia and, eventually, the West. The city that emerged from the ruins of World War II is a bustling center, with the archipelago's best restaurants, nightlife, and shopping.

A long thoroughfare in central Naha, Kokusai-dori (International Street) typifies the new city, with its boutiques and craft shops. The atmosphere along Heiwa-dori market street (to the south, off Kokusai-dori) harks back to an older Naha. Started by widows who had lost their husbands in the Battle of Okinawa, the market is full of Asian aromas, crowded alleys, and stalls selling Okinawan art, crafts, bric-a-brac, and exotic foods.

To the east, along Himeyuri-dori, is the pottery quarter of Tsuboya which dates from the late 17th century. Over 20 workshops still produce wine flasks, tea bowls, and *shisa* (statues of a legendary lion, used all around the island as propitious roof ornaments). You can see examples at the **Tsuboya Pottery Museum**.

Also of interest in central Naha are the Sogen-ji Ishimon Gates. The temple itself, originally a 16th-century memorial to the Ryukyu kings, was destroyed in the war; three of the original arched stone gates have been restored.

The Commodore Perry Memorial by Tomari port marks the point where the commander of the American "black ships" landed on June 6, 1853.

Shuri, the 16th-century former capital, lies 4 miles (6 km) east of central Naha. It contains various shrines, temples, ceremonial gates, and fortifications – a reminder of the sophistication of the Ryukyu kingdom. *Ryusen* and *bingata* (p290) fabrics are made, exhibited, and sold at the **Shuri Ryusen**, where the materials are dyed. With over 4,000 exhibits, the **Okinawa Prefectural Museum & Art Museum** highlights the area's art and culture, and has the original bells from Shuri Castle and the temple Engaku-ji.

Shuri Castle was the headquarters of the Japanese High command during the war, resulting in its total destruction. Shurei-mon, the castle's ceremonial entrance gate, was rebuilt in 1958.

Naha City's imposing
Shurei-mon *(inset)*
leading to Shuri Castle,
with its richly decorated
Seiden (main hall) ↓

Photographs of victims of the Battle of Okinawa at the Himeyuri Peace Museum

Cape Kyan saw some of the fiercest exchanges. Many locals jumped to their deaths here. To the northeast, the Himeyuri no To Monument and the Himeyuri Peace Museum are memorials to a group of young women who died while working as volunteer nurses during the Battle of Okinawa. A total of 136 people died inside a cave while trying to escape from the carnage. Most perished from the effects of a gas bomb fired into the cavern, others committed suicide. Konpaku no To, 1 mile (2 km) south, is a cliffside memorial where 35,000 unknown soldiers and civilians were interred.

One of the heaviest losses of life was on Mabuni Hill. Now a memorial park, it is dotted with monuments dedicated to both military and civilian dead. Photos, memorabilia, and personal accounts of the battle can be seen at the nearby **Peace Memorial Museum**.

Natural disasters and war have led to the constant rebuilding of the 16th-century Benzaiten-do temple, north of the castle park.

Tsuboya Pottery Museum
⊗ 🏠 1-9-32 Tsuboya
📞 (098) 862-3761 🕐 10am-6pm Tue–Sun

Shuri Ryusen
🏠 1-54 Shuri Yamakawacho
📞 (098) 886-1131 🕐 9am-6pm daily

Okinawa Prefectural Museum & Art Museum
⊗ 🏠 3-1-1 Omoromachi
🕐 9am–6pm Tue–Sun (to 8pm Fri & Sat) 🌐 okimu.jp/en

---

②
The Former Japanese Navy Underground HQ
旧日本海軍司令部壕

🅰 F7 🏠 3 miles (5 km) S of Naha 🚌 from Naha bus terminal to Tomigusuku Koen-mae or Uebaru danchi-mae 📞 (098) 850-4055 🕐 8:30am–5pm daily (8:30am–5:30pm Jul–Sep)

Parts of the subterranean rooms and tunnels where the Japanese Navy conducted the closing stages of World War II are open to the public. The Imperial Navy Admiral was one of over 4,000 men who committed suicide here

on June 13, 1945. Many of the officers killed themselves by *seppuku* (ritual disembowelment); others used hand grenades – scorch marks can still be seen on tunnel walls.

---

③
Okinawa Battle Sites
沖縄戦跡国定公園

🅰 F7 🏠 9 miles (15 km) S of Naha 🚌 Bus tour from Naha recommended

At the southern end of the island are various battle sites and memorials to victims and those who committed suicide rather than surrender to advancing American forces.

Peace Memorial Museum
⊗ 🏠 614-1 Mabuni, Itoman
🕐 9am–5pm daily 🚫 Dec 29–Jan 3 🌐 peace-museum.pref.okinawa.jp/english

---

THE BATTLE OF OKINAWA

Few conflicts in modern history have been fought with such ferocity as the Battle of Okinawa. It began when five American divisions landed on the island on April 1, 1945. Although outnumbered, the Japanese fought hard, utilizing flame-throwers, grenades, bayonets, and kamikaze pilots (Japanese suicide bombers). By the end of the 82-day battle, 13,000 American soldiers and 250,000 Japanese soldiers and civilians had died.

↑ A walkway among the rock formations at the vast Gyukusendo Cave

4

Gyokusendo Cave
玉泉洞

F7 **19 miles (30 km) SE of Naha**

Featuring over 460,000 stalactites, this cave system is negotiated with the help of rather slippery pathways and wooden walkways. The stalactites at Gyokusendo Caves have been likened to giant bamboo, wine glasses, organ pipes, and even statues by Rodin.

The cave can be viewed by visiting **Okinawa World**, a park and museum with a large snake collection, including Okinawa's most poisonous reptile, the *habu*.

Okinawa World
1336 Tamagusuku Maekawa, Nanjo **(098) 949-7421** **9am–6pm daily**

> HIDDEN GEM
> **The Shining**
> Seek out the creepy ruins of Nakagusuku Hotel, located on a sacred site near the castle. Its construction was so plagued by accidents that eventually the workers refused to finish the build. It now sits empty.

5

Nakagusuku Castle Ruin
中城城跡

F7 **9 miles (13 km) NE of Naha City, 10-min walk from Nakamura House** **(098) 935-5719** **8:30am–5pm daily (to 6pm May–Sep)**

Built by Lord Gosamaru in the mid-1400s, Nakagusuku was one of the first stone castles in Japan. The views along the east coast of central Okinawa are excellent. The walls are the only structures to survive the ravages of time and the 1458 Amawari Rebellion. Passages link three main compounds, each enclosed by high, fortified walls.

6

Nakamura House
中村家

F7 **9 miles (13 km) NE of Naha City** **(098) 935-3500** **9am–5:30pm Wed–Mon**

A visit to this 18th-century farmhouse, now a museum with exhibits about Okinawan

daily life, offers rare insights into a more refined style of rural architecture. It consists of five buildings around a courtyard. A stone enclosure, with a barrier to repel evil spirits – a typical Okinawan feature – faces the entrance.

7

Ie Island
伊江島

F6 **From Motobu port**

Ie is a picturesque little island ideal for bicycling. Bike rentals are plentiful, and the whole island can be explored in under 8 hours. The north

→ Admiring underwater life at the Okinawa Churaumi Aquarium, Ocean Expo Park

> **The stalactites at Gyokusendo Caves have been likened to giant bamboo, wine glasses, organ pipes, and even statues by Rodin.**

terminates in steep cliffs, while the interior is an expanse of sugarcane, tobacco, and pineapple fields. Gusukuyama, Ie's only hill, provides a first-rate view.

During World War II, Niya-Thiya, a cave in the southwest, was used as a shelter by locals. The Ernie Pyle Monument is dedicated to the US war correspondent who died when his jeep was blown up on the island only a few weeks before the end of the conflict.

---

⑧

Ocean Expo Park
海洋博記念公園

Ⓐ F6 Ⓓ 12 miles (20 km) NW of Nago 🚌 Kinenkoen-mae Ⓞ 8am–7pm (to 8:30pm in summer); some attractions close earlier Ⓦ oki-park.jp/kaiyohaku

The Okinawa International Ocean Exposition was held here in 1975; since then, several new attractions have been added to this coastal park. The Okinawa Churaumi Aquarium houses more than 700 species of fish in three sections (tropical, ocean, and deep sea) and the Oceanic Culture Museum relates the development of the Okinawan people to the maritime culture of Oceania through fishing and navigation exhibits.

The Native Okinawan Village is a faithful reconstruction of traditional 17th- and 18th-century dwellings, featuring sacred springs and forest, places of worship, storehouses, and an arboretum with native plants. On the coast close by is the Tropical Dream Center, a complex of high-tech greenhouses and botanical gardens.

About 19 miles (30 km) to the south of the park, you'll find breathtaking beaches along the coast of Nago Bay. Between Cape Busena and Inbu Beach, **Busena Marine Park** is one of the world's best underwater observatories.

Busena Marine Park
⊘ Ⓓ 1744-1 Kise, Nago Ⓞ 9am–6pm daily (to 5:30pm Nov–Mar) Ⓦ busena-marinepark.com

DRINK

Bar Spade
This dive bar attracts a mixed crowd of all ages with its 500-yen drinks, free popcorn, and open pool table.

Ⓐ F7 Ⓓ Yonaha Buiding 2F, 3-23-10 Kumoji, Naha-shi, Okinawa 900-0015 Ⓦ barspade.com

---

Dojo Bar
"Probably the best karate bar in the world," claims the sign at this pub. Located in Naha - the home of karate - this is the ultimate drinking spot for martial arts buffs.

Ⓐ F7 Ⓓ 101 Asato 1 F, Naha-shi, Okinawa 902-0067 Ⓦ dojobarnaha.com

---

The Smuggler's Irish Pub
This is a great place to enjoy a pint of Guinness and watch the football. The staff are attentive and the crowd friendly.

Ⓐ F7 Ⓓ 1-9-1 Matsuo, Naha-shi, Okinawa 900-0014 Ⓒ (098) 862-0124

→

Tatami-ishi, a rock mosaic resembling a tortoise shell, on an island near Kume

⑨ Kume Island
久米島

🅐 D2 🏠 56 miles (90 km) W of Okinawa Island ✈ From Naha 🚢 From Naha Tomari port 🛈 (098) 985-5288

Volcanic Kume is famous for its sugarcane and pineapple plantations, and Kumejima-*tsumugi*, an exquisite silk pongee. Buses serve many of the island's sights.

The village of Nakadomari, in the southwest, boasts one of the oldest houses in Okinawa, Uezu-ke which was built in the 1700s in the Okinawan samurai style. An extraordinary tree, the Goe-da Pine, whose five separate trunks span upwards, is just a short walk from the house. Rice-planting rituals and prayers for rain are still con-ducted at Chinbei-donchi, the island's foremost shrine, north of Nakadomari. Nearby, the sacred Yajiya-gama Caves were used for burials 2,000 years ago.

To the north, the 650-ft-(200-m-) high Hiyajo Banta cliff affords good views toward the Aguni and Tonaki islands and the barrier reef below.

Nakazato village, in the east of the island, is one of its most traditional settlements, with several well-preserved buildings. You can see women weaving and dyeing Kumejima-*tsumugi* here. Nearby Eef Beach is Kume's largest resort.

Tiny Ou Island is well worth the 20-minute walk across a bridge from Nakazato's Tomari port. In the southwest is a mosaic of over 1,000 pentagonal stones, called the Tatami-ishi, which resemble flattened tortoise shells.

OKINAWAN ARTS AND CRAFT

Okinawan artists and craftsmen are honored as masters or, in a few rare cases, Living National Treasures. The island's textiles are among the finest in Japan, especially the linen-dyed *bingata* and *ryusen* fabrics, *bashofu*, and *kasuri*, a high-quality cloth made from the finest natural fibers. Equally, the glossy, black Okinawan lacquerware has been made for over 500 years, using the wood of the indigenous *deigo* tree as a base. New crafts have appeared since the war, most notably glassware, its vibrant colors reflecting Okinawa's sparkling coral seas.

→

Delicately decorated lacquered box

---

⑩ Kijoka Village
喜如嘉村

🅐 G6 🏠 16 miles (25 km) NE of Nago 🚌 67 from Nago to Daiichi Kijoka

The main reason for a visit to Kijoka Village, in Ogimi, is to watch the making of *bashofu*,

a rare lightweight textile made of plantain fiber, which is used to make Okinawan kimonos. The stages involved in producing this increasingly scarce linen can be seen at the **Bashofu Hall**, a well-known workshop.

Bashofu Hall

🏠 454 Kijoka 📞 (0980) 44-3033 ⏰ 10am–5:30pm Mon-Sat (to 5pm Nov-Mar) 🚫 Obon, Dec 29-Jan 3

11

Nakijin Castle Ruin
今帰仁城跡

🏠 G6 🚗 11 miles (18 km) NW of Nago 🚌 65 or 66 from Nago or express from Naha Airport to Nakijin-jo Ato Iriguchi ⏰ 8am–6pm daily (to 7pm May-Aug) 🌐 nakijinjoseki.jp/en

The foundations, gate, and 4,900-ft (1,500-m) stretch of remaining wall give some

→ The monumental stone remains of the 14th-century Nakijin Castle, near Nago

indication of the original size of Nakijin Castle. It was built in the 14th century by King Hokuzan, founder of the North Mountain Kingdom, an esoteric and short-lived domain.

The entrance, with its flat stone ceiling, is still intact. Because the castle faced the sacred island of Iheya, three wooden shrines were built here to allow the local priest-esses to conduct rituals, but none has survived. There are stunning views across the East China Sea toward several other offshore islands including the Amami and Yoron groups.

12

Cape Hedo
辺戸岬

🏠 G6 🚗 31 miles (50 km) NE of Nago 🚌 67 from Nago to Hentona

The remote, northernmost point of Okinawa Island is a wild and breathtaking area of outstanding natural beauty and, mercifully, few tour buses. A grassy plateau runs to the edge of a steep, 330-ft- (100-m-) high cliff, beyond which are coral reefs. The views of distant Yoron, Iheya, and Izena islands are magnificent. The road to Hedo Point

passes through a number of traditional villages, such as Ogimi, renowned for producing a unique pale yellow *bashofu* cloth. A short distance south of Hedo Point, the site of Uzahama-iseki features the remains of a prehistoric settlement.

Miyako Islands
宮古諸島

⚑ D2 **⌖ 200 miles (330 km) SW of Okinawa Island**

Set amid coral reefs in an emerald sea, Miyako consists of eight perfectly flat islands. Unique customs and a distinct dialect set the inhabitants of Miyako apart from Okinawan mainlanders. Spared the devastation of World War II, traditional houses are one-story buildings with red-tiled roofs and surrounding coral walls that serve as shelters against typhoons.

Hirara town, a former city now merged with other towns in the area to make up the city Miyakojima, is **Miyako Island**'s main area. North of the port is Harimizu Utaki Shrine, dedicated to the two gods who are believed to have created the island. The fascinating mausoleum of the 15th-century chieftain Nakasone Toimiya has graves and tombs that combine local styles with the far more elaborate Okinawan style.

The **Miyakojima City Botanical Garden**, northeast of Hirara, contains over

Did You Know?

Anyone taller than 4 ft 7 in (140 cm) had to pay taxes, according to the Nintozeiseki stone.

40,000 tree and almost 2,000 plant species from around the world.

In the backstreets of Hirara, women dry strips of Miyako-*jofu* indigo cloth. Just north of Hirara is the Nintozeiseki, a 55-in (1.4-m) stone, which was used during the suzerainty of the Satsuma domain in the 17th century.

At the tip of Higashi Henna cape on the east coast you can look out over the Pacific Ocean to the left and the East China Sea to the right. On the southwest coast, facing Kurima island, Yonaha Maehama Beach, a 2-mile (4-km) stretch of pristine white sand, offers swimming, fishing, and diving.

Mostly set aside for sugar-cane plantations, Kurima is of interest to ornithologists as sea hawks rest here for a few days in October on their way to the Philippines. The main sight on Ikema, off the far north of Miyako, is the

Yaebishi (or Yabiji) reef, which emerges in all its splendor during low spring tides. Both Kurima and Ikema can be reached via a road bridge.

Off the west coast, and accessible by boat from Miyako Island, is Irabu, linked by six bridges to neighboring Shimoji. On Shimoji, two deep green lakes called Tori-ike are connected to the sea by an underground river and tunnel.

Miyako Island

✈ From Tokyo, Osaka, Naha, and Ishigaki Island **🛈 At** airport; (0980) 72-1212

Miyakojima City Botanical Garden

⌖ 1166-286 Higashinaka-sonezoe, Hirara **☎ (0980) 76-3184** **⏱ 10am–6pm daily**

Yaeyama Islands
八重山諸島

⚑ D2 **⌖ 270 miles (430 km) SW of Okinawa Island**

The Yaeyamas are Japan's most southerly islands. Some of the finest scuba diving in Asia is found here.

Ishigaki Island's airport and harbor serve the outlying islands in the group. Glimpses of the unique Yaeyama culture

The lighthouse at Higashi Henna, where the Pacific and the East China Sea meet ↑

↑ Glass-bottomed boats at Kabira Bay and scuba diving *(inset)* in the waters off Ishigaki, one of the Yaeyama Islands

can be seen at the **Yaeyama Museum**, near the harbor, which contains Yaeyama-*jofu* textiles, and Polynesian-style canoes. Not far away is **Miyara Dunchi**, a 19th-century noble-man's home. Shiraho Reef, off the southeastern tip of the island, is the world's largest expanse of blue coral. Kabira Bay on the north shore, is full of small islets and supports a cultured black pearl industry.

Meaning "prosperous bamboo," **Taketomi Island** is a quiet, unspoiled island. Its neatness stems from an old custom by which it was, and still is, the responsibility of all householders to sweep the street in front of their own property. The island can easily be explored on foot or by bike. To the west, Kondoi is the island's finest beach; Kaiji

Beach has star-shaped sand – the fossilized skeletons of tiny sea animals. The aqua-marine waters here support bountiful tropical sea life, and brilliantly colored butterflies swarm around the beach.

As much as 90 percent of **Iriomote Island** is forest and jungle. Visitors can take cruises along its two main rivers, the Nakama and Urauchi, where black oyster beds, mangroves, and tropical trees can be seen. The island is the last habitat of the Iriomote wild cat.

Yonaguni offers swordfish and bonito fishing Japan's strongest sake – *hanazake*.

Ishigaki Island
🛪 From Tokyo, Osaka, Nagoya, Naha, and Miyako
ℹ (0980) 87-0971

Yaeyama Museum
◈ 🏠 4-1 Tonoshiro, Ishigaki
📞 (0980) 82-4712 🕐 9am–5pm Tue–Sun

Miyara Dunchi
◈ 🏠 178 Okawa, Ishigaki
📞 (0980) 82-2767
🕐 9am–5pm Wed–Mon

Taketomi Island
⛴ From Ishigaki ℹ (0980) 85-2488

Iriomote Island
⛴ From Ishigaki ℹ (0980) 85-5304

Yonaguni Island
⛴ From Ishigaki ✈ From Naha and Ishigaki ℹ (0980) 87-2402

EAT

Goya
This eatery's namesake is a green bitter gourd. Here, *goya* is deep-fried, pickled, and even made into ice cream.

🏠 D2 🏠 570-2 Hirara Nishizato, Miyakojima-shi, Okinawa 906-0012
📞 (0980) 74-2358

¥ ¥ ¥

NORTHERN HONSHU

The backcountry reputation of Northern Honshu belies its rich history. Long ago, it was home to indigenous people, who may have been from the Ainu ethnic group. In the 12th century, Hiraizumi was the capital of the Northern Fujiwara clan, rivaling Kyoto in splendor, and during feudal times, Morioka, Tsuruoka, Hirosaki, and Aizu-Wakamatsu were thriving castle towns. Foremost, though, was Sendai, ruled by the north's most powerful clan. Despite these significant settlements, when haiku poet Matsuo Basho set out in 1689 on his five-month trek to northern Japan, he likened it to going to the back of beyond. Three centuries later, *shinkansen* lines and expressways provide easy access, and the north is as much a part of the information age as the rest of Japan.

On March 11, 2011, a 9-magnitude earthquake and subsequent tsunami hit this northern part of the country. Much of the area was damaged with some coastal areas completely destroyed. The Fukushima Daiichi nuclear plant was also badly damaged by the tsunami, and the long-term effects of this disaster are still unclear. In 2018, a robotic probe showed that the radio-activity levels inside the plant remain too high for humans to work inside the buildings.

NORTHERN HONSHU

Must See
1 Nikko

Experience More
2 Nikko National Park
3 Mashiko
4 Kitakata
5 Bandai-Asahi National Park
6 Aizu Wakamatsu
7 Matsushima
8 Hiraizumi
9 Tsuruoka
10 Sado Island
11 Dewa Sanzan
12 Sendai
13 Kakunodate
14 Hanamaki
15 Tono
16 Morioka
17 Towada-Hachimantai National Park
18 Oga Peninsula
19 Shimokita Peninsula
20 Aomori
21 Hirosaki

↑ Looking over Lake Chuzenji from the Futara-san Shrine

NIKKO

日光

🅰F4 🏠Tochigi Prefecture 🚃JR and Tobu-Nikko lines
ℹ️At Tobu Nikko Stn; www.nikko-travel.jp/english

Written with characters that mean "sunlight," the mystical town of Nikko has become a Japanese byword for splendor. In 766, the formidable Buddhist priest Shodo Shonin founded the first temple here. This was the first of many and Nikko became a renowned Buddhist-Shinto religious center.

①

Takinoo Shrine

🏠2310-1 Sannai 📞(0288) 21-0765 🕐24 hrs daily

This peaceful, rustic shrine, thought to be dedicated to a female deity, draws women and those looking for love. Toss a stone through the hole in the top of the torii and into the shrine grounds and your wish, they say, will come true.

②

Shinkyo Bridge

This red-lacquered wooden bridge, just to the left of the road bridge, arches over the Daiya River where, legend has it, Shodo Shonin crossed the water on the backs of two huge serpents. The original bridge, which was built in 1636 for the exclusive use of the shogun and imperial messengers, was destroyed by a flood. The current bridge dates from 1907.

③

Futara-san Shrine

🏠2307 Sannai 🕐8am-5pm daily 🌐futarasan.jp

Founded by Shodo Shonin in 782, this shrine is dedicated to the gods of the mountains Nantai (male), Nyotai (female), and Taro, their child. It is actually the main shrine of three; the other two are at Lake Chuzenji and on Mount Nantai. The bronze torii here has been designated as an Important Cultural Property. But the shrine's most interesting feature for visitors is a tall bronze lantern, nicknamed the "ghost lantern", which is said to take the shape of a monster at night. The gashes in the lamp are from the sword of terrified samurai who attacked it when the flame started to flicker in a peculiar way. A vermilion fence now protects the lantern from attack.

④

Rinno-ji

🏠2300 Sannai 🕐8am-5pm daily

The first temple founded at Nikko, by Shodo Shonin in 766, Rinno-ji was originally called Shihonryu-ji. When it became a Tendai-sect temple in the 17th century it was renamed. Its Sanbutsu-do (Three Buddha Hall) is the largest hall at Nikko. It is undergoing major renovations until 2020, but remains open. The three gilt images, of

Amida Buddha, Senju (thousand-armed) Kannon, and Bato (horse-headed) Kannon, enshrined in the hall correspond to the three mountain deities enshrined at Futara-san Shrine. Beyond the hall, the nine-ringed bronze pillar, Sorinto, contains 1,000 volumes of sutras (Buddhist scriptures) and is a symbol of world peace.

The beautiful Treasure Hall (Homotsuden) houses a large and fascinating array of temple treasures, mainly dating from the Edo period. Behind it is the Shoyoen, a lovely Edo-style 19th-century stroll garden that has been carefully landscaped so that it is at its best for every season. The enchanting path through the garden meanders around a large pond, over stone bridges, and past mossy stone lanterns.

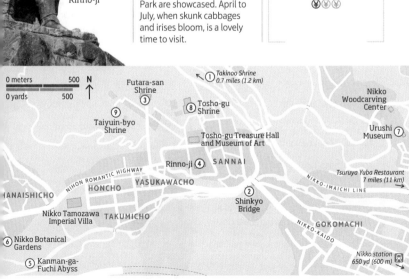

← An imposing statue of Shodo Shonin found near Rinno-ji

⑤ Kanman-ga-Fuchi Abyss

 Nishisando

Lava flows from an old eruption of Mount Nantai combine with the limpid waters of the Daiya River to make these unusual scenic pools. It is not hard to see why the Abyss is a spot sacred to Buddhism. About 70 stone statues of Jizo, the bodhisattva of children, line the path by the river. They are known as phantom statues because their numbers appear to change every time you look.

___

⑥ Nikko Botanical Gardens

🏠 1842 Hanaishicho
📞 (0288) 54-0206
🚉 Nikko Shokubutsuen
🕐 9am-4:30pm Tue-Sun
📅 Dec 1-Apr 14

Some 3,000 varieties of plants and flowers from Japan and around the world are at these gardens, a branch of the Koishikawa Botanical Gardens of the University of Tokyo. Flora from Nikko National Park are showcased. April to July, when skunk cabbages and irises bloom, is a lovely time to visit.

⑦ Urushi Museum

🏠 2829-1 Tokorono
📞 (0288) 53-6807
🚉 Marumi 🕐 Mar 17-Nov 12: Sat, Sun, Mon

This small museum showcases lacquerware arts – *urushi* means lacquer. Used in Japan for over 5,000 years, lacquer has reached the height of refinement only in the past 1,000 years. The museum's collection also includes decorative wares from China, India, and Egypt.

EAT

Tsuruya Yuba Restaurant

This eatery specializes in the local favorite - *yuba* (tofu skins). The menu has everything from *yuba* buckwheat noodles to sweet *yuba* custard pudding.

🏠 10-6 Kawamuro
📞 (0288) 21-7641 🕐 D

¥ ¥ ¥

---

0 meters 500
0 yards 500
N ↑

Futara-san Shrine ③

Takinoo Shrine 0.7 miles (1.2 km) ①

Tosho-gu Shrine ⑧

Nikko Woodcarving Center

Taiyuin-byo Shrine ⑨

Tosho-gu Treasure Hall and Museum of Art

Urushi Museum ⑦

Rinno-ji ④ SANNAI

NIHON ROMANTIC HIGHWAY
YASUKAWACHO
HANAISHICHO HONCHO

Nikko Tamozawa Imperial Villa TAKUMICHO

Shinkyo Bridge ②

Tsuruya Yuba Restaurant 7 miles (11 km) NIKKO-IMAICHI LINE

NIKKO-KAIDO GOKOMACHI

⑥ Nikko Botanical Gardens

⑤ Kanman-ga-Fuchi Abyss

Nikko station 650 yd (600 m)

⑧ 🗺️

TOSHO-GU SHRINE

東照宮

🏠 2301 Sannai 🕐 8am–5pm daily (to 4pm Nov–Mar)
🌐 toshogu.jp/english

Tokugawa Iemitsu set out to dazzle with this mausoleum-shrine for his grandfather Ieyasu. For two years some 15,000 artisans from all over Japan worked, building, carving, gilting, painting, and lacquering, to create this flowery, gorgeous Momoyama-style complex.

Although designated a Shinto shrine in the Meiji period, Tosho-gu retains many of its original Buddhist elements, including the sutra library, which chronicles the temple's history, the Niomon Gate, and an unusual pagoda, with a suspended pilar. The famed *suginamiki* (Japanese cedar avenue) leading to the shrine was planted by a 17th-century lord, in lieu of a more opulent offering. The shrine is undergoing major renovation work, which is scheduled to be completed in 2024, though most of it is still open to visitors. Don't miss the Tokugawa armor in the Treasure Hall or the painted doors in the Museum of Art.

→

The embellished structures making up the Tosho-gu Shrine complex

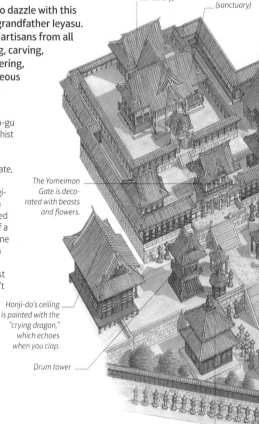

Honden (inner sanctuary)

Haiden (sanctuary)

The Yomeimon Gate is decorated with beasts and flowers.

Honji-do's ceiling is painted with the "crying dragon," which echoes when you clap.

Drum tower

The Rinzo contains a sutra library of Buddhist scriptures set within a revolving structure.

The sacred fountain is covered with an ornate Chinese-style roof. The granite basin (1618) is used for ritual purification.

TOKUGAWA IEYASU

Ieyasu (1543–1616) was a wily strategist and master politician who founded the dynasty that would rule Japan for over 250 years. Born the son of a minor lord, he spent his life accumulating power, before becoming shogun in 1603, when he was 60. He built his capital in the swampy village of Edo (now Tokyo), and his rule saw the start of the flowering of Edo culture. After his death, he was enshrined and given his posthumous name: Tosho-Daigongen, "the great incarnation illuminating the East".

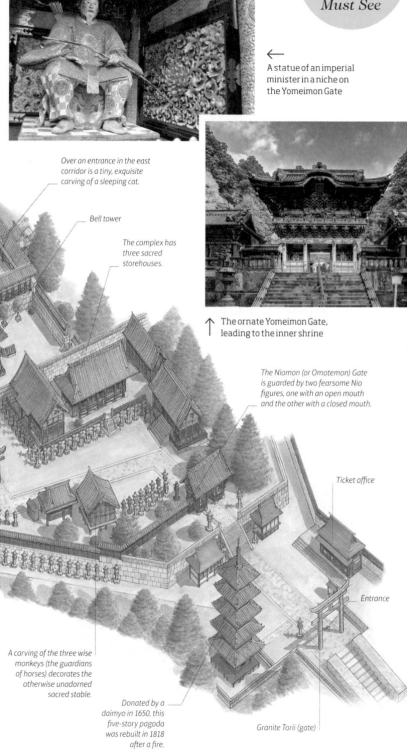

← A statue of an imperial minister in a niche on the Yomeimon Gate

Over an entrance in the east corridor is a tiny, exquisite carving of a sleeping cat.

Bell tower

The complex has three sacred storehouses.

↑ The ornate Yomeimon Gate, leading to the inner shrine

The Niomon (or Omotemon) Gate is guarded by two fearsome Nio figures, one with an open mouth and the other with a closed mouth.

Ticket office

A carving of the three wise monkeys (the guardians of horses) decorates the otherwise unadorned sacred stable.

Entrance

Donated by a daimyo in 1650, this five-story pagoda was rebuilt in 1818 after a fire.

Granite Torii (gate)

9

TAIYUIN-BYO SHRINE

大猷院廟

📍 2300 Sannai 📞 (0288) 53-1567 🕐 8am–5pm daily (to 4pm Nov–Mar)

If Tosho-gu is splendid, Taiyuin-byo is sublime. It was built modestly so that it would not eclipse Tosho-gu, a sign of deep respect to Tokugawa Ieyasu. Despite this restraint, it is still an ornate tomb reflecting the power of the imperial family.

Finished in 1653, Taiyuin-byo is the mausoleum of Tokugawa Iemitsu (1604–51), the powerful third shogun and grandson of Ieyasu, who closed Japan to foreign commerce and isolated it from the world for over 200 years. Tayuin is his posthumous Buddhist name. As with Tosho-gu, Taiyuin-byo has retained many of its Buddhist elements, despite being reconsecrated as a Shinto shrine in the Meiji period. Set in a grove of Japanese cedars, it has a number of ornate gates ascending to the Haiden (sanctuary) and Honden (inner sanctuary). You can admire the grand interior of the Haiden, which has coffered ceilings and carvings, but the Honden is usually closed to the public. The shogun's ashes are entombed beyond the sixth and final gate.

The Honden holds a gilded Buddhist altar with a wooden statue of Iemitsu.

Decorated with carvings of dragons, the Haiden also has some famous 17th-century lion paintings.

Did You Know?

To stop him seizing power, Iemitsu forced his brother Tadanaga to commit seppuku.

1 The drum and bell towers are no longer used, but the drum signifies positivity/birth, while the bell denotes negativity/death.

2 As well as being inlaid with peonies, the Yashamon Gate is also ornamented with four statues of Yasha, a fierce guardian spirit.

3 Marking the main entrance to the shrine, a powerful red-faced Nio warrior god stands guard on either side of the Niomon Gate, frightening away evil spirits.

Entrance

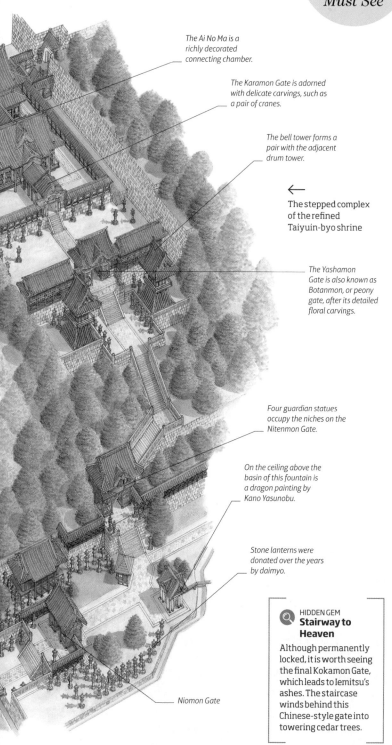

The Ai No Ma is a richly decorated connecting chamber.

The Karamon Gate is adorned with delicate carvings, such as a pair of cranes.

The bell tower forms a pair with the adjacent drum tower.

← The stepped complex of the refined Taiyuin-byo shrine

The Yashamon Gate is also known as Botanmon, or peony gate, after its detailed floral carvings.

Four guardian statues occupy the niches on the Nitenmon Gate.

On the ceiling above the basin of this fountain is a dragon painting by Kano Yasunobu.

Stone lanterns were donated over the years by daimyo.

Niomon Gate

> 🔍 HIDDEN GEM
> **Stairway to Heaven**
>
> Although permanently locked, it is worth seeing the final Kokamon Gate, which leads to Iemitsu's ashes. The staircase winds behind this Chinese-style gate into towering cedar trees.

EXPERIENCE MORE

2
Nikko National Park
日光国立公園

F4 Tochigi, Fukushima, and Gunma Prefectures From Nikko Stn 1404-1 Kinugawaonsen Ohara, Nikko-shi; www.nikko-travel.jp/english

The magnificent national park that includes Tosho-gu and its environs is largely a mountainous volcanic plateau, studded with lakes, waterfalls, and hot springs. For a taste of Oku-Nikko, the mountainous interior, take the bus west to Lake Chuzen-ji. The hairpin curves of Irohazaka, along the old ascent to the sacred Mount Nantai, start at Umagaeshi (horse return), where pilgrims had to give up their horses and walk. At the east end of the lake, the Kegon Falls cascade 315 ft (96 m) to the Daiya River below. An elevator through the cliff runs to an observation deck at the base of the falls.

3
Mashiko
益子

F4 Tochigi Prefecture Local trains only From Tobu-Utsunomiya Stn Next to Mashiko Stn; (0285) 70-1120

Home to the famous potter Shoji Hamada (1894–1978), a founder of the *mingei* (folk art) movement, Mashiko is full of pottery workshops. The **Mashiko Sankokan Museum** contains Hamada's studio, and his eclectic collection of ceramics. The vats of the eighth-generation **Higeta Dyeworks** are sunk in the floor of a thatched workshop.

Mashiko Sankokan Museum
3388 Mashiko
(0285) 72-5300
9:30am–5pm Thu–Tue

Higeta Dyeworks
1 Jonaizaka (0285) 72-3162 Tue–Sun

PICTURE PERFECT
Flaming Bridge

Built in 1636, Shinkyo bridge in the Nikko National Park is among the finest in Japan. Its gorgeous burnt-red span makes a great focal point for a snap, set as it is against the dramatic mountain scenery and lush foliage.

4
Kitakata
喜多方

F3 Fukushima Prefecture 7244-2 Oshimizuhigashi; www.kitakata-kanko.jp

Mud-walled *kura* (storehouses) were long used to keep sake, miso, rice, and other provisions from fire, theft, and vermin. Kitakata has more than 2,600, including a *kura*-style temple. South of the **Kai Honke**, a handsome sake-merchant's

← The Kegon Falls, surrounded by beautiful fall foliage, in the Nikko National Park

↑ Praying at the gravesite of the Byakkotai samurais on Iimoriyama, near Aizu Wakamatsu

house, is a *kura*-lined lane. The **Yamatogawa Sake-Brewing Museum** runs tasting tours. Kitakata is also known for its *oki-agari* dolls, which roll upright when knocked over.

Kai Honke

 📍 1-4611 Kitakata 📞 (0241) 22-0001 ⏰ 10am-4:15pm daily 🚫 Dec-Mar

Yamatogawa Sake-Brewing Museum

📍 4761 Teramachi 📞 (0241) 22-2233 ⏰ 9am-4:30pm daily (book ahead)

---

❺ Bandai-Asahi National Park
磐梯朝日国立公園

🅰 F3 📍 Yamagata, Niigata, and Fukushima Prefectures 🚉 To Fukushima, Tsuruoka, or Inawashiro Stns, then bus 🛈 At Yamagata and Aizu-Wakamatsu Stns

On July 15, 1888, Mount Bandai erupted, killing 477 people. Dammed streams formed hundreds of lakes and marshes, creating the lush natural beauty of the Bandai-Asahi National Park. Crisscrossed by five scenic toll roads, including the Bandai-Azuma Skyline (open April 22 to November 5), the park is studded with hot springs and camping grounds. The best way to explore is by car or bus.

Goshikinuma (five-colored marshes) is a popular 2-mile (4-km) trail starting at the Goshikinuma or Bandai-kogen bus stops.

---

❻ Aizu Wakamatsu
会津若松

🅰 F3 📍 Fukushima Prefecture 🚉 🛈 At Tsuruga-jo Castle; www.samurai-city.jp/en

Once home to the north's second most powerful clan, Aizu Wakamatsu takes pride in its samurai past. With ties to the Tokugawas, the Matsudaira clan bitterly resisted the 19th-century movement to reinstate the emperor. In the 1868 Boshin War, the Byakkotai (White Tigers), a band of teenage samurai fighting against imperial forces, mistakenly thought the castle had fallen and committed mass suicide on Iimoriyama, the hill (east of the station) where they are now buried.

Aizu Wakamatsu's top sights are fairly spread out so buy an all-day bus pass at the bus station office. **Tsuruga Castle**,

the heart of the city for over 600 years, was last rebuilt in 1965 as a museum. To the east is the **Samurai Residence** (Buke-yashiki), a good reproduction of a 38-room samurai manor. Nearby, the **Oyakuen** (medicinal herb garden) of a 17th-century villa contains over 200 herbs.

For shopping, head to Nanukamachi-dori, which is lined with old shops.

Tsuruga Castle

♿ 📍 1-1 Otemachi 🚌 To Tsurugajo Iriguchi 📞 (0242) 27-4005 ⏰ 8:30am-5pm daily

Samurai Residence

♿ 📍 1 Higashiyamamachi Ishiyama 🚌 Aizu bus to Aizu Bukeyashiki-mae 📞 (0242) 28-2525 ⏰ 8am-5pm daily

Oyakuen

♿ 📍 8-1 Hanaharumachi 🚌 Haikarasan bus to Oyakuen-mae 📞 (0242) 27-2472 ⏰ 8:30am-5pm daily

---

↑ Buying fresh oysters at the Shiogama Wholesale Fish Market, in Matsushima

❼ Matsushima
松島

🅰G3 🏠Miyagi Prefecture 🚉To Matsumisha and Matsushima-Kaigan 🚢From Shiogama 🛈By Matsushima sightseeing boat pier; (022) 354-2263

Take a hint from Matsuo Basho's 1689 visit to the bay of Matsushima *(p306)* and make Shiogama your starting point. The busy Shiogama Wholesale Fish Market, active from early morning until about 1pm, is known for its huge tuna auctions. Make time to lunch at one of Shiogama's superb sushi restaurants before taking the ferry to Matsushima.

 HIDDEN GEM
For Sake's Sake

Niigata, set across the water from Sado Island, is known as the home of sake. Founded in 1767, Imayotsukasa offers a free tour that illustrates the history of sake and the brewery, and, of course, with a tasting at the end *(www. imayotsukasa.co.jp/en).*

Although the tsunami of March 2011 caused widespread destruction along Japan's northeast coast, Matsushima was spared thanks to the numerous islands in its bay. These pine-covered islets are the reason Matsushima became renowned as one of Japan's "three famous views."

❽ Hiraizumi
平泉

🅰G2 🏠Iwate Prefecture 🚉 🛈Next to JR Stn; (0191) 46-2110

Nine hundred years ago, the Northern Fujiwara clan, under Fujiwara Kiyohira, made this small town into a cultural and economic capital, second only to Kyoto. Three generations later, Hiraizumi was in ruins. Yoshitsune, Japan's archetypal tragic hero, had sought refuge here from Yoritomo, his jealous brother and Japan's first shogun, but was betrayed by Yasuhira, the last Fujiwara leader, and killed. Yoritomo then turned against Yasuhira and had the clan wiped out.

At its peak, Hiraizumi had a population of 100,000. Wishing to create a Buddhist paradise

on earth, Kiyohira enriched the 9th-century temples Chuson-ji and Motsu-ji. Chuson-ji is five minutes by bus from the station, followed by a long climb lined with towering Japanese cedars. Only two of its many original buildings remain: the small Golden Hall, splendid with gold leaf, lacquer, and mother of pearl, where the first three Fujiwara leaders are buried; and the Sutra Hall. In the Treasure Hall are precious artifacts from the Fujiwara coffins and the temple.

All that remains of the original Motsu-ji (a ten-minute walk from the station) are its foundations and beautiful Heian-period paradise garden, the best in Japan.

❾ Tsuruoka
鶴岡

🅰F2 🏠Yamagata Prefecture 🚉 🛈City Office, 9-25 Baba-cho; (0235) 25-2111

Tsuruoka was the Sakai clan's castle seat. Best of this friendly town's attractions is the **Chido Museum**, west of the former castle grounds. It includes a *kabuto-zukuri* (helmet-style) farmhouse, and marvelous folk objects such as lacquered

sake caskets, bamboo fishing poles, and decorative straw *bandori* (backpacks). Southeast of the castle is the **Chidokan**, a school for young samurai.

Chido Museum

✦ ◉ 10-18 Ienakashinmachi ☎ (0235) 22-1199 ◷ 9am-4:30pm daily ✦ Dec-Feb: Wed

Chidokan

◉ 11-45 Babacho ☎ (0235) 23-4672 ◷ 9am-4:30pm Thu-Tue

Sado Island
佐渡島

◭ E3 ◭ Niigata Prefecture ⛴ Ferry or hydrofoil from Niigata (city) to Ryotsu ✦ 2F Ryotsu port; (025) 927-5000

Though it receives more than a million visitors a year, Sado Island still feels remote. For centuries, this mellow island 37 miles (60 km) off Honshu's northwest coast was home to political exiles, including the emperor Juntoku in 1221, the priest Nichiren in 1271, and Zeami, the Noh actor and playwright, in 1433. Of the 88 Noh theaters once here, about 35 are left. In 1601 the discovery of gold in Aikawa

brought an influx of convicts who were forced to work in the mines.

Buses connect the island's small towns, and tour buses stop at major sites. In the main port of Ryotsu in the east, outdoor Noh performances are held at the Honma Noh Stage. In Aikawa, on the west coast, the touristy **Sado Kinzan Gold Mine** has mechanical dolls recreating the harsh mining conditions. **Aikawa Museum** has exhibits on gold mining, ragweaving, and the local red-clay pottery.

The **Kodo** drumming group is the island's most famous

THE KODO DRUMMING GROUP

Kodo, one of the most dynamic *taiko* drumming groups, is known for performances of drum, flute, song, and dance. Kodo means both "children of the drum" and "heartbeat." The throbbing heart of Kodo is the *o-daiko*, a convex wooden drum used in Japanese folk festivals. Kodo spends much of the year performing in Japan and worldwide, and hosts an annual three-day Earth Celebration, when international musicians come to Sado to perform.

attraction. Based in Ogi, in the southwest, the group has put Sado firmly on the map.

Sado Kinzan Gold Mine

✦ ◉ 1305 Shimoaikawa ⛟ To Aikawa Eigayosho ☎ (0259) 74-2389 ◷ 8:30am-5pm daily

Aikawa Museum

✦ ◉ 20 Aikawa Sakashita-machi ⛟ ☎ (0259) 74-4312 ◷ 8:30am-5pm daily ✦ Dec 29-Jan 3; Dec-Feb: Sat, Sun & public hols

Kodo

◉ 148-1 Kaneta Shinden ⊕ kodo.or.jp

↑ The wild natural landscape of Sado Island, with jagged rocks lining the coastline

↑ The five-story Buddhist pagoda on Mount Haguro, Dewa Sanzan

Dewa Sanzan
出羽三山

🅰F2 🅰Yamagata Prefecture 🚌From S Mall Bus Terminal, near JR Tsuruoka Stn ℹIn front of Tsuruoka Stn; (0235) 25-7678

Dewa is the old name for this region, and Sanzan are its three mountains – Haguro-san (Mount Black Wing), Gassan (Mount Moon), and Yudono-san (Mount Bath) – opened for religious purposes 1,400 years ago by Hachiko, an imperial prince turned wandering priest. The three are sacred to *yamabushi*, mountain ascetics of the Shugendo sect.

The route to the peak of **Mount Haguro** is a climb up the 2,446 stone steps of the Japanese cedar-lined path. Take the bus to Haguro Center to start the climb. At the second stage is a teahouse with a view of the Mogami River valley. A side path goes to the ruins of a temple where poet Matsuo Basho stayed. At the top is the Dewa Sanzan Shrine,

which has the largest thatched roof in Japan, Hachiko's tomb. After the 1868 Meiji Restoration, all Shugendo temples were turned into Shinto shrines. The only true Buddhist structure left is the five-story pagoda at the foot of the stone steps.

Mount Gassan, also topped by a shrine, offers alpine flowers and summer skiing. It is a two-hour trek to the top from the Hachigome bus stop. The shrine on **Mount Yudono**, a 2-mile (2.5-km) hike from the Yudonosan Hotel bus stop, has a sacred hot spring. Mummified priests, examples of *sokushin jobutsu* (living Buddhas), can be seen at the temples of Dainichi-bo and Churen-ji, on the way to Mount Yudono.

Mount Haguro
🕐Apr-Nov: 9am-4:30pm daily; 9:30am-4pm daily

Mount Gassan
🕐Jul 1-fall

Mount Yudono
🕐Late Apr-early Nov

Sendai
仙台

🅰G3 🅰Miyagi Prefecture 🚆🚌 ℹAt 2F JR Sendai Stn; www.sendai-travel.jp/

Laid out in a grid pattern in the 1600s by the dynamic lord Date Masamune, Sendai is the north's largest city. Osaki Hachiman Shrine is a black lacquer architectural beauty in the northwest of the city. Overlooking the ruins of Aoba Castle from 1602 is a statue of the warrior Masamune, nick-named the "one-eyed dragon." The ruins are set in a park that is a bus ride to the west of the station. Nearby, the ornately carved Date mausoleums at Zuihoden, rebuilt after the war, are replicas of Momoyama-period architecture.

In March 2011, Sendai became the epicenter of the worst earthquake and tsunami in recorded Japanese history. The city has made much progress since the disaster and is now a safe place for tourists to visit.

BASHO AND HAIKU

Poet Matsuo Basho (1644-94) perfected the form that came to be known as haiku. A classical haiku is 17 syllables (written 5-7-5), includes a seasonal word, and refers to an objective image in the present. Basho spent most of his life traveling and writing haiku. His travel journal *The Narrow Road to the Deep North* details his five-month pilgrimage in 1689, and has since inspired many people to make the journey for themselves.

BUDDHIST SECTS

In the course of 1,500 years or so, since the first priests from mainland Asia brought Buddhism to Japan in the 6th century, usurping the native Shinto, hundreds of separate Buddhist movements, sects, and subsects developed in the country.

Contrasting beliefs appealed to different groups of nobility, samurai, and commoners, who each adapted practices to their own ends. In the eyes of many visitors today, Zen, one-time favorite of the samurai, is the quintessential religion of Japan, but it is just one of several major movements originating in China, and is itself subdivided into various sects. Of the other movements that flowered in Japan after World War II, the Tendai and Shingon sects of esoteric Buddhism still have millions of devotees.

↑ A man relaxing in the garden of a Buddhist temple

BUDDHIST MOVEMENTS

Zen Buddhism
This school developed during the Kamakura period (1185–1333). There are three main sects: Soto, Rinzai, and Obaku. All place emphasis on *zazen* (sitting meditation) and self-help.

Shingon
Founded in Japan in the 9th century by the monk Kukai, this branch incorporates Hindu elements, such as hand gestures *(mudra)* and the chanting of mantras.

Tendai
Brought to Japan in the 9th century by the monk Saicho, Tendai places emphasis on selfless devotion. From its base at Mount Hiei, Tendai spawned the Jodo, Jodo Shin, and Nichiren sects.

Shugendo
This offshoot of Shingon combines Buddhism and Shinto beliefs, and promotes ascetic practices on mountain retreats.

↑ The contemplative bronze figure of the Great Buddha in Kamakura

↑ Blossoming cherry trees skirting the Hinokinaigawa River banks in Kakunodate

⑬ Kakunodate
角館

🗺️G2 **📍Akita Prefecture** **🚉** **ℹ️At JR Stn; (0187) 54-2700**

Although Kakunodate does not have many of its original samurai houses remaining, this town still evokes the past. More than 150 of the weeping cherries in the Uchimachi district, brought from Kyoto almost 300 years ago, have been designated National Natural Treasures.

This district is also home to many samurai houses that are open to the public. The large **Aoyagi-ke** features ceilings painted with waves as protection from fire. At the classic **Ishiguro-ke**, known for its beautiful garden, the transoms between rooms project shadows by candlelight. Also in Uchimachi, the **Denshokan Museum** has historic exhibits and demonstrations of outstanding local crafts, including *kabazaiku* (objects of polished cherry bark) and *itayazaiku* (baskets and folk objects woven of split maple).

Aoyagi-ke
 🏠3 Omotemachi **🕘9am–5pm daily** **🌐samuraiworld.com/english**

Ishiguro-ke
🏠1 Omotemachi **📞(0187) 55-1496** **🕘9am–5pm daily**

Denshokan Museum
🏠10-1 Omotemachi **📞(0187) 54-1700** **🕘9am–5pm daily**

EAT

Pairon
This is the original home of *jajamen* noodles, served with fried *niku-miso* (miso with mince). After eating the noodles, break an egg into the broth and slurp that, too.

🗺️G2 **📍5-15 Uchimaru, Morioka, Iwate 020-0023** **🌐pairon.iwate.jp/**

> More than 150 of the weeping cherries in the Uchimachi district, brought from Kyoto almost 300 years ago, have been designated National Natural Treasures.

⑭ Hanamaki
花巻

🗺️G2 **📍Iwate Prefecture** **🚇🚉** **ℹ️At JR Shin-Hanamaki and JR Hanamaki Stns; www.kanko-hanamaki.ne.jp/en/**

Kenji Miyazawa (1896–1933), one of Japan's best-loved writers, was born in Hanamaki, a thriving hot-spring town. He wrote more than 1,200 poems and 90 children's stories, and worked to improve conditions for poor farmers in Iwate. The **Miyazawa Kenji Museum** has exhibits that reflect his lifelong interests in minerology, astronomy, wildlife, agriculture, Esperanto, and Buddhism. There is also the Ihatov, a free arts and research center. Ihatov was Miyazawa's Esperanto name for Iwate.

Miyazawa Kenji Museum
 🏠1-1-36 Yasawa 📞(0198) 31-2319 ⏰9am–4:30pm daily

---

⑮

Tono
遠野

🗺G2 📍Iwate Prefecture 🚉
ℹ By JR Stn; (0198) 62-1333

In Tono people still live in rhythm with nature, and observe old traditions. Much has changed, though, since folklorist Kunio Yanagita compiled the *Legends of Tono* in 1910. Few of the *magariya* (L-shaped houses, shared by people and horses) are left, but the mountains ringing the Tono basin are still beautiful.

Tono's attractions are best reached by car or bicycle, both of which can be rented at the station. The **Municipal Museum** in the town center introduces local culture. At Denshoen, local experts teach traditional crafts. A short walk away are Kappabuchi stream and the temple of Joken-ji, both traditionally the home of *kappa* (water imps). Northwest of the railroad station Tono Furusato Village has six *magariya*, where you can see traditional craftwork being made. Hayachine Shrine, a 30-minute drive from the station, is known for its kagura (sacred dances), and Mount Hayachine is popular with climbers.

Municipal Museum
 🏠3-9 Higashidatecho 📞(0198) 62-2340 ⏰Apr-Oct: 9am-5pm daily; Nov-Mar: 9am-5pm Tue-Sun ⏰Last day of month in May-Oct, Mar 1-4, Nov 24-30, public hols

---

JAPANESE DOLLS

Over 1,000 years ago, simple cloth dolls called *sarukko* were attached to babies' clothing as charms against harm. Clay dolls unearthed at Jomon-period sites are also believed to have had symbolic functions. These dolls remind some of *oshirasama* dolls – stick figures, usually of a horse and a girl – still found, and venerated, in parts of northern Japan. Other favorites include the limbless painted *kokeshi* dolls, made at towns around northern Japan, such as Morioka; *ohinasama*, the elaborate tiered arrays of silk court dolls displayed each Girls' Day (March 3); and *anesan ningyo* (big sister dolls), folded from paper.

KOKESHI DOLL

---

⑯

Morioka
盛岡

🗺G2 📍Iwate Prefecture 🚉 ℹ2nd flr, JR Stn; www.morioka-hachimantai.jp/eng/index.html

Once the center of the Nanbu domain, Morioka is now Iwate's capital and a transportation hub for the north, known for its Nanbu *tetsubin* (iron kettles) and Mount Iwate, the volcano that overlooks it. In October salmon run up the Nakatsu River, one of three rivers that bisect the city.

Near the ruins of Morioka Castle is a cherry tree, over 350 years old, that has grown from a crevice in a boulder.

Over Nakatsu River is the **Suzuki Morihisa Iron Studio**, which has superb iron pieces on display. For folk crafts, such as cute *kokeshi* dolls, head for Konya-cho (dyers' street) and Zaimoku-cho (lumber street).

Morioka is home to the noodle-eating tradition of *wanko-soba*. At **Azumaya Soba Shop**, patrons eat as many small bowls of soba buckwheat as possible.

Suzuki Morihisa Iron Studio
🏠1-6-7 Minamiodori 📞(019) 622-3809 ⏰9am-5pm Mon-Sat

Azumaya Soba Shop
🍴 🏠8-11 Moriokaekimaedori 📞(0120) 733-130

→
Bright-red fall leaves surround the poignant ruins of Marioka's castle

Towada-Hachimantai National Park
十和田八幡平国立公園

 G1 Akita, Aomori, and Iwate Prefectures JR Morioka & JR Aomori Stns From Stns to Lake Towada or Hachimantai At Lake Towada; (0176) 75-1015

This national park is in two sections, with the mountainous Hachimantai section 37 miles (60 km) south of the Towada section. The best way to get around the park is by car: trains are limited and buses not available in winter.

Hachimantai offers hiking and ski trails aplenty, frozen lava flows, alpine flora, and mountain views. A favorite with Japanese tourists, it has scenic toll roads, hot-spring and ski resorts, and a variety of tourist facilities. Good stopping places include Goshogake *onsen*, Hachimantai Resort ski complex, and the tourist village of Putaro.

In the Towada section highlights include the lovely Lake Towada. Its symbol, a statue of two maidens (1953) by Kotaro Takamura, is on the southern shore. More dramatic is the 6-mile (9-km) Oirase Gorge to the east of the lake. North of the lake are some atmospheric spa inns, such as the excellent Tsuta Onsen.

Oga Peninsula
男鹿半島

F1 Akita Prefecture JR Oga Stn Next to JR Oga Stn; (0185) 24-4700

Kicking 12 miles (20 km) into the Sea of Japan (East Sea), this foot-shaped peninsula has a scenic rocky coastline, pleasant little fishing villages, good seafood, and hills covered with Akita cedar. The lookout on Mount Kanpu offers a panoramic view of mountains, sea, and spreading rice fields. The peninsula is best known for the Namahage Festival on New Year's Eve, when men dressed in horned masks and straw coats go from house to house, scaring children into being good and idlers into working. A tourist version of the festival, the Namahage Sedo Matsuri, is held at Shinzan Shrine, in the city of Oga.

Shimokita Peninsula
下北半島

G1 Aomori Prefecture JR Ominato Stn Next to JR Shimokita Stn

This axe-shaped peninsula offers unspoiled beauty. In the interior is the desolate Osorezan (Mount Dread), one of three Japanese mountains sacred to spirits of the dead, with a crater lake and sulfur hot springs. It is open from May to October and blind mediums communicate with the spirits from July 22–24. Take the ferry from Sai along the west coast to Hotoke-ga-ura (Buddha Coast), past sea-worn cliffs and rock formations. In the southwest the port of Wakinosawa is home to sassy snow monkeys. A ferry runs from here to Aomori.

Aomori
青森

G1 Aomori Prefecture JR Bus stn bldg; www.en-aomori.com

Aomori is a nondescript city, but it is home to the riotous Nebuta Matsuri and **Sannai-Maruyama**, a Jomon-period site. Since its discovery in 1993, the site has yielded relics and ruins from 4,000 to 5,500 years ago, including a woven pouch, red lacquerware, and clay figures. Most impressive are the reconstructed pit dwellings and a standing-pillar building.

Sannai-Maruyama
3 miles (5 km) SW of city center (017) 734-9924 From Shin-Aomori & Aomori Stns to Sannai-Maruyama Iseki-mae 9am–5pm daily

---

Hirosaki
弘前

F1 Aomori Prefecture Hirosaki Stn; www.hirosaki-kanko.or.jp/en/

The cultural and educational center of Aomori, Hirosaki is a delight to explore. Most

←

Atmospheric waterfall in the forest of Towada-Hachimantai National Park

The moat-surrounded Hirosaki Castle, the former home of the Tsugaru family

streets lead to Hirosaki Park, the old castle grounds of the Tsugaru lords. The castle was destroyed by lightning but its picturesque 1810 keep, some smaller towers, several gates, and three moats remain. Kamenokomon, the imposing main gate, is on the north, where historic samurai houses still stand. Nearby is the **Tsugaruhan Neputa Mura**, displaying the Neputa floats used in Hirosaki's refined summer festival.

The wooded castle park is famous for its cherry blossoms, at their best in late April. The **Municipal Museum**, inside the park, has exhibitions of local history. Twenty-two temples line the approach to **Chosho-ji**, the Tsugaru family temple set on a bluff overlooking the Hirosaki plain and Mount Iwaki. Its handsome two-story

gate has extra-deep eaves because of the heavy snows common in the area. A side hall contains polychrome statues of the Buddha's 500 disciples. The main hall has the naturally mummified body of the 12th Tsugaru lord.

The streets around the castle were designed to twist and turn to confuse enemy forces. The large Kankokan (municipal information center) just south of the park is a good place to get oriented. It also has displays of local crafts. Other craft outlets include Tanakaya, on the corner of Ichiban-cho, with its range of traditional and contemporary Tsugaru lacquerware. Miyamoto Kogei, on Minami Sakura-cho, sells baskets of *akebi*, a vine fruit that grows wild in the mountains.

Tsugaruhan Neputa Mura
61 Kamenokomachi
(0172) 39-1511
9am–5pm daily

Municipal Museum
1-6, Shimoshiroganecho
(0172) 35-0700
9:30am–4:30pm Thu–Wed

Chosho-ji
1-23-8 Nishi-Shigemori
(0172) 32-0813
Mar–Nov: 9am–4pm daily, appt Dec–Feb

HIDDEN GEM
Rice Work!

Inakadate village near Hirosaki is famous for its rice paddy artworks. Perspective drawing methods are used to make the images look their best when seen from the 72-ft (22-m) observation platform.

DRINK

Ichinosuke
This *izakaya* (pub) specializes in Aomori's traditional food and *jizake*, or local artisan-made sake.

G1 1-5-19 Yasukata, Aomori-shi, Aomori 030-0803
(017) 763-0590

Tsugaru Joppari Isariya Sakaba
This farmhouse-style *izakaya* hosts live *shamisen* music.

G1 2-5-14 Honcho, Aomori-shi, Aomori 030-0802 maruto misuisan.jpn.com

---

A-Factory
Learn all about apple-cider brewing at this hip space, which combines a factory and a bar.

G1 1-4-2 Yanakawa, Aomori-shi, Aomori 038-0012
jre-abc.com

HOKKAIDO

First settled 20,000 years ago, this remote northern island became the homeland of the indigenous Ainu people after the 12th century. The Japanese made early forays to Yezo, as the island was called, in ancient times, but it was perceived as remote, inhospitable, and cold. For centuries only the persecuted Ainu, refugee warriors, and banished criminals lived there. In the late 1860s, however, the new Meiji government decided officially to develop the island. Thereafter it became known as Hokkaido, or "north sea road."

Since then, the population has risen to just under 6 million. The few Ainu left number somewhere between 24,000 and 60,000. Fishing, farming, forestry, and mining are the main industries, but tourism draws several million people north each year. The lively capital of Sapporo attracts people with its spectacular festivals, while the island's many national parks offer boundless opportunities for outdoor enthusiasts, including camping, hiking, and hot-spring bathing.

HOKKAIDO

Experience

1. Hakodate
2. Niseko Ski Resort
3. Onuma Quasi-National Park
4. Shikotsu-Toya National Park
5. Sapporo
6. Daisetsu-zan National Park
7. Rishiri-Rebun-Sarobetsu National Park
8. Akan National Park
9. Kushiro Wetlands National Park
10. Nemuro Peninsula
11. Lake Furen
12. Akkeshi Bay
13. Shiretoko National Park

Rebun Island

Kafuka

Rishiri Island

Wakkanai

Wakkanai Airport

Sarufutsu

7 RISHIRI-REBUN-SAROBETSU NATIONAL PARK

Toyotomi

Hamatonbetsu

Horonobe

Teshio

Nakagawa

Enbetsu

Otoineppu

Hako-dake 3,704 ft (1,129 m)

Shosanbetsu

Bifuka

Haboro

Nayoro

Tomamae

Uryu-ko

Shibetsu

Obira

Horokanai

Wassamu

Rumoi

Mashike

Numata

Asahikawa

Shokanbetsu-dake 4,891 ft (1,491 m)

Fukagawa

Asahikawa Airport

Hamamasu

Takikawa

Akabira

Atsuta

Sunagawa

Furano

Tsukigata

Bibai

Yubari-sanchi

Sea of Japan (East Sea)

Yobetsu-dake 4,258 ft (1,298 m)

Shakotan

Otaru

Tobetsu

Iwamizawa

Yoichi

Kamoenai

Ebetsu

SAPPORO 5

Iwanai

Kutchan

NISEKO SKI RESORT 2

Yotei-zan 6,227 ft (1,898 m)

Eniwa

Oiwake

Suttsu

Eniwa-dake 4,331 ft (1,320 m)

Chitose

Hidaka

Kariba-yama 4,987 ft (1,520 m)

Kuromatsunai

Kimobetsu

Lake Shikotsu

New Chitose Airport

4 SHIKOTSU-TOYA NATIONAL PARK

Mu-kawa

Oshamanbe

Toyoura

Lake Toya

Tomakomai

Biratori

Setana

Kunnui

Date

Shiraoi

Oshima-hanto

Yakumo

Noboribetsu

Shizunai

Taisei

Muroran

Kumaishi

Mori

Okushiri

Shikabe

Esashi

Nanae

3 ONUMA QUASI-NATIONAL PARK

Kaminokuni

Kamiiso

Minami-Kayabe

HAKODATE 1

Hakodate Airport

Kikonai

NORTHERN HONSHU
p294

Fukushima

Matsumae

Aomori

Imabetsu

EXPERIENCE

❶

Hakodate
函館

🅰️ A3 📍 150 miles (240 km SW of Sapporo) ✈️ Hakodate 🚃🚌 from Sapporo ⛴️ From Aomori 🚉 JR Stn; www.hakodate.travel/en

Once an island, the fan-shaped city of Hakodate now straddles a low sandbar that links it to the mainland. In 1854, the city was designated one of the first treaty ports in Japan. Fifteen years later the city was the scene of the last battle in Japan before World War II.

Within easy reach of the center is Mount Hakodate, the peak of which can be reached by cable car, road, or on foot. From here, you can see the sea, the mountains, and the unique shape of the city below.

The quiet Motomachi district, nestling beneath Mount Hakodate in the south of the city, is the most attractive area. Western-style buildings are a feature here, a legacy of the treaty-port status. They include the Old Public Hall, with its stately blue-and-yellow clapboarding; the Russian Orthodox Church with its spire and onion domes; and, nearby, the Old British Consulate.

In the north, Goryokaku Park provides a peaceful haven for strolling, and its more than 1,500 cherry trees

GREAT VIEW
Night Vision

The spectacular view from Mount Hakodate of the shimmering city lights fanning out between the two dark arms of the sea is considered one of the finest night views in all of Japan.

create a popular springtime spectacle. The pentangle-shaped Goryokaku Fort was completed in 1864 to defend against the Russians, but it fell to imperial forces in 1869. The Former Magistrate Office sits at the center of the fortress.

Hot-spring enthusiasts will want to stay at the *onsen* resort of Yunokawa 15 minutes from the center. About an hour's drive to the east of the city is the active Mount Esan volcano with nearby azalea gardens and forested slopes.

↓ The star-shaped Goryokaku Fort in Hakodate and the Former Magistrate Office *(inset)*

Niseko Ski Resort
ニセコスキーリゾート

🅰A3 🏠55 miles (88 km SW of Sapporo) 🚉Niseko Stn 🚌From Sapporo

Some of Japan's best skiing can be found in the Niseko mountains. Snowboarders and skiers alike favor this area for its long, cold winter season, numerous slopes, and quality off-piste powder. In summer it offers adventure-sports vacations. Four major resorts are connected at the top of the same mountain and shuttle buses link them at the base. A single pass can be used for all the resorts.

The town of Hirafu is very popular among visitors, and during the skiing season it takes on the character of a lively alpine village.

↑ Downhill skiing on the powdery slopes of Niseko Ski Resort

Onuma Quasi-National Park
大沼国定公園

🅰A3 🏠135 miles (218 km SW of Sapporo) 🚉Onuma-Koen Stn 🚌From Hakodate ℹ️Next to Stn; (0138) 67-2170

Three large, islet-studded lakes – Onuma, Konuma, and Junsainuma – are surrounded by forest and form the Onuma Quasi-National Park. Deer and foxes inhabit the forests, and the lakes support many kinds of waterfowl, particularly during the spring and fall migrations. Wildflowers are abundant in summer and among the rare birds that come to Onuma are the ruddy kingfisher, the white-tailed eagle, and Steller's sea eagle. The graceful form of Mount Komagatake provides a stunning backdrop to the north. An easily followed hiking trail from the north side of Lake Onuma to the upper mountain provides a fabulous view of southwestern Hokkaido.

Shikotsu-Toya National Park
支笏洞爺国立公園

🅰A3 🏠57 miles (92 km SW of Sapporo) 🚉Toya Stn 🚌From Sapporo ℹ️142-5 Toyako Onsen, Toyako-cho, Abuta District; www.toyako-vc.jp/en

The disjointed Shikotsu-Toya National Park is like an open-air museum to vulcanology. It contains the 6,230-ft- (1,900-m-) high Mount Yotei, two crater lakes, and the spa towns of Jozankei in the north and Noboribetsu in the south.

Beside Lake Shikotsu is the popular hot-spring resort of Shikotsu Kohan, as well as the remarkable moss-covered Kokenodomon gorge. The lake is dominated to the north by the rugged peak of Mount Eniwa, and to the south by Mount Fuppushi and Mount Tarumae, with its cinder cone.

Lake Toya, 25 miles (40 km) farther southwest, contains the picturesque group of islands known as Nakajima. Nearby stands Japan's youngest volcano, the bare-sloped Showa Shinzan (it formed between 1943 and 1945), beside the extremely active Mount Usu.

The mountains in the park make for rewarding hikes; trails are well defined, and the views from the tops of Eniwa and Tarumae are superb.

EAT

Hakodate Seafood Market
This famous market (open 5am–2pm) is packed with stalls selling fish, salmon roe, sea urchin, crab, and more. Pick out what you want and have it placed on one of the charcoal grills that dot the street.

🅰A3 🏠9-19 Wakamatsucho, Hakodate-shi, Hokkaido 040-0063 🌐hakodate-asaichi.com

Umizora No Haru
Based on a traditional Ainu house, this restaurant has thatched walls and textiles on loan from Shiraoi's Ainu Museum. The food includes salmon tataki, grilled venison, and dumplings topped with salmon eggs, plus a millet sake.

🅰A2 🏠4-19-1 Minami 3 Jo Nishi, Chuo-ku, Sapporo, Hokkaido 060-0063 🌐umizoranoharu.gorp.jp

5

Sapporo
札幌

 A2 **Hokkaido Prefecture** **Shin-Chitose, Okadama** **Sapporo International Communication Plaza, opposite Sapporo Clock Tower; www.plaza-sapporo.or.jp/en**

Capital of Hokkaido, the modern city of Sapporo lies on the Ishikari plain, straddling the Toyohira River. Four subway lines, streetcars, and a well laid-out grid structure make getting around fairly straightforward. At Sapporo's heart lies the long Odori Park, dominated at the east end by the metal television tower and at the west by a view to the mountains. One block north, opposite the wooden Tokei-dai clock tower, is the Sapporo International Communication Plaza, an essential stop for information on Hokkaido, with friendly staff to help with planning and booking. The city gives its name to the famous local beer; its brewing is shown at the **Sapporo Beer Garden and Museum** north-east of the station. Nightlife is focused on the Susukino area, with thousands of restaurants and bars. Local specialties include "Genghis Khan" –

↑ Sapporo's Odori Park, site of the annual Yuki Matsuri "snow festival"

mutton and vegetables grilled at the table on a charcoal-fired griddle.

A large collection of Ainu artifacts is displayed at the Exhibition Room of Northern Peoples in the **Botanical Gardens**. The gardens themselves are a refreshingly quiet spot, with a representative collection of Hokkaido's flora. The large-scale outdoor sculptures at the **Sapporo Art Park** make for an interesting hands-on excursion.

Lying 9 miles (14 km) east of the city, the **Historical Village of Hokkaido** commemorates the official settlement of the island in the 1860s. This cluster of late 19th- and early 20th-century buildings has been gathered from around Hokkaido. Some have displays of traditional life inside.

Sapporo Beer Garden and Museum

9-1-1 Kita 7-Jo Higashi (011) 748-1876 11am-8pm Tue-Sun

Botanical Gardens

10-min walk from Stn (011) 221-0066 May-Oct: 9am-3:30pm Tue-Sun; Nov-Apr: 9am-3:30pm Mon-Sat

---

SAPPORO SNOW FESTIVAL

Sapporo's annual Snow Festival (Yuki Matsuri) transforms Odori Park and the nearby Susukino area and Makomanai Park into a fairy-tale land of ice sculptures. Watching the making of these carvings (from about a week before the start of the festival) is fascinating. This popular event overlaps with Sapporo White Illumination (mid-Nov-mid-Feb), when strings of white lights adorn Odori Park and Ekimae-dori.

Sapporo Art Park

🅐 2-75 Geijutsunomori
🕐 9:45am–5pm daily
📅 Nov 4–Apr 28: Mon

Historical Village of Hokkaido

◈ 🅐 50-1 Konoppuro
🕐 9am–4:30pm daily 📅 Oct–Apr: Mon 🌐 kaitaku.or.jp

Daisetsu-zan National Park

大雪山国立公園

🅰 B2 🚗 112 miles (180 km) NE of Sapporo ✈ Okadama and Asahikawa 🚉 Obihiro and Asahikawa Stns 🚌 Sounkyo, Kamikawa-cho; (01658) 9-4400

At 890 sq miles (2,310 sq km), Daisetsu-zan is Japan's largest national park. A huge raised plateau ringed with peaks, right in the center of Hokkaido, the park was established in 1934. Asahikawa to the northwest or Obihiro to the south make the best starting points for visiting the park, with easy car access by routes 39 and 273. Buses connect the major *onsen* resorts of Sounkyo, Asahi-dake, and Tenninkyo. The plunging Sounkyo Gorge, with the cascading Ryusei and Ginga waterfalls, is best explored by bicycle or on foot. The ropeway at Sounkyo and the cable car at Asahi-dake tend to be packed but offer quick access; away from the top stations people become scarcer and the views more spectacular.

In Ainu legend the peaks of the Daisetsu mountains are the dwelling places of benevolent but powerful god-spirits who, in human form, helped in times of need. A network of trails across these mountains provides everything from day hikes to week-long tramps, and it is worth taking the time to hike or go by cable car up from the low access roads to the higher levels for the breathtaking views. The dramatic, conical, steam-venting peak of Mount Asahi (or Asahi-dake), Hokkaido's highest at 7,500 ft (2,290 m), offers an uplifting panorama across the high plateau. June and July bring alpine flowers, while fall colors are at their best in late August and September. En route, you may see bears and pika (a rodent), as well as rubythroats and nutcrackers in the trees, among other species.

An excellent route for the fit day-hiker starts from Sounkyo *onsen*. From there take the ropeway and cable car, then hike southwest over Mount Kuro-dake, continuing along well-marked trails to Mount Asahi. From the top, descend via the cable car to Asahi-dake *onsen*. It should take around seven hours.

Located 30 miles (50 km) West of the park, near the pretty town of Biei, the Blue Pond is an unbelievable color.

DRINK

Bow Bar Sapporo

For whisky aficionados, Bow Bar is a must-go spot when in Sapporo. Their selection of rare whiskies is unparalleled.

🅰 A2 🏢 Hoshi Building 8F, 2-7-5 Minami Jonishi, Chuo-Ku ,Sapporo, Hokkaido 064-0804
🕐 7pm–2am
🌐 thebowbar-sapporo.com

Bar Yamazaki

This iconic Sapporo bar was managed for more than 50 years by the legendary bartender Ichiro Yamazaki. His apprentices still serve cocktails in Yamazaki's signature style.

🅰 A2 🏢 3-3 Minami Jonishi, Chuo-Ku, Sapporo, Hokkaido 060-0063 🕐 6pm–2am
🌐 bar-yamazaki.com

↑ Trekking in the mountains of Japan's largest national park, Daisetsu-zan

 7

Rishiri-Rebun-Sarobetsu National Park
利尻礼文サロベツ国立公園

🅰 A1 🏛 240 miles (385 km) N of Sapporo ✈ Wakkanai 🚉 Wakkanai Stn 🚌 From Wakkanai to both islands

Consisting of the Sarobetsu coast and the two islands of Rishiri and Rebun, this park is within sight of the Russian island of Sakhalin. The coastal meadows in the Sarobetsu area and the shores of the

↑ Taking a break on Mount Rishiri, Rishiri-Rebun-Sarobetsu National Park

shallow lagoons in the coastal plain, are carpeted with flowers in summer, including yellow-orange lilies, white cotton grass, white rhododendrons, and purple irises.

About 12 miles (20 km) offshore on the island of Rishiri, the startling 5,650-ft-(1,720-m-) high conical peak of Mount Rishiri (Rishiri-Fuji) appears to rise straight from the sea. A road runs around its coastline, making for incredibly scenic cycling and linking the various settlements including Oshidomari, the main port, and Kutsugata, the second port on the west side. Trails to the top of Mount Rishiri thread through a host of alpine summer flowers. Those less inclined to hike may choose to fish or simply relax and enjoy the excellent fresh fish at local restaurants.

Rebun, Rishiri's partner and Japan's northernmost island, is lowly in comparison but is renowned as the "isle of flowers." Kafuka is its main port; the fishing village of Funadomari is at the opposite, north end of the island. There's great hiking (sometimes hard going), especially on the west coast; the island's youth hostel organizes guided walking groups.

 8

Akan National Park
阿寒国立公園

🅰 C2 🏛 186 miles (300 km) E of Sapporo ✈ Memanbetsu (Abashiri), Nakashibetsu, and Kushiro 🚉 Minami-Teshikaga and Kawayu-Onsen Stns 🚌 From Kushiro Stn 🛈 Near Akan Kohan bus terminal; (0154) 67-2254

This enormous national park in east-central Hokkaido is possibly the most beautiful in Japan. Travel around the park is limited; there are tour buses, but cycling or rental-car are better options.

The western portion, around Lake Akan, is dominated by a pair of volcanic peaks: in the southeast is the 4,500-ft (1,370-m) Mount O-Akan while in the southwest is the still-active Mount Me-Akan, at 4,920 ft (1,500 m). The day hike up Me-Akan from Akan Kohan *onsen* and down the other side on a well-trodden trail to attractive Lake Onneto affords marvelous views in any season, but especially in fall.

East of Akan lies Lake Kusshoro, in a huge caldera with a 35-mile (57-km) perimeter. Beautiful all year,

Winter sun rising over large, volcanic Lake Kussharo, in Akan National Park

Kushiro Wetlands National Park
釧路湿原

🅰 C2 ⏱ 202 miles (326 km) E of Sapporo ✈ Kushiro 🚃 Kushiro Stn 🚌 From Kushiro ℹ JR Kushiro Stn; (0154) 22-8294

If any creature represents Japan, it is the *tancho*, or red-crowned crane, regarded as a symbol of happiness and long life. A large peat swamp, an expanse of undulating reed beds bisected by streams, the Kushiro Wetlands National Park is one of the main homes of these enormous and graceful birds, which stand 4 ft 6 in (1.4 m) high.

In the early 1900s, the cranes were pushed to the verge of extinction in Japan by hunting and loss of habitat, but now protection and provision of food for them during the winter months has boosted the population to around 700 birds.

From December to March, the cranes forage along streams and marsh edges, or fly to one of three major feeding sites north of Kushiro: two in Tsurui village and one in Akan village. These sites

Did You Know?

The harmonics created by pressure in the ice make Lake Kussharo sound as if it is singing.

this vast lake freezes over almost entirely in winter. Thermal vents keep tiny portions ice-free; here flocks of whooper swans remain throughout the winter.

Farther east again lies Lake Mashu. The crater's steep cliffs rise 650 ft (200 m), the water is astonishingly clear, and the lake has no inlets or outlets. The panoramic view from the crater rim takes in Mount Shari to the north, the Shiretoko Peninsula to the northeast, and Lake Kussharo and beyond to the Akan volcanoes in the west.

The park's forests are home to woodpeckers and other birds, red foxes, sika deer, and Siberian chipmunks. There are outdoor hot-spring pools at Akan Kohan, on Lake Akan's south shore, and Wakoto, on Lake Kussharo's south shore.

➡

Elegant red-crowned cranes in the snow at Kushiro Wetlands National Park

TOP 5

HOKKAIDO FOODS

Kaisen don
Kaisen don is a bowl of rice topped with salmon roe and sea urchin.

Hairy Crab
The hairy crab is famed for its sweet flesh and creamy, buttery roe.

Sapporo-Style Soup Curry
A curry-flavored soup served with chicken and flash-fried vegetables.

Sapporo Miso Ramen
Hokkaido's hearty ramen is miso-based and includes sweetcorn.

Yubari Melon
Sweet Yubari melons can cost as much as ¥20,000 each.

offer the best opportunities for viewing the cranes year round. On late winter days, the birds display, calling and dancing to one another in the snow as they prepare for the breeding season ahead.

In summer (May to September), the cranes are territorial, occupying large, traditional nesting grounds where they usually raise just one chick, or occasionally two.

Nemuro Peninsula
根室半島

C2 **280 miles (450 km)** E of Sapporo **Nemuro-Nakashibetsu** **Nemuro Stn** **In front of Nemuro Stn; (0153) 24-3104**

The low-lying Nemuro Peninsula, a coastal plateau carved by streams into steep-sided gullies, is well loved by naturalists. The best way to explore the area is by car.

The red fox is common here and, in forests around Onneto, there are also many sika deer. In summer, lilies, fritillaries, and other wildflowers are plentiful, while in winter, both white-tailed and Steller's sea eagles can be seen. Offshore and in the many sheltered bays, there are flocks of sea ducks, particularly scoters and harlequins, and many other seabirds can be spotted.

Lake Furen
風蓮湖

C2 **263 miles (424 km)** E of Sapporo **Kushiro** **Nemuro Stn**

Situated on Hokkaido's east coast, beautiful Lake Furen is the seasonal haunt of hordes of birds: migrating waterfowl in spring and fall, swans in late fall, sea eagles in winter, and red-crowned cranes in summer.

Nearly 12 miles (20 km) long and up to 2 miles (4 km) wide, the lagoon is only 6 ft (2 m) deep or less in places. It is fringed by forests of fir and spruce, with alder and birch scrub in wetter areas. Some easy forest walks start from the south end of the lake, at Hakuchodai and Shunkunitai, offering a wealth of great bird-watching opportunities and plenty of wildflowers en route. In winter, the frozen lagoon and adjacent areas are good for cross-country skiing.

Akkeshi Bay
厚岸湾

C2 **230 miles (370 km)** E of Sapporo **Kushiro** **Akkeshi Stn** **1st Floor, Akkeshi Gourmet Park, 2-2 Suminoe, Akkeshi-cho, Akkeshi-gun; (0153) 52-4139**

Akkeshi's sheltered tidal lagoon is renowned for its oysters. The bay is extensively farmed, and there is a shrine to the oysters on a rocky islet. Throughout the winter, and during spring and fall migration, whooper swans gather in the inner bay, while in summer red-crowned cranes breed upriver and at the nearby Kiritappu wetland. The scenic coastal road from Akkeshi around to Kiritappu is well worth driving for an insight into the fishing and seaweed-harvesting lifestyles of some of the local people. Walking at the cape beyond Kiritappu is exhilarating, but early summer mornings are best avoided because this is when a sea mist is most likely to conceal the view.

> **Lake Furen is the seasonal haunt of hordes of birds: migrating waterfowl in spring and fall, swans in late fall, sea eagles in winter, and red-crowned cranes in summer.**

← Sailing on the icy waters of the Strait of Nemuro, in the Nemuro Peninsula

 A walkway in the Five Lakes area, Shiretoko National Park

❸

Shiretoko National Park
知床国立公園

C2 🚗216 miles (348 km) NE of Sapporo ✈Memanbetsu (Abashiri) or Nakashibetsu 🚉Shiretoko-Shari Stn 🛈Shiretoko Shizen center; (0152) 24-2114

This rugged finger of land jutting into the Okhotsk Sea was named Shiretoko ("the end of the earth") by the Ainu. Now a World Heritage Site, Shiretoko National Park consists of a well-forested ridge of volcanic peaks dominated by the 5,450-ft (1,660-m) Mount Rausu. The peninsula supports one of the healthiest populations of brown bears left in Hokkaido. Sightings are rare, though the boat ride from Utoro north to the cape during the summer is one possible way of seeing them as they forage along the coastal strip.

Minke whales, dolphins, and porpoises may be seen in summer, too, along with birds such as spectacled guillemots, Japanese cormorants, and short-tailed shearwaters. White-tailed sea eagles nest along the peninsula. In winter their numbers are swollen by hundreds more arriving from Russia. Despite their numbers, they are overshadowed by the arrival of pairs of the world's largest eagle: Steller's sea eagle. Both types of eagles are best seen in winter north of Rausu on the southeast coast.

North of Utoro lie the pretty Shiretoko Five Lakes, reflecting Mount Rausu. An easy 1-mile (2-km) trail starts beyond the visitor center, and *onsen* fans will not want to miss the hot Kamuiwakka waterfall, northeast of here. The high pass from Utoro to Rausu (Route 334) is open from May to October, and the view east from here to Kunashiri island is dramatic. From near the pass, a hiking trail strikes off south for Lake Rausu and Mount Onnebetsu, while another heads north for Mounts Rausu, Io, and Shiretoko, and the cape beyond. Mount Rausu is a day hike along a good trail. The journey to the cape, however, requires several days and careful planning. Note that hiking is possible only from June to September.

NEED TO KNOW

A bullet train speeding past Mount Fuji

Before You Go 328

Getting Around 330

Practical Information 334

BEFORE
YOU GO

Forward planning is essential to any successful trip. Be prepared for all eventualities by considering the following points before you travel.

CURRENCY
Japanese Yen (¥)

AVERAGE DAILY SPEND

SAVE	SPEND	SPLURGE
¥10,000	**¥20,000**	**¥40,000**

BOTTLED WATER	COFFEE	BEER	DINNER FOR TWO
¥100	**¥220**	**¥400**	**¥5,000**

ESSENTIAL PHRASES

Hello	Konnichiwa
Goodbye	Sayonara
Please	Onegaishimasu
Thank you	Arigato Gozaimasu
Do you speak English?	Eigo Hanasemasuka?
I don't understand	Wakarimasen

ELECTRICITY SUPPLY
Power sockets are type A and B. Standard voltage is 100v and the frequency is 50 Hz (east) and 60 Hz (west).

Passports and Visas

For a stay of up to three months for the purpose of tourism, EU nationals and citizens of the US, Canada, Australia and New Zealand do not need a visa. Citizens of some countries, including the UK and EU, may extend this stay by another 90 days at immigration offices in Japan (at least 10 days before the expiration date). Visitors aged 16 or over are fingerprinted and photographed at the point of entry.

Travel Safety Advice

Visitors can get up-to-date travel safety information from the **US State Department**, **UK Foreign and Commonwealth Office**, and the **Australian Department of Foreign Affairs and Trade**.
Australia
w smartraveller.gov.au
UK
w gov.uk/foreign-travel-advice
US
w travel.state.gov

Customs Information

An individual is permitted to carry the following within Japan for personal use:
Tobacco products 400 cigarettes, 100 cigars, or 500g of smoking tobacco.
Alcohol 3 760-ml-bottles of alcoholic beverages.
Cash If you plan to enter Japan with ¥1 million or more in cash, you must declare it upon arrival.
Medicines Some over-the-counter medicines, such as those for sinus problems, and pain killers containing codeine, are prohibited. Prescription drugs are also limited. Contact a Japanese embassy for more information.

Insurance

It is wise to take out an insurance policy covering theft, loss of belongings, medical problems, cancellations, and delays. It is important to confirm that your policy covers medical costs since these can be extremely high in Japan.

Vaccinations

No inoculations are needed for Japan, but it is advisable to be vaccinated against encephalitis if you are planning on staying in the country for over a month or are visiting rural areas.

Money

Although ATMs are common in urban areas, many do not accept foreign credit or debit cards; most post offices and 7-Elevens have machines that will accept them. Cards can also be used at major stations to buy JR train tickets and are accepted by some taxis, but it is still worth carrying around some cash at all times.

Booking Accommodation

As well as Western-style hotels, Japan offers a few idiosyncratic options. *Ryokans* are the most traditional accomodations. These inns usually have an on-site *onsen* and serve breakfast and dinner. At the oppposite end of the scale, capsule hotels are highly modern, and offer inexpensive sleeping pods. Mainly found in entertainment areas and along highways, love hotels are designed for couples, and charge an hourly, as well as nightly, rate for their rooms, which are sometimes themed. For help with booking accomodation, visit the **Japan National Tourism Organization, Rakuten Travel,** or **Japanican.**

Japanican
🌐 japanican.com/en
Japan National Tourism Organization
🌐 jnto.go.jp
Rakuten Travel
🌐 travel.rakuten.com

Travellers with Specific Needs

The visually impaired are well provided for, but people in wheelchairs occasionally have issues at small stations and pedestrian over- and underpasses, despite a 2008 law requiring barrier-free access. **Accessible Tokyo** provides information about disabled access and facilities at individual tourist attractions, parks, and hotels in the capital, as well as Kyoto and Kamakura.

Accessible Tokyo
🌐 accessible.jp.org

Language

Despite the profusion of brand names written in Latin script, visitors may face some language problems outside the main tourist areas. Few locals are comfortable with speaking English, and, when it is spoken, it is generally pronounced as if it were Japanese. For example, taxi becomes *takushi* and hotel is *hoteru*. Even with good English speakers, subtleties may be lost – "yes" often means "I understand," not "I agree," and "it's difficult" usually means no. For clarity, avoid negative and either/or questions.

Closures

Monday Museums, art galleries, and many tourist attractions close for the day; when Monday is a bank holiday, they often close on Tuesday instead.

Saturday Banks, post offices, and offices are closed for the day.

Sunday As well as bank, post office, and office closures, department stores have reduced opening hours.

Public holidays Many attractions are closed on top of banks, post offices, and offices.

PUBLIC HOLIDAYS	
1 Jan	New Year's Day
2nd Mon, Jan	Coming of Age Day
11 Feb	National Foundation Day
20/21 Mar	Vernal (Spring) Equinox
29 Apr	Showa Day
3 May	Constitution Memorial Day
4 May	Greenery Day
5 May	Children's Day
3rd Mon, Jul	Marine Day
11 Aug	Mountain Day
3rd Mon, Sep	Respect for the Aged Day
22/23 Dec	Autumnal Equinox
2nd Mon, Oct	Health and Sports Day
3 Nov	Culture Day
23 Nov	Labor Thanksgiving Day
23 Dec	Emperor's Birthday

GETTING AROUND

Whether you're visiting for a short city break or travelling around the islands, discover how best to reach your destination and travel like a pro.

AT A GLANCE

PUBLIC TRANSPORT COSTS

TOKYO

¥170

A single subway journey

OSAKA

¥180

A single subway journey

KYOTO

¥210

A single subway journey

TOP TIP
Buy a reloadable Suica card for train and bus travel to save time and money.

SPEED LIMIT

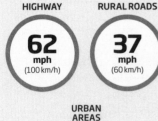

HIGHWAY	RURAL ROADS
62 mph (100 km/h)	**37** mph (60 km/h)

URBAN AREAS

25 mph (40 km/h)

Arriving by Air

The main international gateways to Japan are **Narita International Airport**, located at some distance from Tokyo, **Haneda Airport**, which is smaller but closer to the center, and Osaka's **Kansai International Airport**. Other airports handling international flights (mainly from Asia) include Naha in Okinawa; Fukuoka and Nagasaki in Kyushu; Hiroshima, Nagoya, Niigata, and Sendai in Honshu; and Sapporo in Hokkaido.

Haneda Airport
w haneda-airport.jp
Kansai International Airport
w kansai-airport.or.jp/en
Narita International Airport
w narita-airport.jp/en

Train Travel

Japan's rail system is one of the best in the world in terms of safety, efficiency, and comfort. The Japan Railways Group (JR) is the main operator and runs over 12,400 miles (20,000 km) of tracks, as well as the *shinkansen*. Often, multiple lines run between the same places. As well as the bullet trains, there are *tokkyu* ("limited express," the next fastest), *kyuko* ("express"), *kaisoku* (misleadingly called "rapid"), and *futsu* ("local").

The **Japan Rail Pass** is recommended for those planning to travel extensively, but regional rail passes are also available, such as the **JR East Rail Pass** covering northeast Honshu. There are two types of **JR West Rail Pass**: the Sanyo Area Pass covers Osaka, Okayama, Hiroshima, and Hakata, while the Kansai Area Pass includes Osaka, Kobe, Kyoto, Himeji, and Nara.

Tickets and seat reservations for longer trips can be bought at JR stations, as well as from authorized travel agents. Seat reservations, which are charged at a small extra fee, are recommended for long-distance trips.

Japan Rail Pass
w japanrailpass.net
JR East Rail Pass
w jreast.co.jp
JR West Rail Pass
w westjr.co.jp

Airport	Bus	Taxi	Train	Express
Tokyo (Narita)	¥1,000 (90 mins)	¥20,000 (60 mins)	¥1,200 (90 mins)	¥4,000 (55 mins)
Tokyo (Haneda)	¥1,200 (45 mins)	¥8,000 (30 mins)	¥600 (40 mins)	None
Osaka (Kansai)	¥1,600 (60 mins)	¥15,000 (50 mins)	¥1,200 (70 mins)	¥3,000 (70 mins)

RAIL JOURNEY PLANNER

Plotting the country's main long-distance rail routes, this map is a handy reference for travelling between Japan's main towns and cities by train. Journey times, usually by *shinkansen,* are listed below.

Tokyo to Niigata	4.5 hrs
Tokyo to Nagoya	4.5 hrs
Tokyo to Osaka	6.5 hrs
Tokyo to Kyoto	6 hrs
Kyoto to Kanazawa	3.5 hrs
Kyoto to Matsue	4 hrs
Tokyo to Sapporo	16 hrs
Tokyo to Sendai	4.5 hrs
Sendai to Hakodate	8 hrs
Hakodate to Sapporo	4 hrs
Hakodate to Kushiro	7 hrs
Osaka to Hiroshima	4.5 hrs
Hiroshima to Fukuoka	3.5 hrs
Fukuoka to Nagasaki	2 hrs
Fukuoka to Kumamoto	2 hrs
Fukuoka to Beppu	2 hrs
Kumamoto to Kagoshima	2.5 hrs

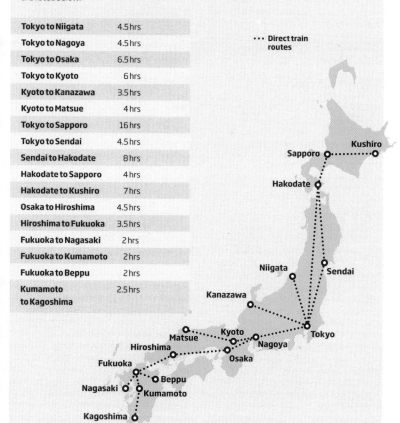

··· Direct train routes

Long-Distance Bus Travel

The efficiency and extent of the rail network means that few visitors use long-distance coaches, but the bus network is comprehensive, and for those without a Japan Rail Pass, a bus is a much cheaper option than the train. While styles and services vary, coaches are uniformly comfortable, and often have toilets. For timetable details contact a local information centers or see **JR Bus Kanto**.

JR Bus Kanto

ⓦ jrbuskanto.co.jp.e.wn.hp.transer.com

Boats and Ferries

It is possible to travel to Japan by ferry from some parts of Asia, including Pusan in South Korea and Shanghai in China. The Far Eastern Shipping Line also connects Japan to Russia.

As an island nation, ferries and boats are a great way to get around Japan. Tickets for boats can be bought at the ferry terminal on the day of departure. Usually, there is a form to fill in, which enables the ferry company to compile a list of passengers. The **Japan National Tourism Organization** (JNTO) produces a travel manual detailing the main services.

Japan National Tourism Organization

ⓦ japan.travel/en

Public Transport

Most cities operate multiple transport services, comprising subway systems, street cars, and buses. The only complication for visitors is in the purchase of tickets: systems vary from city to city; ticket machines tend to be in Japanese, except for at the major train stations in cities; and few staff speak English.

Tickets

Basic fare tickets for short distances are normally bought from ticket machines at stations. At major transportation hubs, these machines will have an English-translation button. Most machines accept ¥1,000 and ¥5,000, some take ¥10,000 notes, and all supply change. Many stations have maps in English, indicating the fares to destinations. If in doubt about the cost of a trip, simply buy a cheap ticket and pay any excess at the destination using the fare adjustment machine near the exit barrier. This machine will supply you with a new ticket. If there is no such machine, station staff will work out the additional charge; you will not be penalized for having the wrong-value ticket.

Many cities have their own special tickets, and local tourist information centers can provide information and advice. In Tokyo, there are a variety of options, including the "Free Kippu",

which allows unlimited travel on most of the subway, bus, and streetcar lines in the city center for 24 hours. But, unless you are planning on making a lot of journeys in one day, use a Suica, or Pasmo, card instead. These electronic cards can be purchased from vending machines at many stations, as well as on the Japan Rail Pass website (p330). You can top them up, using cash, at these machines or on buses. These cards are valid on most forms of city transport. To use it, simply hold your card up against the reader.

Subway

The Tokyo subway system is extensive with color-coded maps matching the color of the subway cars. Other cities, including Osaka, Nagoya, Kobe, Sendai, Yokohama, Fukuoka, Kyoto, and Sapporo, also have subway systems, but their modes of operation differ slightly.

The Japan Rail Pass cannot be used on any subway system. If you do not have a valid pass or reloadable card, buy a ticket from either a vending machine or a ticket window. If you are in any doubt about how much to pay, then simply buy the cheapest ticket and pay the excess at the end of your journey.

Station names are often displayed on platform signboards in romanized form as well as Japanese. All mass-transit systems stop running at around midnight until about 5am.

Streetcars

Modern and old-fashioned streetcars still run in quite a few Japanese cities, including Hiroshima, Nagasaki, Kumamoto, and Sapporo. Tokyo has two streetcar lines, and the Enoden Railway in Kamakura, south of Tokyo, is also classed as a streetcar. Fares and systems for paying on streetcars differ from city to city; some charge a flat fare irrespective of the distance travelled, while others have specific charges for different routes. The fare machine is sometimes manned separately. Follow the example of other passengers as to when to pay, and whether to pay the fare collector or put money into a box.

Bus

Bus depots (basu noriba) are often located outside of train stations in cities. The method of paying fares varies. Some buses are boarded at the front, and the fare – often a flat rate – is deposited into a slot beside the driver. Exit from the door in the middle of the bus.

A second system invites passengers to step aboard toward the center or back of the bus, where a machine distributes numbered tickets. The number on this ticket appears on a screen at the front of the bus, which corresponds to the fare to be paid. Before you disembark, drop the indicated amount and your ticket into the box beside the driver.

Taxis

Taxis come in various colors, but all have a "taxi" sign on the roof. A red sign to the left of the driver indicates that the taxi is free. You can flag a taxi on the street or look for a stand: they are invariably located near main stations. They are expensive, with rates starting at around ¥600–¥700 for the first mile. Fares increase per mile, and are higher at night and on weekends. Fares also increase in standing traffic. Drivers operate taxi doors from inside so you do not need to bother opening and closing them. Few taxi drivers speak much English, so it is best to carry a map marked with instructions in Japanese and the phone number of your destination.

Driving

Japan is an enjoyable and relatively safe country in which to take to the road. In the countryside, renting a car is usually the best and most flexible way to get around.

Driving in Japan
Road surfaces are usually good, and rental cars are very well maintained. The main problem foreign drivers in Japan will face is navigation. It can be difficult trying to find one's way around Japan's towns and cities, which often have complex networks of one-way streets. Only main thoroughfares have names, and although rented cars are usually well equipped with sat-nav systems, these are in Japanese.

Very heavy traffic is a common feature of Japan's major cities. Other problems include hazards such as roads blocked by snow in winter, flooding during the rainy season, and occasional landslides.

Visitors must produce an international driver's license (International Driving Permit), but Japan does not recognize international driving permits from Switzerland, Germany, and Taiwan. However, drivers from these countries are instead allowed to drive in Japan for up to one year with an official Japanese translation of their license, which is available from the **Japan Automobile Federation**, or at their country's embassy or consulate in Japan. A valid passport must be carried at all times.

Japan Automobile Federation
ⓦ jaf.or.jp/e

Car Rental
Vehicles are available for rental at ports of entry, major train stations, and local dealers. Since very few short-term visitors to Japan hire cars, car rental companies are generally not used to dealing with customers in English. Two companies more likely to have English-speaking staff are **Toyota Rent a Car** and **Nippon Rent-A-Car**. There is also a greater chance of finding English-speaking staff with international car agencies, such as **Avis, Budget** and **Hertz**.

Avis
ⓦ avis.com
Budget
ⓦ budgetrentacar.co.jp/en
Hertz
ⓦ hertz.com
Nippon Rent-A-Car
ⓦ nrgroup-global.com/en
Toyota Rent a Car
ⓦ rent.toyota.co.jp/eng

Parking
Public parking is available but it tends to be expensive – and the parking fee rises as you move closer to the city center. There are cheaper car parks in neighborhoods on the city fringes, but these may be hidden away on backstreets and difficult to find. On-street parking is not permitted in Japan, and parking meters are a rarity. To overcome the problem of a lack of sufficient space, the Japanese have developed various innovative parking solutions, such as lifts and rollover systems.

Rules of the Road
For visitors who wish to acquaint themselves with driving conditions in Japan, the Japan Automobile Federation publishes "Rules of the Road" in five languages. This can be purchased for ¥1,000 from its regional offices, which are listed on its website.

The Japanese drive on the left side of the road. Drivers may not turn left on a red light. Drivers tend to be considerate while on the road, and although most drivers adhere to the laws, some tailgate, speed, and have a habit of driving over intersections after a light has turned red. It is not a good idea to follow suit. Vehicles to the front and rear should be observed carefully when approaching traffic lights.

Cycle and Scooter Hire

As indicated by the often large bicycle parks outside big stations and the huge numbers of bikes parked on the streets of Japan's cities, cycling is an extremely popular way of getting around – even though there are few cycle paths to speak of. There are often bicycle-rental companies in tourist areas. A good option in the capital is **Tokyobike Rentals**.

Sidewalks are frequently used by cyclists, despite the fact that it is illegal to do so. However, this is not strictly enforced and some towns prefer cyclists to use sidewalks rather than roads.

Tokyobike Rentals
ⓦ tokyobikerentals.com/en

PRACTICAL INFORMATION

A little local know-how goes a long way in Japan. Here you will find all the essential advice and information you will need during your stay.

AT A GLANCE

EMERGENCY NUMBERS

GENERAL EMERGENCY	COAST GUARD
119	**118**

FIRE AND AMBULANCE	POLICE
119	**110**

TIME ZONE
JST
There is no daylight saving time.

TAP WATER

Unless stated otherwise, tap water in Japan is safe to drink.

TIPPING
Tipping is not part of the culture in Japan. Attempts to do so could lead to confusion, embarrassment, and misunderstanding.

Personal Security

Thefts and muggings do occur at times in Japan. There are also sporadic incidents of bag snatching and pickpocketing in crowded areas. It is generally safe to walk around at night, but be careful in Tokyo's Roppongi entertainment district.

Health

All visitors should take out comprehensive travel insurance before traveling. If you are sick, consult a doctor at a local clinic; for minor problems, see a pharmacist. For hospitals and other medical services in Tokyo, see **Himawari**.
Himawari
W himawari.metro.tokyo.jp

Smoking, Alcohol, and Drugs

Japan has a zero-tolerance policy toward the possession of even small amounts of narcotics. The punishment is a jail sentence and heavy fine.

Japan has a strict limit of 0.03 percent BAC (blood alcohol content) for drivers. If a driver exceeds this limit, they will face a heavy fine and up to five years in prison.

In many Tokyo wards, smoking on the street is banned (sometimes punishable by on the spot fines), except in specially designated areas. Smoking is banned on buses and trains (except for some long-distance trains, such as *shinkansen*, which have smoking cars), as well as in most stations, but smoking is usually permitted in bars and restaurants.

Local Customs

The traditional greeting in Japan is a bow, its depth reflecting the relative status of participants. Foreigners, however, rarely need to bow; a handshake is fine. In many situations, bows are part of the service, for instance, in elevators, department stores, restaurants, and hotels. They can be ignored or met with a brief smile. If you feel the need to bow, hold your arms and back straight, bend from the waist, and pause for a moment at the low point.

Be mindful of the etiquettes relating to hygiene in Japan. Bodily emissions are considered very rude, though anything drawn inward is acceptable; sniffing is fine, but blowing your nose in public is reviled. Shoes are an important element of etiquette, and it is a serious mistake to wear them indoors. When you enter a building, take off your shoes and put on slippers. If no slippers are provided, or if they are too small, you can wear socks. The principle is not to contaminate the interior with dirt from outside.

When it comes to table manners, there are several rules to be observed when using chopsticks. If you touch food in a communal dish with your chopsticks, you must then take it. You should also avoid passing food with your chopsticks, gesturing, and pointing with them, and shoveling food direct from bowl to mouth.

LGBT+ Safety

Same sex couples traveling around Japan are unlikely to encounter any problems, but displays of affection should be avoided outside the major cities. **Utopia Asia** is a comprehensive guide to Japan's LGBT+ scene.
Utopia Asia
🆆 utopia-asia.com

Visiting Sacred Sights

The atmosphere in Buddhist temples and Shinto shrines is informal, and there are no clothing restrictions. Visitors should show respect, and not be noisy, but there are few of the taboos found in some other Buddhist nations. Remember to remove your shoes when you enter sacred buildings, leaving them at the entrance or carrying them with you.

Cell Phones and Wi-Fi

Foreign cell phones may not work in Japan. Check with your cell operator before traveling. If you aren't covered, you can rent a cell phone from companies such as **Rentafone Japan**.

Some cafés offer free or inexpensive WiFi. For a list of WiFi hotspots, check **Freespot**.
Freespot
🆆 freespot.com/users/map_e.html
Rentafone
🆆 Japan rentafonejapan.com

Post

Post offices (*yubin-kyoku*) and mailboxes are identified by the character looking like a "T" with an extra horizontal bar across the top. Main post offices are usually open 7am–11pm on weekdays with shorter hours at weekends. Some large central post offices are open 24 hours a day. Smaller post offices may open 9am–4pm on weekdays but are often closed on weekends. Stamps are also sold at convenience stores, and large hotels. Make sure any mail is addressed correctly and legibly, paying particular attention to the postal code.

Taxes and Refunds

All visitors must pay a ¥1000 tourist departure tax. A consumption tax of 8 percent is charged on goods and services. Claiming back this money is a relatively simple process. There is no need to show customs your products and receipts at the airport; instead, you can apply for a cash refund as soon as you have made your purchase at one of the tax refund counters found in shopping centres and malls.

Discount Cards

Several cities offer a Welcome Card to visitors, and a number of different ones are available for a set fee. Intended to reduce the cost of a visit, the card can be used to obtain discounts on entry to museums, galleries and sites, as well as accommodations, shopping, food and drink, and transportation. Many of the cards can be printed out from the Welcome Cards page of the JNTO website (*p332*).

WEBSITES AND APPS

Japan Times
Visit www.japantimes.co.jp for Japan's leading English-language newspaper.
Sushi Dictionary App
This app tells you everything you need to experience sushi to the max.
Yomiwa App
Simply take a picture of any Japanese text and this clever app will translate it, no internet connection needed.

INDEX

Page numbers in **bold** refer to main entries.

21st Century Museum of Contemporary Art (Kanazawa) **166**
88-Temple Pilgrimage (Shikoku) 60, **258-9**

A

Abe, Shinzō 77
Accommodation
    booking 329
    see also Hotels; Ryoken
Ainu people 315, 321
Air travel 330, 331
Aizu-Wakamatsu 295, **305**
Akan National Park **322-3**
Akasaka District (Tokyo) **96-7**
Akihabara Electronics District (Tokyo) **118**
Akiyoshi-dai Tablelands **241**
Akkeshi Bay **324**
Alcohol 334
Amakusa **57**
Amami Oshima Island **279**
Amanohashidate Sandbar **238-9**
Ameyoko Market (Tokyo) **134**
Anderson, Wes 47
Ando, Tadao 90, **250**
Anime 10, 52, 62, 118, 143
Antiques 114
Aomori **312**
Aoshima Island 57, 277
Apps 335
Arakawa Tram Line (Tokyo) **142**
Arashiyama Bamboo Grove (Kyoto City) **202**
Arashiyama District (Kyoto City) **202-3**
Arcades 52
Architecture **36-7**
    gassho-zukuri houses **173**
    Zen Buddhist temples **177**
Art
    Japan for Art Lovers **68-9**
    Mount Fuji in **159**
    painters of the Kano School **184**
Art galleries see Museums and galleries
Asakusa neighborhood (Tokyo) 133
Asuka Plain **233**
Atomic bombs 76, 228, 261
    Atomic Bomb Museum (Nagasaki) **268**

B

Bandai-Asahi National Park **305**
Bars
    Central Honshu 171
    Hokkaido 321
    Kobe 223
    Kyoto City 192
    Northern Honshu 313
    Okinawa 289
    Osaka 221
    sports bars 67
    Tokyo 67, 89, 141
    types of Japanese 96
    Western Honshu 221, 223, 239
    see also Nightlife
Baseball 67
Basho, Matsuo 47, 235, 295, 306, **308**
Beer 64, 142-3, 320
Benesse Art Site Naoshima **250-51**
Beppu **271**
Bicycle hire 333
Boats and ferries 332
Boat trips
    Dotobori River Night Cruise (Osaka) 57
    Sado Island 56
    Sumida River (Tokyo) 116
    Yaeyama Islands 293
Bookshops 113
Buddhism
    sects **309**
    see also Temples and shrines
Budget travel **44-5**
Bunraku **115**, 220
Busena Marine Park 289
Bus travel 45, 332

C

Cafés, themed 63
Camping 43
Cape Hedo **291**
Cape Nosappu 324
Capsule hotels 45, 329
Car rental 333
Castles and fortifications 10
    Goryokaku Fort (Hakodate) 318
    Hikone Castle 239
    Himeji-jo **224-7**
    Honmaru Goten (Kawagoe) 168
    Inuyama Castle 171

Castles and fortifications (cont.)
    Kanazawa Castle **166**
    Kochi Castle 255
    Kumamoto Castle 274
    Matsue Castle 240, 241
    Matsumoto Castle 174
    Matsuyama Castle 256
    Nagoya Castle 170
    Nakagusuku Castle Ruins **288**
    Nakijin Castle Ruin **291**
    Nijo Castle (Kyoto City) **184-5**
    Okayama Castle 236
    Osaka Castle **218**
    Samurai 50
    Shuri Castle (Naha City) 286
    Tsuruga Castle (Aizu Wakamatsu) 305
Cat islands 57
Caves
    Akiyoshido Cave 241
    Gyokusendo Cave **288**
    Nippara Caves 175
Cell phones 335
Cemeteries
    Aoyama Cemetery (Tokyo) 93
    Boso no Mura (Narita) 168
    Foreigners' Cemetery (Yokohama) **153**
    Yanaka Cemetery (Tokyo) 134
Central Honshu 17, **148-79**
    bars 171
    hotels 169
    itinerary 28-9
    map 150-51
    restaurants 157, 175
    shopping 167
Charms, good luck **121**
Cherry blossom 12, 126, 234, 310, 318
Chichibu 149, 175
Chichibu-Tama-Kai National Park **175**
Chidokan (Tsuruoka) 307
Children **52-3**
Chinatown (Kobe) **222**
Chion-in Temple (Kyoto City) **190**
Chiran **279**
Christianity 57, 261, 266, 268, 269, 275
Chuo Toshokan Kitakyushyu (Kokura) 270
Confucius Shrine (Nagasaki) **268**
Coppola, Sofia 47
Cosplay 52, 62

Crafts **54-5**
 Bashofu Hall (Kijoka Village)
  291
 fabric dyeing 54, 304
 gold leaf 167
 Hagi's ceramic arts **242**
 Japanese dolls **311**
 Kumamoto Traditional Crafts
  Center 274
 Kurumu Regional Industry
  Promotion Center 272
 lacquerware 55, 176
 Moriyana Kasuri Workshop
  272
 Okinawan arts and crafts
  290
 paper making 55, 272
 pottery 55, 167, 242, 273,
  281, 286
 Saga Pottery Towns Tour
  280-81
 Shuri Ryusen (Naha City)
  286, 287
 textiles 54, 272, 286,
  290-91
 Yosegi-Zaiku marquetry
  169
 see also Shopping
Currency 328
Customs information 328
Cycling
 cycle hire 333
 Takayama 161

D

Daigo-ji (Kyoto City) **204**
Daisetsu-zan National Park
 321
Daitoku-ji (Kyoto City) **198**
Dance see Entertainment
Dazaifu **273**
Dejima (Nagasaki) **266-7**
Department stores 106, 108-
 109
Dewa Sanzan **308**
Diet Building (Tokyo) **116-17**
Disabled travellers 329
Diving women 57
Domoto, Insho 201
Dosojin stones **174**
Drink see Food and drink
Driving 332-3
Driving tours
 Ise Peninsula Tour 244-5
 Kiso Valley Tour 178-9
 Saga Pottery Towns Tour
  280-81
Drugs 334

E

Earthquakes 77, 103, 171, **223**,
 308
Ebisu District (Tokyo) **142-3**
Economy 76-7
Edo Period 75, 149
Eihei-ji **176**
Electricity supply 328
Electronic goods 118
Emergency numbers 334
Engaku-ji (Kamakura) **157**
Entertainment
 Awa-Odori dancing **255**
 geisha, geiko and maiko
  193
 Japanese traditional theater
  115
 Kabuki-za Theater (Tokyo)
  114
 karaoke and J-Pop 13, 62
 Kodo Drumming Group **307**
 Kongo Noh Theater (Kyoto
  City) **194-5**
 National Bunraku Theater
  (Osaka) **220**
 shamisen 115, 167
 Tokyo Opera City **95**
 Uchiko-za 257
Etiquette 334-5

F

Fashion 63, 94, 95
Ferries see Boats and ferries
Festivals and events 11, **70-
 71**
Film **46-7**
 Samurai movies 50
Fishing industry 138
Fish, popular varieties **140**
Floating Garden Observatory
 (Osaka) **220**
Flower arranging (Ikebana)
 48
Fly fishing 43
Food and drink
 Azumaya Soba Shop
  (Morioka) **311**
 bento boxes **188**
 budget 44
 Gifu foods **172**
 Hokkaido foods **323**
 Japan for Foodies **40-41**
 Japan in a Glass **64-5**
 Kyoto specialities **194**
 nabemono (hotpot) 41
 roast sparrows 186
 shochu 275, 278

Food and drink (cont.)
 sushi and sashimi 40, **140**
 tea ceremony **197**
 wellness 61
 yatai (Fukuoka) 41, 264
 see also Restaurants; Sake
Foreigners' Cemetery
 (Yokohama) **153**
Former Japanese Navy
 Underground HQ **287**
Fuji Five Lakes **158-9**
Fuji, Mount see Mount Fuji
Fukiya **238**
Fukuoka **264-5**
Fukuoka Asian Art Museum
 69, **265**
Fukuoka City Museum **264**
Fukuoka Tower **264**
Fukushima Daiichi nuclear
 plant 295
Fukushima Sargenten
 (Kanazawa) **167**
Funeral customs **134**
Fushimi Inari Shrine (Kyoto
 City) **186-7**
Futara-san Shrine (Nikko)
 298

G

Gallery of Horyu-ji Treasures
 (Tokyo National Museum)
 130-31
Gardens see Parks and
 gardens
Geiko **193**
Geisha 167, **193**
Ghibli Museum (Tokyo) 46,
 143
Gifu **172**
Ginkaku-ji (Silver Pavilion)
 (Kyoto City) **195**, 208, 209
Ginza (Tokyo) **106-7**
 walk 108-109
Gion District (Kyoto City) **192**
Glover Garden (Nagasaki)
 269
Golden Gai (Tokyo) **96**, 98, 99
Gotoh Museum (Tokyo) **141**
Great Buddha (Kamakura)
 154
Great Buddha (Nara) 216-17
Great Hanshin Earthquake
 223

H

Hagi **242-3**
Haiku 47, **308**

Hakata Machiya Folk Museum (Fukuoka) **265**
Hakodate **318**
Hakone 149, **168-9**
Hama-rikyu Gardens (Tokyo) **116**
Hanamaki **310-11**
Harajuku District (Tokyo) **94-5**
Hase-dera Temple (Kamakura) **154**
Health 329, 334
Hearn, Lafcadio **240**
Hegura **57**
Heian Period 73
Heiseikan (Tokyo National Museum) 130-31
Hida Folk Village (Takayama) **161**
Hideyoshi, Toyotomi 74, 170, 186, 204, 234, 266
Hieizan Enryaku-ji (Kyoto City) **204-5**
Higashi Hongan-ji (Kyoto City) **190-91**
Higeta Dyeworks (Mashiko) 304
Hikawa Maru (Yokohama) **153**
Hiking
    Chichibu-Tama-Kai National Park 175
    Japanese Alps 42
    Kamikochi 175
    Mount Aso 276
    Mount Fuji 42, 158
    see also National parks; Walks
Himeji-jo **224-7**
Hiraizumi 295, **306**
Hirohito, Emperor 76
Hirosaki 295, **313**
Hiroshige 159
Hiroshima 76, 211, **228-9**
Hiroshima Peace Memorial Park 37, **228-9**
Historic buildings
    Aoyagi-ke (Kakunodate) 310
    Buke Yashiki (Matsue) 240, 241
    Chiiori House (Tokushima) 255
    Diet Building (Tokyo) **116-17**
    Garyu Sanso (Ozu) 256
    Gyobu-tei (Kumamoto) 274
    Hirokane-tei (Fukiya) 238
    Ishiguro-ke (Kakunodate) 310
    Kai Honke (Mashiko) 304-5
    Katsura Imperial Villa (Kyoto City) 36, **203**
    Kikuya House (Hagi) 242, 243

Historic buildings (cont.)
    Lafcadio Hearn Memorial Hall (Matsue) 241
    Lafcadio Hearn Residence (Matsue) 240-41
    Meimei-an Teahouse (Matsue) 240, 241
    Mekata House (Iwakuni) 242
    Miyara Dunchi (Ishigaki) 293
    Nishimura House (Kyoto City) 198
    Nomura Family Samurai House (Kanazawa) 164
    Samurai Residence (Azai Wakamatsu) 305
    Sannai-Maruyama (Aomori) 312
    Seisonkaku Villa (Kanazawa) **164**
    Seki-sho Barrier Gate (Hakone) 169
    Shugaku-in Imperial Villa (Kyoto City) **204**
    Takayama Jinya **161**
    Toro ruins (Shizuoka) 171
    Yoshinogari Ruins **275**
    see also Castles and fortifications; Palaces; Temples and shrines
History **72-7**
Hokkaido 21, 43, **314-25**
    bars 321
    foods 323
    hotels 325
    map 316-17
    restaurants 319
Hokoku-ji (Kamakura) **156**
Hokusai, Katsushika 159, 174-5
Hollander Slope (Nagasaki) **269**
Honkan gallery (Tokyo National Museum) 128-31
Honshu see Central Honshu; Northern Honshu; Western Honshu
Horseback archery 50
Horyu-ji **232-3**
Hotels
    Central Honshu 169
    Hokkaido 325
    Kyoto City 189
    Northern Honshu 305
    Okinawa 291
    Shikoku 253
    Tokyo 93, 117, 145
    Western Honshu 234
Hot springs
    Beppu spas **271**
    Boiling Hells (Beppu) 271
    Dogo Onsen Honkan (Matsuyama) 47, 247, 256

Hot springs (cont.)
    Gifu 172
    Hakone 168-9
    Izu Peninsula 170
    Kirishima-Kinkowan National Park 278
    Kurokawa 276
    Myoban Hot Spring 271
    onsen 13, 61, 276
    rotenburo 38
    Spa World (Osaka) **220**
    Suginoi Palace (Beppu) 271
    Takegawara Bathhouse (Beppu) 271
    Unzen Spa 275
Huis ten Bosch (Nagasaki) **269**

I

Ie Island **288-9**
Iemitsu, Tokugawa 300, 302, 303
Ieyasu, Tokugawa 74, 126, 184, **300**
Iga-Ueno **235**
Ikebukuro District (Tokyo) **142**
Ikigai 61
Imperial Palace (Tokyo) **112-13**
Inaricho District (Tokyo) **135**
Insho Domoto Museum (Kyoto City) **201**
Insurance 328
Inuyama **171**
Iriomote Island 293
Irises (Korin) 68
Ise 245
Ise Peninsula Tour **244-5**
Ishigaki Island 292, 293
Ishikawa Museum of Traditional Arts and Crafts (Kanazawa) **165**
Islands **56-7**
Isozaki, Arata 270
Isui-en Garden (Nara) **214**
Itineraries **22-35**
    2 Days in Kyoto 30-31
    2 Weeks in Japan 22-5
    5 Days in Central Honshu 28-9
    5 Days in Tokyo 26-7
    5 Days in Western Honshu 32-3
    7 Days in Kyushu 34-35
    see also Driving tours; Walks
Itsukushima Shrine (Miyajima Island) **230-31**
Iwakuni **242**
Izumo **241**

Izumo Taisha Grand Shrine (Izumo) 121, 241
Izu Peninsula **170**

J

Japanese Alps 42, 149, 161, 175
Japan Folk Art Museum (Osaka) **220**
Japan Folk Crafts Museum (Tokyo) **141**
Jimmu, Emperor 211, 261
Jinbocho Booksellers' District (Tokyo) **113**
Jomon Period 72, 261

K

Kabuki **115**
Kabukicho district (Tokyo) 98, 99
Kabuki-za Theater (Tokyo) **114**
Kaga-Honda Museum (Kanazawa) **166**
Kagoshima 261, **278-9**
Kakunodate **310**
Kamakura 50, 149, **154-7**
  map 155
  restaurants 157
Kamakura Period 73
Kamikaze pilots 279
Kamikochi **175**
Kamo Shrines (Kyoto City) **198**
Kanazawa 149, **164-7**
  map 165
Kanazawa Castle **166**
Kanda Myojin Shrine (Tokyo) **120**
Kanman-ga-Fuchi Abyss **299**
Kano School painters **184**
Kansai 57
Kantei-byo Temple (Yokohama) **153**
Kappabashi-dori (Tokyo) **135**
Karaoke 13, 62
Kasuga Taisha Shrine (Nara) **215**
Katsura Imperial Villa (Kyoto City) 36, **203**
Kawagoe **168**
Kencho-ji (Kamakura) **156**
Kendo 66
Kenroku-en Garden (Kanazawa) 49, **165**
Kii Peninsula **235**
Kijoka Village **290-91**
Kikumasamune Shuzo Kinenkan (Kobe) **223**
Kimonos 54, 164
Kinkaku-ji (Golden Pavilion) (Kyoto City) **199**
Kirishima-Kinkowan National Park **278**

Kiso Valley 149
  tour **178-9**
Kitakata **304-5**
Kitano-cho (Kobe) **222**
Kitanomaru Park (Tokyo) **118-19**
Kitano Tenman-gu Shrine (Kyoto City) **198-9**
Kitaro, Nishida 209
Kiyomizu-dera Temple (Kyoto City) **191**
Kobe 211, **222-3**
Kobe City Museum **222**
Kochi **254-5**
Kofuku-ji (Nagasaki) **267**
Kofuku-ji (Nara) **214**
Koka Ninja Village 51, **233**
Kokura **270**
Kongo Noh Theater (Kyoto City) **194-5**
Korin, Ogata, *Irises* 68
Koryu-ji (Kyoto City) **201**
Koshikawa Korakuen Garden (Tokyo) **117**
Kotohira **252**
Kukai 72, 188, 234-5, 247
  pilgrimage 255, 258-9
Kumamoto 261, **274**
Kuma Shochu Museum (Kumamoto) **275**
Kume Island **290**
Kurama District (Kyoto City) **203**
Kurashiki **237**
Kurokawa **276**
Kurume **272**
Kusama, Yayoi 251
Kushiro Wetlands National Park **323**
Kyoto City 12, 17, **180-209**
  bars 192
  food 194
  history 72, 73, 74, 75, 181
  hotels 189
  itinerary 30-31
  map 182-3
  restaurants 195
  shopping 201
  walks 206-9
Kyoto Imperial Palace **195**
Kyoto National Museum **188**
Kyoto Station **189**
Kyushu 19, **260-81**
  drink 275
  itinerary 34-35
  map 262-3
  restaurants 265, 267, 277
  shopping 272

L

Lake Biwa **239**
Lake Furen **324**

Lakeside (Seiki) 128
Landmark Tower (Yokohama) **152**
Language 329
  essential phrases 328
LGBT
  nightlife 59
  safety 335
Liberty Osaka (Osaka Human Rights Museum) **221**
Lion Dance Ceremony Exhibition Hall (Takayama) **161**
Literature **46-7**
Local customs 334-5

M

Maiko **193**
Manga 10, 62, 118, 203
Manshu-in Temple (Kyoto City) **204**
Maps
  Central Honshu 150-51
  Fukuoka 265
  Hokkaido 316-17
  Ise Peninsula Tour 245
  Japan 14-15
  Journey Planner 331
  Kamakura 155
  Kanazawa 165
  Kiso Valley Tour 179
  Kobe 223
  Kyoto City 182-3
  Kyushu 262-3
  Nara 215
  Nikko 299
  Northern Honshu 296-7
  Okinawa 284-5
  Osaka 219
  Saga Pottery Towns Tour 281
  Shikoku 248-9
  Takayama 161
  Tokyo 80-81
  Tokyo: Beyond the Center 137
  Tokyo: Central Tokyo 104-5
  Tokyo: Northern Tokyo 124-5
  Tokyo: Western Tokyo 84-5
  Western Honshu 212-13
  Yokohama 153
Markets
  Ameyoko Market (Tokyo) **134**
  Oedo Antique Market (Tokyo) 114
  Toyosu Fish Market (Tokyo) **138-9**
  Wajima Market **176**
Marunouchi District (Tokyo) 117

Mashiko **304**
Matsue **240-41**
Matsumoto **174**
Matsushima **306**
Matsuyama **256**
Meditation 60
Meigetsu-in Temple (Kamakura) **156-7**
Meiji Emperor 75, **86**
Meiji Restoration 75
Meiji Shrine (Tokyo) **86-7**
Meriken Park (Kobe) **223**
Metabolism 36, **37**, 106
Minami-Aoyama District (Tokyo) **92-3**
Minamoto clan 73, 155, 247
Miyajima Island **230-31**
Miyake, Issey 90
Miyako Islands **292**
Miyazaki 43, 52, 277-8
Miyazaki, Hayao 46
Miyazawa, Kenji 310-11
Mobile phones 335
Money 328, 329
Mongol invasions 51, 73, 261
Monorail (Tokyo) 145
Mori Art Museum (Tokyo) 68, 90, **91**
Morioka 295, **311**
Mori Tower (Tokyo) 36, 91
Mount Aso 261, **276**
Mount Fuji 42, 149, **158-9**
Mount Gassan 308
Mount Haguro 308
Mount Koya **234-5**
Mount Unzen 275
Mount Yudono 308
Murakami, Haruki 46
Muromachi Period 74
Museums and galleries
  21st Century Museum of Contemporary Art (Kanazawa) **166**
  Aikawa Museum 307
  Asakura Museum of Sculpture (Tokyo) 134
  Atomic Bomb Museum (Nagasaki) **268**
  Basho Memorial Museum (Tokyo) 47
  Benesse Art Site Naoshima **250-51**
  Boso no Mura (Narita) 168
  Chichu Art Museum (Naoshima) 250
  Chido Museum (Tsuruoka) 306-7
  City Museum of Art (Kagoshima) 279
  Costume Museum (Kyoto City) 203
  Crafts Gallery (Tokyo) 119

Museums and galleries (cont.)
  Cup Noodle Museum (Yokohama) 152
  Daimyo Clock Museum (Tokyo) 134
  Denshokan Museum (Kakunodate) 310
  Design Festa Gallery (Tokyo) 94, 95
  Edo-Tokyo Museum 144
  Fukuoka Asian Art Museum 69, **265**
  Fukuoka City Museum **264**
  Gekkeikan Okura Sake Museum (Kyoto City) 203
  Ghibli Museum (Tokyo) 46, **143**
  Gotoh Museum (Tokyo) **141**
  Hakata Machiya Folk Museum (Fukuoka) **265**
  Hakone Art Museum 169
  Hakone Open-Air Museum 69, 169
  Hakushu Kinenkan (Yanagawa) 275
  Hayashibara Museum of Art (Okayama) 236
  Hida Folk Village (Takayama) **161**
  Historical Village of Hokkaido 320, 321
  Hokusai Museum (Nagano) 174-5
  Iga Ninja Museum (Iga-Ueno) 235
  Insho Domoto Museum (Kyoto City) **201**
  Ishibashi Bunka Center (Kurume) 272
  Ishii Tea Bowl Museum (Hagi) 242, 243
  Ishikawa Museum of Traditional Arts and Crafts (Kanazawa) **165**
  Iwakuni Art Museum 242
  Japan Folk Art Museum (Osaka) **220**
  Japan Folk Crafts Museum (Tokyo) **141**
  Japan Rural Toy Museum (Kurashiki) 237
  Japan Ukiyo-e Museum (Matsumoto) 174
  Kaga-Honda Museum (Kanazawa) **166**
  Kobe City Museum **222**
  Kumamoto Prefectural Art Museum 274
  Kuma Shochu Museum (Kumamoto) **275**
  Kumaya Art Museum (Hagi) 242, 243

Museums and galleries (cont.)
  Kurashiki Archaeological Museum 237
  Kurashiki Folk Art Museum 237
  Kura-Zukuri Shiryokan (Kawagoe) 168
  Kyoto International Exhibition Hall (Miyako Messe) 196
  Kyoto International Manga Museum 203
  Kyoto Municipal Museum of Art 196
  Kyoto National Museum **188**
  Kyushu National Museum (Dazaifu) 273
  Lake Biwa Museum 239
  Liberty Osaka (Osaka Human Rights Museum) **221**
  Lion Dance Ceremony Exhibition Hall (Takayama) **161**
  Local History Museum (Fukiya) 238
  Mashiko Sankokan Museum 304
  Matsumoto Folkcraft Museum 174
  Meiji Mura (Inuyama) 171
  Miho Museum (Uji City) 240
  Miyazawa Kenji Museum (Hanamaki) 310-11
  Mori Art Museum (Tokyo) 68, 90, **91**
  Mori Ougai House (Tsuwano) 243
  Mount Aso Volcanic Museum 276
  Municipal Museum (Hirosaki) 313
  Municipal Museum (Tono) 311
  Museum of Oriental Ceramics (Osaka) **219**
  Museum of Weaponry (Himeji-jo) 224
  Nakamura House **288**
  Naoshima Contemporary Art 250
  Nara National Museum **214**
  Narukawa Art Museum (Hakone) 169
  National Art Center (Tokyo) 90, 91
  National Museum of Art (Osaka) **219**
  National Museum of Emerging Science and Innovation (Tokyo) 145

Museums and galleries (cont.)
National Museum of
    Japanese History
    (Narita) 168
National Museum of Modern
    Art (Kyoto City) 196
National Museum of Modern
    Art (Tokyo) 119
National Museum of Nature
    and Science (Tokyo) 126,
    127
Nezu Museum (Tokyo) 68,
    92, 93
Nishi House (Tsuwano)
    243
Nishijin Textile Center
    (Kyoto City) 203
NYK Maritime Museum
    (Yokohama) **152**
Ocha no Sato (Shizuoka)
    171
Ochaya Shima Geisha House
    (Kanazawa) **167**
Ohara Museum of Art
    (Kurashiki) 237
Okaya Prefectural Museum
    of Art 236
Okinawa Prefectural Museum
    & Art Museum (Naha City)
    286, 287
Okinawa World 288
Open-Air Museum (Ogimachi)
    172
Orient Museum (Okayama)
    236
Osaka Museum of History
    218
Peace Memorial Museum
    (Hiroshima) 37, 228
Peace Memorial Museum
    (Okinawa) 287
Sado Kinzan Gold Mine
    (Aikawa) 307
Sakamoto Ryoma Museum
    (Kochi) 255
Samurai Museum (Tokyo)
    51, **96**
Sapporo Beer Garden and
    Museum 320
Science and Technology
    Museum (Tokyo) 118–19
Sex Museum (Uwajima)
    257
Shiki Masaoka Museum
    (Matsuyama) 256
Shitamachi Museum (Tokyo)
    134
Sueda Art Museum (Yufuin)
    270, 271
Sumo Museum (Tokyo)
    144
Suntory Museum of Art
    (Tokyo) 90

Museums and galleries (cont.)
Suzuki Morihisa Iron Studio
    (Morioka) 311
Sword Museum (Tokyo) 51,
    144
Taiji Whale Museum 235
Takamatsu Heike Monogatari
    Wax Museum 253
Takayama Festival Floats
    Exhibition Hall **160**
Tanabe Art Museum (Matsue)
    240, 241
Taro Okamoto Memorial
    Museum (Tokyo) 92, 93
Togugawa Art Museum
    (Nagoya) 170
Tokyo National Museum 126,
    128–31
Tokyo Photographic Art
    Museum 142
Trick 3D Art Yufuin Museum
    270, 271
Tsuboya Pottery Museum
    (Naha City) 286, 287
Tsugaruhan Neputa Mura
    (Hirosaki) 313
Ukiyo-e Ota Memorial
    Museum of Art (Tokyo)
    94, 95
Urushi Museum (Nikko)
    299
Watari-um (Tokyo) 92, 93
Yaeyama Museum (Ishigaki)
    292–3
Yamatogawa Sake Brewing
    Museum (Kitakata) 305
Yebisu Beer Museum (Tokyo)
    142–3
Yokohama Museum of Art
    152
Yokohama Ramen Museum
    53
Yushukan (Tokyo) 120
Music see Entertainment
Myohon-ji (Kamakura) **154**
Myoshin-ji (Kyoto City) **–201**

N

Nagamachi Samurai Quarter
    (Kanazawa) **164**
Nagano **174–5**
Nagasaki 76, 228, 261, **266–9**
    foreigners in **269**
    map 267
    restaurants 267
Nagoya 149, **170**
Naha City 283, **284–5**
Nakagin Capsule Tower
    (Tokyo) 106
Nakagusuku Castle Ruins **288**
Nakamura House **288**
Nakasendo 149

Nakijin Castle Ruin **291**
Nametoko Gorge 257
Nanzen-ji (Kyoto City) **194**,
    208
Naoshima 68, **250–51**, 252
Nara 211, **214–17**
    map 215
Nara National Museum **214**
Nara Park (Nara) **214**
Nara Period 73
Narita **168**
Naruto Whirlpools **254**
National Bunraku Theater
    (Osaka) **220**
National Museum of Art
    (Osaka) **219**
National Parks
    Akan National Park **322–3**
    Bandai-Asahi National Park
        305
    Chichibu-Tama-Kai National
        Park **175**
    Chubu Sangaku National
        Park **175**
    Daisetsu-zan National Park
        321
    Ise-Shima National Park
        245
    Kirishima-Kinkowan National
        Park **278**
    Kushiro Wetlands National
        Parks **323**
    Nikko National Park **304**
    Onuma Quasi-National Park
        319
    Rishiri-Rebun-Sarobetsu
        National Park **322**
    Shikotsu-Toya National Park
        319
    Shiretoko National Park
        325
    Towada-Hachimantai
        National Park **312**
    Unzen-Amakusa National
        Park 275
Nemura Peninsula **324**
Nichinan Coast **277**
Nightlife **58–9**
    Tokyo 90
Nihonbashi District (Tokyo)
    112–13
Nijo Castle (Kyoto City) **184–5**
Nikko **298–303**
    map 299
Nikko Botanical Gardens **299**
Nikko National Park **304**
Ninja 51, 233, **235**
Ninna-ji (Kyoto City) **200**
Niseko Ski Resort 39, **319**
Nishi Hongan-ji (Kyoto City)
    190
Nobunaga, Oda 74, 170
Noh **115**, 194–5

Northern Honshu 20, **294–313**
  bars 313
  hotels 305
  map 296–7
  restaurants 299, 310
Noto 149
Noto Peninsula **176**
Nuclear disaster 295
NYK Maritime Museum (Yokohama) **152**

O

Ocean Expo Park **289**
Ochaya Shima Geisha House (Kanazawa) **167**
Odaiba (Tokyo) **145**
Off the Beaten Path **56–7**
Oga Peninsula **312**
Ogasawara Islands **56**
Ohara District (Kyoto City) **205**
Ohori Park (Fukuoka) **264**
Okayama **236**
Okazaki Area (Kyoto City) **196**
Okinawa 20, 42, **282–93**
  bars 289
  hotels 291
  map 284–5
  restaurants 293
Okinawa, Battle of 283, **287**
Olympic Games (Tokyo, 1964) 37, 66, 83, 96
Onaruta Suspension Bridge 254
Ōnin War 74, 181
Onta **273**
Onuma Quasi-National Park **319**
Osaka 211, **218–21**
  bars 221
  map 219
Osaka Castle **218**
Osaka Museum of History **218**
Otaku (Geek culture) 10, **118**
Oura Catholic Church (Nagasaki) **268**
Outdoor activities **42–3**, 53
Ozu **256**

P

Palaces
  Imperial Palace (Tokyo) **112–13**
  Kyoto Imperial Palace **195**
Parking 333
Parks and gardens
  Arashiyama Bamboo Grove (Kyoto City) **202**
  Botanical Gardens (Sapporo) 320

Parks and gardens (cont.)
  Dazaifu Government Ruins 273
  Glover Garden (Nagasaki) **269**
  Hama-rikyu Gardens (Tokyo) **116**
  Hiroshima Peace Memorial Park 37, **228–9**
  Imperial Palace (Tokyo) 112–13
  Isui-en Garden (Nara) **214**
  Japan's Gardens **48–9**
  Kairaku-en (Mito) 49
  Katsura Imperial Villa (Kyoto City) **203**
  Kenroku-en Garden (Kanazawa) 49, **165**
  Kitanomaru Park (Tokyo) **118–19**
  Kokura Castle Japanese Garden 270
  Koraku-en Garden (Okayama) 49, **236**
  Koshikawa Korakuen Garden (Tokyo) **119**
  Meiji Shrine (Tokyo) 86–7
  Meriken Park (Kobe) **223**
  Mikayo-jima City Botanical Garden 292
  Nara Park (Nara) **214**
  Nikko Botanical Gardens 299
  Ocean Expo Park **289**
  Ohori Park (Fukuoka) **264**
  Oyakuen (Aizu Wakamatsu) 305
  Paradise gardens 48
  Peace Park (Nagasaki) **268**
  Rikugi-en Garden (Tokyo) **144**
  Ryoan-ji rock garden (Kyoto City) 200
  Sankai-en Garden (Yokohama) **153**
  Sapporo Art Park 320, 321
  Sengan-en (Kagoshima) 278, 279
  Shiba Park (Tokyo) **118**
  Shugaku-in Imperial Villa (Kyoto City) **204**
  stroll gardens 49
  Suizen-ji Jou-en Garden (Kumamoto) 274
  tea gardens 49
  Ueno Park (Tokyo) **126–7**
  Yoyogi Park (Tokyo) 37, **96**
  Zen gardens 12, 48
  Zuisen-ji (Kamakura) **155**
Passports 328
Peace Park (Nagasaki) **268**
Pearl cultivation 245, 247

Perry, Commodore Matthew 75, 286
Pilgrimages 60, 258–9
Poetry 115
Pokemon 62
Pontocho Alley (Kyoto City) **191**
Pop culture **62–3**
Postal services 335
Prices 328
Public holidays 329
Public transport 45, 330, **332**

R

Rail travel 10, 330
Reasons to Love Japan **10–13**
Refunds, tax 335
Religion see Buddhism; Shinto
Restaurants
  Central Honshu 157, 175
  Hokkaido 319
  Kyoto City 195
  Kyushu 265, 267, 277
  Northern Honshu 299, 310
  Okinawa 293
  Shikoku 257
  Tokyo 40, 96–7, 110, 119, 128, 143
  vending machine 44
  Western Honshu 237
Rice cultivation 176
Rickey, George, *Three Squares Vertical Diagonal* 250–51
Rikugi-en Garden (Tokyo) **144**
Rinjo-ji (Nikko) **298–9**
Rishiri-Rebun-Sarobetsu National Park **322**
Robots 63
Roppongi District (Tokyo) 36, **90–91**
Rugby 66
Rules of the road 330, 333
Russo-Japanese War 75
Ryoan-ji (Kyoto City) **200**
Ryogoku District (Tokyo) **144**
Ryokan 10
Ryoma, Sakamoto 255

S

Sado Island 56, **307**
Safety
  LGBT 335
  personal security 334
  travel safety advice 328
Sagano District (Kyoto City) **202**
Saga prefecture 280–81
Sake 11, **65**, 86, 203
  Imayotsukasa (Nigata) 306
  Kikumasamune Shuzo Kinenkan (Kobe) **223**

Sake (cont.)
  Yamatogawa Sake Brewing
    Museum (Kitakata) 305
Sakuda Gold Leaf Store
  (Kanazawa) **167**
Sakurajima Volcano 261, 278,
  279
Samurai **50–51**, 164, 242, 307
  Aizu Wakamatsu 305
  Chiran 279
  Himeji-jo 224
  Kakunodate 310
  Samurai Museum (Tokyo) 51,
    96
Sanjusangen-do Temple (Kyoto
  City) **189**
Sankai-en Garden (Yokohama)
  153
Sannai-Maruyama (Aomori)
  312
Sapporo 315, **320–21**
Sashimi 138, **140**
Scooter hire 333
Seiki, Kuroda, *Lakeside* 128
Seisonkaku Villa (Kanazawa)
  164
Sekigahara, Battle of 224
Sendai 295, **308**
Sengaku-ji (Tokyo) **143**
Senso-ji (Tokyo) **132–3**
Seto Inland Sea 247, 250, **252**,
  254
Shiba Park (Tokyo) **118**
Shikibu, Murasaki 47
Shikoku 19, **246–59**
  hotels 253
  map 248–9
  restaurants 257
Shikoku Mura 253
Shikotsu-Toya National Park
  319
Shimabara Peninsula **275**
Shimokita Peninsula **312**
Shingon sect 309
Shinjuku Station (Tokyo)
  92
Shinkyo Bridge (Nikko) **298**
Shinto **121**
  see also Temples and
    shrines
Shin-Yakushi-ji (Nara) **215**
Shinzuoka **171**
Shiretoko National Park **325**
Shisen-do Temple (Kyoto City)
  202
Shitamachi Museum (Tokyo)
  134
Shitenno-ji (Osaka) **221**
Shizuoka 149
Shofuku-ji (Fukuoka) **265**
Shogunates 73–5
Shokawa Valley 149, **172**
Shonin, Shodo 298, 299

Shopping
  Central Honshu 167, 176
  Kanazawa 167
  Kyoto City 201
  Kyushu 272
  Tokyo 106, 113, 118, 108–109,
    134
  Western Honshu 243
  see also Crafts; Markets
Shoren-in Temple (Kyoto City)
  196
Shrines *see* Temples and
  shrines
Shugaku-in Imperial Villa (Kyoto
  City) **204**
Shugendo sect 309
Silk 149, 164, 173
Silk Road 214
Sino-Japanese War 75
Skiing 39, 53, 174, 319
Smoking 334
Snorkelling 42
Snow Festival, Sapporo 39,
  320
Sofuku-ji (Nagasaki) **267**
Soto Zen 176
Spas *see* Hot springs
Specific needs, travellers
  with 329
Spectacles Bridge (Nagasaki)
  266
Speed limits 330
Sports **66–7**
Streetcars 332
Subways 332
Sugimoto-dera Temple
  (Kamakura) **156**
Sugimoto, Hiroshi 69, 250
Sumida River 116
Sumo wrestling 67, **144**
Surfing 43
Sushi 13, 138, **140**
Suwa Shrine (Nagasaki) **267**
Swords, Samurai 50, 51

T

Taira clan 73, 247, 270
Taiyuin-byo Shrine (Nikko)
  302–3
Takachiho **276–7**
Takamatsu **253**
Takao District (Kyoto City)
  203
Takayama 149, **160–63**
  map 161
  walk 162–3
Takayama Festival Floats
  Exhibition Hall **160**
Taketomi Island 293
Takinoo Shrine (Nikko) **298**
Tange, Kenzo 36, 37, 88, 96,
  152

Tap water 334
Taxes 335
Taxis 332
Tea 65
Tea ceremony 195, **197**, 240
Temples and shrines
  88-Temple Pilgrimage
    (Shikoku) 60, **258–9**
  architecture 37
  Byodo-in (Uji City) 240
  Chion-in Temple (Kyoto
    City) **190**
  Chosho-ji (Hirosaki) 313
  Confucius Shrine (Nagasaki)
    268
  Daigo-ji (Kyoto City) **204**
  Daitoku-ji (Kyoto City) **198**
  Dazaifu Tenman-gu 273
  Eihei-ji **176**
  Engaku-ji (Kamakura) **157**
  Fushimi Inari Shrine (Kyoto
    City) **186–7**
  Futara-san Shrine (Nikko)
    298
  Ginkaku-ji (Silver Pavilion)
    (Kyoto City) **195**, 208, 209
  Hase-dera Temple
    (Kamakura) **154**
  Hieizan Enryaku-ji (Kyoto
    City) **204–5**
  Higashi Hongan-ji (Kyoto
    City) **190–91**
  Hokoku-ji (Kamakura) **156**
  Horyu-ji **232–3**
  Itsukushima Shrine (Miyajima
    Island) **230–31**
  Izumo Taisha Grand Shrine
    (Izumo) 121, 241
  Kamigamo Shrine (Kyoto
    City) 198
  Kamo Shrines (Kyoto City)
    198
  Kanda Myojin Shrine (Tokyo)
    120
  Kantei-byo Temple
    (Yokohama) **153**
  Kasuga Taisha Shrine (Nara)
    215
  Kencho-ji (Kamakura) **156**
  Kinkaku-ji (Golden Pavilion)
    (Kyoto City) **199**
  Kitano Tenman-gu Shrine
    (Kyoto City) **198–9**
  Kiyomizu-dera Temple
    (Kyoto City) **191**
  Kofuku-ji (Nagasaki) **267**
  Kofuku-ji (Nara) **214**
  Koryu-ji (Kyoto City) **201**
  Manpuku-ji (Uji City) 240
  Manshu-in Temple (Kyoto
    City) **204**
  Meigetsu-in Temple
    (Kamakura) **156–7**

Temples and shrines (cont.)
Meiji Shrine (Tokyo) **86-7**
Mount Koya **234-5**
Myohon-ji (Kamakura) **154**
Myoshin-ji (Kyoto City)
200-201
Nanzen-ji (Kyoto City) **194**, 208
Ninna-ji (Kyoto City) **200**
Nishi Hongan-ji (Kyoto City) **190**
Rinjo-ji (Nikko) **298-9**
Ryoan-ji (Kyoto City) **200**
Sanjusangen-do Temple (Kyoto City) **189**
Sengaku-ji (Tokyo) **143**
Senso-ji (Tokyo) **132-3**
Shimogamo Shrine (Kyoto City) 198
Shin-Yakushi-ji (Nara) **215**
Shisen-do Temple (Kyoto City) **202**
Shitenno-ji (Osaka) **221**
Shofuku-ji (Fukuoka) **265**
Shoren-in Temple (Kyoto City) **196**
Shrine to the 26 Martyrs (Nagasaki) **266**
Sofuku-ji (Nagasaki) **267**
Sugimoto-dera Temple (Kamakura) **156**
Suwa Shrine (Nagasaki) **267**
Taga-jinja shrine (Uwajima) 257
Taiyuin-byo Shrine (Nikko) **302-3**
Takachiho Jinja 277
Takinoo Shrine (Nikko) **298**
temple stays and retreats 60
Todai-ji (Nara) **216-17**
Toji Temple (Kyoto City) **188**
Tokei-ji (Kamakura) **157**
Toshodai-ji (Nara) **215**
Tosho-gu Shrine (Nikko) **300-301**
Tosho-gu Shrine (Tokyo) 126, 127
Tsurugaoka Hachiman-gu Shrine (Kamakura) **155**
Udo Jingu 277
visiting 335
Yakushi-ji (Nara) **215**
Yasaka Shrine (Kyoto City) 192
Yasukuni Shrine (Tokyo) 120
Zen Buddhist **177**
Zeni-Arai Benten Shrine (Kamakura) **157**
Zuisen-ji (Kamakura) **155**
Tempozan Harbor Village (Osaka) **221**

Tendai sect 309
Terumasa, Ikeda 224
Theater *see* Entertainment
Theme parks 53
Huis ten Bosch (Nagasaki) **269**
Meiji Mura (Inuyama) 171
Universal Studios Japan (Osaka) **220-21**
Three Squares Vertical Diagonal (Rickey) 250-51
Tickets, public transport 332
Time zone 334
Tipping 334
Todai-ji (Nara) **216-17**
Toji Temple (Kyoto City) **188**
Tokaido Highway 149, 274
Tokei-ji (Kamakura) **157**
Tokushima **255**
Tokyo 16, **78-145**
bars 67, 89, 141
Beyond the Center **136-45**
budget tips 45
Central Tokyo **102-21**
food tour 40
history 75
hotels 93, 117, 145
itinerary 26-7
map 80-81
map: Beyond the Center 137
map: Central Tokyo 104-5
map: Northern Tokyo 124-5
map: Western Tokyo 84-5
nightlife 90
Northern Tokyo **122-35**
restaurants 40, 96-7, 110, 119, 128, 143
shopping 106, 134
Walks 98-101
Western Tokyo **82-101**
Tokyo City-i 117
Tokyo International Forum **114**
Tokyo National Museum 126, **128-31**
Tokyo Opera City **95**
Tokyo Skytree 36, **135**
Tokyo Stock Exchange 110
Tokyo Tower **118**
Tono **311**
Toshodai-ji (Nara) **215**
Tosho-gu Shrine (Nikko) **300-301**
Tosho-gu Shrine (Tokyo) 126, 127
Tottori Sand Dunes **238**
Towada-Hachimantai National Park **312**
Toyokan (Tokyo National Museum) 130-31
Toyosu Fish Market (Tokyo) **138-9**
Trains *see* Rail travel
Trams 142

Travel
getting around **330-33**
safety advice 328
Tsunamis 77, 295, 308
Tsurugaoka Hachiman-gu Shrine (Kamakura) **155**
Tsuruoka 295, **306-7**
Tsuwano **243**
Tuna fish **138**

U

Uchiko **257**
Ueno, Battle of 123, 126
Ueno Park (Tokyo) **126-7**
Uji City **240**
Ukai (cormorant fishing) 172
Universal Studios Japan (Osaka) **220-21**
Urushi Museum (Nikko) **299**
Usa **270**
Usuki Stone Buddhas **272**
Uwajima **257**
Uzunooka Onarutokyo Memorial Hall 254

V

Vaccinations 329
Visas 328
Votive tablets **121**

W

Wajima 55, 176
Walks
A Long Walk: The 88-Temple Pilgrimage (Shikoku) 258-9
A Short Walk: Eastern Gion and the Higashiyama (Kyoto City) 206-7
A Short Walk: East Shinjuku (Tokyo) 98-9
A Short Walk: Ginza (Tokyo) 108-109
A Short Walk: The Philosopher's Walk (Kyoto City) 208-9
A Short Walk: Shibuya (Tokyo) 100-101
A Short Walk: Takayama 162-3
see also Hiking
War criminals 120, 142
Warring States Period 74
Weather 39, 52
Websites 335
Weddings 86
Wellness **60-61**
Western Honshu 18, **210-45**
bars 221, 223, 239
hotels 234

Western Honshu (cont.)
  itinerary 32-3
  map 212-13
  restaurants 237
  shopping 243
West Shinjuku (Tokyo) **88-9**
Whiskey 65
Wi-Fi 335
Wildlife
  Aquarium (Sunshine City,
    Tokyo) 142
  Busena Marine Park 289
  Kagoshima Aquarium 279
  Okinawa Churaumi Aquarium
    289
  Okinawa World 288
  see also National parks
Wine 64

Winter **38-9**
World War II 76, 171
  Battle of Okinawa 283, **287**
  Former Japanese Navy
    Underground HQ **287**
  Hiroshima **228-9**
  kamikaze pilots 279
  Nagasaki 261, 266, **268**
  Yasukuni Shrine (Tokyo)
    120

Y

Yaeyama Islands **292-3**
Yakushi-ji (Nara) **215**
Yakushima forests 43
Yamaguchi **241**
Yamato clan 211

Yanagawa **275**
Yanaka District (Tokyo) **134**
Yasukuni Shrine (Tokyo) **120**
Yayoi Period 72, 275
Yokohama 149, **152-3**
Yokohama Museum of Art **152**
Yonaguni Island 293
Yoshino **234**
Yoshinogari Ruins **275**
Yoyogi Park (Tokyo) 37, **96**
Yufuin **270-71**

Z

Zen Buddhism 309
Zeni-Arai Benten Shrine
  (Kamakura) **157**
Zuisen-ji (Kamakura) **155**

PHRASE BOOK

The Japanese language is related to Okinawan and is similar to Altaic languages such as Mongolian and Turkish. Written Japanese uses a combination of three scripts: Chinese ideograms, known as *kanji*, and two syllable-based alphabet systems known as *hiragana* and *katakana*. These two latter are similar, *katakana* functioning as italics are used in English. Traditionally, Japanese is written in vertical columns from top right to bottom left, though the Western system is increasingly used. There are several romanization systems; a simplified version of the Hepburn system is used as the base for this guide. To simplify romanization, macrons (long marks over vowels to indicate longer pronunciation) have not been used. Japanese pronunciation is fairly straightforward, and many words are "Japanized" versions of Western words. This Phrase Book gives the English word or phrase, followed by the Japanese script, then the romanization.

GUIDELINES FOR PRONUNCIATION

When reading the romanization, give the same emphasis to all syllables. The practice in English of giving one syllable greater stress may render a Japanese word incomprehensible.

Pronounce vowels as in these English words:

a   as the "u" in "cup"
e   as in "red"
i   as in "chief"
o   as in "solid"
u   as the "oo" in "cuckoo"

When two vowels are used together, give each letter an individual sound:

ai   as in "pine"
ae   as if written "ah-eh"
ei   as in "pay"

Consonants are pronounced as in English. The letter *g* is always hard as in "gate," and *j* is always soft as in "joke." *R* is pronounced something between *r* and *l*. Similarly, *f* is pronounced somewhere between *f* and *h*. Whereas "*SI*" always becomes "*shi*," and *V* in Western words (e.g., "video") becomes *b*. If followed by the consonants b, p, or m, *n* usually becomes *m*, although there are some exceptions to this rule.

All consonants except *n* are always either followed by a vowel or doubled; however, sometimes an *i* or *u* is barely pronounced.

DIALECTS

Standard Japanese is used and understood throughout Japan by people of all backgrounds. But on a colloquial level, there are significant differences in both pronunciation and vocabulary, even between the Tokyo and Osaka-Kyoto areas, and rural accents are very strong.

POLITE WORDS AND PHRASES

There are several different levels of politeness in the Japanese language, according to status, age, and situation. In everyday conversation, politeness levels are simply a question of the length of verb endings (the longer *masu* ending is, as a rule, more polite), but in formal conversation you will notice that entirely different words and phrases *(keigo)* are used. As a visitor, you may find that people try to speak to you in formal language, but there is no need to use it yourself; the level given in this Phrase Book is neutral yet polite.

IN AN EMERGENCY

Help!	助けて!	Tasukete!
Stop!	止めて!	Tomete!
Call a doctor!	医者を 呼んでください!	Isha o yonde kudasai!
Call an ambulance!	救急車を 呼んでください!	Kyukyusha o yonde kudasai!
Call the police!	警察を 呼んでください!	Keisatsu o yonde kudasai!
Fire!	火事!	Kaji!
Where is the hospital?	病院はどこに ありますか?	Byoin wa doko ni arimasu ka?
police box	交番	koban

COMMUNICATION ESSENTIALS

Yes/no.	はい／いいえ	Hai/iie.
... not ...	・・・ない／・・・ません	... nai/ ... masen
I don't know.	知りません。	Shirimasen.
Thank you.	ありがとう。	Arigato.
Thank you very much.	ありがとう ございます。	Arigato gozaimasu.
Thank you very much indeed.	どうもありがとう ございます。	Domo arigato gozaimasu.
Thanks (casual).	どうも。	Domo.
No, thank you.	結構です。	Kekko desu.
Please (offering).	どうぞ。	Dozo.
Please (asking).	お願いします。	Onegai shimasu.
Please (give me or do for me).	・・・ください。	... kudasai.
I don't understand.	わかりません。	Wakarimasen.
Do you speak English?	英語を 話せますか?	Eigo o hanesemasu ka?
I can't speak Japanese.	日本語は 話せません。	Nihongo wa hanasemasen.
Please speak more slowly.	もう少しゆっくり 話してください。	Mo sukoshi yukkuri hanashite kudasai.
Sorry/Excuse me!	すみません。	Sumimasen!
Could you help me please? (not emergency)	ちょっと手伝って いただけませんか?	Chotto tetsudatte itadakemasen ka?

USEFUL PHRASES

My name is	私の 名前は・・・です。	Watashi no namae wa ...desu.
How do you do, pleased to meet you.	はじめまして、 どうぞよろしく。	Hajimemashite, dozo yoroshiku.
How are you?	お元気ですか?	Ogenki desu ka?
Good morning.	おはようございます。	Ohayo gozaimasu.
Hello/good afternoon.	こんにちは。	Konnichiwa.
Good evening.	こんばんは。	Konbanwa.
Good night.	おやすみなさい。	Oyasumi nasai.
Good-bye.	さようなら。	Sayonara.
Take care.	気をつけて。	Ki o tsukete.
Keep well (casual).	お元気で。	Ogenki de.
The same to you.	そちらも。	Sochira mo.
What is (this)?	(これは) 何 ですか?	(Kore wa) nan desu ka?
How do you use this?	これをどうやって 使いますか?	Kore o doyatte tsukaimasu ka?
Could I possibly have ...? (very polite)	・・・をいただけますか?	... o itadakemasu ka?
Is there ... here?	ここに・・・が ありますか?	Koko ni ... ga arimasu ka?
Where can I get ...?	・・・はどこに ありますか?	... wa doko ni arimasu ka?
How much is it?	いくらですか?	Ikura desu ka?
What time is ...?	・・・何時ですか?	... nanji desu ka?
Cheers! (toast)	乾杯!	Kampai!
Where is the restroom/toilet?	お手洗い／おトイレは どこですか?	Otearai/otoire wa doko desu ka?
Here's my business card.	名刺をどうぞ。	Meishi o dozo.

USEFUL WORDS

I	私	watashi
woman	女性	josei
man	男性	dansei
wife	奥さん	okusan
husband	主人	shujin
daughter	娘	musume
son	息子	musuko
child	子供	kodomo
children	子供たち	kodomotachi
businessman/ woman	ビジネスマン／ ウーマン	bijinessuman／ wuman
student	学生	gakusei
Mr./Mrs./Ms. ...	・・・さん	...-san
big/small	大きい／小さい	okii/chiisai
hot/cold	暑い／寒い	atsui/samui
cold (to touch)	冷たい	tsumetai
warm	温かい	atatakai

good/	いい／	ii/
not good/	よくない／悪い	yokunai/warui
bad		
enough	じゅうぶん／結構	jubun/kekko
free (no charge)	ただ／無料	tada/muryo
here	ここ	koko
there	あそこ	asoko
this	これ	kore
that (nearby)	それ	sore
that (far away)	あれ	are
what?	何？	nani?
when?	いつ？	itsu?
why?	なぜ／どうして？	naze?/doshite?
where?	どこ？	doko?
who?	誰？	dare?
which way?	どちら？	dochira?

SIGNS

Open	営業中	eigyo-chu
closed	休日	kyujitsu
entrance	入口	iriguchi
exit	出口	deguchi
danger	危険	kiken
emergency	非常口	hijo-guchi
exit		
information	案内	annai
restroom, toilet	お手洗い／手洗い／	otearai/tearai/
	おトイレ／トイレ	otoire/toire
free (vacant)	空き	aki
men	男	otoko
women	女	onna

MONEY

Could you	これを円に	Kore o en ni
change this into	替えてください？	kaete kudasai?
yen please?		
I'd like to cash	この	Kono
these travelers'	トラベラーズチェック	toraberazu chekku o
checks.	を 現金にしたいです。	genkin ni shitai desu.
Do you take	クレジットカード／	Kurejitto-kado/
credit cards/	トラベラーズチェックで	toraberazu-chekku
travelers'	払えますか？	de haraemasu ka?
checks?		
bank	銀行	ginko
cash	現金	genkin
credit card	クレジットカード	kurejitto-kado
currency	両替所	ryogaejo
exchange office		
dollars	ドル	doru
pounds	ポンド	pondo
yen	円	en

KEEPING IN TOUCH

Where is a	電話はどこに	Denwa wa doko ni
telephone?	ありますか？	arimasu ka?
May I use your	電話を使っても	Denwa o tsukatte mo
phone?	いいですか？	ii desu ka?
Hello, this is ...	もしもし、…です。	Moshi-moshi,
		...desu.
I'd like to make	国際電話、	Kokusai denwa,
an international	お願いします。	onegaishimasu.
call.		
airmail	航空便	kokubin
e-mail	イーメール	i-meru
fax	ファックス	fakkusu
postcard	ハガキ	hagaki
post office	郵便局	yubin-kyoku
stamp	切手	kitte
telephone booth	公衆電話	koshu denwa
telephone card	テレフォンカード	terefon-kado

SHOPPING

Where can I	…はどこで	... wa doko de
buy ...?	買えますか？	kaemasu ka?
How much does	いくらですか？	Ikura desu ka?
this cost?		
I'm just looking.	見ているだけです。	Mite iru dake
		desu.
Do you have ...?	…ありますか？	... arimasu ka?
May I try this	着てみても	Kite mite mo
on?	いいですか？	ii desu ka?
Please show me	それを	Sore o
that.	見せてください。	misete kudasai.
Does it come in	他の色も	Hoka no iro mo
other colors?	ありますか？	arimasu ka?
black	黒	kuro
blue	青	ao
green	緑	midori
red	赤	aka
white	白	shiro

yellow	黄色	kiiro
cheap/expensive	安い／高い	yasui/takai
audio equipment	オーディオ製品	odio seihin
bookstore	本屋	honya-ya
boutique	ブティック	butikku
clothes	洋服	yofuku
department store	デパート	depato
electrical store	電気屋	denki-ya
fish market	魚屋	sakana-ya
folk crafts	民芸品	mingei-hin
ladies' wear	婦人服	fujin fuku
local specialty	名物	meubutsu
market	市場	ichiba
menswear	紳士服	shinshi fuku
newsstand	新聞屋	shimbun-ya
pharmacist	薬屋	kusuri-ya
picture postcard	絵葉書	e-hagaki
sale	セール	seru
souvenir shop	お土産屋	omiyage-ya
supermarket	スーパー	supa
travel agent	旅行会社	ryoko-gaisha

SIGHTSEEING

Where is ...?	…はどこですか？	... wa doko
		desu ka?
How do I get	…へは、どうやって	... wa doyatte
to ...?	いったらいいですか？	ittara ii desu ka?
Is it far?	遠いですか？	Toi desu ka?
art gallery	美術館	bijitsukan
reservations	予約窓口	yoyaku-madoguchi
desk		
bridge	橋	hashi/bashi
castle	城	shiro/jo
city	市	shi
city center	町の中心	machi no
		chushin
gardens	庭園／庭	teien/niwa
hot spring	温泉	onsen
information	案内所	annaijo
office		
island	島	shima/jima
monastery	修道院	shudo-in
mountain	山	yama/san
museum	博物館	hakubutsukan
palace	宮殿	kyuden
park	公園	koen
port	港	minato/ko
prefecture	県	ken
river	川	kawa/gawa
ruins	遺跡	iseki
shopping area	ショッピング街	shoppingu-gai
shrine	神社／神宮／宮	jinja/jingu-gu
street	通り	tori/dori
temple	お寺／寺	otera/tera/dera/ji
tour, travel	旅行	ryoko
town	町	machi/cho
village	村	mura
ward	区	ku
zoo	動物園	dobutsu-en
north	北	kita/hoku
south	南	minami/nan
east	東	higashi/to
west	西	nishi/sei
left/right	左／右	hidari/migi
straight ahead	真っ直ぐ	massugu
between	間に	aida ni
near/far	近い／遠い	chikai/toi
up/down	上／下	ue/shita
(top/bottom)		
new	新しい／新	atarashii/shin
old/former	古い／元	furui/moto
upper/lower	上／下	kami/shimo
middle/inner	中	naka
in	に／中に	ni/naka ni
in front of	前	mae

GETTING AROUND

bicycle	自転車	jidensha
bus	バス	basu
car	車	kuruma
ferry	フェリー	feri
baggage room	手荷物	tenimotsu
	一時預かり所	ichiji azukarijo
motorcycle	オートバイ	otobai
one-way ticket	片道切符	katamachi kippu
return ticket	往復切符	ofuku kippu
taxi	タクシー	takushi
ticket	切符	kippu
ticket office	切符売場	kippu uriba

TRAINS

What is the fare to ...?	・・・まで いくらですか？	... made ikura desu ka?
When does the train for... leave?	・・・行きの電車は、 何時にですか？	... yuki no densha wa nanji n desu ka?
How long does it take to get to ...?	・・・までの時間は どのくらい かかりますか？	... made jikan wa dono gurai kakarimasu ka?
A ticket to ..., please.	・・・行きの切符を ください。	... yuki no kippu o kudasai.
Do I have to change?	乗り換えが 必要ですか？	Norikae ga hitsuyo desu ka?
I'd like to reserve a seat, please.	席を 予約したいです。	Seki o yoyaku shitai desu.
Which platform for the train to ...?	・・・行きの電車は、 何番ホームですか？	... yuki no densha wa nanban homu desu ka?
Which station is this?	ここは、 どの駅ですか？	Koko wa dono eki desu ka?
Is this the right train for ...?	・・・へは、 この電車で いいですか？	... e wa kono densha de ii desu ka?
bullet train	新幹線	shinkansen
express trains:		
"limited express" (fastest)	特急	tokkyu
"express" (second)	急行	kyuko
"rapid" (third)	快速	kaisoku
first-class	一等	itto
line	線	sen
local train	普通／各駅電車	futsu/ kaku-ekidensha
platform	ホーム	homu
train station	駅	eki
reserved seat	指定席	shitei-seki
second-class	二等	nito
subway	地下鉄	chikatetsu
train	電車	densha
unreserved seat	自由席	jiyu-seki

ACCOMMODATIONS

Do you have any vacancies?	部屋がありますか？	Heya ga arimasu ka
I have a reservation.	予約を してあります。	Yoyaku o shite arimasu.
I'd like a room with a bathroom.	お風呂付の部屋 お願いします。	Ofuro-tsuki no heya, onegaishimasu.
What is the charge per night?	一泊 いくらですか？	Ippaku ikura desu ka?
Is tax included in the price?	税込みですか？	Zeikomi desu ka?
Can I leave my luggage here for a little while?	荷物をここに ちょっと預けても いいですか？	Nimotsu o koko ni chotto azuketemo ii desu ka?
air-conditioning	冷房／エアコン	reibo/eakon
bath	お風呂	ofuro
check-out	チェックアウト	chekku-auto
hair drier	ドライヤー	doraiya
hot (boiled) water	お湯	oyu
Japanese-style inn	旅館	ryokan
Japanese-style room	和室	washitsu
key	鍵	kagi
front desk	フロント	furonto
single/ twin room	シングル／ ツイン	shinguru/ tsuin
shower	シャワー	shawa
Western-style hotel	ホテル	hoteru
Western-style room	洋室	yoshitsu

EATING OUT

A table for one/two/three, please.	一人／二人 三人、 お願いします。	Hitori/futari/ sannin, onegaishimasu.
May I see the menu.	メニュー、 お願いします	Menyu, onegaishimasu..
Is there a set menu?	定食が。 ありますか？	Teishoku ga arimasu ka?
I'd like	私は・・・が いいです。	Watashi wa ... ga ii desu.
May I have one of those?	それをひとつ、 お願いします？	Sore o hitotsu, onegaishimasu.
I am a vegetarian.	私は ベジタリアンです。	Watashi wa bejitarian desu.
Waiter/waitress!	ちょっと すみません！	Chotto sumimasen!
What would you recommend?	おすすめは 何ですか？	Osusume wa nan desu ka?
How do you eat this?	これは、どうやって 食べますか？	Kore wa, doyatte tabemasu ka?
May we have the check please.	お勘定、 お願いします。	Okanjo, onegaishimasu.
May we have some more ...	もっと・・・、 お願いします。	Motto ..., onegaishimasu.
The meal was very good, thank you.	ごちそうさまでした、 おいしかったです。	Gochiso-sama deshita, oishikatta desu.
assortment	盛り合わせ	moriawase
boxed meal	弁当	bento
breakfast	朝食	choshoku
buffet	バイキング	baikingu
delicious	おいしい	oishii
dinner	夕食	yushoku
to drink	飲む	nomu
a drink	飲み物	nomimono
to eat	食べる	taberu
food	食べ物／ ごはん	tabemono/ gohan
full (stomach)	おなかがいっぱい	onaka ga ippai
hot/cold	熱い／冷たい	atsui/tsumetai
hungry	おなかがすいた	onaka ga suita
Japanese food	和食	washoku
lunch	昼食	chushoku
set menu	セット／ 定食	setto/ teishoku
spicy	辛い	karai
sweet, mild	甘い	amai
Western food	洋食	yoshoku

PLACES TO EAT

Cafeteria/ canteen	食堂	shokudo
Chinese restaurant	中華料理屋	chuka-ryori-ya
coffee shop/ cafe	喫茶店／ カフェ	kissaten/ kafe
local bar	飲み屋／ 居酒屋	nomi-ya/ izakaya
noodle stall	ラーメン屋	ramen-ya
restaurant	レストラン／ 料理屋	resutoran/ ryori-ya
sushi on a conveyor belt	回転寿司	kaiten-zushi
upscale restaurant	料亭	ryotei
upscale vegetarian restaurant	精進料理屋	shojin-ryori-ya

FOODS

apple	りんご	ringo
bamboo shoots	たけのこ	takenoko
beancurd (tofu)	豆腐	tofu
bean sprouts	もやし	moyashi
beans	豆	mame
beef	ビーフ／ 牛肉／	bifu/ gyuniku
beefburger (patty)	ハンバーグ	hanbagu
blowfish	ふぐ	fugu
bonito, tuna	かつお／ ツナ	katsuo/ tsuna
bread	パン	pan
butter	バター	bata
cake	ケーキ	keki
chicken	とり／鶏肉	tori/toriniku
confectionery	お菓子	okashi
crab	かに	kani
duck	カモ	kamo
eel	うなぎ	unagi
egg	卵	tamago
eggplant/ aubergine	なす	nasu
fermented soybean paste	みそ	miso

fermented soybeans	納豆	natto
fish (raw)	刺身	sashimi
fried tofu	油揚げ	abura-age
fruit	くだもの	kudamono
ginger	しょうが	shoga
hamburger	ハンバーガー	hambaga
haute cuisine	会席	kaiseki
herring	ニシン	nishin
hors d'oeuvres	オードブル	odoburu
ice cream	アイスクリーム	aisu-kurimu
jam	ジャム	jamu
Japanese mushrooms	まつたけ／しいたけ／しめじ	mats'take/shiitake/shimeji
Japanese pear	梨	nashi
loach	どじょう	dojo
lobster	伊勢海老	ise-ebi
mackerel	さば	saba
mackerel pike	さんま	samma
mandarin orange	みかん	mikan
meat	肉	niku
melon	メロン	meron
mountain vegetables	山菜	sansai
noodles:		
buckwheat	そば	soba
Chinese	ラーメン	ramen
wheatflour	うどん／そうめん	udon (fat)/somen (thin)
octopus	たこ	tako
omelet	オムレツ	omuretsu
oyster	カキ	kaki
peach	桃	momo
pepper	こしょう	kosho
persimmon	柿	kaki
pickles	漬物	tsukemono
pork	豚肉	butaniku
potato	ジャガイモ	jagaimo
rice:		
cooked	ごはん	gohan
uncooked	米	kome
rice crackers	おせんべい	osembei
roast beef	ローストビーフ	rosutobifu
salad	サラダ	sarada
salmon	鮭	sake
salt	塩	shio
sandwich	サンドイッチ	sandoichi
sausage	ソーセージ	soseji
savory nibbles	おつまみ	otsumami
seaweed:		
laver (dried)	のり	nori
kelp (chewy)	こんぶ	kombu
shrimp	海老	ebi
soup	汁／スープ	shiru/supu
soy sauce	しょうゆ	shoyu
spaghetti	スパゲティ	supageti
spinach	ほうれん草	horenso
squid	いか	ika
steak	ステーキ	suteki
sugar	砂糖	sato
sushi (mixed)	五目寿司	gomoku-zushi
sweetfish/ smelt	鮎	ayu
taro (potato)	里芋	sato imo
toast	トースト	tosuto
trout	鱒	masu
sea urchin	ウニ	uni
vegetables	野菜	yasai
watermelon	すいか	suika
wild boar	ぼたん／いのしし	botan/inoshishi

DRINKS

beer	ビール	biru
coffee (hot)	ホットコーヒー	hotto-kohi
cola	コーラ	kora
green tea	お茶	ocha
iced coffee:		
black	アイスコーヒー	aisu-kohi
with milk	アイスオーレ	kafe-o-re
lemon tea	レモンティー	remon ti
milk	ミルク／牛乳	miruku/gyunyu
mineral water	ミネラルウォーター	mineraru uota
orange juice	オレンジジュース	orenji jusu
rice wine (non-alcoholic)	酒（甘酒）	sake (ama-zake)

tea (Western-style)	紅茶	kocha
tea with milk	ミルクティー	miruku ti
water	水	mizu
whiskey	ウイスキー	uisuki
wine	ワイン／ぶどう酒	wain/budoshu

HEALTH

I don't feel well.	気分がよくないです。	Kibun ga yokunai desu.
I have a pain in ...	・・・が痛いです。	... ga itai desu.
I'm allergic to ...	・・・アレルギーです。	... arerugi desu.
asthma	喘息	zensoku
cough	咳	seki
dentist	歯医者	haisha
diabetes	糖尿病	tonyo-byo
diarrhea	下痢	geri
doctor	医者	isha
fever	熱	netsu
headache	頭痛	zutsuu
hospital	病院	byoin
medicine	薬	kusuri
Oriental medicine	漢方薬	kampo yaku
pharmacy	薬局	yakkyoku
prescription	処方箋	shohosen
stomachache	腹痛	fukutsu
toothache	歯が痛い	ha ga itai

NUMBERS

	Japanese	Romaji
0	ゼロ	zero
1	一	ichi
2	二	ni
3	三	san
4	四	yon/shi
5	五	go
6	六	roku
7	七	nana/shichi
8	八	hachi
9	九	kyu
10	十	ju
11	十一	ju-ichi
12	十二	ju-ni
20	二十	ni-ju
21	二十一	ni-ju-ichi
22	二十二	ni-ju-ni
30	三十	san-ju
40	四十	yon-ju
100	百	hyaku
101	百一	hyaku-ichi
200	二百	ni-hyaku
300	三百	san-byaku
400	四百	yon-hyaku
500	五百	go-hyaku
600	六百	roppyaku
700	七百	nana-hyaku
800	八百	happyaku
900	九百	kyu-hyaku
1,000	千	sen
1,001	千一	sen-ichi
2,000	二千	ni-sen
10,000	一万	ichi-man
20,000	二万	ni-man
100,000	十万	ju-man
1,000,000	百万	hyaku-man
123,456	十二万三千四百五十六	ju-ni-man-san-zen-yon-hyaku-go-ju-roku

TIME

Monday	月曜日	getsuyobi
Tuesday	火曜日	kayobi
Wednesday	水曜日	suiyobi
Thursday	木曜日	mokuyobi
Friday	金曜日	kinyobi
Saturday	土曜日	doyobi
Sunday	日曜日	nichiyobi
January	一月	ichi-gatsu
February	二月	ni-gatsu
March	三月	san-gatsu
April	四月	shi-gatsu
May	五月	go-gatsu
June	六月	roku-gatsu
July	七月	shichi-gatsu
August	八月	hachi-gatsu
September	九月	ku-gatsu
October	十月	ju-gatsu
November	十一月	ju-ichi-gatsu
December	十二月	ju-ni-gatsu
spring	春	haru

summer	夏	natsu
fall/autumn	秋	aki
winter	冬	fuyu
noon	正午	shogo
midnight	真夜中	mayonaka
today	今日	kyo
yesterday	昨日	kino
tomorrow	明日	ashita
this morning	今朝	kesa
this afternoon	今日の午後	kyo no gogo
this evening	今晩	konban
every day	毎日	mainichi
month	月	getsu/tsuki
hour	時	ji
time/hour (duration)	時間	jikan
minute	分	pun/fun
this year	今年	kotoshi
last year	去年	kyonen
next year	来年	rainen
one year	一年	ichi-nen
late	遅い	osoi
early	早い	hayai
soon	すぐ	sugu

ACKNOWLEDGMENTS

The publisher would like to thank the following for their kind permission to reproduce their photographs:

Key: a-above; b-below/bottom; c-centre; f-far; l-left; r-right; t-top

123RF.com: 501room 71tr, 126-7b; Steve AllenUK 65br; Leonid Andronov 214t; Nattee Chalermtiragool 152t; coward_lion 127tl; Diego Grandi 186bl; Pablo Hidalgo 52-3t; jaimax 268bl; Nattachart Jerdnapapunt 70cl; kawamuralucy 114tl; liligraphie 40-1b; Sanchai Loongroong 309tr; Luciano Mortula 186crb, 217bl; mtaira 173bl; oleandra 82-3; ookinate23 39crb; orthone 127br; Sean Pavone 26t, 235tl; PaylessImages 41crb; Chan Richie 286crb; Pandech Saleewong 34tl; Chanon Tamtad 22bl; Sompob Tapaopong 253t; tomas1111 132c; Yiu Tung Lee 220tr; tupungato 32crb; yusukerf 43tr.

4Corners: Massimo Borchi 136; Maurizio Rellini 326-7.

Alamy Stock Photo: Stuart Abraham 43cl; AF archive 47cl; Aflo Co. Ltd. 11br, 55tr, 59crb, 62b, 66-7t, / Hiroyuki Sato 28cr, / Nippon News 255tr; age fotostock / Javier Larrea 201b; All Canada Photos 38-9t; Arif Iqball Photography - Japan 70clb; ART Collection 73cb, 224fbl; Askanioff 216clb; Aurora Photos 53cl; David Ball 310t; Patrick Batchelder 8cl; Blue Jean Images 254tr, 308tl; Tibor Bognar 160br, 162bl, 242br; Dominic Byrne 322-3t; Pocholo Calapre 36tc; Nano Calvo / © 2010 Olafur Eliasson Colour activity house, 2010 166-7t; Jui-Chi Chan 119t; David Cherepuschak 175tr; Chon Kit Leong 202-3t; Trevor Chriss 74cb; Chronicle 75tr, 75cr, 240tr; Classic Image 73br, 74-5t; coward_lion 46-7b, 170bc, 195t, 198tl; adrian davies 71crb; Design Pics Inc 91tr; Terry Donnelly 324b; Paul Dymond 291br; EDU Vision 141bl, 241tr, 300bc, 308tr; Ei Katsumata - FLP 244; Robert Evans 4, 134br; Everett Collection Historical 76tl; F1online digitale Bildagentur GmbH / D.Fernandez & M.Peck 323br; Malcolm Fairman 70cla, 73tl, 190bl; FantasticJapan 157tr; Food for Thought 140bl; Fabio Formaggio 61cl; Miyoko Fukushima 77br; Granger Historical Picture Archive 74tl; Harry Green 87cra; Hemis 93br, 111crb, 194clb, 306tl; Brent Hofacker 61br; Camilla Hohmann 290bc; Horizon Images / Motion 231cla, 279tr; Peter Horree 111cr; Image navi - QxQ images 43crb, 140cl, 293t; imageBROKER 193tr; Haiyun Jiang 72bc; jirobkk 312bl; John Frost Newspapers 76cr; Jon Arnold Images Ltd 320bc; Juite Wen 172t; Yoshiyuki Kaneko 311br; Keystone Pictures USA 86tr; Hideo Kurihara 88clb, 111bl, 114br; Lebrecht Music & Arts 47tr, 73tr, 76bc; Chu-Wen Lin 318clb; LOOK Die Bildagentur der Fotografen GmbH 159b, / Axel Schwab 168b; Ivan Marchuk 72br; Iain Masterton 61tr, 63br, 107, 235br, 240b; Michael Matthews 227tr; mauritius images GmbH 22t, 92t, 196b, / Jose Fuste Raga 116-7b; Mint Images Limited 54-5b, 55br; Trevor Mogg 237tr; Moonie's World 119cra; Tuul and Bruno Morandi 243br; Geoffrey Morgan 265cl; myLAM 92bl; Roland Nagy 96tl; paolo negri 307cra; Newscom 44br, 106clb, 110-111t, / BJ Warnick 196cr; Nic Cleave Photography 233br; Niday Picture Library 72t; Old Paper Studios 75clb; Panther Media GmbH / Pius Lee 171bl; Alberto Paredes 184tr; Sean Pavone 12-3b, 94-5t, 118br, 135, 170t, 188bl, 190-1t, 194bl, 198-9b, 238-9b, 256br, 274b, 278-9b, 313t, 318b, 320t; Miguel A. Muñoz Pellicer 121t; Photononstop 25tr, / © Estate of George Rickey / VAGA at ARS, NY and DACS, London 2019 Three Squares Vertical Diagonal, 2007 250-1b; tawatchai prakobkit 192b; Prisma by Dukas Presseagentur GmbH 76crb, 130tl, 219tr, / Raga Jose Fuste 145b; QEDimages 200bl; Alex Ramsay 198c; Cheryl Rinzler 67cla; Magda Rittenhouse 69br; robertharding 67crb, 276tl, 325t, Ian Robinson 259br; Prasit Rodphan 17bl, 180-1; Ralph Rozema 159c; Darby Sawchuk 45br; Pietro Scòzzari 287tl; Alex Segre 130-1b; Skye Hohmann Japan Images 171cr; SOURCENEXT 13t, 56-7t, / MIXA 97clb; dave stamboulis 281bl, 322clb; John Steele 97b, 258clb; StockFood Ltd. 140cla; StockShot 319tr; Jeremy Sutton-Hibbert 52bl, 55cl; TCD / Prod.DB 46tl; The Picture Art Collection 68-9b, 73cla, 128cdb; Top Photo Corporation 269b; Travel 53bc; travelbild-asia 128-9t; Jorge Tutor 131tr; Leisa Tyler 40crb; Lucas Vallecillos 10clb, 59tr, 115t, 202bl, 231ca,

268tr; Ivan Vdovin 128bl, 131cb; Chris Willson 12clb, 280, 293cl; Peter M. Wilson 98bl; World Discovery 113tr; World History Archive 216fclb, 224fbr, 287br; Masayuki Yamashita 45cl, 89br, 142-3; Ka Wing Yu 271tl; Philipp Zechner 311tr.

AWL Images: Jan Christopher Becke 290-1t; Marco Gaiotti 17t, 148-9; Gavin Hellier 191cra.

Bridgeman Images: Pictures from History 224bl.

Depositphotos Inc: javarman 177tr; kadsada23@gmail. com 288t; leungchopan 276br; nicholashan 30t; parody 301tl; sepavone 215cr; Torsakarin 2-3; yoshiyayo 77cb.

Dreamstime.com: Aaa187 229; Akiyoko74 70cr; Leonid Andronov 37bl; Sittichan Ausavakornthanarat 34-5ca; Kristopher Bason 21, 314-5; Beatricesirinun 24cla; Bennymarty 12t, 26crb, 63cl, 90-1b, 116tl, 155cra, 156-7b; Evgenia Bolyukh 91cla; Shubhashish Chakrabarty 169tr; Checco 228clb; Cowardlion 68tl, 86-7b, 143bl, 163tl, 185tl, 221bl, 302clb, 302cb, 302bc, 305tl, / Louise Bourgeois © The Easton Foundation / VAGA at ARS, NY and DACS, London 2019 Maman 90cl; Leo Daphne 266br; Eudaemon 115cr; Eyeblink 292b; F11photo 32cr, 309b; Ioana Grecu 36-7t; Angela Ho 41cl; Thomas Humeau 74br; Ixuskmitl 206bl, 272-3b; Jonkio4 87tl; Kan1234 57bt, 270br; Thitichot Katawutpoonpun 275tl; Patryk Kosmider 204bl; Erik Lattwein 49bl; Chon Kit Leong 232bl; Bo Li 65tr; Lumppini 50-1b; Luciano Mortula 218-9t; Mrnovel 28bl, 216crb; Roland Nagy 8cla; Naruto4836 140br; Ngo Pang Ng 286b; Thanathorn Ngammongkolwong 306-7b; Sean Pavone 10ca, 20bl, 24-5t, 36bl, 41tr, 48bl, 49crb, 64-5b, 76-7t, 100bl, 102-3, 132cb, 158-9t, 164t, 165tr, 166bl, 225, 231tl, 242-3t, 252b, 264t, 266t, 294-5, 298t, 301cra; Phuongphoto 24tl, 144-5t; Picturecorrect 58-9t; Pipa100 228br; Platongkoh 32bl; Psstockfoto 299cl; Prasit Rodphan 48-9t; Eq Roy 64tr; Somchai Sanguankotchakorn 154t; Seiksoon 39cl; Siraanamwong 185cla; Strixcode 51br; Ignasi Such 160-1t; Aduldej Sukaram 77cra; Parinya Suwanitch 108bl; Tktktktk 22cr, 28crb; Jens Tobiska 50tr, 71cr; Torsakarin 177cra, 226-7t; Tungtopgun 112-3b; Tupungato 121cr, 309cr; Vincentstthomas 44-5t; Krisada Wakayabun 42-3t; Chun-Chang Wu 251cra; Asyraf Yatim 70cra.

Getty Images: a-clip 10-11b, 13br; AFP / Kazuhiro Nogi 62tl, 250clb, / Martin Bureau 54tl, 57cla, / Toshifumi Kitamura 139cra; Corbis Documentary / B.S.P.I. 238bc; Carl Court 122-3; Yongyuan Dai 77tr; De Agostini Picture Library 55cl; Fine Art 159tr; Glowimages 224cra; Taro Karibe 60tl; Kyodo News 142bl; John S Lander 56b, 205cra; National Geographic Image Collection / Gianluca Colla 288-9b; Denis O'Regan 216fcrb; Pozland Photography Tokyo 109br; Print Collector 75br; Raga 60-1b; Jeremy Sutton-Hibbert 193br; The Asahi Shimbun 63t, 138-9b, 139tl, 139tr.

iStockphoto.com: 10max 254-5b; 4X-image 132cl; akiyoko 11t; AlexStoen / Yayoi Kusama Pumpkin, 1994 251tl; aluxum 70crb; ColobusYeti 62cra; coward_lion 74cla, 115br, 127cra, 174b, 236-7b; Yongyuan Dai 101br; DanielBendjy 40tl; DavorLovincic 30cr, 32t, 277t; electravk 309cra, 309crb; enviromantic 185cra; finallast 224br; FotoKOT 197bl; gyro 178; Hakase_ 71tl; helovi 309cl; iconogenic 272tl; japanthings 121br; JavenLin 112-3t; kanonsky 35tr; kiennews 51tr; Korkusung 22crb, 95br; kyonntra 71clb; lisegagne 51cl; MasaoTaira 176tr; Masaru123 66b; Miknos 8clb; mrtom-uk 224crb; Tamaki Nakajima 42-3b; Nayomiee 140t; nicholashan 30bl; Nikada 24-5ca; oluolu3 197t; paprikaworks 256-7t; Sean Pavone 6-7, 8-9, 120b, 222-3t, 234b, 238t; petesphotography 20t, 282-3; preuk13 304xb; Ratth 133bc; recep-bg 58bl; RichLegg 13cr; Rixipix 106br; sara_winter 207cra; SeanPavonePhoto 11cr, 19cb, 189t, 200tr, 209b, 260-1; sheilades 146-7; shirophoto 28t; somchaij 26bl; spastonov 140clb; superjoseph 186-7; tanukiphoto 34-5t; TommL 16, 78-9; VittoriaChe 26cr; JianGang Wang 71cl; whitewish 188cra; winhorse 99br; xavierarnau 18, 210-1.

Rex by Shutterstock: Snap Stills 47br.

Robert Harding Picture Library: Photo Japan 205t.

Penguin Random House

Main Contributers Matthew Wilcox, John Hart Benson Jr., Mark Brazil, Jon Burbank, Angela Jeffs, Emi Kazuoko, Stephen Mansfield, Bill Marsh, Catherine Rubenstein Jaxquelne Ruyak

Senior Editor Ankita Awasthi Tröger

Senior Designer Owen Bennett

Project Editor Rebecca Flynn

Project Art Editors Dan Bailey, Sara-Louise Brown, Bharti Karakoti, Mark Richards, Priyanka Thakur, Vinita Venugopal

Designer William Robinson

Factchecker Masumi Kamozaki, Simon Scott

Editors Ankita Awasthi Tröger, Elspeth Beidas, Alice Fewery, Emma Grundy Haigh, Rachel Laidler, Lucy Sara-Kelly, Lucy Sienkowska, Lauren Whybrow, Sylvia Tombesi-Walton

Proofreader Susanne Hillen

Indexer Helen Peters

Senior Picture Researcher Ellen Root

Picture Research Marta Bescos, Sumita Khatwani, Harriet Whitaker

Illustrators Richard Bonson, Gary Cross, Richard Draper, Paul Guest, Claire Littlejohn, Maltings Partnership, Mel Pickering, John Woodcock

Cartographic Editor Casper Morris

Cartography ERA-Maptec Ltd, Simonetta Giori, Zafar-ul-Islam-Khan

Jacket Designers Bess Daly, Maxine Pedliham, Simon Thompson

Jacket Picture Research Susie Peachey

Senior DTP Designer Jason Little

DTP George Nimmo, Neeraj Bhatia, Mrinmoy Mazumdar, Azeem Siddiqui, Tanveer Zaidi

Senior Producer Stephanie McConnell

Managing Editor Hollie Teague

Art Director Maxine Pedliham

Publishing Director Georgina Dee

First edition 2000

Published in Great Britain by Dorling Kindersley Limited, 80 Strand, London, WC2R 0RL

Published in the United States by DK Publishing, 1450 Broadway, 8th Floor, New York, NY 10018

Copyright © 2000, 2019 Dorling Kindersley Limited
A Penguin Random House Company
19 20 21 22 10 9 8 7 6 5 4 3 2 1

A CIP catalog record for this book is available from the British Library.

A catalog record for this book is available from the Library of Congress.

ISSN: 1542 1554
ISBN: 978 0 2413 6533 5

Printed and bound in Malaysia.

www.dk.com

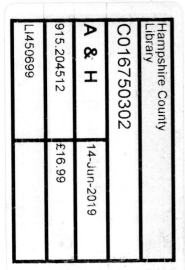